Modern Naval History

Modern Naval History

Debates and Prospects

RICHARD HARDING

Bloomsbury Academic
An imprint of Bloomsbury Publishing Plc

B L O O M S B U R Y
LONDON · OXFORD · NEW YORK · NEW DELHI · SYDNEY

Bloomsbury Academic
An imprint of Bloomsbury Publishing Plc

50 Bedford Square	1385 Broadway
London	New York
WC1B 3DP	NY 10018
UK	USA

www.bloomsbury.com

BLOOMSBURY and the Diana logo are trademarks of Bloomsbury Publishing Plc

First published 2016

© Richard Harding, 2016

Richard Harding has asserted his right under the Copyright, Designs and Patents Act, 1988, to be identified as Author of this work.

All rights reserved. No part of this publication may be reproduced or transmitted in any form or by any means, electronic or mechanical, including photocopying, recording, or any information storage or retrieval system, without prior permission in writing from the publishers.

No responsibility for loss caused to any individual or organization acting on or refraining from action as a result of the material in this publication can be accepted by Bloomsbury or the author.

British Library Cataloguing-in-Publication Data
A catalogue record for this book is available from the British Library.

ISBN: HB: 978-1-4725-7908-9
PB: 978-1-4725-7909-6
ePDF: 978-1-4725-7911-9
ePub: 978-1-4725-7910-2

Library of Congress Cataloging-in-Publication Data
Harding, Richard, 1953-
Modern naval history : debates and prospects / Richard Harding.
pages cm
Includes bibliographical references and index.
1. Naval history, Modern. I. Title.
D215.J37 2015
359.009'04–dc23
2015012099

Typeset by Deanta Global Publishing Services, Chennai, India
Printed and bound in India

For Anne, Rebecca and Hannah

CONTENTS

List of Illustrations ix
Preface xi

Introduction: Debates and prospects for naval history 1
Purpose and rationale 1
Structure: Three themes 8

1 Sea power and international relations: History in the service of policy 13
The emergence of modern naval history 13
The French Revolutionary and Napoleonic Wars (1793–1815) and their impact on naval history 15
Naval operations during the war, 1793–1815 18
Pax Britannica and naval history, 1815–1914 25
Technology, innovation, ideology and naval power, 1850–1914 28
The First World War: Navalism and the impact of modern naval warfare, 1914–18 42
Coming to terms with new realities, 1919–39 47
The Second World War and naval power, 1939–45 49
Historians, strategists and naval power, 1945–2010 57
Conclusion 62

2 Navies, politics and government, 1500–1789 65
Maritime empires, confessional politics and navies, 1500–1650 66
Navies, state-building and the fiscal-military state debate, 1650–1750 75
England, sea power and the Anglo-Dutch Wars, 1649–74 78
The military or naval revolution 81
The dominance of the line of battle fleet and the alternatives, 1650–1750 83

Global reach: Logistics and bureaucracy, 1713–89 86
The triumph of sea power, 1739–83: The continental versus maritime war debate and the decisiveness of naval war 91
The apogee of naval competition during the Age of Sail, 1763–93 104

3 Navies and societies: The widening research agenda 109
Navies and globalization from the fifteenth to the twenty-first century 109
Maritime economies, industrial revolution and the engine of growth 111
Science, technology and technological determinism in naval history 113
Navies as complex organizations (structures, systems and expertise) 114
The officer corps and naval leadership 118
Manpower and navies 121
Health and medicine in navies 122
The sailor at sea and ashore 123
Navies and cultures 127

Conclusion: The future of naval history? 131

Notes 135
Select Bibliography 197
Index 257

LIST OF ILLUSTRATIONS

Figure 1   The eighteenth-century line of battle in action: the Battle off Cape St Vincent, 14 February 1797. © National Maritime Museum: ID PW5795   19

Figure 2   The impact of sea power: an inshore squadron under Vice Admiral Horatio Nelson, blockading Cadiz, July 1797. © National Maritime Museum, Greenwich, London. ID BHC0499   21

Figure 3   An ambiguous precedent. The Austrian battleship *Erzherzog Ferdinand Max* moves astern after ramming the Italian battleship *Re d'Italia*. The latter sank in a few minutes. Von Teuffenbach, A. *Oesterreichs Hort: Geschichts Und Kulturbilder Aus Den Habsburgischen Erblandern*. 2nd edn. 2 vols. Vienna: Patriotische Boltsbuchhandlung 1910, opposite p. 160   31

Figure 4   The line of battle in the twentieth century: the Royal Navy's 2nd Battle Squadron at Jutland, 31 May 1916. © Trustees of the National Museum of the Royal Navy (Portsmouth)   41

Figure 5   Naval war in three dimensions. HMS *Ark Royal*, the surface ship designed to project air power from the seas, listing to starboard after being torpedoed by U81 on the afternoon of 13 November 1941 in the Mediterranean. She capsized and sank on the morning of 14 November while under tow to Gibraltar. © Trustees of the National Museum of the Royal Navy (Portsmouth)   50

Figure 6   The impact of sea power: a Japanese merchantman sinking by the bows after being torpedoed by a US submarine. Seen from the periscope of the submarine, November/December 1943. National Archive   54

Figure 7   The impact of sea power: amphibious Invasion, Normandy, 6 June 1944. © Trustees of the National Museum of the Royal Navy (Portsmouth)   56

LIST OF ILLUSTRATIONS

Figure 8	Coexisting expressions of power: an English three-decker and a galley in an Italian port, unknown artist, c. 1680. © National Maritime Museum. ID BCHO 935	71
Figure 9	The spectacle of sea power: Phineas Pett and the *Sovereign of the Seas*, c. 1637. © National Maritime Museum. ID BHC 2949	72
Figure 10	The Battle of Scheveningen 31 July 1653, Willem Van de Velde the Elder, 1655. © National Maritime Museum. ID B8318	80
Figure 11	A chase action: first Battle of Finisterre, 3 May 1747 by Samuel Scott. © National Maritime Museum. ID BHCO 369	95
Figure 12	Another chase action: the Battle of Quiberon Bay (or les Cardinaux), 20 November 1759. © Trustees of the National Museum of the Royal Navy (Portsmouth)	98
Figure 13	The impact of sea power: the British landing at Kipps Bay, New York Island, 15 September 1776. © National Maritime Museum. ID 2891	103
Figure 14	Navies as industrial enterprise: Planned extension to Portsmouth dockyard, 1786. Trustees of the National Museum of the Royal Navy (Portsmouth)	115
Figure 15	Naval power as advertising power: Player's cigarettes metal and enamel sign, 1890s. © Trustees of the National Museum of the Royal Navy (Portsmouth)	126

PREFACE

During 2010/2011 the Society for Nautical Research celebrated its centenary. As chairman of the Society at the time, I was particularly intrigued by the Society's role in stimulating a public consciousness of maritime history over those 100 years. The world had changed dramatically in the period, and so had the study of history. The Society's own centenary publications reflected on this change, but naval history has gone through changes in emphasis and significance that seemed to be worthy of examination in more detail. It remains a subject of immense public interest, for both popular consumption and informing policy. Yet it is also a subject that seemed to have lost some connection with both its popular audience and policy makers. To many, there was little to distinguish it from popular fiction in its tales of derring-do and less to recommend it in comparison with the claims to certainty and prediction of the modern social sciences. I am convinced navies and maritime power will have a vital role to play in the world that is emerging in the twenty-first century and that naval history is still important to public understanding of the world. This work is intended as a contribution to that process. It is aimed at prospective researchers in history and social sciences and at the interested layman. Whether interested in politics, economics, diplomacy or cultures, there is a maritime dimension. By exploring the debates that have informed and shaped the writing of naval history it is intended to encourage new scholars to engage rigorously with the subject. Naval history has a global spread and, with its vast archival resources, it has the ability to shine a light onto significant aspects of contemporary societies in the process of globalization. Furthermore, we have so far, as historians, only scratched the surface of the research needed to understand how navies have influenced the societies which they serve.

Throughout this project a simple metaphor has constantly reoccurred to me – trying to see the woods for the trees. Naval history is now such a dense forest – an amorphous, ambiguous, dynamic sub-discipline, deeply connected to other scholarly endeavours – that any attempt to define its limits, assert its essentials or make claims for its contributions to wider bodies of scholarship is immediately contested by other scholars who survey the same wood. Similarly, picking out the individual works that make up the most significant trees in that wood brings forth dissension and alternatives. Such is one of the genuine delights of the subject for the researcher and the enthusiast.

My view of this particular wood is, therefore, partial and will, no doubt, change as I get to know it better and differently. Over the four years' gestation of this work, the world has changed as long-term economic and political trajectories unfold and unpredictable crises emerge. Both are enforcing an important rethinking of naval power. There is nothing intrinsically new in this process, but it shows how priorities shift and how understanding history is an essential aspect of the modern world. In presenting this view of the current state of research in naval history to others, I have sought to limit idiosyncrasies by seeking the opinions of friends and colleagues who have contributed so much to the present state of the subject. Particularly, I am indebted to Professors John Hattendorf, Roger Knight, Andrew Lambert, Nicholas Rodger, Jeremy Black, John Beeler and Eugene Rasor, and Drs David Davies, Peter Le Fevre, Roger Morriss and Malcolm Murfett. Together they have eliminated errors and widened my perspectives for this survey. I am also extremely grateful to two anonymous referees who had the patience to provide detailed critiques of this work. The errors, omissions and ambiguities that remain are entirely my own. Whatever the reader may make of it, I hope that it is stimulating or challenging enough to encourage more work, discussion and comprehension of the naval dimension of human life.

I have been greatly assisted in my search for appropriate images by Dr Duncan Redford and his colleagues at the National Museum of the Royal Navy, and by the staff of the National Maritime Museum. The staffs of the US History and Heritage Command and the National Archive, Washington DC also responded quickly and positively to my requests and queries. To all of them I am very grateful.

This work would not have been possible without the great assistance of the library staff at the University of Westminster, who cheerfully and promptly responded to my constant enquiries and requests. On remarkably few occasions were they unable to locate or advise on works that I needed. Finally, my wife Anne and our daughters Rebecca and Hannah had to watch as more of our home became submerged in paper and books. Without them, this book would never have seen the light of day.

Richard Harding
February 2015

Introduction: Debates and prospects for naval history

Purpose and rationale

In 1981 a historian of the Russian navy lamented that his subject had not fared well in recent decades. For the most part, histories were scoreboards of defeats and victories, reiterations of sea battles and the doings of naval heroes.[1] To the public and many scholars, this is still what naval history is all about. While naval history is interesting, even exciting, it is limited in content, context and (for some scholars) theoretical underpinning. On the other hand, naval historians see it very differently. As a historian of the late-seventeenth-century English navy put it in 1953, 'If national history may be compared to a cake, then naval history is not a layer but a slice of that cake.'[2] In other words, naval history cannot be understood unless the multiple contexts (social, economic, technological, cultural, political and diplomatic) in which navies are constructed and put to sea are also understood. To this must be added that if naval conflict and sea power are to be understood, then multiple national contexts and navies have also to be understood.

While naval history has always been distinct, its connections with other sub-disciplines are so close that the precise limits of the subject are impossible to define.[3] For example, a short time spent browsing *The Oxford Encyclopaedia of Maritime History* soon demonstrates how deeply embedded naval history is in so many aspects of world history. Diplomatic, political, economic, social and, particularly, the broader notion of maritime history share content and method with naval history.[4]

Over the last sixty years, naval history has emerged as a complex sub-discipline with its dedicated practitioners. Their growing self-consciousness has also involved a widening and deepening of connections with other sub-disciplines such as those mentioned above and now including the newer sub-discipline of cultural history, as well as social sciences such as international relations and organizational studies. Naval historians have long been aware that they are working in a vast, fascinating and expanding arena. By its nature, it is international in scope. The English-speaking scholar is fortunate in that much is available in English, but much more has not been translated from other languages. The subject is now also intercultural and interdisciplinary which places additional demands on scholars to understand the discourses of other disciplines and cultures.

This book is an attempt to encourage and inform potential researchers about the opportunities naval history presents. It seeks to explain how it has developed, what its contribution has been and thus what are the lacunae, the opportunities for new questions, new research and even a new agenda for naval history.

At the root of any research endeavour must be the driving interest of the researcher. Naval historians have engaged with the subject for its intrinsic value; for curiosity, entertainment or inspiration; and for its extrinsic importance in providing insights and answering questions about contemporary society. Like all history, it has been written to provide stories to inspire and entertain. Indeed, the popular market for naval histories is so close to that for naval novels that the public have been known to confuse the two. For example, during the 1950s the Horatio Hornblower novels by C. S. Forrester were a staple of naval fiction. In 1970, Cecil Northcote Parkinson wrote a spoof biography of the dashing hero, whose existence had become embedded in the popular mind. The book was reviewed as a work of non-fiction in the *Times Literary Supplement* and the staff of the National Maritime Museum, where Hornblower's papers were supposed to have been deposited, had to fend off persistent requests to see the manuscripts.[5]

Although in Western societies few communities actually draw a living directly from the sea, economic and cultural globalization has made the sea an integral and essential part of their lives. Digital media enable the public vicariously to experience life on, in and around the sea in the past and the present. The actions of navies, historically and in the news, across the world are part of this global digital exposure. The public can be extremely passionate about naval history. The notorious and continuing debate regarding a supposed world voyage by a Chinese fleet under Zheng He between 1421 and 1423 is only one of the most extreme examples of how public interest can be fired by an imagined naval past.[6] The problem of 'history' or 'historical method' being mimicked by writers of fiction, fantasy or obsession is not unique to naval history and is possibly a testimony to the enduring appeal of the sea and navies.[7]

Despite cyberspace, the sea is still the essential physical environment which modern international commerce and diplomatic action must traverse. Over 90 per cent of global trade is carried by sea, and the volume of that trade has expanded over 300 per cent since 1970.[8] Despite the economic downturn in 2008, the world commercial fleet has expanded by 37 per cent since that date.[9] Future maritime security for global energy supplies is now one of the most pressing concerns of defence policy makers. However, the sea is not just a vital (if mundane) highway, which, if disrupted, can cause rapid and powerful fluctuations in standards of living within the globalized economy; it is also the setting for many exotic, unfamiliar and surprising encounters in contemporary culture.

This is not new. Naval history, like all history, evolves from an exploration of the past by scholars informed by their contemporary concerns or perspectives. The merging of cultural, political and economic understandings of the sea was an essential part of the development of modern naval history in the last decades of the nineteenth century. The naval history we have today is the result of at least four generations of endeavour, bringing past and present together, overlaying and entwining their interests, discoveries and conclusions. Thus, while naval historians are working in a modern globalized context, the output is currently still dominated by an English speaking and European focus engendered in the struggle of the imperial powers after 1870.

Modern naval history owes a great deal to those who wrote to inform public policy in the decades before the First World War, the significance of which will be discussed in the next chapter. However, those statesmen could not have enacted that policy without popular political approval, and the writing of naval history for popular audiences was an essential part of the genre. Between the two poles of popular and professional naval history, there lies of range of studies that has been of growing significance to other scholars over the last 140 years. Diplomatic history relies to an extent on an understanding of naval warfare. The histories of Europe, the Americas, the 'Atlantic World' or Asia would be incomprehensible without an understanding of naval history.

There is a growing body of historians and social scientists whose primary interests lie elsewhere, but who are working on the sea and, by extension, navies. There has always been a close relationship between maritime economic history and naval history, but more recent interest among economic and cultural historians in global networks for transmission of wealth and ideas has reinforced and widened this interest.[10] The mass participation of populations in military organizations during the twentieth century lends itself to oral history projects, and thus naval history is being integrated into the methodology and concerns of oral historians. The popularity of genealogy and its relationship to heritage have a direct impact on research and the writing of naval history. Even the traditional dominance of the narrative in naval history has the potential for extensive debate with the philosophers of history. For naval historians, the value of this new work lies in exposing the limitations of traditional popular and professional naval histories, providing new insights and suggesting fruitful new areas for research.[11]

This makes a tight definition of naval history both impossible and undesirable. Nevertheless, a broad definition is helpful to position an understanding of its historical evolution. Very few societies or nations have exercised significant sea power in a global or even an extensive regional context, but many societies use navies in riverine or coastal environments, which are still largely neglected in historical studies. At its core, current naval history is predominantly about the application of force at sea or from the sea, and the resolution of conflict by the use of sea power. This is a deceptively simple statement of what, for most of recorded history, has been one of the most complex and difficult human endeavours. The sea is a hostile environment. Exercising sustainable, decisive force upon other societies over the sea requires levels of investment, organization and specialist training that have few parallels on land. Nevertheless, it has been the subject of chronicles and historical narratives since the earliest recording of civilizations in the Western world. The societies of the Mediterranean archipelagos and peninsulas that provided the cultural foundations of Western Europe depended on the sea for their wealth and power. The political histories of the Peloponnesian (431–404 BCE) and Punic (219–167 BCE) Wars had an essential naval dimension.[12]

It is, therefore, a very old subject. The literate public were well used to naval romances and tales of daring, and from classical times the sea and sailing were common metaphorical devices in literature.[13] By the early seventeenth century, the gradual linking of the globe via the oceanic sea routes since the 1450s had exposed a much larger proportion of the world's population to the fruits of maritime commerce, and naval power began to play a far more prominent role in how some societies defined themselves. This was particularly the case in England.[14] As this self-conscious relationship to the sea evolved in the next 200 years of commercial and colonial conflict, more explicit naval histories or narratives began to be written and exploited in political discourse. By the middle of the nineteenth century, political perceptions of naval and maritime affairs were a large and essential part of the diplomatic agendas that then spanned the globe.

By the early 1880s the trajectory of European expansion overseas was clear to contemporaries, as was the acceleration of its competitive pace. For much of the period since the fifteenth century this expansion was explained by beneficent Providence or commercial necessity. In the nineteenth century Social Darwinist theory pointed to the apparent inevitability of conflict and reinforced perceptions of European superiority, as evidenced by imperial power, industrialization and the application of advanced technologies. After a series of revolutions and wars of unification that had buffeted Europe since 1789, nations were again looking overseas as a natural and necessary extension of their ambitions.

The paradigm for the new imperial powers was Great Britain. It was axiomatic that sea power was at the foundation of European transoceanic, global empires. That there was a causal relationship between the British Empire, the most globally extensive empire the world had ever seen, and the dominant position of the Royal Navy was taken for granted. The question was: why had Britain emerged so predominant and successful? The technologies of wood and sail were then giving way to steam and steel – would this undermine British power and provide the space for others to compete on more equal terms? Science had unlocked the technologies of the new navies, and it was believed that the scientific approach to history could also hold the key to the hidden principles of sea power. Thus, the British Royal Navy became the central element of the establishment of modern naval history.[15]

The scientific approach to history, based upon rigorous analyses of surviving documentary sources, had been developing over the previous three decades. State archives were gradually opened to scholars and private collections of papers were being opened to public access. History schools were developing in universities, moving the study from the strong literary bias of the first half of the century to a much more scientific, legalistic focus on the provenance and meaning of individual documents.[16]

In the twenty-five years between 1889 and the outbreak of the First World War, naval history developed as both a serious scholarly and a popular study. The modern scientific study of naval history seemed to offer critical insights for the present. Uncovering the principles of naval warfare was the task that dominated the work of the most famous naval historians and contemporary strategists of the period: Captain Alfred Thayer Mahan, Sir John Knox Laughton, the Colomb brothers and Sir Julian Corbett. Some of their works, particularly Mahan's *The Influence of Sea Power upon History* (1890), crossed over from professional interest into influencing a far wider body of policy makers and the public at large.[17]

Very closely allied to this professional interest in naval history was a broader public interest. In Britain, the Navy League (established in 1895) was a political lobbying organization pushing for the naval defence of the nation.[18] Similar movements were emerging in Germany.[19] Antiquarians, artists, journalists and the public generally began to take a deeper interest in naval history. The Navy Records Society (established in 1893) printed collections of documents illustrating naval history ranging from the Armada to the loss of Minorca in 1756. In 1911 the Society for Nautical Research was established to publish on nautical matters of all periods and all nations, of which naval history was an essential part. These groups brought information to the public, stimulated interest and helped create a publishing environment receptive to naval history.[20]

By 1914 naval history had evolved from a marginal narrative of great deeds, designed to stir the hearts of potential naval officers and to illuminate for the general public the providential rise of the British Empire, to a rich, varied and solidly researched literature that made claims to explain the broader trajectory of world history and the proper course of contemporary strategy.

The First World War proved that the predictive power of this history was overstated and optimistic.[21] In the pre-war years of powerful diplomatic navalism, naval history had become a truly international study, but its integration into the wider body of civilian historical scholarship and policy making withered in the face of the realities of 1914–18. Naval history continued to have its specialist publications, which focused primarily upon ship technologies, tactics, strategy and operational narratives. The results of this research continued to spread over into the academic imperial and political histories of the day, but its influence on policy drifted from the centre of affairs.[22]

To the public, the contribution of naval power to Allied victory in the First World War was obscured by the tragic, but decisive, operations on the Western Front. The role of blockade and convoy in tipping the balance of resources in the Allies' favour was understood, but difficult to emphasize in the wake of the unprecedented slaughter on the front lines of Europe. The Second World War was different. The ejection of the Allies from Europe and the Japanese attack on the Allies across the Pacific and China Sea ensured that this war was fought with a highly visible naval dimension, made easier to comprehend and more dramatic by advances in film and newsreels. The Battle of the Atlantic and the campaigns in the Central and Southwest Pacific could be witnessed and were understood as essential prerequisites for the Western Allies' land operations against the Axis powers. Seeing the terrible conditions experienced on the Murmansk convoys (1941–5), which took war supplies to Russia, also served to educate the public in the West about the global role of sea power in defeating Nazi Germany.

While naval history informed many of the decision-makers involved in these campaigns, it was investment in material and practical experience of contemporary problems that principally underpinned the growing capability of the Allied naval forces. After the war the result was a resurgence in memoirs and amateur and professional studies of the war at sea. The Second World War remains one of the staples of historical publishing seventy years on and is a major proportion of the current output of naval historical studies. It also remains a key reference point for the public in their conception of contemporary naval power.[23]

Given the success of naval history at a popular level after 1945, it is striking that it did not make the same impact within the expanding world of professional academic history. In this, it is no different from military history generally. In the wake of the turmoil generated by two world wars and the continuing tension of the Cold War, historical interest had many alternative foci. The economic, social and political causes of international conflict, struggles of domination and liberation were of greater interest than the conduct of past wars. The new nuclear balance seemed to invalidate the historical experience for policy makers and in the schools of political science and international relations. New methods, borrowed from social sciences, facilitated a stronger focus on the experience of the individual and the group rather than the elites or states. Against this background much naval history seemed limited, irrelevant and biased. The focus on ships and the technology of shipping was important, but had limited relevance to historians asking broader questions. The 'rivet-counters' were more akin to the nineteenth-century antiquarian than in tune with the critical questioning of late-twentieth-century historians.[24] The operational histories, often written by servicemen, gave an opportunity to understand specific victories or defeats, but did not explain the close relationship between these outcomes and the societies from which the armies and navies sprang.

Nevertheless, good, analytical naval and military history was being written, and it would touch the mainstream as fashions changed over the next thirty years. For example, post-1945 interest in the historical development of the modern state led to studies in the growth of bureaucracy in which it was impossible to ignore naval forces. They have become integrated into the long-running debates on state-building, the 'military revolution' of the sixteenth and seventeenth centuries and the 'fiscal-military state' in the eighteenth. They are now informing the debate on the nineteenth-century administrative revolution. Navies also played a role in assisting capital accumulation and thus the beginnings of industrial revolution. As large-scale consumers of manufactured products and raw materials, and as organizers of large manufacturing efforts, navies have something to tell us about industrial change. Interest in the lives of ordinary people is also illuminated by studies of naval history. State naval archives provide unparalleled insights into the lives of seamen as wage labourers and life in port communities over a period of about 400 years. All of this is now interesting economic and social historians.

The end of the Cold War in 1991 and the subsequent acceleration of economic globalization also had implications for the study of naval history. Naval power was important in the collapse of the Soviet Union and the realignment of world diplomacy. Consequently, contemporary Western naval history has not entirely escaped a whiff of triumphalism. The victory of open maritime societies over authoritarian continental powers played well into a narrative that linked the collapse of Napoleonic France, Imperial and Nazi Germany and the Soviet Union. It reinforced the ill-defined link claimed to exist between maritime nations, political democracy and economic success, which underpins a thalassocratic view of the world. Thalassocracy is a mid-nineteenth-century term, originating in the combination of the Greek for 'sea' and 'rule'. It is applied to states claiming or exercising dominion over bodies of water rather than land.[25] That such states are distinctive in that they are shaped by their relationship with the sea, rather than the land, goes back at least as far as Athenian political culture, and this thread continues to be influential in modern political philosophies. For some historians it provides a key causal link between naval power and political liberty. Seeing a progressive trajectory of world history in terms of European maritime expansion raises serious concerns for other historians. It ignores the experience of the vast majority of the world's population. By changing perspective from a spatial to a demographic focus, world history looks very different.[26] Today, the economic rise of China and the concurrent development of the People's Liberation Army Navy (PLAN) are causing

Western strategists to look again at historical precedent and to ask whether traditionally continental or authoritarian powers can build and sustain sea power to compete with more open, traditionally defined, thalassocratic societies.[27]

With over 130 years of accumulated development, naval history is only a little less venerable than the core subjects of European politics and diplomacy. It has probably as much accumulated output, with as much dross and as many gems, as any other part of the discipline. Its relevance to contemporary society is as strong now as it was at the beginning of the twentieth century. The prospects of high-intensity naval conflict may be temporarily low, but in the globalized, interdependent world economy conflict in the maritime sphere, from diplomacy through police actions to low-intensity warfare, is a constant possibility. Relatively minor disruption in this sphere, for example maritime energy routes, can have political and economic consequences out of all proportion to the actions taken. Navies and naval power impinge on so many aspects of life across so many centuries that an examination of their progress and processes provides important insights into many other concerns. Contemporary naval strategists and historians are in a continual dialogue as needs are redefined, resources constrained and contexts shifted.[28]

Structure: Three themes

With such a wide and deep field of study, the question is how to present it. A large bibliography proved unavoidable in a project such as this, but to produce an annotated bibliographic volume did not seem practicable or desirable. Bibliography is the work of a lifetime. There are numerous bibliographies, which are interesting in themselves in that they give insights into the concerns and preferences of the compiler. One of the most important bibliographers of the twentieth century was Robert Albion, whose annotated bibliography went into four editions between 1951 and 1973. After Albion's death in 1983, a supplement was produced by B. W. Labaree.[29] At present, the *Tijdschrift voor Zeegeschiedenis* and the *Mariner's Mirror* both publish annual bibliographies on naval and maritime history. The growing popularity of genealogy has led to a new type of guide, which is also useful for naval researchers.[30] However, as digital technologies make the maintenance of bibliographies much easier and more current, the bibliographer's art is going to be increasingly web based. Although the current estimate of the average life of a web page is approximately seventy-five days, there are excellent bibliographic sites, such as that of US Naval History and Heritage Command and the Rasor Bibliography, hosted by the Centre for Maritime Historical Studies at the University of Exeter. Museums, national libraries, defence institutions, journals and individuals are increasingly posting indices of their own holdings or publications, making it possible for researchers, equipped with modern search engines, to identify materials and collate relevant primary and secondary sources with a few clicks of a mouse.[31]

The purpose of this work is not, therefore, to provide a comprehensive bibliography or a detailed chronological narrative, but to explore the debates that naval history has stimulated, and the understanding of the world to which this history has contributed. Naval history has progressed from its focus on daring deeds or searching for the enduring principles of naval power. Battle, campaigns and operations are still fruitful and central, but in the last fifty years naval historians have enriched their field of study by embracing different methods and foci to answer a much wider range of questions. In the United States, particularly, the contribution of naval history has been critically examined. From the end of the Cold War, historians have been active in reflecting upon history and historical method as a means of illuminating the present and, possibly, the future. Collections of essays on the contributions of Mahan, Corbett and Richmond, based on colloquia at the Naval War College, provide evidence of this serious reflection.[32] In 1994 the proceedings of another international colloquium on the state of naval history provided an important snapshot of the discipline across the globe.[33] This was followed in 1995 by another collection of essays from an international array of scholars, reflecting on the methods, biases and interdisciplinary connections of naval history.[34]

These works have greatly influenced my interest and thinking, and so this volume owes a great deal to all those scholars. The work of one author cannot hope to be as comprehensive as that of a number, but I want to bring up to date some of those reflections and provide a slightly different balance to the review of the subject in order to address a wider audience.

This work has been structured around three themes, which follow the evolving contribution of naval history to a wider body of scholarship and a changing world. The first theme, *Sea Power and International Relations*, is an exploration of the support naval history has provided for policy and diplomacy in international relations. Historians have been essential in the construction of modern doctrines of sea power and informed decisions that have led to the construction and deployment of navies. This remains at the core of the subject today. The Anglo-centric or US-centred domination of the subject remains, but there are now excellent studies of other European navies at different periods, ranging from the Dutch navy of the seventeenth century, to the French and Spanish navies of the eighteenth century, to the German, Russian, Chinese and Japanese navies of the nineteenth and twentieth centuries. Comparative studies of how naval power, or sea power, was exercised and what it was intended to achieve are now beginning to appear and give us a richer picture than the old histories that focused on the ultimate triumph of the capital ship.

The second theme, *Politics and Government*, deals with navies as one of the great departments of state. Navies do not only have an impact on international politics. They also have significant influence on the political structures of their host societies. Navies have always been major consumers of resources, which has evident political and economic consequences. They are different from armies and present different bureaucratic and political imperatives. Consequently, navies play an important, distinctive role in the debates concerning state-building, bureaucratization and democratization.

The third theme, *Navies and Societies*, emerges from the second. Navies are themselves some of the most complex organizations that humans have created. To exercise sustained power over massive distances on an element inimical to normal human existence is an activity demanding intense concentration of effort. Understanding how societies did this, and why, is an important question for modern economic, social, cultural and organizational historians. Navies can be studied as organizations that were the most complex of their time. How they operated tells us about contemporary norms and attitudes, which are only now being explored in any detail. How navies related to the other elements of their host societies has been at the centre of claims to a thalassocratic social culture. Yet the detailed research to investigate these hypotheses has yet to be carried out.

The study of navies encompasses the experiences of the people who served on the ships. The social structure of navies is now a thriving area of study, moving from traditional concerns about manpower and officership to the social construction of the naval seaman, with the racial and gender issues underpinning their working lives. The shoreside activities of navies, particularly the political, diplomatic, logistical systems, have been a long-standing concern of naval historians. More recently, studies of the labouring and commercial communities that supported dockyards have enriched our understanding of the social and economic impact of navies.

These three themes go to the heart of some of the most interesting subjects in modern history: the nature of international relations, the state and the economy, of social and political attitudes, of norms and cultural influences, of employment practices and administrative systems, and of technological innovation and global relations. That navies provide insights into these questions is not just because of their role in those aspects of society, but because they have, unlike many private organizations, left behind them a mass of documentation ready to be explored and interpreted. These documents were not preserved for the convenience of future historians, but their survival in such quantity and variety is a treasure that is almost unmatched by any other organization. Rarely, outside naval history, can a historian recover a level of detail varying from individuals' service lives to the assessment of the global impact of a voyage. This is what is available to the naval historian and what naval history has to offer to contemporary scholarship.

Nonetheless, naval history still has its difficulties. The study of war, with all its connotations of propaganda, the glorification of aggressive nationalism and destruction, is looked upon with some distaste in centres of liberal learning.[35] As one eminent naval historian has commented, unlike researchers into cancer, researchers into war and conflict are assumed to be in favour of their subject matter. A body of scholarship which has been built up with the explicit didactic intent of instructing naval officers and politicians on how to be more effective, or by antiquarians intent on pursuing some nationalist or patriotic project, does not sit easily within a discipline that struggled to free itself of teleological distortions. Naval history generally, but particularly British naval history at the popular end of the spectrum, with its overwhelmingly Anglo-centric corpus of research and triumphalist tone, stands at odds with the more comparative, culturally nuanced and socially focused interests of many historians today.

Shaking off the perception of a narrow technical, nationalist study, like challenging any stereotype, is a task of years and immense effort. Nevertheless, as the paragraphs above have indicated, this has been going on for some decades, and there are reasons why naval history now provides a fruitful, challenging and diverse study.

CHAPTER ONE

Sea power and international relations: History in the service of policy

The emergence of modern naval history

Today, naval history is a truly international project. However, its modern origins are very much rooted in the British experience. By 1880 the great continental heartlands of the globe were experiencing a period of relative stability. Europe had emerged from decades of conflict and revolution that accompanied the wars of unification. From Spain eastwards to Russia, with the exception of the Balkans, a social and diplomatic status quo had finally settled across Europe. Similarly, after the destructive Civil War (1861–5), the United States had expanded its control across the continent, creating a union of states and territories that was unbroken from the Atlantic to the Pacific. In Asia, the Chinese Quing emperor had suppressed revolts with the help of Western forces, and Japan had emerged from its civil wars as a unified state under the Meiji emperor.

However, the politically conscious populations across the world were not looking forward to a prolonged period of stability and peace. Technological change was accelerating across Europe and America, creating extensive industrialization and with it massive social dislocation and economic opportunities. The intellectual context of the time was one in which science and technology promised massive leaps forward in wealth and power for those that exploited it and spelt ruin for those that did not. Framed by the social application of the Darwinist theory of evolution, the world was conceived as the setting for a highly competitive global race for survival.

How that competition was to be played out was unclear. The creation of the new, unified and increasingly bureaucratized nation-states, such as Germany and the United States, highlighted the potential economic and political power of organized, continental polities. On the other hand, the glaring example of the British Empire, a linked global trading organization, suggested that greater power rested in the opportunities for materials and markets on a world scale. For British scholars and statesmen the truth of this was axiomatic. It had been the foundation of 250 years of policy,[1] and it was all predicated on the dominance of British naval power, which had been firmly consolidated during the long wars against Revolutionary and Napoleonic France (1793–1815). Even when free trade finally supplanted imperial mercantilist economic policy during the first half of the nineteenth century, a world commercial order, guaranteed by the Royal Navy, was the basic assumption of British economic and political thought.

Nonetheless, the challenge posed by the new continental powers was disturbing. In 1881, Sir John Seeley, the Regis Professor of History at Cambridge, delivered an influential series of lectures on the British and their empire, comparing it with previous empires and speculating about its future. He found no special virtues in the imperial conquests or economic organization, but firmly concluded that the old British-settled empire was a network of societies, a Greater Britain, spreading across territory, much like the contemporary United States. From this expanding base, Seeley concluded that the moral mission of Britain was to tighten the bonds in that common British society and spread its influence to other societies, principally India and later Africa, for the mutual benefit of all.[2] This historically argued imperial vision could be just as easily adopted by any other power convinced that its moral purpose and economic interests went conveniently hand in hand. It explained Britain's global economic dominance and helped justify the rapid European conquest of Africa and parts of Asia between 1880 and 1914.

While Seeley identified many factors that had created the British Empire, one of the key instruments was the Royal Navy, which, between 1650 and 1815, won the maritime wars against Spain, the United Provinces (the Netherlands) and France to establish a naval supremacy.[3] While it was never universally accepted, even in Britain, that maritime rather than continental dominion was the way to future prosperity and power, it was the message that had the most persuasive diplomatic and political appeal.[4] Whether or not 'Pax Britannica' was really the phenomenon that underpinned the global (as opposed to regional) diplomatic system of the nineteenth century did not matter – 'navalism' dominated late-nineteenth-century great power politics.[5]

Given the perceived importance of sea power, discovering its mechanics was essential for the modern sea officer and statesman, and history was an obvious means of illuminating its principles. History had always served to provide lessons of morality, behaviour and the essential legends to bind societies, but now history became the explicit servant of policy – to explain the correct course of action for nations engaged in the great struggle for survival. It was a task undertaken by many historians at the time, working in many countries, but it was Captain Alfred Thayer Mahan of the United States Navy who provided the neat, popularly packaged explanation of the true way. In his book, *The Influence of Sea Power upon History, 1660-1783*, published in 1890, Mahan highlighted the persistent British focus on the battle fleet. The sheer scale of British investment and the competence of its crews, its officers and, later, its administrators ensured that it had the power, the resilience and the range to outperform any of its rivals. Under its protection the British maritime economy had flourished out of proportion to competitors.

The apogee of this process and the demonstration of its truth were the French Revolutionary and Napoleonic Wars. It was self-evident to contemporary Europeans that Britain had emerged from those wars as the unparalleled global imperial power, whose wealth and empire continued to expand during the century. The story of those wars was the subject of Mahan's subsequent volumes in 1892.[6]

The French Revolutionary and Napoleonic Wars (1793–1815) and their impact on naval history

In Mahan's view, even before 1789, 'The overwhelming sea power of England was the determining factor in European history.'[7] Extensive as this claim was, Mahan was only building on a shared nineteenth-century perception of how the 'Great War', as the French Wars were commonly known, shaped contemporary Europe. In Britain, at least, the vital role of the Royal Navy in these wars was already firmly embedded in the national legend. On the eve of the French Revolution, European investment in navies was running at a historically high level. Britain had ended the American War of Independence (1775–83) with more ships than her taxpayers were willing to support, and although numbers fell, there was continued investment in maintaining the infrastructure with a large and active fleet.[8] In France and Spain, the momentum of building and the development of naval infrastructure continued.[9] The Revolution changed all this. France, which had turned away from the problems of central Europe after the Seven Years' War (1756–63), found herself the target of the European powers which were determined to eliminate the new republic after the deposition of Louis XVI in August 1792. France became absorbed in European warfare until the fall of Napoleon in 1815. The effectiveness of the French navy crumbled even before war broke out, as most of the noble officer corps fled France in 1790–1. Despite the huge energy displayed by the French Revolutionary authorities during 1793–4, it was impossible to rebuild either the officer corps or the administrative infrastructure that had sustained a large and credible battlefleet.[10]

The scale of the wars, their length, and the political forces of liberalism, nationalism and romanticism which they released, created shifts in the European political and diplomatic environment that resonated throughout the rest of the nineteenth and into the early twentieth centuries. Two apparent consequences are of particular note for naval historians. The first was the confirmation of Britain's maritime hegemony. Despite repeated victories in Europe, France and its allies or vassal states could not overcome the naval power of Great Britain. Although there were scares in 1796–7 and 1804–5, Britain remained beyond French domination. Furthermore, from that secure base, British policy was consistently able to mobilize and finance opposition to France, which ultimately led to the coalition that overthrew Napoleon in 1814. Sea power, it seems, had been the fundamental determinant of the fate of Europe.

Alongside political independence, the British economy was rapidly outpacing its rivals. While Europe was consumed by wars, Britain, which fought France for longer than any other nation during this period, was expanding economically at an unprecedented rate. The apparent linkage between economic acceleration and Britain's naval dominance was too strong not to assume a direct causal relationship in the minds of contemporaries and historians.

Politically and economically, therefore, these wars provided the foundations for historians working on naval power and navies. British naval power was the model for emulation or analysis. During the second half of the nineteenth century, as technological changes and the absence of long naval conflicts made the future conduct of naval warfare more difficult to predict, the experiences of the wars of 1793–1815 were the most convenient analytical frame for servicemen and politicians.

It was an exceptionally long war, particularly for Britain, which only once made a peace treaty with France (1802–3). It took three more coalitions from 1804 to destroy the Napoleonic Empire. The crucial victories were won in Germany and France in 1813–14 primarily by the armies of Russia, Austria and Prussia, but the long duration of the conflict was an ideal environment within which to display the less dramatic, but critical, impact of sea power. With Britain controlling the world sea lines of communication, France could not invade Britain, nor, despite the size of the Imperial Army and its confederates, could it prevent British merchants from trading around the European littoral. Britain was thrice blessed by these circumstances. They kept the war off home soil and gathered the riches of trade from colonies and collaborators across the globe, which, in turn, enabled the financing of Napoleon's enemies, who, ultimately, brought down the Empire on the battlefields of Europe. This was the perfect demonstration of Mahan's analysis of sea power.

The power of the French Wars lay not just in the elegance of the story of sea power that could be woven around them, but in the impact they had on the British political psyche. This was not a one-sided war, with Britain able to stand completely aside while Europe burned. It required an unparalleled mobilization of national resources.[11] The social mobilization required by the war has been commented upon, but the specific naval dimension of this experience has not yet been fully explored by historians.[12]

This mobilization included a major propaganda effort to bring the population behind the state in order to generate the necessary financial resources over a prolonged period. The French Wars mark the point at which naval history and contemporary political and strategic dialectics begin to elide. For the first time, substantial contemporary history was being written to influence the public view of a current war. Once the war was over, the lessons of this history were employed as a means of defining a nation in its international relations.[13]

The naval narrative became an important element within this effort. Contemporary narratives, such as *The Naval Chronicle* (1799–1818), fed public perceptions of Britain as a natural naval power.[14] This was taken up by contemporary historians, such as William James in his *The Naval History of Great Britain,* published between 1822 and 1824.[15] James was particularly exercised to see that the Anglo-American War of 1812–14 was portrayed as a naval victory by the Americans. James was able to demonstrate that, while the United States achieved spectacular early successes in naval actions, which became part of the founding legend of the United States Navy, the British had, by 1814, imposed an effective blockade of the Eastern Seaboard, making the continuation of the war impossible for President Madison's government.[16]

For politically aware Britons of the mid-nineteenth century the Great French Wars had confirmed that economic prosperity, imperial expansion and diplomatic power rested on British naval power. It was an understanding that was increasingly shared by other nations as they surveyed the global environment. As the certainty of British naval dominance began to fade during the last quarter of the century and other nations turned their resources towards navies, the history of the Great War with France to understand (and to propagandize) the new threat or opportunities became more important. Furthermore, the growth of literacy, the franchise and the imperial dynamic within European politics all fed into a situation in which the demand for naval history expanded and evolved.

At the end of the nineteenth century, most naval history was being carried out in the naval war colleges. Nevertheless, the concurrent rise of modern academic, or 'scientific', history schools in European universities also promoted history as an intellectual grounding for contemporary statecraft and the elaboration of the national story. Until 1914 the French Wars were an essential part of this narrative, and in Britain they provided the best examples of long-term, long-range naval warfare.[17] The naval war was an essential part of the political and diplomatic narrative, linking the professional, the academic and the popular interest in naval history, but was never quite integrated into the mainstream of British academic historical studies. This surprising lack of integration remains unchanged to this day.

Naval operations during the war, 1793–1815

While the impact of the naval war on British society and European diplomacy is still relatively under-researched, the operational history of the Royal Navy in the war is at the heart of perceptions of sea power.

Britain joined the war against Revolutionary France in February 1793, and initially events in the continental war were critical to the naval balance. In alliance with Spain and the United Provinces, the Royal Navy was more than able to hold its own against France. The Royal Navy gave Britain and her allies the ability to strike at France from multiple directions, but it was never able to create the decisive impetus once ashore. An attempt to take Toulon in 1793 was defeated by events ashore, not at sea. The expeditions to support Royalist insurrections in the Vendee in 1795 foundered on the lack of support for the cause. The difficulties experienced by major expeditions to the West Indies were, with the exception of Victor Hughes' resistance on Guadeloupe, caused more by climate and slave rebellions than by French opposition.[18]

However, events in Europe were gradually reducing the support Britain received on land and at sea. The French occupation of the United Provinces in 1796 and the withdrawal of Spain from the war in 1795 had a dramatic impact on the balance of the war at sea. By 1796 France and her allies had a nominal numerical advantage in line of battle ships. The late 1790s were very difficult times for Britain, with French forces dominating Europe. Almost the entire Atlantic coastline (excluding Portugal) was in hostile hands. British ability to influence events ashore seemed extremely limited as finally Austria, the last great power holding out against France, signed the Treaty of Campo Formio in October 1797.

Difficult as it appeared for Britain, the state of Europe in 1802 hid the significance of its naval strength. The Royal Navy had entered the war well funded, well organized and well balanced. In almost every encounter with the weakened French navy it emerged successful. Major battles were rare, but decisively won. Lord Howe's victory over the French squadron defending an important grain convoy returning to France, the Glorious First of June 1794, imposed serious losses on the French navy, although the grain convoy got through.[19] The navy was able to impose an effective and sustained blockade along the French coast.[20]

The accession of the United Provinces (now the Batavian Republic) and Spain to alliances with France in 1796 provided the latter with only weak naval reinforcements. These navies could not be concentrated easily. Both the Batavian Republic and Spain had serious fiscal difficulties. The Dutch navy was defeated in a hard-fought battle off Camperdown (11 October 1797), losing nine of the fifteen line of battle ships engaged. In 1799, after a mutiny, most of the rest of the Dutch navy was captured at anchor by the British at Den Helder.[21] After Admiral Sir John Jervis's victory

FIGURE 1 *The eighteenth-century line of battle in action: the Battle off Cape St Vincent, 14 February 1797.* © *National Maritime Museum: ID PW5795.*

over a Spanish squadron off Cape St Vincent on 14 February 1797, the Spanish navy was effectively immobilized and the British could re-enter the Mediterranean. Campaigning there in 1798, Vice Admiral Horatio Nelson inflicted a crushing defeat on the French squadron that had covered Napoleon Bonaparte's invasion of Egypt, at Aboukir Bay near Alexandria (1 August 1798).[22] Nelson subsequently supported a revolt against French occupation in Malta and helped overthrow (temporarily) the pro-French republican government in Naples.

Ultimately, the War of the Second Coalition (1798–1800) did little to restore the balance of power in Europe, but British naval power was reinforced throughout European waters. The French were driven out of Egypt during 1801.[23] French attempts to invade the British Isles, while mostly seriously intended, were poorly executed and easily defeated.[24] A second League of Armed Neutrality in the Baltic fell apart shortly after a squadron under Admiral Sir Hyde Parker and Nelson destroyed the Danish floating batteries and warships defending Copenhagen (2 April 1801),[25] but what role the victory or the subsequent presence of the British squadron in the Baltic played in the critical political event in the collapse of the Neutrality – the assassination of Tsar Paul – is still a point of contention.[26]

The Treaty of Amiens (27 March 1802), which ended the Anglo-French war, only lasted until May 1803. With the Royal Navy dominating most waters, but without European allies, the threat of invasion was Britain's principal concern. Both naval and diplomatic histories of the Revolutionary War (1793–1802) are mostly in agreement with this conclusion,[27] but the lack of modern work on the French amphibious capabilities and the need for a broader integration of the European and imperial conditions into the analyses of naval power suggest that far more work needs to be done.[28]

In October 1804 Spain joined a French alliance against Britain. While French invasion planning continued during 1804 and into 1805, British diplomatic effort was successful in raising a third coalition, including Austria, Russia and Sweden. The year 1805 was to be one of the most significant years of the war. Napoleon's complex grand plan for invading Britain was finally executed, but collapsed during the course of the year, and ended for the Franco-Spanish combined fleet in the catastrophic Battle of Trafalgar (21 October 1805). By this time, Napoleon's attention had been drawn to the Danube, where Austrian forces had been assembling in preparation for an invasion of the Rhineland. This campaign, which saw an Austrian army surrender at Ulm (17 October 1805) and the main Austro-Russian army crushed at the Battle of Austerlitz (2 December 1805), ended with Napoleon's empire firmly established in Germany and Italy. The Third Coalition collapsed as Austria withdrew, and a belated attempt by Prussia to reverse the settlement led to disaster at the Battle of Jena-Auerstadt (14 October 1806). Russia made peace after a final campaign in Poland and defeat at the Battle of Friedland (14 June 1807).

Britain was not saved from invasion by Trafalgar in 1805, but now that Napoleon's attention could be turned back to Britain, the Royal Navy made it impossible for the emperor to revive his invasion plans. Almost all of Europe was under French imperial control and subject to the economic Decrees of Berlin and Milan, which prohibited commerce with Great Britain. Britain, however, could exert pressure on all Europe's overseas trade. British forces tightened their grip on the West Indies, the Cape of Good Hope and the East Indies, placing almost all oceanic trade under her surveillance.

Unlike the period from 1793 to 1805, naval operations after Trafalgar have been examined far less intensely and by relatively few scholars. This is curious, as the post-1805 period is one of unparalleled British naval and maritime domination, and it is here that the evidence of the decisive impact of sea power which Mahan claimed should be found. Once established by decisive fleet battle, the 'noiseless, steady, exhausting pressure with which sea power acts' could be brought to bear upon the enemy's economy and society by blockade, raids and diversions.[29] There is a distinct lack of studies for the period in which the presumed pressure of sea power should be at its most evident. Most of the studies we have are operational, which are excellent in explaining how sea power was exercised, but do not get to the crucial matter of what impact this power had upon the courts and markets of Paris, Vienna, St. Petersburg, Berlin and others. Only recently have the mechanics of European trade become the focus of historians' attention.[30] Piers Mackesy has produced an excellent history of operations in the Mediterranean, but detailed studies of the impact of the blockades are still needed.[31] The war in the Far East is broadly covered by C. N. Parkinson in his *War in the Eastern Seas, 1793-1815*. More recently, the period up to 1805 has been re-examined by Peter Ward, and the dramatic events of 1809–10 in the Indian Ocean have been recounted by Stephen Taylor.[32] Yet a fuller examination of the impact of events in that theatre from 1805 to 1815 awaits its historians. The West Indies after 1801 has attracted very little attention, despite two important operations against Guadeloupe and Martinique in 1809 and 1810. The Baltic has been better served. A. N. Ryan's work has recently been enriched by Tim Voelcker and James Davey, but how these operations influenced the behaviour of the Russian and Nordic courts is still only partially examined.[33]

After Trafalgar, the Royal Navy was absorbed by the unglamorous but essential activities of applying sea power to undermine the enemy. It was a war of convoy and blockade. The dominance of the British battle squadrons across the globe provided security for the ports and centres of population. The sea lines of communication between those ports could never be so securely patrolled. Privateers and small raiding squadrons continued to get to sea. Although they could not destroy British commerce, they could impose heavy costs upon it. Convoys, covered by escorting naval vessels, reduced those costs. British naval patrols off the coasts of French-dominated Europe imposed tremendous costs upon French commerce. Together, convoy and blockade determined the trajectory of maritime commerce for the rest of the war. Napoleon reorientated the French economy towards central Europe, but Europeans, as consumers, did not wish to isolate themselves from the global

FIGURE 2 *The impact of sea power: an inshore squadron under Vice Admiral Horatio Nelson, blockading Cadiz, July 1797.* © *National Maritime Museum, Greenwich, London. ID BHC0499.*

markets. Ultimately, this tension made French imperial policy untenable and provided the context for the fatal over-extension of Napoleonic ambition in Russia in 1812.[34]

For Mahan the privateers were of little interest, as they 'produced no results, [and] had absolutely no effect on the issue of the war'.[35] While this remains the dominant view, it has never been universally shared. French naval historians, like those of all countries, are involved in a discourse concerning the apparent lessons learnt from British naval domination and their own national experiences. Just as the Anglo-French struggle between 1688 and 1815 provided the context for Mahan's history, so the French navy emerges most clearly on the losing side. Rather than simply seeing this as the demonstration of an eternal truth of naval strategy, which Mahan claimed, French historians and policy makers have been more interested in understanding why France went down the developmental route it did, and what advantages this might have brought.

Defeat is far more difficult to explain than victory, as counter-factual arguments are insecure and highly contestable. Thus, as the distinguished French naval historian Hervé Coutau-Bégarie noted, the French naval narrative is more fragmented than the dominant Anglo-American narrative of battlefleet success.[36] From the late 1690s, when France was faced with defeat in battlefleet actions (*guerre d'escadre*), she consciously turned to the privateering or cruising war against trade (*guerre de course*). This presented an apparent dichotomy between concentrating on the battlefleet and investment in a cruising naval force. In the period between 1880 and 1900, the time when Mahan was making his case for the battlefleet, these were presented as alternative strategies – the *jeune école* of the cruising fleet opposed to the *vielle école* of the dominant battlefleet. France was not alone in this. Other nations, such as Italy, Russia and Germany, explored the options these strategies presented, provoking a previously unseen intellectual ferment around naval operations. Ultimately, by 1905, the *vielle école* emerged triumphant in this debate, but whether privateering of cruising warfare was the right or wrong policy to adopt is dependent on context, and continued work upon it has produced a rich historiography that links maritime capacity and social and economic pressures to naval strategies. It continues to provide a stimulus to serious historical studies of commerce warfare, trade protection, and the role of navies in dominating the dynamics of international trade.[37]

After 1805 the exertion of sea power did not rest purely on blockade. While there was no longer the prospect of significant fleet action, the potential for Napoleon to rebuild his naval forces had grown rather than diminished as a result of his victories between 1805 and 1807, and the British reacted fiercely to this threat. They captured the Danish fleet in 1807 after a severe bombardment of Copenhagen (September 1807).[38] Other operations were less decisive. A large expedition was mounted to the island of Walcheren. Although it neutralized Flushing as an enemy assembly point, it was unsuccessful in destroying the shipbuilding facilities in Antwerp (July to October 1809).[39] Throughout the war, Venetian shipyards remained a small but unsuppressed threat. Napoleon never completed his plans for a vast imperial fleet, but how far this was due, directly or indirectly, to British naval or to completely different causes, such as Napoleon's mercurial attitude to naval power, remains to be explored. The answers lie in the French archives, if anywhere.[40]

Napoleon's attempts to create a fortress of Europe based on the Continental System were fatally undermined by European demand for overseas produce and British manufactures, together with endemic corruption in the imperial customs service. The desire to close off Portugal, the only British access point to Europe not under French control, led to an invasion in November 1807 and a war in the Peninsula that ended only with the fall of Napoleon. It is, therefore, possible to infer that it was sea power that led to the first significant over-extension of the Napoleonic Empire. Once the campaign had started, the Royal Navy played a crucial role in providing the logistical support for British operations in the Peninsula, from the first operations around the Tagus in 1807 to Wellington's march across the Pyrenees in 1814.[41]

Sea power was also an important factor in the fatal over-extension – Napoleon's invasion of Russia on 24 June 1812. Napoleon's fruitless attempts to stop Russia trading with Britain were one important factor in the gradual collapse of Franco-Russian relations.[42] As the war consumed Europe, Britain grew wealthy on colonial conquests and an expanding manufacturing sector – the produce of both being smuggled to Europe under the eye of the Royal Navy. Subsidies, arms and uniforms began to flow into Europe to supplement goods and produce, first to Portugal and Spain, and later, from 1813, to Austria and Prussia as the campaigns against Napoleon developed. British naval power did not cause the coalitions that brought down Napoleon, but it did ensure that material and financial aid flowed to the allies when the coalitions were formed.

Other vital work was done supporting amphibious operations or armies ashore in Spain, Portugal, Italy, Egypt, and the West and East Indies.[43] There were some defeats (most significantly, Buenos Aires and Naples in 1806, Walcheren in 1809 and Mauritius in 1810), but for the most part, this period saw the most extensive and effective control of maritime trade ever exercised up to that date.[44]

From this perspective, the story of sea power looks central to the fate of Europe, and there is no doubt that Britain did manage to wield sea power with a sophistication and range never before seen. However, while much effort has been put into understanding the processes or mechanics of how Britain exercised its extensive sea power, much less has been devoted to how this pressure was experienced and understood within the French Empire and the courts of Europe. Action can only be understood if the impact it has on its target group is fully explored. On the whole, historians of sea power have not yet engaged with the diplomatic archives adequately to test rigorously the claims of sea power. Also, diplomatic and military historians have tended not to look beyond the towering personality of the emperor and the direct diplomatic exchanges, to absorb the indirect influence of sea power into their perceptions of interstate conflict and the fate of Europe.

In 1812, as the war was reaching a climax in Europe, a simmering dispute between Britain and the United States erupted into war. While the war was a sideshow for the British, who were still focused upon defeating Napoleon, it was vitally important for the future of the United States. In the United States, unlike Britain, there was a real and deep political divide between the 'navalists', who saw America's future as being linked to expanding world commerce, and the 'anti-navalists', who were more concerned with consolidating the American nation across the great continent. Even among 'navalists', opinion had been split ever since 1793 over the best way to defend the growing trade to Europe and the Caribbean. French privateers, Barbary pirates and the Royal Navy all posed threats and obstacles. The results of a 'quasi-war' with France, between 1798 and 1801, in the West Indies demonstrated some disproportionate successes but also distinct limitations of the rapidly expanded American squadrons.[45]

This conflict did not resolve a long-running debate within Congress on the appropriate size, structure and function of a United States Navy. Rising tensions with Britain over the economic blockade of Europe and the impressment of Americans into the Royal Navy were real points of tension between the two nations, particularly when they exploded into violent confrontation. One such confrontation occurred in June 1807 when the British fourth-rate HMS *Leopard* (50) attacked the US frigate *Chesapeake* (44) off Cape Henry in search of deserters.[46] *Chesapeake,* although a 44, was not one of the formidably armed 24 lb frigates which later became so famous, and was caught unprepared. She surrendered almost immediately, much to the fury of the American public.

However, there were other domestic political pressures in America. The pressure for expansion into Canada and the West was equally significant in the eventual declaration of war. On the whole, the naval causes of the war of 1812 have had the most prominence in the diplomatic histories, as they neatly fitted the navalist, diplomatic narrative of historians working at the end of the nineteenth century. However, the balance is being redressed by some of the many works stimulated by the recent bicentenary of the war.[47]

Early action at sea surprised the British. The large, well-armed American frigates performed well in single-ship actions. The destruction of the *Guerriere* (38) by the *Constitution* (44) (19 August 1812) and the capture of the *Macedonian* (38) by the *United States* (44) (11 October 1812) and the *Java* (38) by the *Constitution* (44) (22 December 1812) are still important symbols in the United States Navy's history. Their smaller vessels on the coasts and in the Great Lakes performed equally well.[48] In the end, superior numbers told on the high seas. The American cruising strategy of 1812–13 failed to disrupt British maritime trade significantly, and British control of the Eastern Seaboard was reasserted, largely closing American trade and making the whole coast vulnerable to destructive raids. The burning of Washington in August 1814 was a potent signal of the re-established naval order.[49]

However, Americans could take a great deal of pride in the performance of their small navy. The navalists had not wanted the war, but events had given their perspective of American naval policy a boost. The anti-navalists' gunboat navy that had dominated the political debate since 1807 had not done as badly as navalists had feared, but by the end of the war America was completing three ships of the line.[50] The investment did not last, but over the next five years it enabled the United States to act independently in the Atlantic and Caribbean.[51] Ultimately, the political rationale for such a navy proved difficult to sustain with the realization that US and British policies were consistent and a large navy unnecessary. The role of the navy expanded again from the 1830s, but it was not until the emergence of what Symonds has called 'emotional navalism' in the 1880s that the navalist ideology decisively won the battle for US policy.[52]

Pax Britannica and naval history, 1815–1914

So many of the key themes that were to dominate the writing of naval history and navalist thinking were embedded in the period from 1792 to 1815. It demonstrated the essential navalist proposition – naval power had enabled Britain to stand apart from the catastrophic land wars that had consumed Europe. It protected maritime commerce, which was the root of financial power. This financial power, in turn, underpinned the Royal Navy and sustained the coalitions against Napoleon. It even determined the broader diplomatic terms by which those allies did most of the land fighting.[53] Although the proposition that global power is founded on financial strength and immunity from land attack, the rise of the United States to economic and diplomatic dominance since 1939 has powerfully demonstrated it to the point where there is almost a complete geopolitical consensus on the symbiosis of sea power, economic weight and diplomatic punch.[54]

The French Wars also provided a clear narrative to embed public interest in navies. They were broad, wide-ranging conflicts with decisive fleet battles, dramatic frigate actions, amphibious operations and even close encounters with national catastrophe. The intensity of the wars created the need for national heroes and provided the opportunities for them. Naval officers become national heroes, and Horatio Lord Nelson became the iconic symbol of sea power.[55] With his death in this battle, Nelson was transformed from an exceptionally capable, if humanly flawed, officer into an international symbol of ultimate naval virtue. The literature on Nelson is now enormous, and he has a following of his own that is unique among naval officers.[56]

Biographies have continued to appear with great regularity, and the bicentenary of Trafalgar in 2005 stimulated a range of new studies.[57] During his life, Nelson adroitly promoted his own public image, and his efforts were rewarded, as they resonated with a contemporary demand for modern heroic figures.[58] He was an avid correspondent, and his papers have been published in collections since the middle of the nineteenth century.[59] The Royal Navy had become 'Nelson's Navy' in popular understanding.

In recent decades the complexities of wielding a weapon like the Royal Navy over the world's oceans during the period 1793–1815 have been the subject of more detailed and rigorous study, but the fighting officer of this period remains the quintessential naval hero. Frigate commanders such as Thomas Cochrane, Edward Pellew, Graham Moore, Sydney Smith, Philip Broke, William Hoste and James Gordon were heroes of that cast. Over the past two centuries, others, including French and Spanish officers, have been added to the martial pantheon of an age that has captured and still enthrals the public imagination. Men such as St Vincent, Collingwood, Keith, Cotton, Gravina, Latouche-Tréville and Willaumez have full studies devoted to them, and many more have substantial biographical essays.[60] Naval biography remains a vibrant aspect of modern naval historical studies, even if the impact of this genre on naval history is still very much under-researched.

The Battle of Trafalgar itself has taken on a life of its own. The myths that surrounded it grew rapidly in the nineteenth century as it was integrated into the British national story and, very quickly, it was absorbed into the institutional myths of the naval service, not just in Britain but in other states as well.[61] The navy's supposed role in saving the nation, the climactic annihilation of the Combined Fleet, and the sacrifices on both sides provided a ready market for memoirs, histories and representation in the arts. At the beginning of the twentieth century the battle had a special position in the strategic thinking within the Royal Navy.[62] So significant had it become in the debates on contemporary naval tactics that in 1913 the Admiralty commissioned a detailed investigation of Nelson's tactics on the day, and the failure of the navy to inflict another Trafalgar on the German High Seas Fleet in the First World War was a major element in post-war re-evaluations of the service.[63] The battle has inevitably become weighed down with generations of myths and stories. The work carried out by historians of many nations during the bicentennial commemoration of the battle has done much to strip away layers of national and service narratives to put it more accurately into the geopolitical context of 1804–6. The battle did not save Britain from invasion. It did not prevent Napoleon from attempting to resurrect a battlefleet from European yards between 1808 and 1814, but it did make that task incredibly difficult and, ultimately, unachievable. The battle has also become the focus for historians exploring the life experiences of seamen and officers who served at sea in this period.[64]

After the exhausting wars since 1792, only Britain emerged diplomatically and economically enhanced. The wars had left her as the paramount naval power, with an expanded extra-European empire and with the most advanced economy in the world. The European order established by the Congresses of Vienna (1814–15) was the basis of the diplomatic order that endured up to 1914, and it was against this background that naval power must be considered. In the years after 1815 there were too many unresolved issues within Europe and too little appetite for naval expansion among the continental powers to disturb Britain's naval hegemony.[65] However, it did not go unnoticed. The coincidence of naval power, economic advance, political liberalism, imperial expansion and diplomatic strength was a mix that contemporaries could not ignore. Britain's influence on the great European powers waned after 1815 with the termination of the subsidy treaties, but Britain was able to order the wider world to her own ends with minimal expenditure of resources for the next forty years.[66]

During these years of the 'Pax Britannica' the flexibility of naval power allowed Britain to intervene at critical points in the Spanish and Portuguese Civil Wars (1834–9 and 1827–34), the Greek War of Independence (1821–32) and the Belgian Revolution (1830–2). British naval bombardments of Algiers in 1816 and 1826 and their operations at Beirut and Acre in 1840 in support of the Ottoman Turks all helped adjust international relations towards British objectives. Similarly, British support for the independence movements in South America (1807–25) effectively made the re-establishment of Spanish or Portuguese rule on the continent impossible.[67] Britain was also able to impose her own priorities, such as the abolition of the slave trade, upon other nations.

Despite the importance of this, there was a huge gap in historical studies of this period. Peace never generates as much historical interest in navies as war, and most naval history has been primarily concerned with seizing or maintaining naval dominance by war. Nevertheless, it is in the exercise of sea power, rather than the desperate struggles for it, that the validity of the navalist argument is really tested.

With the end of the Cold War and the unchallenged dominance of Western naval power, historians have turned their attention more towards the use of navies as diplomatic tools in situations short of war.[68] Yet, deterrence or diplomatic suasion by naval means across the centuries is only just receiving the attention it deserves.[69] The dramatic struggle for naval dominance has always overshadowed the study of the exploitation of sea power and its contribution to diplomacy. Diplomacy entails the interaction of two or more actors, each with their own objectives, priorities and interpretations. At its centre lies the dialogue through which each party seeks to be understood by the others. The results have to be interpreted or understood by domestic and foreign audiences. Britain was one actor among many, and its sea power was one factor within a situation. Deterrence has always been part of this, but it is a particularly slippery concept.[70] The dominance of the British navalist narrative within naval history has troubled diplomatic historians for some decades. Gerald Graham pointed out that the 'three rings' of commerce, colonies and sea power were never as tight as British opinion held, and that British influence depended as much on global conditions as British policy.[71] While we now know a great deal about how British naval power was exercised, we still have a lot to learn about its impact. The best study that we have is related to Anglo-French rivalry. British and French interests were most closely linked and often in conflict. Naval power was an effective lever given the proximity of the states and the maritime dimension of the issues at stake, for example in the Mediterranean, where relations with North Africa, Greece, Italy, Turkey and Russia were involved.[72] However, we need studies of other nations and regions, where Britain did and did not intervene, to understand more fully how naval deterrence may have worked in the nineteenth century.

Technology, innovation, ideology and naval power, 1850–1914

While Britain dominated the world's oceans after 1815, it was not a period of unchanging domination. The commercial exploitation of steam power, through the production of paddle steamers, soon had naval applications. Used as river boats, despatch boats and towing vessels, paddle steamers provided additional naval manoeuvrability in the littoral environment.

The new technologies had an influence on the local balance of naval power. The Royal Navy used them successfully at Algiers in 1824 and during the Portuguese Civil War in 1828.[73] In May 1830, seven steam vessels served as couriers and towed flat boats during the French invasion of Algeria.[74] They were used as transports when the French sent troops to the Papal States in April 1849. The US invasion of Vera Cruz in March 1847 was assisted by paddle and screw steam ships. Paddle steamers effectively supported Danish and Austro-German operations during the war with Prussia over Schleswig-Holstein in 1848–9.[75] Britain used steamers in her campaigns in China in 1840–2, and also used them in both her official and unofficial campaigns there in 1860–2.[76]

While the advantage of manoeuvrability conveyed by steam was clear, the impossibility of continuing to mount large broadside batteries on paddle steamers was also obvious. Interest grew in smaller numbers of heavier guns, ranging up to the muzzle-loading 68 lb. The shell gun, which had been in development since 1809, attracted more attention than others. Shell guns were not used in action until 1838, when a French naval force bombarded St Juan d'Ulloa, Vera Cruz, and forced its capitulation in a matter of hours.[77] However, initial unreliability and short range dampened enthusiasm for the gun. Neither shell guns nor smaller numbers of heavy guns were yet a match in action for a well-handled battery of 32 lbs. The advent of the effective screw propeller in the 1830s revived the prospects of broadside batteries.[78] The real potential of the shell gun was not proven until 30 November 1853, when the Russian Black Sea fleet under Vice Admiral Nakhimov destroyed almost an entire Turkish-Egyptian squadron off Sinope during a six-hour battle.[79]

Much of the naval history of the nineteenth and twentieth centuries has been framed in terms of technology adoption and a race between offensive and defensive technologies.[80] Dramatic technological shifts, whether from sail to steam or from surface to submarine or aviation platforms, have been presented as major adjustments to the contemporary balance of naval power. Ship design and technology is now a major thread in naval history. The warship, and the ship more generally, attracts attention as a designed industrial product, a symbol of power and a feat of engineering or industrial organization. The survival of engineering drawings, constructor notes, sea trials, operational testing, original, high-quality photography and, most recently, digital publication techniques has made this an extremely popular and fruitful area for naval historians. There are now thousands of publications which cover naval history from the perspective of a ship, ship type or design. The results differ according to the emphasis on technology, application, typology or representation and the audience which is being addressed.[81]

Technological advances of the nineteenth century were accessible to great and small navies. Paddle steamers could be purchased, sailing ships could be converted to screw steamers and experiments could be undertaken with heavy cannons and shell guns. As some technologies gradually matured, others emerged in response to them. The introduction of the ironclad warship began in the 1850s, as did the first iron-hulled frigates. The announcement in May 1858 of a French ironclad line of battle ship, *La Gloire*, sent a wave of concern through Britain and an accelerated drive to experiment with iron armour plate. Britain was able to respond rapidly with its own design, the *Warrior*, and, in due course, out-built the French with potent new designs. However, the shock of 1858–60 was another step in the growing complexity, potency and destabilizing impact of evolving warship design.[82]

By the late 1860s warship design was going through a period of major change. The screw propeller dominated, but almost all other aspects of naval construction were in a state of flux. By the mid-1870s individual artillery pieces, increasingly breech-loaders, were becoming heavier, more reliable and effective at longer ranges, so the options for mounting these guns became more complex and pressing.[83] Turret, central battery, casemate, breastwork, citadel and barbette mountings were designed to protect these weapons and provide them with maximum flexibility between 1860 and 1890. Associated with this was the need to protect the ship as a whole from the impact of powerful shells. As the use of iron and, later, steel armour developed, the overall look of the warship gradually changed from the archetype of the eighteenth-century ship of the line to the mastless steel warship of the twentieth century.

Throughout the nineteenth century, developments in metallurgy and chemical and electrical technologies made new and better armour and arms available, enabling adjustments in ship design and capability. This also stimulated the emergence of different weapons and ship types. The self-propelled torpedo, developed in the 1860s, began to have an impact on ship design. By the end of the 1870s Britain, France and Russia had torpedo boats, and within a decade they had torpedo boat destroyers in service.[84] Perhaps the most studied new weapon of the period was the submarine. The challenge of underwater operations and the knowledge of its impact on the twentieth century have made this weapon one of the most popular subjects of naval historians. While most histories focus on the German U-boat activities of the two world wars, the US campaign against Japan and, latterly, the role of the submarine in the Cold War, there are important studies that deal in a popular manner with the principles of submarine development and their early evolution.[85]

As technologies spread, there were conflicts in which they were used, and some conclusions could be drawn by anxious diplomats and naval officers. The Russian War of 1854–6 provided an opportunity to see new technologies intensively employed. This was a war in which modern sea power played a crucial role. Anglo-French naval forces got an army to the Crimea and maintained it there for two years. Despite its victory at Sinope, the Russian Black Sea fleet did not come out of Sevastapol and challenge the Anglo-French squadrons. The same was the case in the Baltic, where the Russian fleet sheltered behind the works of Sveabourg and Kronstadt. In both seas the war was mostly remarkable for the experience it provided for the inshore work of new gunboats and mortar vessels. Steam frigates, corvettes and the gunboats could impose an effective blockade, inflict damaging bombardments and support landings, which had a critical impact on the war.[86] The Russian Baltic fleet was forced to remain in harbour while the Allies threatened St Petersburg. Russia, despite its vast resources and its history of successful engagement in Europe, was exposed as having fallen behind the technological and organizational changes that had occurred in Western Europe. Similarly, during the Franco-Austrian War of 1859, the Austrian navy in the Adriatic was too weak to take on the Franco-Piedmontese fleet. The Austrians were compelled to reinforce the coastal defences of the Adriatic, diverting critical reinforcements to the decisive theatre in Lombardy.[87]

If the wars of the 1850s had proved the value of recent technological changes in coastal operations, the question of their significance for fleet action remained unanswered. A battle between a modern, powerful, but poorly trained and led Italian fleet and an Austrian squadron off Lissa on

FIGURE 3 *An ambiguous precedent. The Austrian battleship* Erzherzog Ferdinand Max *moves astern after ramming the Italian battleship* Re d'Italia. *The latter sank in a few minutes.* Von Teuffenbach, A. Oesterreichs Hort: Geschichts Und Kulturbilder Aus Den Habsburgischen Erblandern. 2nd edn. 2 vols. Vienna: Patriotische Boltsbuchhandlung 1910, opposite p. 160.

20 July 1866 only served to confuse opinion. The Austrians broke through the Italian line and hours of gunnery proved indecisive. Each side attempted to ram the other, but only the Austrian flagship *Erzherzog Ferdinand Max* succeeded in ramming and sinking the Italian *Re d'Italia*. At the end of the battle, the Italians had lost two ships and the Austrians none. The Austrians were left in control of the Adriatic, ensuring that Italian expansion into the eastern littoral was halted.

Steam gave the warship a manoeuvrability that made ramming possible, and for the next decade the potential of gunnery was blurred by the apparent lesson of the pell-mell engagement at short range.[88] Although subsequent events proved the concept of ramming a tactical dead-end, the power of the ram could not be dismissed. On 22 June 1893, HMS *Victoria* was accidently rammed by HMS *Camperdown* during a manoeuvre off the coast of Syria, tearing a hole in the starboard side from her fo'castle deck down to twelve feet below her waterline. *Victoria* sank in about ten minutes with the loss of over 350 officers and men – far more quickly than if the ship had been engaged by gunfire. *Camperdown* was not under full power, but the kinetic energy was formidable, seeming to provide confirmation that the ram was a decisive weapon in modern sea warfare.[89]

The American Civil War (1861–5) saw the most intensive use of new naval technologies of the mid-century. It has attracted a great deal of attention and continues to stimulate important new studies.[90] A littoral, riverine and high-seas war was important to both sides. For the Union, the advantages of naval power were expected to be decisive. The 'Anaconda' strategy was based on strangulating the Confederacy by controlling the Mississippi in the west, the Gulf of Mexico in the south and the Atlantic seaboard in the east. It failed to deliver the results as quickly or as bloodlessly as anticipated in 1862, but by 1865 it had produced the conditions in which a weakened Confederacy buckled under the onslaught of Union armies.[91]

Whether or not the US government ultimately possessed the strategic vision or the political or operational control to make combined or amphibious operations a decisive factor in the war is still contested, but its naval forces developed a powerful capability for executing such operations. However, this was not the only innovation that emerged from the war. Far more startling to public and professionals alike was the advent of river ironclads and coastal monitors. On 8 March 1861 the casemated ironclad CSS *Virginia* rammed and sank the US sloop *Cumberland* in Hampton Roads. The following day, she sallied out again and was met by the Union ironclad turret ship USS *Monitor*. The engagement lasted for four hours at close range, but neither vessel inflicted fatal damage on the other.[92] Sailing ships remained the dominant weapon in both navies, but ironclads and paddle and screw steamers were now essential elements in the naval war. Steam gave the United States Navy improved capacity to stay on blockading station in poor weather. For the Confederacy, it fed into new designs for fast steamers, which broke the blockade and continued to supply the Confederacy until the last months of the war.[93] Ironclads with heavy guns gave a better opportunity to attack fortified coastal positions, inflict greater harm and sustain more punishment.

Although steps had been taken to outlaw privateering at the Treaty of Paris in 1856, the United States was not a signatory, and the Confederate States also recognized the importance of disrupting Northern commerce.[94] On the outbreak of war, the Confederacy licensed privateers, but more importantly, it commissioned its own state warships as commerce raiders. The small, local privateers had some impact on US shipping, but it was the oceanic raiders such as the *Florida*, *Tallahassee* and *Alabama* that made the greatest impression on public opinion in Europe and America. Over half of the US merchant fleet disappeared during the war. The cruisers took about 110,000 tons, another 800,000 tons was sold to foreign owners, and an unknown quantity was shifted to foreign registries to gain the cover of neutrality.[95] This kept US trade flowing, as the Confederacy was never capable of blockading northern ports to prevent neutral shippers from maintaining trade, but it was a spectacular blow to the US merchant marine. To some, this was the most powerful lesson of the naval war.[96] In 1874, Admiral David Porter, the United States' most senior naval officer, noted: 'One vessel like the *Alabama* roaming the ocean, sinking and destroying, would do more to bring about peace than a dozen unwieldy ironclads cruising in search of an enemy of like character.'[97]

In defending their coastline, the Confederate States employed contact and electric mines anchored to the sea or river bed. They experimented with submersibles. The USS *Housatonic* became the first ship to be sunk by submarine, when attacked by CSS *H.L. Hunley* on 17 February 1864 with a spar torpedo. *Hunley* was also lost in the attack. By the end of the war, all types of submarine weapon had destroyed forty-three US vessels, far more than all the ships of the Confederate navy put together.[98]

Dramatic as these new weapons were, they were still too few or too ineffective to have a decisive impact on the overall balance of the war at sea. Nevertheless, they complicated the United States Navy's task of blockading the Confederacy. The South had few ports with the infrastructure to support international commerce and effectively distribute goods inland. Direct amphibious action had been the preferred strategy early in the war. The capture of New Orleans in April 1862 by the West Gulf Squadron under Rear Admiral David Farragut (1801–70) and a small army under General Benjamin Butler was an important blow to Confederate access to international markets. This was followed by an advance 400 miles up the Mississippi to Vicksburg in support of a drive southward by a Union army in the Kentucky theatre, under General Ulysses S. Grant, which was supported by a Union river squadron under Charles Davis.[99] This squadron captured Memphis in June 1862. Farragut managed to bypass Vicksburg for a temporary link-up with Davis' squadron, but Grant's campaign floundered around Corinth. It was not until July 1863 that Vicksburg finally fell, effectively cutting the Confederacy in two and reopening the Mississippi under Federal control. New Orleans was a great triumph for Farragut, but naval attacks on other important ports, particularly Charleston (April 1863), failed. It took assaults from the landward side to capture the last refuges of the blockade runners, Wilmington (Fort Fisher, January 1865) and Charleston (February 1865).

The American Civil War is full of interest and relatively well explored. It will continue to generate much more writing as new gaps in our knowledge of the naval war are continually being identified. The war influenced design of ships, provided a testing ground for weapons systems, and produced lessons in the their deployment. The period also saw dramatic developments in the recording and dissemination of information. The telegraph, the camera and the newspaper press provided materials and means to inform a wider public about the course of the war and its weapons. The rise of professional military and naval staffs brought with it a more intense desire to observe and to accumulate and organize information to be used for official staff histories. These public and the professional developments in the recording and analysis of military events culminated in the compilation of official histories for public consumption after the First World War. In the mid-nineteenth century this process was still unfolding. European observers reported their impressions, which prompted tantalizing speculations, but rarely did these reflections prove unambiguous. The ironclad monitor was, of course, the most dramatic example of design innovation, but its high-seas application failed to live up to the original speculation or potential diplomatic significance.[100] The 'science of coast defence' had been revived by Farragut's capture of New Orleans, but the balance of power between ships and shore fortifications remained disputed. The potential of the torpedo or mine was intriguing but ultimately unproven.[101]

The focus of these near-contemporary debates was largely on the operational and tactical lessons of the war. Union naval operations made the Mississippi campaign possible and were an essential element in weakening the Confederacy in 1863. The potential for a more decisive impact existed. If the blockade of the South had been effective, the Confederacy would not have been able to sustain the war for many months. Operationally, this proved beyond the capability of the United States Navy, and therefore the Confederate efforts to break this blockade were vital to the prolongation of the war. It did not prevent the military defeat of the Confederacy, but, counter-factually, had the political will been weaker in the North, it might have sustained Confederate resistance long enough to make a political settlement attractive to the Federal government.

Far less attention was paid to the strategic and diplomatic impact of the naval war on the overall outcome of the struggle. More than any other aspect of the war, the naval war could have caused an international crisis by forcing Britain to abandon its neutrality.[102] Confederate expectations that British demand for raw cotton would force it to join the Southern cause, or that Confederate attempts to build their navy in British yards would push Britain into direct conflict with the Union, came to nothing. For Britain, the conflict posed serious questions, ranging from the economic significance of 'King Cotton' and the rights of neutrals, through imperial defence, to the abhorrence of slavery in the Southern states. Naval power could have been employed to resolve one or other of these matters, but not all simultaneously.

Elsewhere, smaller conflicts provided other examples of how naval war was changing, but none provided a clear view of how tactics or operations at sea should respond to the technological opportunities, or how deeply naval operations could influence events ashore. The Spanish-Peruvian/Chilean War (1864–6), the Brazilian-Paraguayan War (1864–70), the Chilean-Peruvian War (1879–84), the Sino-French War (1884–5) and the Chilean Civil War (1891) all saw new technologies employed. The last was particularly instructive. On 23 April 1891, the Chilean battleship *Blanco Encalada* became the first warship to be sunk by self-propelled torpedo. There were lessons to be learnt regarding landings and naval supporting fire with modern weapons.[103] Coastal mobility gained by naval forces was an important factor in the outcome of the Chilean Civil War.[104]

In Europe, after the Crimean War, the Russian navy had been hobbled by the provisions of the Treaty of Paris of 1856, which had neutralized the Black Sea and limited Russia to just ten small coastal policing vessels in those waters.[105] Despite every Russian intention to reverse this, little progress was made. When Russia declared war on Turkey in support of Serbia in April 1877, the Turks had complete control of the Black Sea. However, the Russians proved expert in skirmishing with small ships, torpedoes and mines throughout the war on the Danube and in coastal areas. Turkish naval forces maintained the supply and reinforcements to their army fighting the Russians in the Danubian provinces, but the Russians conducted a highly successful campaign against them with small vessels, while the Turks did not exert any significant naval pressure on the Russians. Ultimately, it was Turkish defeat on land that determined the shape of the peace in January 1878.[106] British intervention to protect Constantinople from further Russian advances brought a Royal Navy squadron there in January 1878. What would have been its impact if the Tsar and the Turks had not been equally determined to make peace and how this fleet would have fared if war had expanded down the Gallipoli peninsula are difficult to determine.[107] The Russians had plans to mine the Sea of Marmora in order to keep the British out of the Black Sea, and for the mobilization of twenty-two cruisers as worldwide commerce raiders.[108] Slowly, attention is being focused on the Russian and Turkish navies, particularly with regard to the design and numbers of ships they possessed.[109] However, more work is needed to understand Russian and Turkish perceptions of naval power as a factor in diplomatic and strategic decision-making during the last quarter of the nineteenth century.

The final stages of the wars of unification in Europe also gave a few hints for the future. The Danish navy was effective along the coast and at the mouth of the River Elbe against the Austro-Prussian forces in 1864, but was not equipped to resist modern land-based artillery in riverine operations, and so was unable to make a decisive impact on events ashore.[110] French warships from Brest and Toulon mounted an effective blockade of northern Germany for a few weeks in 1870, but, with the collapse of the French army after Sedan, it had little effect on the outcome of the Franco-Prussian War.

It was clear that the new steel and steam navies were having an impact on warfare. It was all highly suggestive of potential, but at no point was there decisive evidence of the impact of these new weapons, doctrines or tactics. It was not until the end of the century that three conflicts provided this evidence. The first was the Sino-Japanese War of 1894–5. The modernization of the Japanese navy under the restored Meiji dynasty after 1868 is, for naval historians, one of the major events of the period. The Chinese made a faster start at building armoured warships, but these were small, coastal vessels. Most of the Chinese ocean-going fleet still consisted of unarmoured ships, and Chinese industry was not equipped to build a new generation of modern armoured ships. The Japanese relied heavily on foreign shipbuilding, but had developed their navy as an imperial service commanded by a Japanese officer corps modelled on the discipline and professionalism of its Western contemporaries.[111] The political position of the navy in Japanese society at this time has not yet been explored to the same depth as that of the army, but Japanese society managed to integrate the needs of modern naval war more effectively than the Chinese.[112]

The Battle of the Yalu River on 17 September 1894 was a serious defeat for the Chinese fleet. A heterogeneous Chinese squadron of two ironclad battleships, four cruisers and some torpedo boats successfully covered the landing of troops in northern Korea, but on their homeward voyage they found a smaller Japanese cruiser force blocking their path. This was to be the first high-seas squadron battle since Lissa in 1866. The Chinese approached in line abreast, or wedge formation, following the example of the Austrians at Lissa, to be met by the Japanese, who manoeuvred in two lines ahead, on either side of the Chinese force. The well-drilled Japanese cruisers, equipped with quick-firing guns, wreaked havoc on the Chinese. The six-hour artillery duel cost the Chinese four cruisers and a fast sloop sunk. The two battleships escaped to Wei-Hai-Wei. The defeat left the Chinese and Korean coasts open to Japanese landings. Japanese forces landed on the Liaotung peninsula and captured Taiwan and the Pescadores Islands. Eventually, the Chinese warships were blockaded in Wei-Hai-Wei and besieged by Japanese troops on land. When Wei-Hai-Wei fell, all the Chinese ships were captured and incorporated into the Japanese navy when peace was finally negotiated.[113]

Despite the clear impact of the battle, the artillery duel at the Yalu River had, again, not proved decisive and the lessons were unclear. Primitive fire control limited the accuracy of gunfire. The armour of both Chinese and Japanese ships, although none of it was of the latest type, proved reasonably effective. One lesson that did seem to emerge was the importance of a relatively homogeneous squadron of ships capable of manoeuvring and fighting as a cohesive body. The Japanese had this advantage in 1894, and it was a relative advantage the United States had in its war with Spain in 1898. After the Civil War, the United States Navy had been allowed to atrophy while domestic political attention was turned to the interior of the country, and American mercantile interests seemed perfectly well protected by the British Navy. A political battle, of which Mahan was part, to equip the United States with an oceanic navy was started in the 1880s and won by the mid-1890s. Congress supported the growth of a modern, oceanic battlefleet, and the new capital ships were in service by the late 1890s.

Like a number of European fleets, the Spanish fleet had been built up during the experimental years since 1860. The Spanish fleet was large, fourth or fifth by tonnage in the world, containing both large and small vessels. However, budgetary constraints after the revolution of 1868 had meant that the Spanish navy had not kept up with all the new types, or maintained its existing ships well. Like many of the designs between 1870 and 1900, some were not as seaworthy as anticipated. The foundering of the *Regina Regente* in July 1895 with the loss of her entire crew caused losses greater than the entire naval battle casualties of the 1898 war and boded ill for the ships following on in that class.[114] By the 1890s, the Spanish did not have ships equal to the best of the new American warships, but had ships with greater speed and heavier guns than their enemies.[115]

In 1897, unrest in Cuba was tending towards Civil War and tension between Spain and the United States was rising. American public opinion and strategic interests sided with the dissidents. On 25 January 1898 the USS *Maine* arrived in Havana harbour. She was there to show the flag and provide protection to US nationals and property should the need arise. The *Maine*, one of the first of the new modern battleships authorized by Congress, was a potent symbol of US power. On 15 February, the *Maine* was torn apart by a huge explosion, killing over 260 seamen. The United States quickly concluded it was the result of a mine, and the incident became the trigger for popular furore that led to a declaration of war on Spain on 21 April 1898.

US naval forces were mobilized in both the Atlantic and the Pacific. On 1 May 1898, at Manila Bay, the American Asiatic Squadron engaged the anchored Spanish force and by the end of the day, six of the eight Spanish ships had been sunk by gunfire and the last two scuttled. The American ships were armoured cruisers, fitted with medium-size quick-firing guns rather than the larger guns of the battleship. The accuracy of American fire was not good, but their rate of fire, like that of the Japanese at the Yalu River, more than compensated. In the Atlantic, the Spanish sent a squadron to reinforce their garrison on Cuba, but their ships were no match for the American vessels. Blockaded in Santiago de Cuba and besieged by American troops who had been landed on the island, Rear Admiral Pascual Cervera broke out of the harbour on the morning of 3 July 1898. Pursued by the blockading squadron, the ships were overhauled and destroyed by rapid gunfire.[116] As in the wars of liberation in South America earlier in the century, and like the Chinese in 1894, once the sea communications were disrupted, it was impossible for the Spanish to reinforce their colonial garrisons. Eventually Spain was compelled to cede independence to Cuba, and surrendered the Philippines, Guam and Puerto Rico to the United States.[117]

After 1895, the Japanese continued to expand and improve their navy with the latest designs from Britain, Germany, France and the United States, as well as developing their own warship shipbuilding capacity. Russo-Japanese tension over Manchuria led to a surprise Japanese naval attack on the Russian naval base at Port Arthur on the Liaotung peninsula on 8 February 1904. Japanese landings in Korea and advance into Manchuria left the Russians fighting to defend the Liaotung peninsula. The Russian squadrons based at Port Arthur and Vladivostok sortied out, but were unable to break the Japanese blockade of Port Arthur. Eventually, the Russian squadron in Port Arthur was demobilized to assist with the land defences, and the ships were gradually sunk by Japanese land-based artillery before the Russians surrendered the town in January 1905. The Russian Baltic fleet was by then on its way around the world to relieve Port Arthur. It was a mixed force of thirty-eight warships, with only a handful of modern battleships at its core.

They met the Japanese fleet off Tsushima on 27 May 1905. The faster, more modern and better-served Japanese warships crushed the Russian squadron. Only one small vessel made its way through to Vladivostok. All the rest were sunk, captured or interned. The Japanese lost only three torpedo boats and had three armoured cruisers badly damaged. It was a stunning victory. The damage inflicted on the Chinese by the Japanese armoured warships was as catastrophic as that inflicted by the Russians on the Turks at Chesme in 1770 and Sinope in 1853, or achieved by Nelson at Aboukir Bay in 1798 and Trafalgar in 1805.[118]

Between 1856 and the late 1870s Britain stood aside from these conflicts, not because she was disinterested, but because her hegemonic naval power enabled her to use this force as a deterrent rather than being compelled to engage in operations.[119] As long as the naval wars were relatively small in scale and British interests were relatively tangential to the core objectives of the belligerents, naval action could be limited to demonstration. Similarly, British building capacity had a deterrent effect on emergent arms races. Throughout the period, Britain was able to maintain a comfortable advantage over its most feared rivals, France and Russia. Occasionally, France posed a threat, as she possessed both a productive capacity to expand her fleet and a technological capability to change the nature of the race, but she was never able to bring her battlefleet close to parity with the Royal Navy.

Overall, changing technologies did not pose a particularly serious threat to Britain. Britain had the technological know-how and the industrial capacity to meet any qualitative or quantitative challenge to her supremacy. Britain preserved her naval supremacy by adopting and integrating new designs and technologies faster than her potential enemies. A lag in the initial adoption of a technology could be rapidly closed by the flexibility of the Royal Navy in adaptation and integration.[120] After 1840, the strategy of adaptation worked well, as steam, the screw propeller and the heavy shell gun quickly demonstrated their universal applicability. Later, it was more worrying. From the 1870s, the radically changing design of the armoured battleship made it difficult to predict how it would perform in fleet action. Similarly, from the 1880s, the development of new types of vessel such as the torpedo boat, which exploited the self-propelled torpedo, and the fast unarmoured cruiser made it possible to conceive of a new strategy which did not depend on the battleship. By the end of the century, the submarine was emerging as a practicable technology. However, for the most part, the strategy of adaptation served Britain well, and these technologies assisted the prosecution of imperial policing missions and minor clashes with other powers. Gunboats supporting littoral actions, naval brigades and artillery ashore became important elements of sea power in the second half of the nineteenth century.[121]

For Britain, the most significant naval problem during this period was the revival of French naval ambition. The key naval problem related to the French ports. For the British, it was how to impose an effective blockade or attack

French ports.[122] For the French, it was how to break that blockade. Britain proved well equipped to deal with any threat from this direction and effectively countered French building and technological developments. The Franco-Prussian War (1870–1) was such a disaster for France that any idea of creating a battlefleet to challenge the Royal Navy after 1871 was impractical. The rising threat of a new Italian navy and German domination of central Europe were by then of greater significance than any immediate point of friction with Britain.[123]

Nevertheless, the period between 1870 and 1900 was one of flux, in which viable strategic alternatives presented themselves. The huge investment in large battleships was questionable. The development of heavy guns seemed to make the battleship extremely vulnerable unless adequate armour could be provided at all weak points. The potential of torpedoes, mines and smaller craft had been suggested in numerous ways from the 1860s. Particularly, the value of commerce raiders, which could evade blockading squadrons and disrupt enemy commerce, had been demonstrated in the American Civil War. This commerce-raiding strategy fed well into the older French tradition of the *guerre de course*, which from the 1690s to 1815 had played an important role in anti-British naval policy. These vessels seemed to provide an alternative to the prohibitively expensive and seemingly unwinnable race for battleships. The *jeune école* of French naval strategists who linked the traditional *guerre de course* with the new designs for armoured cruisers to threaten the sea lanes, or ocean-going torpedo boats whose speed and manoeuvrability could force battlefleets to release their blockade of ports, provided an attractive alternative to the battlefleet theorists.[124] The theory was also attractive to other nations that could not hope to gather the maritime and financial resources essential to building a battlefleet. It was a debate that raged from the 1880s through to about 1898. Both the adherents of the *jeune école* and their opponents, the classical *vielle école*, could turn to contemporary technology and to the lessons of history to support their arguments. The new weapons could occasionally make a great *éclat* of publicity both in manoeuvres and in the small conflicts around the globe. However, nothing during the period decisively undermined the classical argument that, ultimately, sea power rested on the domination of the battlefleet.

This was the context for the turn to naval history in the last decades of the nineteenth century. Naval history was coming of age as a modern discipline based upon rigorous documentary analysis, contributing to the solution of some of the most pressing military questions of the day. With so little that was certain about the power of the new weapons or designs, naval officers and statesmen hoped some universal laws could be discovered from the past. This was not an abstract scientific enquiry. It was an intensely political debate, fought out in various nations with their own domestic and diplomatic agendas. The sea was assuming a wider role in national politics and diplomacy than it had ever enjoyed before. Technological possibilities, state finance, and economic and social necessity were all brought into a mix of ambiguity and anxiety. History was to provide the examples of nations that were 'natural' sea powers, depending on the sea of defence, economic necessity and tradition, of which Britain was the archetype.

In Britain, the debate was characterized by the fear of losing its long-established naval dominance, starting with the 'naval scares' of 1878 and 1884 and not ending until the outbreak of the First World War.[125] Japan saw itself as a mirror image of Britain and framed its need for naval power in terms similar to Britain.[126] For France, the question related to resolving the daunting problems of facing the world's largest navy on a global scale while containing a growing Italian navy in the Mediterranean. Even here, the birthplace of the *jeune école*, the evident power of the modern battleship in imperial diplomacy by the late 1890s was causing professional and political attention to focus again on the battlefleet.

Other powers were coming to terms with the new conditions in which they found themselves. Italy, unified in 1866, had over 3,000 miles of vulnerable coastline to defend and had inherited the navies of Sardinia and Naples, whose traditional commitment to the battleship was to influence the navy of the new kingdom.[127] Austria-Hungary had lost its last Italian possessions in 1866, and with them the Venetian tradition of seafaring. Nonetheless, it retained significant interests in the Mediterranean and Balkans, which would be threatened or lost unless it preserved its control of the Adriatic. The strategy for doing this was fought over within Austrian ministries for the next forty years.[128] Russia was uncertain about its naval requirements, with a powerful Germany to the west and complex problems on its southern and eastern borders. It was not driven to a maritime strategy by either economic or diplomatic necessities. However, the experience of the 1877–8 war with Turkey indicated that the *jeune école* offered an effective strategy at an affordable price – at least until the need to counter the threat from Japan in the Far East began to be understood in the 1890s.[129]

In the United States, a new continental power secure in its relative isolation, there was a fear that foreign naval power was growing in reach and effectiveness. The continent was no longer isolated, and US interests across the world were under threat. Great power status and a popular concept of manifest destiny demanded that the United States be an actor in the global expansion, not a passive victim of it.[130] Germany was likewise a new continental power. Its need for naval power was limited and seen by navalist theorists as artificial. The threats to Germany did not come from the sea, but from Europe, and the solutions to those threats did not lie at sea. Nevertheless, the lure of maritime power as the expression of modern great-power virility had been gradually influencing German public opinion since 1870 and, most importantly, provided one of the key diplomatic assumptions of Kaiser Wilhelm II (1888–1918).[131]

British sea power provided the archetype and persuasive evidence that it rose, fell and rose again with the power of the battle fleet. Mahan captured

FIGURE 4 *The line of battle in the twentieth century: the Royal Navy's 2nd Battle Squadron at Jutland, 31 May 1916. © Trustees of the National Museum of the Royal Navy (Portsmouth).*

this phenomenon so well in his writings. He was not an archival historian like some of his contemporaries, but his work, based on the secondary and contemporary printed sources, encapsulated so clearly the centrality of the battlefleet to sea power that it won him immediate international acclaim. By the late 1890s the battle for history and its lessons had been effectively won, and despite the continued development of new weapons and the lack of definitive evidence in support of the battlefleet thesis, the size and strength of the battlefleet again became the definitive measure of naval power in the final years of the century. By the time Mahan died in 1914, his stature as the leading exponent of sea power was unchallenged, and his ideas continue to resonate deeply in navies to this day.[132]

By 1900, Italy, the United States, Germany, France and Japan were turning significant resources towards the building or purchase of battleships. They were becoming regional, if not global, naval powers. For Britain, whose policy since 1815 had been predicated on a theoretical 'two power standard' of a fleet capable of facing the next two naval powers together, the world was changing. From the 1860s, the question of imperial defence had concerned British governments, and by 1887 at the latest, an integrated structure for defence, based upon naval power, existed.[133] Rising public anxiety about naval defence culminated in the 1889 Naval Defence Act. Yet, British naval potential proved not to be the deterrent it had been. Growing German, American and Japanese naval power posed regional threats that were too significant and strategic problems too complex to be contained with the mantras of either a 'splendid isolation' or a 'two power standard'. The reordering of British foreign and naval policy during the period from 1890 to 1914 has been extensively studied. The ceding of primacy in the West Indies to the United States, the alliance with Japan in 1902 to protect Far East interests, and, eventually, the concentration of the fleet in home waters from 1904 and an Anglo-French entente were pragmatic policy responses.[134]

By 1905, the ambiguity and confusion over the future shape of naval warfare with these new, powerful and still-evolving warships had all but disappeared. The Spanish-American War of 1898 and the Russo-Japanese War of 1904–5 had demonstrated the dominance of well-handled, homogeneous battle squadrons. Coastal operations carried out by the Japanese in Manchuria gave important hints of the decisively destructive power of modern naval weaponry as well as the flexibility and speed of warships. Defeat left Spain too weak financially and industrially to take up the challenge of rebuilding a modern balanced fleet.[135] However, in the wake of defeat, Russian naval policy centred on the battleship. Then, in 1906, came the launch of two new classes of warship – the *Dreadnought* and the battlecruiser. *Dreadnought*, the generic name of an all-big-gun battleship, named after the first of its type to enter the Royal Navy, was a design development occurring contemporaneously in a number of countries. Its launch spelt the obsolescence of other battleship designs, and naval power was redefined around the possession of this class of ship.[136] In Britain, the battlecruiser, a vessel designed to combine the speed of the cruiser with the firepower of a battleship, was championed by Admiral Sir John Fisher. As First Sea Lord of the Admiralty, Fisher was at the centre of naval policy from 1904 to 1911.

It was a period in which new designs and technologies were introduced alongside strategic repositioning and changes to the education and status of the officer corps, and the period ended in 1914 with a major war, for no navy had precedent upon which to work. All history is by definition an *ex post facto* exercise, and in the light of the First World War, it is not surprising, therefore, that the years from 1900 to 1914 have excited some of the most intense debate among naval historians.

The First World War: Navalism and the impact of modern naval warfare, 1914–18

The First World War has a massive literature devoted to it, which can barely be touched upon in a work such as this.[137] Apart from the constant thirst for dramatic battle narratives, ranging from individual ship actions, such as the hunt for the *Emden*, to squadron actions like Coronel and the Falklands, to the single great sea battle of the war off Jutland in 1916, there are two major revisionist themes that have dominated the historiography.

The first relates to Jutland and the failure of the great battlefleets to fight a decisive campaign in four years of conflict. When war broke out, Trafalgar and Tsushima provided the dominant mental models informing expectations of the conduct of the war. Fleet action would bring about a decisive naval battle, which would then determine the key context in which the war on land would be played out. This did not happen, and the British and German main fleets appeared surprisingly inert during a catastrophically bloody conflict on land. This concerned contemporaries. The principles confidently deduced from historical precedents were obviously untrue, or at least the practitioners, from the historians, like Sir Julian Corbett, to the naval commanders, had been inexpert in articulating or acting on them.

A reckoning was inevitable. Why had there been no second Trafalgar, and had historians, particularly Sir Julian Corbett, whose sophisticated historical interpretation of sea power had influenced many senior officers since 1900, undermined the fighting instinct of the Royal Navy?[138] The question has taken historians into a detailed re-examination of navies from 1906 to 1914 and has provoked probably the most vigorous revisionist debates in naval history, which continue to this day.

Although important contributions to the question were made before 1939, it was not until the 1960s that distance from the events and access to new materials enabled substantial new scholarship to develop. The most significant was Arthur Marder's *From Dreadnought to Scapa Flow*, which provided a detailed study of British naval policy from 1905 until 1918 in five volumes published between 1961 and 1970.[139] In the 1970s, Holger Herwig's work shone new light on Tirpitz and the development of the German navy, which has continued in the work of Michael Epkenhans and Matthew Seligmann.[140]

Marder's views dominated the debate from the 1960s, and with them Sir John Fisher's technical and strategic domination of naval development while First Sea Lord from 1904 to 1910 remained central. However, in 1989 Jon Sumida's *In Defence of Naval Supremacy* appeared.[141] With a greater focus on the political, financial and economic constraints facing the Liberal government, Sumida produced a more nuanced picture of the motivations and limitations of Fisher's tenure at the Admiralty. Fisher's role was also re-examined by Nicholas Lambert.[142] Both Sumida and Lambert demonstrated the importance of the personalities, the social and professional pressures, and contemporary political debates in driving naval policy. From their work has emerged a story that is far less focused on the apparent technological superiority of the *Dreadnought*, and far more conditioned by political considerations. Lambert sought to show how Fisher was forced to dissemble his views on maintaining naval supremacy in the face of entrenched opposition in the navy and politics. Sumida's original work highlighted how this led to sub-optimal decisions in the great naval race with Germany, particularly in the choice of fire-control systems. The Admiralty's ultimate decision to favour the Dreyer system over the Argo system of the civilian Arthur Pollen was, in Sumida's view, a critical factor in the relative failure of British gunnery at the Battle of Jutland.

It has led to further work on Jutland by John Brookes, who has taken issue with Sumida on the fire-control controversy.[143] Matthew Seligmann has questioned the revisionist interpretation of Fisher's shift in strategy towards the North Sea.[144] Battleships and gunnery systems are not the only aspects of Edwardian naval power that have undergone re-evaluation. Organization and leadership have also been the foci of recent studies. The failure to adopt effective staff structures, which were becoming common in modern armies, has been a long-standing criticism of navies at the turn of the nineteenth century.[145] Fisher's resistance to such a staff and his influence on planning have been a point of controversy among historians and biographers of that contentious admiral. This now has a good study in Nicholas Black's work.[146] The British Royal Navy officer corps as whole is the focus of Andrew Gordon's *The Rules of the Game: Jutland and British Command*. Gordon's work, which involves another technical system, that of signalling, contends that the effectiveness of the Royal Navy was diminished by a cultural clash of command, based on a long-standing tension between the need for obedience and the requirement for aggressive initiative.[147]

The second theme relates to blockade, convoy and economic warfare. Ultimately, the naval blockade of Germany had catastrophic effects on the German economy. It was an aspect of the war that was central to British naval planning, and, lacking the dramatic narrative of decisive sea battles, it was a story that could be presented to the public as a shining example of how sea power worked constantly to preserve British supplies of food and raw materials while slowly, but decisively, strangling the enemy. In recent years, historians have revised interpretations of both the defensive and offensive policies, demonstrating that the British were less sure footed than the immediate post-war narratives claimed. The defence of British trade was precarious until the middle of 1917 as the British sought a means to counter the German U-boats. It was not until the adoption of convoys after the crisis of April 1917 that the threat was overcome.[148] The offensive, founded on an aggressive plan of economic warfare, rapidly collapsed under US and domestic pressures. It struggled on as a series of improvisations, and its ultimate effectiveness owed as much to German agrarian inefficiencies as to a tight maritime grip on a major industrial economy.[149]

A range of minor themes (in terms of historical attention given to them) have also had some good work done on them in recent years. Paul Halpern has covered the naval war in the Mediterranean.[150] The war in the air at sea has had some attention, particularly its significance for the control of the English Channel.[151] The Gallipoli campaign has its own large literature, but after the abortive attempt to force the Straits on 18 March 1915, these histories focus mostly on the army's campaign on the Peninsula. Aside from participants, such as Churchill, Keyes and Wemyss, writing after the war, the naval contribution to the overall campaign has not attracted a great deal of attention.[152] Combined operations generally in the war still need modern studies.[153]

The war ended without a decisive naval victory that the public could applaud. Navalists could argue that although there had been no climactic fleet battle, naval power had determined the environment, which proved fatal to Germany in the long run. The naval blockade crippled the German economy and forced her to act in a manner which brought the United States into the balance against her.[154] The Japanese navy proved a potent force in the China Sea and the Pacific. America's naval ambitions were clear before it entered the war when, in 1916, Congress approved the greatest expansion of the battlefleet in its history and continued that trajectory into 1918.[155]

Despite these signs of the obvious vitality of naval power, its significance was far more open to question than in 1914, and in the aftermath of the war the public wanted to know a great deal about it. From the official point of view, it was important that the public understood how their sacrifices in treasure and blood had been expended. From the last quarter of the nineteenth century, historical studies of campaigns designed to identify lessons from the conflict had become a standard feature of military staff activity. Early in the First World War there was a conscious policy to preserve a mass of documentation for these traditional purposes, but it was also decided to produce official histories of the war for the public. The British official history, edited by Sir Julian Corbett until his death in 1922, and then by Sir Henry Newbolt, *The History of the Great War: Naval Operations*, appeared in five volumes between 1920 and 1931.[156] But the histories of the land war were not completed until 1948.[157] The German official history, *Der Krieg zur See, 1914-1918*, was a much larger undertaking, at twenty-two volumes, and more slowly constructed, the last volume only appearing in 1966.[158] The Italian navy's official history, *La Marina Italiana nella grande Guerra*, in eight volumes, was completed in 1942.[159]

Public interest in the war was not confined to an official interpretation. Mass public participation in this war, combined with rising literacy, meant that the conflict stimulated a huge range of memoirs. Many of these were partisan accounts intended to justify an individual's role. Almost as soon as the war ended, prominent memoirs appeared. In 1919, those of Jellicoe, Reginald Bacon, von Tirpitz and William Sims were on sale.[160] All had points to make. Jellicoe had been relieved of command of the Grand Fleet in 1917, to be replaced by the flamboyant Admiral David Beatty, whose Battlecruiser Fleet had cut a dash with the British public. Beatty's behaviour at Jutland was controversial and, in Jellicoe's view, highly damaging, but his flair for publicity never left him after his rise to commanding the Grand Fleet and then First Sea Lord in 1919–27. It left a scar within the officer corps.

Bacon, in command of the Dover Patrol between 1915 and 1917, had come out on the wrong side of received opinion regarding the effectiveness of the anti-submarine barrage in the Channel and was dismissed in December 1917, at the same time as his friend Jellicoe was. Tirpitz was out of office by 1914, but the complete failure of the High Seas Fleet left him with a reputation to defend. In 1920 the United States was embarked on an expansion of its battlefleet, which had not played any obvious role in the world war. Admiral William Sims, commander of the US Atlantic Squadron, provided the public with the essential narrative about the defeat of the U-boat and the opening of the way to transporting two million American troops to France. Fisher died in July 1920 without leaving an autobiography, but had authorized two eclectic volumes of anecdotes in the previous year.[161] Winston Churchill, who had been First Lord of the Admiralty between 1914 and 1915, produced a multi-volume history of the world war, *The World Crisis*, between 1923 and 1931. The volume covering 1915 was an unsubtle defence of his role in the Dardanelles campaign, which went down very badly with some naval officers.[162] Beatty, who continued to serve after the war, did not publish his own autobiography, but vigorously defended his role at Jutland against the champions of Jellicoe, such as Reginald Bacon.[163] Admiral Roger Keyes, who had played an important role at Gallipoli in 1915 and commanded the daring raid on Zeebrugge in April 1918, also continued to serve and did not publish his autobiography, *The Naval Memoirs of Admiral of the Fleet Sir Roger Keyes*, until after his retirement in 1931.[164] There are many more examples of memoirs. For some it was a vital exercise in putting the record straight, for others it was a potentially lucrative opportunity to reminisce. The memoirs and biographies continued to accumulate up to the outbreak of the Second World War, and some even appeared in the 1950s. However, so far very little research has been conducted into the question of how or whether these memoirs shaped perceptions of naval power, and how this may have varied across the belligerent nations.

Before the First World War, the disputes between the historical school and the 'materialists', who based their prescriptions for naval policy on the inherent or expected capabilities of technological weapons or systems, were irresolvable without the experience of operations. The war provided that experience. It turned out to be inconclusive, but certainly undermined faith in the extrapolation of principles from historical studies. Staff histories remained central to recording and learning lessons from the conflict, but other disciplines were beginning to show their value to planners. Rudimentary psychology and more sophisticated economic analysis provided contemporary data for planners against which the claims of the materialists could be judged. Processes and systems were used that would provide the model for renewed attention to problems in 1939. History became relatively less important as the planners' tool. It is a change that has not yet received as much attention as it deserves from naval historians.[165]

Coming to terms with new realities, 1919–39

In 1919 it was unclear what role navies had in the new world order. On the one hand, the cost of the war had been horrific. It was not immediately obvious that the great battlefleets had been worth the investment nor that the exhausted nations could sustain further naval competition. Britain was still the pre-eminent global naval power, but the public was no longer very much convinced of the need for active imperial adventures or of the effectiveness of traditional naval power. Submarines and, to a lesser degree, aircraft had emerged to offer the prospect of cheaper alternative, or complementary, sources of sea power. On the other hand, competition had not disappeared. The United States had emerged from the war with ambitions to be second to none in naval terms. Japan had more limited ambitions, but was now a naval–imperial power of some weight.[166] Yet the war and the economic depressions of the early 1920s and early 1930s provided the context for restrained naval expenditure.

In Britain, the very scale of the problem – maintaining a pre-eminent navy in these economic conditions – was a subject of urgent analysis. Admiral Sir Herbert Richmond, one of the most intellectual, if awkward and undiplomatic, officers of his generation, had been a leading light of the naval historical fraternity before 1914. He continued to lead the way in using history for his analysis of contemporary British naval requirements.[167] The main historiographical theme of this period is the need to meet global naval strategic needs with finite and depreciating naval resources.[168]

In the United States the shifting balance of power was also an important subject for examination.[169] The diplomatic imperative of containing competition by agreement and conflicts by negotiation dominated the period. The Washington Naval Treaty (22 February 1922) provided the basis of a world naval order in which Britain, the United States, Japan, France and Italy accepted, more or less reluctantly, no new building of capital ships for ten years and that a stable naval balance was preferable to unlimited competition. The details of these treaties, whether individual nations accepted ratios prejudicial to their national interests in one or another class of vessel, or accepted limitations on their naval bases, were disputed at the time and remain controversial.[170]

While navies chafed at it, the Washington Treaty was not entirely destructive. A new naval race could have had crippling consequences. Reconstructions were permitted to incorporate improvements within aerial and underwater technologies. Aircraft carriers were not limited by the Treaty, and the hulls of uncompleted battleships provided the platforms for the development of aircraft carriers in Britain, the United States and France into the 1920s. The number of cruisers in navies was not limited by the Treaty. Although limits were placed upon the size and calibre of guns on cruisers (10,000 tons and 8-inch guns), they were not so constraining as to prevent the steady, if unspectacular, development of this class of ship.

The vessel which had the most striking impact on naval warfare between 1914 and 1918, the submarine, was initially unaffected by the Treaty. In Britain some wished and others hoped for the abolition of the type, but no nation voluntarily abandoned it.[171] Germany was prohibited from acquiring them by the Treaty of Versailles, but other navies gradually developed the submarine's capability to meet their particular naval needs.[172]

Between 1918 and 1930 Britain had been a major beneficiary of the international agreements that limited construction and competition. It had consolidated a status quo at a point at which Britain was disproportionally powerful. This could not last forever. Germany (not a signatory to the Washington Treaty) began to build again in 1929 by laying down the *Deutschland*, an 11,000-ton warship, larger than a treaty cruiser. Japan was increasingly resentful about its enforced inferiority to Britain and the United States.[173] France was wary of German intentions, while Italy distrusted French plans for building.[174] The protracted ratification proceedings following the 1930 London Naval Conference showed that tensions were rising among the signatory nations, opening the way for renewed naval competition. When the treaty participants met again in London in 1936, they had to accept that the non-signatories were now driving up tonnage and gun sizes, which they had to match. Japan had left the treaty in 1935, and in the same year Germany negotiated the right to build up to 35 per cent of the strength of the Royal Navy, with an option to build to parity in submarines.[175]

The treaty limitations were never scrupulously followed by any nation, but as the cooperative naval environment began to fragment into unrestricted competition, nations had to make choices in line with their financial and industrial bases. With war appearing increasingly likely and the demands of land and air services equally pressing, a new generation of warships was laid down, but most were not completed by the time war broke out in September 1939.

Despite the budgetary constraints, it was a period in which technological change did not slacken. However, the ability of navies to absorb, understand and adapt to these changes was limited, as resources were not available for extensive experimentation and operational testing.[176] The changing technology of air power from the mid-1930s was the most obvious expression of this. Aircraft were changing significantly, but no navy had the means to test the precise impact this would have on naval operations.[177] Against this background, the aircraft carrier evolved slowly under a continuing debate about the effectiveness of air power at sea. German air power over the sea rested on land-based aircraft and only really developed during the Second World War.[178] Similarly, the struggle between the submarine and anti-submarine forces continued a slow evolution in the absence of intense operational pressures.[179]

During the interwar years the relative importance of the battleship, the submarine and the aircraft in future combat was the subject of extensive speculation. The same was not true of amphibious operations. Such operations had not played a major role in the First World War.[180] While it is not true that the experience of the British at Gallipoli in 1915 effectively ended naval interest in such expeditions, there were very few opportunities to test or develop technique, doctrine or equipment.[181] Only the US Marine Corps (USMC) had a clear mission, for which amphibious operations were central to their existence.

The historiography of the period 1919–39 is dominated by financial restraint, the naval treaties and, later, the rearmament process. The Royal Navy, the United States Navy and the Imperial Japanese Navy, particularly, each have a solid body of literature to support further research, as intense competition between them remained diplomatically significant throughout the period.[182] Similarly, the evolving naval strategies of Britain and the United States, in response to the rising power of Japan, Italy and Germany, have been studied in some detail.[183]

There is a growing literature dealing with the French and Italian navies of the 1930s. The role of the Italian navy in Mussolini's increasingly bellicose foreign policy now has some very good studies.[184] French naval policy is less well covered.[185] The revived German navy has studies devoted to it as well as its own place in the history of the rearmament of the Third Reich. While some works on the *Reichsmarine* and *Kriegsmarine* treat the interwar period as simply a preamble to the campaigns and ships of 1939–45, there are now some excellent studies that place the growth of this navy in the overall strategic context of the times.[186] The history of the Soviet navy has generally been neglected, reflecting the lack of interest in naval affairs in Russia after 1917 and the secrecy of that state. Works by Donald Mitchell, Jürgen Rohwer and Mikhail Monakov provide the basic narrative of the period, and Admiral Sergei Gorshkov himself gives a version that illuminates the problems of Russian commitments to naval power.

The Second World War and naval power, 1939–45

The Second World War was the defining event of the twentieth century. The First World War had shaken the European imperial state system, but the second shattered it. Out of the ruins in 1945, European empires were fatally weakened and disintegrated in the coming decades. Political survival for the western European nations had come at the cost of economic devastation. The United States and the Soviet Union had experienced very different wars, but they had emerged the clear victors. The Soviet Union had suffered immense devastation but had destroyed the bulk of the German Army and now dominated Eastern Europe. The United States had responded to the war, becoming the arsenal for the United Nations. US forces also provided the essential numbers for the liberation of Western Europe. US economic power continued to provide the underpinning for the recovery of Western

Europe. The campaign in the Pacific had ended with the occupation of Japan and the United States dominating the Asia-Pacific Rim.

Compared with the First World War, naval power was less obviously a cause of the conflict, but more obviously a decisive factor in its course and result. The naval war saw the fruition of many technological and operational trends. The coming of age of the aircraft carrier and naval air power, ending the domination of the big gun battleship, had been apparent from 1940 and was demonstrated decisively at the Battle of Leyte Gulf in October 1944. The submarine had developed into an oceanic warship capable of long-range patrols, great submerged capability and high speeds. The battle between submarines and escort vessels had seen major developments in weapons technology. Radio, radar, sonar and an embryonic missile technology all took naval warfare more deeply into a three-dimensional environment. Carrier-based task forces could operate effective air power over land masses more completely than ever before. Amphibious capability, which was limited in the 1930s, had grown to bringing armies across oceans and putting them ashore successfully against heavily defended positions.

The Second World War is probably the single most widely researched and published period of naval history. Access to this past is vast. Biography,

FIGURE 5 *Naval war in three dimensions.* HMS Ark Royal, *the surface ship designed to project air power from the seas, listing to starboard after being torpedoed by U81 on the afternoon of 13 November 1941 in the Mediterranean. She capsized and sank on the morning of 14 November while under tow to Gibraltar.* © Trustees of the National Museum of the Royal Navy (Portsmouth).

autobiography, popular history, official history, oral histories and technical, operational, tactical, industrial, economic and political studies abound for almost all nations which participated in this conflict. The scale of the surviving evidence, official and personal, written, photographic and voice-recorded, exceeds anything that preceded it. The technology and the will were there to preserve the historical record. However, the ambition to control it was greater than ever before. History has always been the battleground for ideologies and the vehicle of national pride or mourning. Institutional and personal reputations, contemporary budget allocations and projections for future strategies or policies lay in the historical narrative.[187] This was never more so than after 1945. History was too important to be left to chance. The writing of the official histories was a matter of vital importance, undertaken with more vigour than after 1918.[188] Individuals were determined to dominate the historical record. Churchill was a past master of the art, but he was run a close race by commanders like Field Marshall Bernard Montgomery. In 1963, Air Chief Marshal Lord Tedder, commander of the Allied air forces during the invasion of Sicily (July 1943), wrote to the journalist and historian, Basil Liddell Hart:

> I wonder if it has struck you that there is a remarkable likeness between Monty and Winston in their respective attitudes to history. In other words, each of them determined so far as it lay within his own power, to make sure that 'his story' should record his own version of events rather than history. It was quite early days in the Desert War – even before Montgomery arrived – that one saw this process of adjustment in motion and it was early days when I was forced to the conclusion that the chances of true history being recorded of that campaign were slight indeed. Nothing has happened since has made me less pessimistic on that subject. Indeed, while it is evident that Winston's story will in due course be disentangled, on the other hand, as regards Monty the record was so skilfully adjusted at the time that I see little if any prospect of the truth being disentangled from the story.[189]

Written history is always a partial view of events, but the sheer scale and complexity of the campaigns, the number and power of interested parties, and the importance of the war in the collective psyche of a traumatized post-war world have made the Second World War the most problematic period in naval history. On the other hand, there is so much to discover, to re-evaluate and explore, that the options for the historian seem almost limitless. Even by reducing this discussion to a bare review of the most significant themes, we can barely scrape the surface as a point of illustration.

In the mass of research and publication on the naval war, there are two campaigns that stand out most strongly in the historiography of the war at sea – the Battle of the Atlantic (1940–5) and the Pacific campaign (1941–5). For Britain, the Battle of the Atlantic was a vital struggle for foodstuffs, fuel and raw materials that would enable her to keep fighting. For the United Nations, success in this battle enabled the build-up of materials and manpower to defeat German forces in the West. For Germany, it provided the most likely means of bringing Britain to terms and preventing the opening of a second front. The long campaign between the U-boats and Allied antisubmarine forces, which turned decisively against Germany in May 1943, has a mass of literature, including major printed sources.[190]

Since 1945 the submarine has remained one of the most important weapons in international maritime policy. Although the technologies have changed dramatically, the Battle of the Atlantic provides the most recent experience of high-intensity submarine warfare. The link between past and present is evident, and every year new studies, from popular histories, to technical, economic or operational studies, to biographies and reminiscences, appear in print and digital media.

The battle was the greatest contribution of the Royal Navy and the Royal Canadian Navy to victory in the Second World War. For the *Kriegsmarine*, the battle was the tragic, but important, redemption of its martial reputation after the humiliation of 1914–18. The Atlantic sea lanes between Europe and the United States remained a critical element in the Cold War. The battle's historical and contemporary significance has maintained it as a major source of historical debate. The contribution of the Royal Air Force to the battle remains a major point of contention. Whether the delay in assigning long-range bombers to attack U-boats at sea or the aerial mining of the Baltic effectively prevented the operational deployment of the advanced Type XXI U-boat are matters of debate that require more analysis.[191]

Perhaps the most significant historiographical revision that has occurred in the last forty years was the revelation of ULTRA in 1974 and the importance of signals intelligence in this campaign.[192] As time has passed and new concerns, such as digital battle-space, permeate current debates, so the significance of factors such as ULTRA assumes greater prominence in writers' minds, taking centre stage in the narrative of the battle.[193]

Histories, even of such well-known campaigns as the Battle of the Atlantic, have to be read in the light of these gaps, biases and changing priorities. An interesting example is the dominant narrative of the Battle of Britain (June–September 1940), in which so much of the institutional history of the Royal Air Force is invested. The campaign takes on a different complexion when the frame of analysis is shifted. Instead of the invasion of Britain being defeated in the skies over southern England between July and September, it has been argued that the crippling damage inflicted on the *Kriegsmarine* during the campaign around Norway between April and June effectively made covering and sustaining an invasion force by sea or air in the face of the Home Fleet a hopeless proposition – something of which the *Kriegsmarine*, if not the *Luftwaffe*, was fully aware.[194]

Today, the Battle of the Atlantic is an exemplar of how history is written and contested, from the minutiae of daily lives to grand strategy. The event, in its drama and significance, is well known to the public. The struggle for survival and its contribution to the overall victory is clearly understood. Yet the scale of operations, evidence it has left behind and the questions it raises for contemporary defence policy provide scope for new discoveries, perspectives and disputes.

The other long decisive campaign was in the Pacific. The campaign is now a fundamental element in the institutional identity of the United States Navy, with nine of the fifteen volumes of the US official history of naval operations devoted to it. The destruction of the Japanese navy in three years of war was the key to the collapse of the Japanese Empire. The gradual destruction of the Japanese surface fleet, through the battles of attrition in the Southwest Pacific and the critical clashes in the Central Pacific at Midway (4–7 June 1942), the Philippine Sea (19 June 1944), Leyte Gulf (24 October 1944) and, finally, off Okinawa (April–June 1945) brought American air power within range of the Japanese home islands, cut the vital sea lines of communication to the Philippines and the Dutch East Indies and presented the Japanese with imminent invasion.

Even more than the Battle of the Atlantic, the literature is vast and the story deeply embedded in public understanding of the war. The scale of the campaign, with its closely linked air, surface and submarine operations, makes it the largest and most sophisticated oceanic campaign of conquest ever undertaken. The US government was quick to ensure that the lessons of this campaign were presented to the American public by sponsoring the official service histories of naval and amphibious operations. These provided the narrative spine for much that has followed. Even while the war was in progress, print and film, drama and documentary brought the naval campaign alive to the public. Even though the United States has, since 1945, engaged in several relatively high-intensity campaigns with a powerful naval dimension, the Pacific campaign still stands out as the most intense, and the most unambiguous in terms of its success, purpose and consistency with the national narrative of democracy and liberty, of much that has followed. However, more recently, Japanese sources and scholarship have been incorporated into works in English, which is leading to some significant revisions. For example, the Battle of Midway, the most decisive naval battle of the campaign, has been thoroughly re-examined in the light of Japanese sources by Parshall and Tully in *Shattered Sword: The Untold Story of the Battle of Midway*, leading to a re-evaluation of individuals and events.[195] Re-evaluations of other battles have been less ambitious regarding new sources, but nonetheless have presented new perspectives. For example, the battle of Leyte Gulf has recently been re-examined by Hugh Willmott in *The Battle of Leyte Gulf: The Last Fleet Action*.[196] Part of this complex battle involved the last ever battleship to battleship engagement on the night of 24/25 October 1944, which is examined in detail by Tully in *Battle of Surigao Strait*.[197] The Battle of the Philippine Sea (19–21 June 1944) has also been recently re-evaluated by

Barrett Tillman in *Clash of Carriers: The True Story of the Marianas Turkey Shoot of World War II*.[198]

The Pacific campaign was founded on three key operational systems – the carrier task group, the submarine and the amphibious landing force. New scholarship is constantly developing the history of the campaign. Access to new sources and reinterpretations have provided recent major studies of most of the major naval battles. Most significantly, the incorporation of Japanese sources and scholarship into works in English is leading to some significant revisions.[199] Technology, naturally, dominates much of the literature. The spectacular appearance of the aircraft carrier, its obvious role in the Pacific War and its continued centrality to US naval strategy have all contributed to a massive outpouring of work on this particular type of warship.[200]

Although it has attracted far less attention than the U-boat campaign in the Atlantic, the US submarine service was extremely effective against enemy shipping. By March 1945 Japanese merchant tonnage had been reduced to 12 per cent of its 1941 volume.[201] However, this vital campaign is in need of significant historical examination. Unlike the dramatic demise of the Imperial Japanese Navy in battle with US forces, the slow collapse of Japanese merchant capacity and detailed historical analysis of the measures taken to combat the submarine are still largely neglected.[202]

Amphibious operations, on the other hand, have taken their place alongside the carrier task group in dominating the historical narrative of

FIGURE 6 *The impact of sea power: a Japanese merchantman sinking by the bows after being torpedoed by a US submarine. Seen from the periscope of the submarine, November/December 1943. National Archive.*

the war. Amphibious operations rolled back the Japanese conquests in the Southwest Pacific, ejected them from their mandates in the Central Pacific and took US forces to the Ryukyu Islands, under 400 miles from Kyushu. They marked the maturing of modern amphibious capability.[203] It was a massive joint service effort that had to be worked out as the campaigns proceeded. The success of these operations entrenched the USMC in the political culture of the United States. When the US flag was raised on Mount Suribashi, Iwo Jima, on 23 February 1945, Secretary for the Navy James Forrestal was watching the progress of the battle from offshore with General Holland Smith. He commented to Smith that 'the raising of that flag means a Marine Corps for the next five hundred years'.[204] The photograph captured by Joe Rosenthal subsequently became the iconic symbol of the Marine Corps and the Pacific campaign as a whole. The campaign in the Southwest Pacific is inextricably associated with General Douglas MacArthur, and much of the work on the drive from New Guinea to the liberation of the Philippines is told in this context.

Like the Battle of the Atlantic, the Pacific campaign has sustained a continuous flow of scholarship and popular history for over seventy years. As the primary example of a transoceanic campaign of high-intensity warfare between industrialized states, its history is both compelling and important for contemporary naval strategists. In the light of this, it is curious that a fundamental aspect of this campaign seems to have attracted so little attention. This is the logistical systems that supported the campaign. Although some work has been done on the US naval logistics, almost no work has been done to provide a comparative analysis with Japanese capabilities.[205]

Apart from the two great oceanic campaigns, the naval history of the Second World War has had mixed attention. By comparison with almost any other period, it is, of course, extensive. For example, outside the Pacific, amphibious warfare has not received the attention it deserves. Despite some useful works, British historiography is scanty for the late nineteenth and twentieth centuries.[206] A huge amount has been written on Operation Overlord (Normandy 6 June 1944), but far less on Operation Neptune (the naval operation to land the forces on D-Day). The naval aspects of other important landing operations, such as Sicily (July 1943), Madagascar (June 1942), Salerno (September 1943), Anzio (January 1944) and Walcheren (November 1944), are usually only a small part of the wider story. The existing literature seldom addresses the operational and developmental aspects of the experiences of Allied amphibious power, or how events did or did not turn out as expected.[207]

Unlike the USMC, the Royal Marines have also suffered from relative historical neglect. Before the Second World War, there were very few general histories of the corps, and those that were produced were directly linked to the campaign to preserve the Royal Marines from impending budget cuts.[208] The Royal Marines had a range of roles within the navy and on land

FIGURE 7 *The impact of sea power: amphibious invasion, Normandy, 6 June 1944.*
© *Trustees of the National Museum of the Royal Navy (Portsmouth).*

during the First World War, but it was the Second World War that raised the profile of the corps as specialist amphibious soldiers, which remains central to their identity to the present day. Narratives of their battles and weapons, and the individuals who served, continue to grow, but detailed analyses of operations, organizations and effectiveness are far less common.

Equally important, defence against amphibious operations has had very little serious consideration.[209] There are plenty of works relating to coastal defences as battlefield archaeology, but the whole matter of coastal defence lacks the drama to encourage detailed comparative study. Another example of relative neglect is the history of coastal forces. In Britain, the literature dedicated to them is often by veterans for veterans: anecdotal and popular rather than analytical. The British coastal motor boats had found fame in August 1919 with their daring attack on the Kronstadt naval base, but they quickly faded from the limelight. The drama of the war in the high-speed motor boat has an appeal to popular audiences in all nations, but comparative analyses are almost non-existent.[210] Equally neglected are the dangerous, but less dramatic, mine-laying and mine-sweeping campaigns, usually undertaken by reservists and even fishermen. Similarly, while carrier air power is extensively covered, the role of land-based air power in operations at sea is in need of further exploration. Also, as with the Pacific campaign, the naval logistical support networks in the European and Mediterranean theatres are in need of good modern studies.[211] Until recently, another relatively neglected aspect was the British naval contribution to the war in the Far East. Still, given the complexity of the diplomatic and military situation from India to the Central Pacific and the particular problems it posed for the Japanese navy, it would repay more work.[212] The adjustments of navies to war and then peace, to victory and defeat, pose important questions that are also in need of further examination.[213]

Furthermore, while the navies of Britain, the United States, Germany, Japan and, to a lesser degree, France have extensive literatures devoted to them, the navies of other combatants, and particularly neutrals, have barely been considered. The Russian navy has some good scholarship now available in English, and the Italian navy is at last receiving the attention it deserves.[214] Other navies have yet to be explored in appropriate detail.

Naval histories of the Second World War are more abundant than for any other period (followed closely by the French Wars of 1793–1815). They are particularly rich as they encompass the interests and efforts of a wide range of historians, from popular historians through to scholars of contemporary strategic studies. Popular histories reach a wider audience, generating greater public interest and understanding of naval warfare. Although much of the content is anecdotal, personal and antiquarian in its focus on individuals, weapons or great dramas, it does have its advantages over the dry, unemotional official documentation, which can be equally partial and biased. Studies based on archival holdings of official documents used to examine policy, plans and evaluations, and narratives of those who experienced the reality of those plans, both have their place. Writing that aims to bridge that gap, that is both critical and analytical, as well as conveying the drama of real lives, is still very much needed.

Historical works on the Second World War at sea are unlikely to diminish in the near future, and the heavy weighting towards the great oceanic battles and campaigns, with the supporting technologies, will, no doubt, continue. However, as time passes, the amount of material available to historians is expanding and the questions being asked of naval history do change. A number of historians are working on archives outside the English-speaking countries, and so the gaps and biases are becoming more evident and new perspectives are still emerging. Altogether, this suggests that the naval history of the Second World War has much more to be explored.

Historians, strategists and naval power, 1945–2010

By 1945, the capabilities of naval power exceeded anything that had preceded it. Naval power had created and then destroyed the Japanese Empire in the Pacific and Southeast Asia. It had ensured that the economic and human resources of the North American continent could be transported to influence decisively war and peace in Europe. On the other hand, the

Second World War had changed the balance of power more generally. Air power had developed even more dramatically since 1939 than sea power. The vulnerability of ships to aerial attack, an open question in 1939, was indisputable by 1945. The air-dropped atomic bomb now appeared to be the ultimate arbiter of states. Sea power, which had been one of the key symbols of great power status since the seventeenth century, now appeared a secondary support to membership of the nuclear club.[215] The cost of warfare had crippled almost every economy that had engaged in the Second World War, and the future costs of war on land, sea and air could only increase.

The post-war bi-polar diplomatic settlement consolidated around the United States and the Soviet Union, dominating international relations until 1991. The creation of North Atlantic Treaty Organization (NATO) and the Warsaw Pact reinforced the dynamic of coalition naval operations which had developed during the Second World War, leaving little room for independent action by medium and small powers. For Britain, the demands imposed by the withdrawal from empire and playing a full naval role in NATO provide the backdrop for most of the period.[216]

There was also a question over the role of history in this new world, which had been lingering since 1918. At the beginning of the twentieth century, navies and statesmen had turned to historical examples in the absence of practical experience in operating the new steam navies. By 1945, huge experience now existed of 'hot war'. The technologies had been developed, tested, evaluated and integrated into the post-war force structures. Other experiences of war, such as the Korean War (1950–3) or the Suez operation of 1956, provided lessons that were obvious and applicable.[217] Therefore, did the study of naval history have anything to tell the new generation operating aircraft, missiles and submarines under a nuclear umbrella? The answer was unequivocally yes.

History and historians provided the essential narrative for public understanding of these calamitous events. Official histories projected the approved narrative. The United States moved faster than Britain in producing its official history, leaving the British to play catch-up to ensure that their version of the war at sea was embedded in the public mind.[218] The USMC official history of the Korean War (1950–1) appeared in five volumes in 1957. The United States Navy's role in Vietnam up to 1965 was completed by 1976. The history of the USMC in Vietnam was published in nine volumes between 1977 and 1997. The United States Naval Historical Center now has good bibliographies of these conflicts on line, as well as some digital volumes. Similarly, the USMC has a well-developed historical division, which provides a valuable web resource.[219]

The British official histories are less well supported. The two volumes on the British involvement in the Korean War did not appear until 1990s, but the official history of the Falklands War (1982) is now in its second edition.[220]

During the early years of the Cold War, the naval problem for NATO was very similar to that which had existed prior to 1945 – ensuring the security of the sea lines of communication across the Atlantic and projecting power regionally with carrier task forces and amphibious units.[221] After the death of Stalin in 1953, the Soviet navy shifted from being principally a littoral defence force towards using a large and diverse submarine fleet to challenge NATO at the world maritime trade choke points and to force the carriers away from the Soviet land mass. This drive was accelerated both quantitatively and qualitatively under the direction of Admiral Sergei Gorchakov between 1966 and 1972. From the mid-1970s until 1989, there was a sustained naval arms race. Although the strategies and technologies shifted, the lessons deduced by Mahan and Corbett remained valid. Historians could say something about arms races, continually changing technologies and the general use of sea power in low-level intensity conflicts, but there were few new, detailed analytical cases to round out or challenge the general consensus on what navies could or should do.

This suddenly changed with the collapse of the Soviet Union at the end of 1991. Navies that for forty years had organized and prepared for large-scale oceanic coalition warfare suddenly found themselves without a potent enemy. Winning the Cold War was a major psychological boost to the West, particularly the United States, which was recovering from the trauma of defeat in Vietnam. To build on this success, there was a powerful stimulus to return to history, to find the new mission or to justify the size and structure of the naval forces. Starting around 1990, there has been a steady flow of naval history coming out of the service academies or closely linked organizations. The importance of history to strategy has been re-established.[222]

It did not take long until the new mission emerged. The new world order, free of Cold War alignments, was not peaceful. Regional, ethnic and religious fissures, international crime and piracy demanded persistent low-intensity policing of the common maritime environment. Occasionally, violent conflicts in the Balkans (1994–9), West Africa and the Gulf (1990) demanded more formal expeditionary or blockading capacity. After 9/11 naval conflict was given more definition, less by a nebulous 'War on Terror' and more by specific long-term interventions in Afghanistan (2001 to date) and Iraq (2003–13).

Navies contracted in size, but in the twenty-five years following the end of the Cold War, they grew massively in capability and technical sophistication. Just as in the period of major technological evolution between 1840 and 1890, this change has been accompanied by no significant operational application in high-intensity naval war. Strategists now have at their disposal highly sophisticated war games to model behaviours, scenarios and doctrine, but they still do not have current data to confirm hypotheses. Historical example is still useful to produce a baseline for positioning strategic possibilities. Mahan and Corbett were doing exactly this in the early twentieth century, and both still explicitly influence the writing of contemporary strategists, who are dealing with new challenges like the rise of the PLAN of China.[223]

For the historian of contemporary international relations and strategy, access to participants is a luxury of which historians of earlier periods can only dream. However, other sources, often critical ones, are withheld, and triangulating evidence from multiple sources can be more difficult. The 'Hot Wars' of the period, Korea, Vietnam, the Falklands and, to a lesser extent, the First Gulf War, are becoming more distant, and with the passage of time, the accumulation of accessible evidence is occurring. Often starting with personal memoirs, biography, interviews and informed journalism, access to the past expands via the declassification of operational and technical documents and the publication of official histories to more nuanced studies of naval affairs.

The expanding literature on the post-1945 conflicts is important, but gaps are still there. The role of the United Nations navies in the Korean War is under-researched. There are many accounts of ships, aircraft and personal memoirs, but overviews of the campaign from the perspective of the various United Nations are still very rare. Access to North Korean archival sources is still a long way in the future. The Falklands War (1982) is rather different. It was the last truly naval and amphibious campaign. Even though it was fought out of sight of both Britain and Argentina, modern democratic societies with excellent media communications receive information about military affairs quickly and can respond to them in real time. The tension this creates between operational planners and those managing the political/diplomatic dimensions of the campaign was evident during the Vietnam War, and the sinking of the Argentine cruiser *General Belgrano* on 2 May 1982 by HMS *Conqueror* remains an excellent example of the rapid effects of naval operations on domestic political and diplomatic decision-making. Operation Corporate was a tremendous success, after the expeditionary force was hastily assembled, but it also exposed the fragility of British naval power in this type of war. The weaknesses in ship design and the need for better shipboard air defence in the face of missile attack were clear. The lack of preparedness and training in amphibious operations was exposed. The difficulties of operating civilian ships in a war zone posed problems that had to be resolved when the conflict ended. Yet Argentinean operational and strategic studies are still needed to balance the British studies.[224]

The Cold War is now distant enough for solid work related to naval strategy and operations on both sides of the ideological divide to be undertaken, at least for the earlier part of the period. For NATO the preservation of the Atlantic sea lines of communication was vital, which made the anti-submarine campaign an essential strategic element, which in turn made the lessons of 1939–45 of continuing relevance. The projection of carrier-based air power and amphibious incursions, such as Suez in 1956 or Lebanon in 1958, were also important elements in national strategy.[225] British and American naval strategy in the Cold War is now part of the historical debate.[226] However, much more is needed to put the Cold War naval strategic balance into perspective. Studies of Soviet naval strategy are still heavily reliant upon Western interpretations formulated during the Cold War. Histories of the naval strategies of the smaller navies of NATO, the Warsaw Pact and non-aligned countries during the Cold War are growing in number and detail, but more work is needed to position them properly in the overall naval balance.[227] As with earlier periods of naval history, it will only be when scholars from many countries, working with familiarity and access across archives, bring the fruits of their research together that we are going to approach a satisfactory history of this period.

The need for a common forum is not just to understand national approaches to strategy. There may be a broad consensus that 'seapower (or, more precisely, ocean power) is the sine qua non of action in global politics',[228] but strategy emerges from an appreciation of many military, political and economic capabilities. Naval power is just one of these, and to understand both the naval contribution to strategies and the impact of other factors on naval strategy, it is essential that rigorous studies of all elements in the strategic equation are incorporated into the historical debate.

The value of naval power to diplomacy is its flexibility. From demonstration off the coast and blockade beyond the horizon to amphibious landing and devastating bombardment, naval power has far more capacity than land or air power to send messages of varying strength to a potential opponent. The 'gunboat diplomacy' of the nineteenth century has its equivalents in the twenty-first, ranging from massive humanitarian assistance or suppression of piracy, people trafficking, migration and environment protection to direct intervention by air or landings. Only navies can provide such flexible power.[229]

Sea power remains extremely expensive, but navies shaped to meet local and regional needs are an essential part of the security apparatus of any state with a significant coastline. The shifting centre of economic gravity from the West to the Pacific has raised the significance of the developing navies in that region. For contemporary strategists, the importance of placing the PLAN of China into its historical context has provided a growing link between naval historians and policy makers.[230] The development of the Indian navy and its role in creating an impact on the politics of the Indian Ocean is leading to the building of a literature devoted to the subject.[231]

Historians and strategists are working together to pose questions and interrogate evidence. By far the most extensive work is on naval technologies – where policy concerns and popular and political interests coincide. The 'Revolution in Military Affairs', which has dominated professional military thinking since the 1990s, has powerful echoes in the popular interest in technology.[232] The importance of bringing together an understanding of contemporary technology and the historical context is evident from some of the ten volumes in the Brassey's series *Seapower: Naval Vessels, Weapons Systems and Technology*, published in the mid-1990s. Since 1945, the

United States has led the way in technological development, and its history dominates the contemporary history of sea power. From ship design to naval weapons and sensor technologies, the history of the United States Navy is now the centrepiece of historians' concerns.[233] The technological advances of most other navies have had much less attention, although the development of the British Royal Navy to become a nuclear-powered and nuclear-armed force has been recorded in some detail.[234]

Operational aspects of naval policy have also attracted some attention. Despite the overwhelming dominance of US naval power, the continuing diplomatic advantages of coalition warfare have become clear since 1990. Historians are helping to explore the strengths and weaknesses of coalitions in naval affairs.[235] Understanding power projection by amphibious force and carrier air groups links historians and strategists.[236] In the absence of hot wars and the need for rapid response, intelligence gathering has become a major aspect of operations for post-war navies.[237]

Less attention has been paid to the financial and economic underpinning of naval strategy, but it has not been ignored. Budgetary constraints and the limitations of industrial capacity are a central theme of the history of the British Royal Navy of the twentieth century, and also form part of the stories of the US, German, Italian, Austro-Hungarian, French and Spanish navies of the preceding century.[238]

Nevertheless, given the importance of industrial, financial and organizational infrastructures to our understanding of how navies interact with their host societies, they remain subjects in need of significant development.

Economics and finance are not the only constraints on strategies, and historians are now borrowing from social scientists to frame questions and seek answers to how nations innovate or maintain naval capability in rapidly changing technological or operational environments. Systems approaches to understanding innovation processes are beginning to emerge. A particularly striking example of innovation, which has brought together thinking from social scientists and historians, is the development of the submarine-launched nuclear missile. How this weapon system (Polaris A1 to Trident II) emerged from the political and budgetary battles from 1955 to 1990 is an excellent case study of historians and social scientists.[239] There are, therefore, hopeful signs of fruitful and growing interests shared by the historians of contemporary naval history and strategists.

Conclusion

This chapter has tried to provide an overview of the writing and research in naval history as it emerged from the late nineteenth century to aid navies, statesmen and other professional strategists in the formulation and conduct of international relations. Naval historians try to present insights into the complex phenomenon of sea power which are intelligible and interesting to the professionals and the public. The tempo of that research and the subjects examined have been synchronized to their needs ever since. To this end, naval history has focused largely on the operational aspects of navies, exploring technologies, strategies and tactical deployments. It has provided the public at large with essential national narratives to underpin the economic and fiscal cases for contemporary navies. For the public around the world, operations naturally lie at the centre of their interest, because of both the drama of the events and the obvious application of sea power. The result is a vast literature, continues to grow and shows no sign of declining. As such, the subject is in a very healthy condition.

Yet there is still a serious question to be asked about naval history in this context. Naval history was, and continues to be, seen as an important element in the creation and sustenance of naval power. It facilitates judgements on past conflicts that inform decision-making in contemporary navies, and it provides the narrative that legitimates political decisions regarding public investment in navies. Is it still effective in this role? In other words, are the producers of naval history (historians primarily connected to navies and popular historians informing the public) still well connected to their intended audience (naval services, politicians and public)?

The answer to the question will be different in every society navies serve, but there are reasons to fear that the connections are not as strong as the volume of historical studies might suggest. The current state of the art is still heavily skewed towards the navies of Great Britain and the United States and is unbalanced in its emphasis on the battle. Battle is the ultimate expression of naval power, where the genius, courage, fortitude and suffering of those involved are most clearly shown. However, if sea power is perceived as the output of dynamic economic, political and social systems, which more or less contribute to the net power of a navy, its complexity becomes more obvious and the gaps in our understanding stand out more starkly. Operational history is only fully comprehensible when all the actors in a particular conflict are sufficiently understood. This is not the case for most conflicts in history. The performance of navies can only be understood in relation to the tasks they are asked to achieve and the organizational and institutional strength that they possess. This institutional strength is partly determined by the robustness of the internal systems within navies that generate the fighting edge of the force. A great deal of research has focused on this, but it remains patchy across time and societies. It is also determined by the power navies exercise within their host societies, which influences the critical political and economic resources granted to them to ensure long-term investment and support of their organizational systems. Less research has been focused upon this.

The importance of this cannot be over-emphasized. In the last decades of the nineteenth century, navies were becoming institutionally entrenched in societies. This had long been the case in Britain. The importance of naval power was a deeply held assumption in British political thinking, and was becoming so in the United States, France, Germany, Italy, Spain, Japan and Russia, to name but the most significant. What was required from historians at that time, given the massive technological changes of the period, was to help produce an understanding of how to maximize the operational strength of the new steam and steel warships. Today, the situation is very different. Operationally, navies are highly capable professional organizations, expert at adaptation and innovation, with huge potential force. However, the institutional strength of navies is far less than it was. The purpose and process of naval power are poorly understood by the general public, and the rising cost of effective sea power, relative to the economic growth of states, is becoming more transparently burdensome. The destruction that can be wrought from the sea is now greater than at any time in history, but the expectation of having to defend against such an attack, be it an economic assault on maritime trade communications or a direct assault on territory, is remote among the populations of maritime nations. An historical understanding is now needed less for its operational lessons or principles of naval power and more for its political legitimacy in a globalized world. To address public 'sea-blindness', historians need to engage with issues they have not traditionally focused upon, but which lie at the centre of the institutional strength of navies – the interplay of naval and other concerns in domestic political and social agendas. To despair about the public failure to understand naval warfare is not adequate. The thalassocratic argument needs to rest less on generic assumptions and more on detailed comparative archival work. Important work is being done to redress this, which will be discussed in Chapter 3, but more needs to be done. Only when we understand how naval power worked within individual states across large time spans can we assess the evolving significance of naval power.

CHAPTER TWO

Navies, politics and government, 1500–1789

The purpose of the previous chapter was to explore how naval history has been shaped and influenced by the concerns of its principal producers and audiences – naval officers, statesmen and the politically aware public at large. Naval history was and still is vocational education, public information and entertainment. However, audiences are never as hermetically separated as this simplified classification implies. Naval officers wrote and read naval history for professional and leisure purposes. The public read it for leisure and to inform themselves of the civic expectations of their societies. Nevertheless, the distinction is useful, particularly as it enables us to highlight the apparent absence of another audience and producer – the community of academic historians. Although operational naval history or naval strategy has never firmly established itself as a major sub-discipline with civilian history departments around the world, it has played and is playing an important part in the interests of historians. It is largely this group of scholars that has broadened the significance of naval history. From traditional diplomatic, political and economic histories to more recent cultural and social histories, naval history is present, posing questions, pointing to neglected archival sources and suggesting answers for a wide range of scholars.

International trade, state formation and colonial expansion were themes clearly relevant to the new history schools of the nineteenth century. They were there, after all, to inform and educate the administrative and political classes about these phenomena; a core curriculum in Britain that only changed significantly in the last years of the twentieth century. The British Empire has been described as having an 'almost metaphysical presence' to Victorian historians.[1] The culmination of this focus and energy occurred between the two world wars in monumental works such as *The Cambridge History of the British Empire* (published between 1929 and 1936 and reprinted in the

1950s–1960s) and *The Oxford History of England* (published between 1934 and 1939, with later editions and reprints). American scholarship was almost equally focused on the history of the colonial institutional and economic origins of the nation.

Naval history was an essential element, but had probably never recovered from the disaster of Montagu Burrows' appointment as the first Chichele Professor of Modern History at Oxford. Burrows, an ex-naval officer, was so deeply unimpressive that the chair was 'sterilized for more than a generation by a clownish first appointment'.[2] Nevertheless, the subject was clearly important, and in 1919 a new chair, the Vere Harmsworth of Imperial and Naval History, was established at Cambridge, although the fact that only one naval historian ever held the chair indicates the subordinate role of the naval to the imperial dimension of scholarship. More recently, imperial history, traditionally seen almost exclusively from the perspective of the metropolitan state, has given way to more nuanced and sensitive histories of relations with the periphery, with different social groups and from different perspectives of empire.[3] As will be shown, naval history, on the coat-tails of this phenomenon, is following a similar path. Thus, navies and naval power, while seldom explicitly explored in detail, are still deeply embedded in the history curriculum.

Maritime empires, confessional politics and navies, 1500–1650

The need to control violence on the sea has been a perennial concern of societies ever since mankind took to the water for migration or trade. From antiquity, robbery at sea and raiding were common ways of making a living, but the cost and complexity of sustaining a major presence at sea could only be borne by relatively few sophisticated societies. Societies around the China Sea were capable of projecting formidable naval power from the thirteenth century AD, which made those waters a vital contested space for centuries. For a short period between 1417 and 1423, the Ming Empire dominated the waters as far as the western edge of the Indian Ocean.[4] In Europe, cities such as Venice and Genoa or confederations like the North German Hansa League were important actors in their regional maritime environments.[5]

By the 1520s, three new factors were at play in Europe. First, the discovery, between the 1470s and the 1490s, of the oceanic trade routes to the Far East and to America had unleashed massive expectations regarding the economic potential of global trade. Second, the Reformation from 1517 had begun to split Europe into hostile camps based on deep convictions far exceeding the usual dynastic rivalries that had divided Europeans for centuries. Third were the changes in warfare being experienced as a result of technological, economic and political changes. Historians have focused on these three dimensions of European society in their quest to understand the development of the early modern world, and continue to contest their relative significance.

Navies, or naval power, are part of that contest. Navies had played a role in the Habsburg–Valois struggles over Italy, Flanders and Burgundy between 1495 and 1559. As the French and imperial courts vied to contain the English and Turkish forces on their maritime peripheries, the sea became a significant element in the struggle between them. As Europe descended into the more complex and wider-ranging wars of religion in the second half of the century, the importance of naval power became even more evident. Sea communications were vital to Spanish interests in the Americas and the Netherlands. The collapse of Valois control over the coastal regions of France made them vulnerable to seaborne interventions by their enemies. By 1530, Sweden had moved from the periphery to the centre of European politics as it established itself on the southern Baltic shores. From then on, sea power was vital to preserve Sweden's position in Livonia and Estonia, and to defend against a hostile Denmark.[6]

The conflicts that ranged across Europe had a significant impact on maritime commerce. Europe was bound by a long-established and stable rhythm of trade by the end of the fifteenth century.[7] Reciprocal trade between the Baltic and the Mediterranean had evolved in the Middle Ages. The European littoral and the great river systems enabled the movements of goods from far inland and provided a network that tied European commercial interests together. The first dramatic blow to this network occurred in 1453 when Constantinople fell to the Ottoman Turks. Within ten years the great trading empire of Venice, which had dominated the Levant Trade, was under threat from Turkish fleets pressing towards the Adriatic, and by 1502 it had lost the last of its strongholds on the Morea.[8]

These great arteries of commerce were also the highways for the projection of naval power. Whether for the disruption of commerce, the plundering of wealth or the landing of armies, naval power was a flexible and effective weapon.[9] However, navies are complex and expensive organizations. Far more than armies, which were, by the sixteenth century, changing dramatically, navies relied on relatively specialized expertise from mercantile and maritime communities. States needed money and permanent administrative infrastructures in order to work with these communities to build and supply warships for the state and to ensure the hire or requisition of additional merchant ships. In this period it was becoming clear that conducting business effectively was as important as traditional military acumen in the long-term maintenance of naval power. Early modern states gradually developed this expertise, which was to be one of the major factors in the development of sea power until the nineteenth century.[10]

By the beginning of the seventeenth century, the great oceanic voyages to Africa, the Far East and the Americas had opened up trading opportunities to Europeans, particularly the Portuguese, Spanish, Dutch, English and French.[11] The tendency to overstate the significance of the European technological superiority in shipping and guns continued into the 1980s, but is now strongly disputed.[12] For most of the world, the advantage did not lie overwhelmingly with the Europeans. Outside the Americas, Europeans were confined to coastal regions by powerful local forces and disease.[13]

Nevertheless, by the mid-1560s, Spain had established the first truly global trading empire. Silver mined in South and Central America was carried across the Pacific to Manila to pay for spices, silks, gold and porcelain from China. These in turn were taken back to Central America.[14] From there, together with more silver, these cargoes paid for goods brought from metropolitan Spain. The wealth generated by this commerce had a fundamental impact on international relations. The silver and trade goods immensely reinforced the power of the Spanish Habsburg monarchs, making the King of Spain both the envy and the dread of other states. The solution for those other powers was to take as much of that trade as they could, generating a constant low-level warfare at sea and occasional major operations between Europeans across the globe. Successful war at sea against Catholic Spain became a central part of the national legends of Protestant England and the Dutch Republic. The English raids into the Caribbean, particularly the exploits of Sir Francis Drake and the defeat of the Spanish Armada in 1588, linked maritime commerce, wealth and national defence as the central virtuous conditions of England's rise to economic supremacy and political liberty.[15] In 1940, during the deep crisis of that summer, this legend provided the theme for the Ford Lectures at Oxford. James Williamson surveyed the 'oceanic interest' that came to dominate Britain from the sixteenth century. Britain was vulnerable, but oceanic enterprise

> had produced the means of defending it. Three of those means may be enumerated; the most efficient fighting fleet the world has seen, its sea-talent as well as its material having common origin with those of the innumerable merchant fleets that traversed every ocean; an elastic and expanding wealth, ill-distributed, no doubt, but unprecedented in bulk and resilience to disaster; and a tradition of statesmanship, an instinctive strategy, guiding even mediocre men to do the right thing, bred from two centuries of familiarity with the whole earth as a field of play, and proving able after anxious years to use the sea-power and the wealth to overcome the greatest military ascendancy that continental Europe had produced.[16]

Similarly, the Dutch depredations on Spanish commerce, their massive expansion of colonial possessions at the expense of the old Portuguese empire (incorporated into the Spanish orbit in 1580) and their defeat of a Spanish Armada at the Battle of the Downs in 1639 provide a similar narrative for the emergence of their Golden Age in the second half of the seventeenth century.[17]

These events provided the focus for many of the early histories of navies and naval warfare. They are an essential part of the national myths which had crystallized by the end of the nineteenth century. In Britain, the ultimate success of the Protestant northern states against Catholic Spain and the explicit link between trade, expanding wealth and sea power provided a firm foundation to complement the dominant ideology that contrasted Protestant freedom and work ethic with Catholic autocracy and stultifying hierarchy.[18] The legend matured over two centuries, and by 1900 was so axiomatic in British political thinking that the ideological assumption truncated the analysis. The economic analyses that could have underpinned the claimed causal relationships were absent in the early histories. The purpose of these histories, founded on a long-standing antiquarian tradition, was to present the evidence through a narrative that explained the present situation of the nation.[19] As a result, a great deal is known about how the 'Navy Royal' operated, how it was organized, resourced, led and, to a lesser degree, manned. There is now a mass of literature and printed documents on the Tudor navy, published in the first half of the twentieth century, by bodies such as the Hakluyt Society and the Navy Records Society, which provided a core for the more critical study of the phenomenon by imperial and naval historians during the second half of the century. The output on the subject continues to expand. The current historiography of the Tudor navy provides an excellent example of the changing emphases in the study of naval history. From ships and guns it has moved to the mobilization of shipping and seamen in the maritime communities; from the perspective of monarchs to the nature of local contractual and obligatory relationships; and from assumptions of national characteristics to conjectures about levels of efficiency and effectiveness.[20]

French and Spanish naval history underwent a similar construction in the latter part of the nineteenth century. Until the 1980s, the monumental *Historia de la Armada Española* (1898–1900) by Cesaro Fernández Duro was the most important history of the Spanish navy.[21] While Duro's narrative is still the best single work on the scale and scope of Spanish naval commitments between 1450 and 1833, there is a growing body of work that is giving a far richer understanding of the key elements of the Spanish naval power – its relationship to the Crown, the officer corps, manning and logistics.[22] Some specific operations, such as the great Armadas of 1588 and 1639, have been covered in far more depth from the Spanish sources, and for Spain generally there is now a more complete view of many aspects of regional naval power, such as the Spanish forces in the Mediterranean or the Caribbean Barlovento Squadron. As we begin to understand more about the long-term development of Spanish naval power during the sixteenth and seventeenth centuries, and the priorities placed upon the naval problems by the Spanish Crown, we get closer to understanding the dynamics of the naval force under the Habsburg monarchy, and thus we are coming closer to being able to make some comment about the comparative problems, objectives, efficiency and effectiveness faced by English, Dutch and Spanish naval forces.

French scholars were no less interested in origins of their state navy. Unlike Spain, which had no national navy until the accession of the Bourbons in 1713, the navy played an important part in the consolidation of the French state in the seventeenth century. It was always a factor, if not a central one, first in Richelieu's defeat of internal and foreign enemies and later in Louis XIV's assertion of French power, at least until 1696. Charles de la Ronciere's six-volume *Histoire de la marine française,* published between 1899 and 1932, provided the core narrative of the development of the navy from the Middle Ages to 1714. Generations since have developed that broad narrative.[23]

The same process is happening with other navies. The dominance of British naval history, written from the perspective of nineteenth-century navalist scholars, seriously misconstrued the nature of naval warfare in the Mediterranean and the Baltic. The British problem of the late nineteenth century – that of a global, oceanic trading empire, highly dependent for its wealth, basic sustenance and domestic security on its sea communications – was not a common phenomenon. The Baltic and the Mediterranean in the early modern period were ringed by societies that did not necessarily depend on maritime trade for their survival. Naval capability was important for defence and offensive operations, but long-term blockade or battles of decisive annihilation did not possess the operational logic that had developed on the Atlantic seaboard. To the navalist scholars looking back to the period 1500–1800, the survival of the Mediterranean galley until the mid-eighteenth century appeared an anachronistic folly. They failed to see how warfare in the Mediterranean was conditioned by the geography and social and economic structures. The galley was well adapted for the Mediterranean, in which low-level conflict at sea was endemic along the whole littoral and was factored into the economic calculations of the galley owners and the states that hired them. While heavy cannon remained expensive and scarce, galleys provided a more reliably manoeuvrable platform than the high-sided sailing ship, which carried no more guns and presented a better target than the galley. It was not until merchant ships began to carry significant numbers of cheap, heavy, iron cannon for defence in the mid-seventeenth century that the galley began to lose its edge.

Galleys also had a cultural and social rationale. The Ottoman Turks had been a constant threat in the Mediterranean since the fall of Constantinople in 1453. The galley was the warship that represented both the threat and the defence in this religious conflict. The galley fleets of the French and Spanish Crowns, as well as the militant religious orders, such as the Knights of St John at Malta or St Stephen at Leghorn (Livorno), conferred a combined martial and confessional status that attracted aristocratic officers from

FIGURE 8 *Coexisting expressions of power: an English three-decker and a galley in an Italian port, unknown artist, c.1680.* © National Maritime Museum. ID BCHO 935.

across Catholic Europe.[24] In 1571 the Counter-Reformation was beginning to gather its intellectual and artistic pace, and the *Real*, the flagship galley of Don Juan of Austria, the commander of the Holy League fleet, at Lepanto in October of that year, was a deliberate expression of naval power, religious conviction and contemporary humanism. Built at Barcelona in 1568, and decorated in Seville, the *Real* was an exceptionally large vessel of its type. Greek and Roman images and motifs adorned the vessel. Images of successful commanders from classical times to the present reminded the commander of his heritage. Over it all were the three twelve-sided lanterns, inscribed with religious verse.[25]

From the Battle of Lepanto (1571) to the mid-eighteenth century, the galley fleets were the shield of Christendom against the Ottoman Turks. Command conferred spiritual and temporal status, and while service at the oars and in the arsenals was a mixture of free and forced labour. Hard unforgiving labour for Protestant recusants or Muslim captives in the service of the Catholic faith seemed a proper and redeeming fate.[26]

It was not just in the Mediterranean that the warship was seen as a symbol of religious devotion. The ocean was a wild, chaotic and barbarous environment. God's protection was essential, and success on the sea was a signal of divine approbation. The mounting of the Great Armada of 1588 and its dispersal by the winds in the English Channel was seen on both sides as a divine salvation or retribution. Although, generally, Protestant powers did not choose religious names for their ships, the expression of divine and secular power was important to friend and foe. The forty-four-gun Swedish warship *Vasa*, which sank on her maiden voyage in Stockholm harbour on 10 August 1628, shows this clearly. She was adorned with mythical, Biblical and abstract figures in bright colours, designed to inspire wonder. The intention was to proclaim the martial valour of Gustavus Vasa by association with the Biblical characters of King David and Gideon, the mythical Hercules and the great Roman emperors. The enemy was ridiculed with the crouching figure of a Polish nobleman, located next to the heads, crushed by the cathead, which supported the anchor.[27] In 1637, the *Sovereign of the Seas*, built by Phineas Pett for Charles I, asserted the monarch's power over the waters, although it was an empty boast which could not be maintained in practice.

The situation in the eastern Baltic was also conducive to the use of war galleys. The many islands, archipelagos and shallow waters made the galley an essential component of naval operations that continued until the 1790s, almost fifty years after the demise of the Mediterranean galley squadrons.[28] Thanks, particularly, to the work of Jan Glete, we now have a better understanding of what contemporaries considered to be a balanced

FIGURE 9 *The spectacle of sea power: Phineas Pett and the* Sovereign of the Seas, *c. 1637.* © *National Maritime Museum. ID BHC 2949.*

naval force for the Baltic navies. However, work on the social composition of the officer corps and the seamen in these navies is still in its infancy.[29]

The growing number of regional and national studies of naval forces is encouraging and valuable, but, on the whole, the naval history of this period from 1600 to 1650 remains underdeveloped. It has not captured the imagination of scholars of imperial power or state-building in the way that the navies of the formative period in the sixteenth century and the dramatic clashes of the eighteenth century have done. Although the Thirty Years' War (1618–48) has been seen as the first European conflict fought on a global scale, the war on land dominates the historiography.[30]

For naval historians, the historiography of the English Civil War (1640–8) is rather more developed than that of the wider European conflict. It was in the Civil War and during the English Republic (1649–60) that the early naval historians found important building blocks of subsequent British naval hegemony. During the war, the navy played an extremely important part in isolating the Royalists from Continental support and preserving the financial base of London for the Parliamentarian cause. The New Model Army undoubtedly brought about the ultimate defeat of the Stuart cause, but it was the navy that 'held the ring' and tilted the advantage massively in favour of Parliament.

The period also saw important developments in ship design. The high sides of the 'great ships' of the early seventeenth century were intended to provide an advantage in battles of boarding and infantry fighting. Gradually, 'race built' ships or galleons with lower freeboard were constructed to improve speed and manoeuvrability while carrying an equivalent punch in cannons and weight of shot.[31] During the 1640s, Spanish light, single-deck, relatively narrow warships, armed with lighter guns operating first out of Dunkirk and then Irish ports, caused serious problems for the English, particularly in their reconquest of Ireland.[32] The English began to build similar ships to supplement their heavier vessels. During the 1650s, these 'frigate' designs were blended with the galleon design to create an English frigate-type warship, little smaller in tonnage than the galleon, with a similar battery of heavy guns, but with a narrower profile and with greater manoeuvrability.[33] This was the period in which the distinctive, purpose-built line of battle ship and cruising frigate began to emerge as the dominant weapons in the naval arsenal. With this, there was a demand for changing tactics and naval leadership. Increasing in size, carrying more and heavier guns, ships of the line made it impossible to rely any longer on converting merchantmen to warships in time of need as the basis for naval power; the purpose-built warship and the professional naval officer were beginning to emerge as distinctive types.[34]

The significance of the English Civil War to British naval historians has ensured that there has been a steady, if small, stream of work on the first half of the seventeenth century. The Council of the Navy Records Society, established in 1893 to ensure that there were good source materials readily available for the professional study of naval history, recognized the importance of the period. The Tudor navy was well covered in the early years of the Society, but over time, the Society also published some important collections on the early Stuart period, including fighting instructions, operations and, most significantly, naval administration.[35] Good modern studies are rare. The most recent full-length study of the Civil War at sea is now over fifty years old.[36] However, the overall narrative has been enriched over the decades by biographies and articles on specific incidents by historians such as Michael Baumber, J. R. Powell and R. C. Anderson.[37] There are, additionally, articles and books focusing on English politics or economics, which necessarily provide important insights into matters of naval administration or operations.[38]

By the end of the Civil War, the English navy was having a growing impact on domestic politics. The maritime community, from which the seamen for the state's ships were drawn, was confessionally close to the moderate Presbyterians, and distrustful of the radical Independents who were dominating Parliament with the support of the army. Changes in the naval command, in which the popular Sir William Batten was replaced as vice admiral by the Independent Republican Colonel Thomas Rainsborough, fractured command and control in the parts of the fleet. During the first half of 1648, Royalist sympathizers encouraged riots in the southeast of England. Sandwich and Walmer Castles fell into their hands, and sailors on six warships at Deal mutinied. This was followed by other mutinies on ships in the North Sea. Eighteen out of a total of thirty-nine warships in the summer guard were lost to Parliamentary control, ten of which eventually sailed to join the Royalists in Wales or Holland. Although the revolt was crushed and the Royalist naval threat of blockade or landings petered out after an abortive raid up the Thames, the potential threat to the vital commerce of London was clear.[39]

The purge of the House of Commons that followed the end of the Royalist revolt left the Independents dominating the Rump Parliament. They had solid support from the army, but their hold on the navy was far more questionable. After the execution of King Charles I on 30 January 1649, the new Republic was faced by the hostility of most European powers. Defence of the Republic and the elimination of the residual Royalist forces in the colonies and Europe would depend on the fleet. Before the Civil War, the Navy Royal had seemed to have slipped into torpor. By 1639, the Crown could not prevent Barbary corsairs from raiding the coast of the British Isles. Nor could it stop Dutch or Spanish forces using English waters with impunity. By 1650, however, the English navy was the largest in Europe in terms of tonnage, and within four years the English Republic emerged as a naval power of major stature.

At home, the power of the Republic rested firmly in the New Model Army, but it was the effective use of the navy that projected that power diplomatically across the European and Atlantic worlds. The ability of the

Parliamentary administrative system to construct, maintain and organize a major navy is one of the great achievements of the Republic and highlights one of the most important aspects of navies in the building of the modern nation-state.

Despite this, the naval history in the period from 1600 to 1650 is still neglected. The founding myth of British sea power was closely associated with the Tudor state, its long maritime resistance to the power of Catholic Spain and its initial steps towards an imperial future. The period after the 1603 peace with Spain offered nothing like the same drama until the Civil War, when the impact of naval power could again be clearly traced. Until recently, the Thirty Years' War, both as an interstate conflict and as a series of civil wars, has been viewed predominantly in terms of land campaigns. This is now changing, thanks to the work of scholars like Jan Glete, Jaap Bruijn, Carla Rahn Phillips, Jean Meyer, J. Alcala-Zamora, Alan James and others. Important gaps have been filled, but we are not yet at a point where a deep comparative study of the naval dimension of the Thirty Years' War can be confidently attempted.

Navies, state-building and the fiscal-military state debate, 1650–1750

The Thirty Years' War ended in 1648. Europe desperately needed peace. For 150 years Europe had been convulsed by crises – economic, fiscal, social, religious and political conflicts had opened, intertwined and fed upon one another. By the end, the unity of Christendom was irrevocably shattered and the factions stood in militant, if exhausted, opposition. The once dreaded prospect of a Spanish hegemony had faded, but had been replaced by a Europe riven by unresolved conflicts. Traditional political consensuses had been shattered and new political equilibriums had yet to be established. Naval and maritime affairs have not usually been seen as important in these great events, but navies played a part.

The political history of the period has been dominated in the last half of the twentieth century by two linked debates – the rise of the absolutist monarchies and the fiscal-military state. Both are concerned, in part, with how states responded to the fiscal and economic crises caused by the increasing costs of warfare. The scale and cost of warfare during the sixteenth and seventeenth centuries demanded ever more resources, which stretched the fiscal and financial systems of early modern states to breaking point on a number of occasions. The way in which states struggled to avoid bankruptcy and maintain an effective foreign policy has interested scholars of state formation for a number of decades. Centralization of the state bureaucracy, territorial consolidation and political absolutism have been the three main explanatory tools for the emergence of the modern European state.[40] Together or separately, they are supposed to have facilitated the greater capability of the state to extract tax revenues, which funded the growth of the military, which in turn assisted in further centralization, consolidation and absolutism. This simplistic circle of state growth has not gone unchallenged, and explanations have become increasingly sophisticated and conditional as the limitations of all three concepts have been exposed and redefined.[41]

Why absolutism seemed to triumph in some countries, such as Spain, France, Prussia and the Habsburg Empire, while it failed in others, principally England and the United Provinces, has fuelled historical discourse since the eighteenth century. Indeed, some of these debates feed off much older thalassocratic theory. The argument runs that the need to centralize, consolidate or impose absolutism was directly linked with needs for fiscal extraction. The weaker the fiscal base, the more vigorous states had to be in these activities, leading to either the destruction of local liberties or the failure of the state to maintain itself among the ranks of the major powers. Thus, absolutism thrived in traditional agrarian societies, dominated by a landed aristocracy served by a mass peasant population. There may have been violent and bloody resistance, but, ultimately, the strong central authority of the monarch was established, which enabled the state to extract all the resources it required from its domestic population. There was no need for alternative methods of acquiring revenues to preserve the state.[42] On the other hand, where that strong central power failed, as it did in England and the United Provinces, usually as the result of resistance from a wealthy commercial middling order, then a search had to be made for resources outside the domestic economy. Fortunately, that same middling order of people, the merchants and mariners, provided the means for gathering those resources by overseas trade and colonial expansion. Political liberties, commerce, and naval and maritime power were symbiotically linked and provided a direct contrast to absolutism and commercial stagnation.

The power of this analysis is tremendous. It was consistent with the influential historical sociology of Max Weber. It supported the political ideology of nineteenth-century liberalism and traditional thalassocratic beliefs. Naval power becomes the defining feature of political liberty and economic well-being in the modern world. It is the cause and the consequence of economic and political liberty.

This conclusion has been attacked from a number of directions as more detailed research has continued. The assumption that representative institutions survived because local tax resources were less has not turned out to be universally true. Absolutism did not destroy representative institutions or regionalism in many countries, nor was the existence of representative institutions incompatible with a centralized, geographically homogeneous state. The relationship between state and society which governed the extraction of tax revenues and the construction of armed forces was far more varied and nuanced than the original explanation allowed.[43]

This is also picked up in the work of John Brewer, whose *Sinews of Power: War, Money and the English State, 1688–1763*, published in 1989, did a great deal to focus attention on the close relationship between the growth of English fiscal power and its conversion into effective military and naval force. His conclusion was that England was not driven to overseas expansion by state weakness, but chose it as a pathway facilitated by state strength. The state's ability to extract taxation was greater than that of its absolutist rivals. This fiscal power underpinned a credit market that enabled long-term borrowing at low rates of interest. The expansion of credit was vital for the institutional stability of naval force, which required massive investments in infrastructure and commercial contracts.[44] This was the fiscal-military state, or, as it has been more recently formulated by Roger Knight and Martin Wilcox, the contractor state.[45]

This conclusion has been supported by Jan Glete's work on Sweden and the Dutch Republic. The army, usually seen as the servant of absolute monarchs, had as important a role in the United Provinces. Far from being weaker states, Glete found that both Sweden and the Dutch Republic were domestically stronger than the Spanish monarchy, and thus political weakness could not account for their maritime expansion. Furthermore, too little account had been taken of per capita income figures in assessing the value of revenues generated.[46] In the case of England, James Wheeler demonstrated it was the long-term development of strong fiscal and financial institutional power between 1640 and 1690 that provided the foundations of English naval power.[47] On the other hand, investigations of merchant communities also established that merchants do not all have the same political and economic interests. The great merchants who dominated the monopoly companies had little in common with the interlopers and smaller merchants trading to different parts of the world. To ignore conflict between merchant communities is to impose a homogeneity of outlook and interest on these communities that did not exist.[48]

More recently, attention is being paid, not just to the nature of revenue-raising activities of states, but to their expenditure patterns. Military or naval power could only be created from the industries and merchant communities that provided the maritime and martial products. The power of the state did not just depend upon the political structure, but on the economic networks that underpinned it. Armies might be created from relatively narrow and weak commercial networks, so a small nation like Prussia could be seen in the eighteenth century as an army with a state rather than the other way around. Navies could not be so easily constructed. They required a wide-ranging industrial and commercial base. Few states, if any, were self-contained in these resources, and investment in naval resources had different impacts on societies.[49]

The role of institutions in shaping societies is also under-researched. The long-held belief that navies were institutions intimately linked to commercial and political liberty, as distinct from armies, which derived their institutional weight from a landed aristocracy, autocracy and tradition, is not as simple as it was once thought. It is still a strongly held belief in some quarters, and there is intuitive logic to support such ideas, but the more opportunities we take to examine specific navies in societies at defined chronological points, the more likely it is that we will find that this simple dichotomous assumption is at best partial and at worst completely misleading.

Historical fashions come and go, and at present, it seems that interest has moved on from historical institutionalism.[50] However, naval historians must return to it. One of the most important questions that can be asked about any organization is: What impact does it have on its host society? Not only is it important for our understanding of how the seventeenth-century state developed across Europe, but also, if we are to understand navies and navies wish to be understood by their societies, it is a question that needs answering for every period up to the present day.

England, sea power and the Anglo-Dutch Wars, 1649–74

In England, by 1649, the navy of the new Republic had become the major arm of the state. After the mutiny of 1648, the Council of State took great care to ensure its political reliability and effective force by expanding both the financial resources committed to it and the number of ships in service. In the 1640s and 1650s, the English navy pursued exiled Royalists to the Scillies, Jersey, Barbados and Virginia. It drove the small Royalist naval force under Prince Rupert from Holland, Ireland and Portugal into the Mediterranean, where Rupert was finally compelled to disband his forces in 1653. It put pressure on French shipping, played an important part in compelling Cardinal Mazarin to recognize the Republic in 1652 and was an element in the eventual decision of Louis XIV to expel Charles II from France.[51]

Spain initially courted the English Republic in the hope of getting support for a reconquest of Portugal and operations against France, but instead became a victim of the Republic's increasing closeness to France. In 1655, an English expedition conquered Jamaica, giving England a position in the Central Caribbean.[52] English ships blockaded the Spanish coasts and destroyed a treasure fleet sheltering in Santa Cruz Bay in the Canaries. Thereafter, the Anglo-Spanish war continued indecisively, with mounting losses to the commerce of both sides, until after the death of Cromwell in 1658. After the Restoration, the American colonies, which had their civil disturbances reflecting the upheavals in Britain, were secured by naval and military force.[53]

However, for the early British naval historians, the most important conflicts in this period were the three Anglo-Dutch Wars (1652–4, 1664–8,

1670–2). These wars demonstrated with great clarity the link between naval power, maritime commerce and national wealth. Unlike the French and Spanish fleets, which went into a decline in the late 1640s and 1650s, the Dutch continued to dominate world commerce and kept an expanding fleet to protect it.[54] English maritime commerce had done well during the course of the seventeenth century, and although England and the United Provinces shared a common Protestant religion and hostility to Catholic France and Spain, they were also deadly commercial rivals.[55]

Each of the wars had its own specific causes, but each was underpinned by the commercial rivalry that drove it on and determined how the war was to be conducted. The English objective was always to break the Dutch domination of maritime trade by attacking it as it came through the Channel or the North Sea. It was the key battleground upon which domestic security and prosperous trade depended. The Dutch fought with similar objectives and intent – to cripple English trade, cut off the money that was the 'sinews of war' and threaten the coasts. The wars were largely fought in the narrow confines of these waters.[56]

For the early naval historians, these wars provided the context for four important developments in naval warfare during this period: the growth of the state's own battlefleet, the role this investment had in the development of the state, the emergence of a new tactical approach that was to dominate naval war and the increasing range of state naval power.

By the 1660s, the western European economies were increasingly reliant on overseas trade for bullion. While wealth still lay in the land, cash, and thus liquidity and credit, lay in commerce. Credit and liquidity were essential for trade, and trade generated that liquidity by returning profits in the form of bullion. Contemporary economic orthodoxy saw the volume of this bullion as generally fixed, so that the gains of one individual or state must come at the expense of another. The states that could channel that bullion would, therefore, exercise power in excess of their nominal domestic resources and diminish those of their rivals.

All three of the wars saw Dutch commerce fractured by English warships. English commerce suffered as well, and by the end of the wars the English had not replaced the Dutch as the world's prime carriers, but the balance of power had changed. The English invested in their navy, in bigger and more heavily armed ships. The numbers of private ships of war in the English fleet gradually declined. These state-owned warships, acting together from 1653 in a line of battle, could generally outfight the more numerous but smaller Dutch adversaries in the First War. The Dutch built larger ships before the Second War, which redressed the balance. In the Third War, French pressure on the Dutch landward borders limited Dutch activities. The results appeared to confirm that the state's resources were strongly influenced by maritime commerce. Thriving maritime commerce was the bedrock of financial liquidity and provided the industrial resources for building, fitting out and manning the larger two-and three-deck warships. A strong and focused state was needed to provide the legal, social and political frameworks to mobilize those resources. Then, these powerful ships, which only a truly wealthy state could afford in large numbers, proved themselves capable of effectively controlling maritime commerce as it traversed the choke points of trade in the North Sea, the Sound, the Channel and the Straits of Gibraltar.

During the second half of the seventeenth century, warships grew in size and firepower. The backbone of European battlefleets was the powerful sixty-to eighty-gun two-deckers with main batteries of 18 lb to 32 lb cannons. However, navies began to return to the three-deck ships. These vessels, capable of mounting ninety or more guns, had been designed as statements of royal power in the first half of the century.[57] By the end of the century, Dutch, French and English warships were capable of major fleet action in most European waters and were beginning to exploit sea power effectively in the Americas and the East Indies.[58] Sweden, Denmark-Norway, Spain, Portugal, Turkey and Venice all had navies with line of battle ships capable of exercising significant regional power.

The Second Dutch War saw the maturing of the line of battle, which was to remain the dominant tactical formation as long as warships were armed primarily with the smooth-bore, muzzle-loading cannon. Defensively, a line of powerful ships (or ships of the line), each with up to three decks of cannons, formed powerful, mutually supporting sets of batteries, almost impossible to break with the pell-mell boarding tactics of the smaller ships in earlier decades. In offence, these battle squadrons were effective in breaking

FIGURE 10 *The Battle of Scheveningen 31 July 1653, Willem Van de Velde the Elder, 1655.* © *National Maritime Museum. ID B8318.*

up convoys of enemy merchantmen or invasion flotillas. However, these ships were expensive to build, maintain and man. The costs of naval warfare were, consequently, rising, and decisions to commit to this expenditure became both more important to the long-term development of individual navies and more problematic as the costs of warfare generally rose. Spain, already suffering from acute fiscal problems, was not able to maintain the naval force that it required for its trans-Atlantic empire from the 1620s. By 1678, France possessed the most powerful navy in Europe, requiring both the Dutch and English navies to keep it in check.[59]

The three Dutch Wars produced no decisive victor, but it appeared to the naval historians of the late nineteenth century that they presaged a clear historical trajectory from which the growth and sustenance of naval power might be inferred. The virtuous helix could start anywhere, but must include all elements – thriving maritime commerce, determined government and powerful ships of the line. Constitutionally, the Dutch lacked the centralized power to create a sustainable navy based on the large line of battle ship.[60] In the 1670s, Louis XIV and his great minister Colbert created a navy that eclipsed the English navy in number, but ultimately, France lacked the deep maritime economy or infrastructure to support their ambitions. By the 1660s, Spanish finance had been shattered by war and the last Habsburg monarchs lacked the will at the centre of government to address the fiscal, administrative and operational problems that they faced in building a modern navy.

By this process of elimination, England, the possessor of all three elements, seemed destined to emerge as the pre-eminent naval power. The British experience became the core evidence for a thesis of naval power that remained largely unchallenged until the latter part of the twentieth century. As has been mentioned in relation to the debate about state-building and institutionalism, comparative studies are still needed to clarify, confirm or refute our understanding of this process. Jan Glete, Jean Meyer and Etienne Taillemite have all cast doubt upon both the process and the objectives of states in raising or maintaining large navies.[61] Other debates are also beginning to have an impact on our understanding of early modern naval power.

The military or naval revolution

All debates which include the word 'revolution' become tangled in questions of speed, chronology, geography and impact of the perceived change. The military revolution debate is no exception. It had its origins in changes noticed in land warfare. In 1955, Michael Roberts proposed that a revolution in infantry tactics, primarily in Sweden and Holland, had taken place between the 1590s and the 1630s. These new tactics demanded more professional soldiers and, in the end, much larger armies. In 1976, Geoffrey

Parker revisited the concept and proposed that a revolution had taken place in the use of cannon and gunpowder between 1450 and 1530 which demanded greater investment in new types of artillery fortification: the *trace italienne*. Since then, historians have found revolutions, or denied them, in a wide range of societies and military organizations. Revolutions include tactical, organizational and technical innovation, with impacts from battle outcomes to shifting the entire political and economic power structures of early modern states.[62]

Given that navies were highly capital and technology intensive, and that they had far greater geographical mobility than armies, it is surprising that until recently relatively little attention was paid to them. The second half of the seventeenth century saw a rapid expansion in colonial commerce. Increasingly, this commerce had to be supported by naval forces as European powers competed for its fruits. This was the period in which the line of battle began to dominate naval warfare and the galley faced a major decline in its effectiveness in the Mediterranean. Intuitively, the obvious differences in ship design, the handling of fleets and expansion of naval power projection suggest some sort of military revolution. However, naval historians have not found revolution to be a particularly useful explanatory tool for the entire 1650–1815 period. The changes required for extending effective naval power projection were the product of decades and an iterative process of invention, experimentation and adaptation. Success in transoceanic conquest or commerce required far more than a limited shift in a single technology or organizational process. Isolating a single shift as a causal stimulus in the maritime context is problematic. Each of those single shifts usually required the development of skills within different maritime communities over long periods. These skills could not be manufactured by state decree and imposed as easily as they could be upon an army.

The discussion of military revolution moved on from specific technologies or organization to explore how the spread of any change was conditioned by the social forces that fostered or inhibited adoption of innovation. Both John Guilmartin and Jeremy Black emphasized the spatial or geographical limitations of innovation.[63] Military change was the result of different societies and communities acting on one another, either in conflict or in cooperation. As this interchange of ideas, practices and experiences evolved, Europe became more homogeneous as a military environment that gradually outpaced other regions on its peripheries, such as the Balkans, North Africa or the Middle East. As these regions adapted to European pressures and even adopted the military/naval systems, so the balance of power altered again and the homogeneous military/naval community expanded. Where it came into conflict with regions completely unfamiliar with it, such as South America or Oceania, the result was catastrophic. It was navies, rather than armies, that had the geographical reach to bring these unacclimatized societies into rapid and dramatic conflict with European methods of warfare.[64]

Overall, the current consensus seems to be that it was not new technologies or systems by themselves that made the difference, but the absorption of many new weapons or military/naval systems into the European social context, and then their employment in environments that were completely unused to them.

Nevertheless, it must be accepted that, given the wealth of archival material available, much more could be done to understand any 'naval revolution', and more work might reveal the process of change as being more revolutionary during some periods or places than is currently accepted. Furthermore, this perspective is solidly Western focused. We still know far too little about how the communities feeling the impact of the military or naval revolutions perceived them, and how far the adjustments they made were founded on local and traditional practices rather than adoption of Western systems. Once again, the historical debate seems to have run its course. Navies and naval history have been touched by it, but as yet, both have more to offer and there is much more to learn.

The dominance of the line of battle fleet and the alternatives, 1650–1750

The battlefleet dominates conceptions of naval force during this period. The melée battles of the Anglo-Dutch Wars merged into more organized artillery duels of ships in line of battle as this tactical method proved its power and resilience. Yet it was only one element of contemporary naval power. The battlefleet worked best in deep waters, where it could be supported locally from the shore and at choke points in the trade or invasion routes where convoys could be predicted. The North Sea, the Channel, the western Baltic and the western Mediterranean were ideal operating waters. In the shallows or the open oceans, where the enemy could retire from contact and evade the deep-drafted battleships, the battlefleet was less effective. In the Mediterranean and the eastern Baltic, galley squadrons were effective for inshore work among archipelagos and shallows. In the Mediterranean, their role was gradually declining, but they continued to be important in the Swedish and Russian navies, even experiencing a revival at the end of the eighteenth century.[65] Smaller, cruising warships, sloops and frigates provided important services inshore, particularly reconnaissance and general duties on distant stations. From the 1680s, specialist bomb vessels provided navies with additional power for direct attacks on ports.[66]

Despite this growing specialization of function in naval vessels, and the increasing size of the line of battle ship, navies still relied on mobilizing the resources from their maritime communities. Warships were built in private yards as well as royal or state yards. In the seventeenth century, the English Crown had relied upon both royal dockyards and private shipbuilders to construct its warships. During the first quarter of the eighteenth century, naval ships were built exclusively in the royal yards. However, as the century progressed a greater proportion of warship building reverted to the private shipyards, so that by 1815, the fleet which dominated the world's oceans, the Royal Navy, was essentially a privately built force.[67] Throughout the eighteenth century, essential stores were purchased on the increasingly sophisticated international markets. All states relied on seamen to man the ships, who had to be drawn from the international seafaring populations. Research is now being done on all these subjects, but far more is needed before we have a comprehensive picture of the international and private commercial links in the chain of naval power on any meaningful comparative basis.

An important element in sea power during this period was the privateer. These private men-of-war were fitted out at the expense of the owners in the hope of capturing rich prizes from the enemy. The literature on privateering is now extensive.[68] If one of the key purposes of sea power was to disrupt the commerce of the enemy and protect one's own commerce, the privateer was, in theory, as capable as a state navy might be. State battlefleets were excellent for breaking up the large Atlantic convoys of merchantmen at choke points, but were less effective in disrupting the routine trades that were the life blood of commerce in the Mediterranean and the West Indies. In the last years of the seventeenth century it was far from clear how these two elements of naval force, the battlefleet and the privateers, could be best combined to provide the most effective naval power.

Two major wars, the Nine Years' War (1689–97) and the War of Spanish Succession (1701–13), absorbed the energies of much of Europe and were stimuli to the growth and experience of naval forces. However, at the end of these conflicts it was not self-evident that the battlefleet would, in future, be the overwhelming tool of naval power. In the right places, the battlefleet provided a powerful defence against invasions or attacks on trade. For nations like Britain, Denmark-Norway and Sweden, investment in this expensive, complex weapon made perfect sense. In the case of Britain, invasion had to come over the sea, and sea communications were essential for the burgeoning Atlantic commerce. England had been invaded in 1688, and the threat of French invasion in support of the restoration of the Stuart dynasty remained a constant fear until the end of the Jacobite Rebellion in 1746. The Royal Navy's battlefleet remained the primary defence against periodic invasion threats from France or Germany until 1945. The English political public had also been made painfully aware, particularly in the war of 1689–97, that their overseas trade was vital to both the general health of their economy and the prosecution of war. Naval defence of this trade was an essential prerequisite of domestic security and economic stability in times of war, becoming a major subject of political debate and division between 1688 and 1713.[69]

Both Denmark-Norway and Sweden recognized that the maintenance of the Swedish empire in northern Germany depended on sea communications.

Other states, such as France, Portugal, Spain, the United Provinces and Ottoman Turkey, all had important requirements for sea commerce, but they all had to balance this with the threats posed by their landward borders. The privateer provided a means of prosecuting a maritime war against the enemy that did not cost the state treasury money, and could even enrich the state's coffers while damaging the enemy's commerce and finances.[70]

Furthermore, the battlefleet had yet to prove that it could be universally decisive as an offensive weapon. During the wars of 1689–97 and 1701–13, there were very few battles between large squadrons, and those that did occur had very limited diplomatic impact. The battles of Bantry Bay (1 May 1689) and Beachy Head (30 June 1690) were won by French fleets against English and Anglo-Dutch squadrons respectively, but on neither occasion were the French capable of capitalizing on their victories to influence the war on land. The Anglo-Dutch fleet won a decisive victory at Barfleur and La Hogue (19, 23 and 24 May 1692), which did begin to change French thinking about naval power, but did little to alter the diplomatic balance in the short run. In August 1704, the only major sea battle of the War of Spanish Succession, the Battle of Malaga, was a tactical draw, but gave the allies control of the western Mediterranean for the rest of the war. Still, it had a limited impact on the wider balance of power in the Mediterranean.[71]

Between 1689 and 1697, four English and four French expeditionary forces were sent to the West Indies. Admiral Francis Wheeler's expedition of 1692 also went to North America in the expectation of supporting a colonial attack on Canada. Between 1701 and 1713, twelve British and ten French expeditions departed for the Americas, including one to attack Quebec in 1711.[72] None of these had the impact that had been hoped for.

By the end of these wars, colonial conquests had been made and trade had been disrupted, but those achievements had been won by battlefleets working in conjunction with local colonial forces and privateers. Commerce was threatened as much by privateers as by royal or state warships.[73] The contributions of the battlefleet and commerce raiders to the overall outcome of the wars remained unclear.

A similar pattern emerged from the conflicts in the Baltic. The Skane War (1675–9) saw considerable fleet and other naval action by the Swedes against the Danes, Dutch and Brandenburgers. A series of naval reverses caused the Swedes to lose control of the Baltic and suffer a Danish invasion of the Scanian provinces. Still, the Swedes were able to fight on. It was only diplomatic movements outside the Baltic that finally forced Charles XI to accept peace in 1679. The Great Northern War (1700–21) between Sweden and an alliance led by Denmark and Russia saw the emergence of Russia as a great naval power in the Baltic. There was again considerable action at sea as the powers contested the sea communications between Scandinavia and the Danish–North German/Swedish–Polish littoral. The decisive battle of Poltava in the Ukraine (1709) occurred a year before the first Russian line of battle ships appeared in the Baltic. However, from then on, there was increasing naval pressure on Sweden. In 1714, it was a Russian galley squadron, moving within the Finnish archipelago, complemented at a distance by sailing battleships, that beat the Swedes off Hango Head, opening the way for an invasion of Finland and the ravaging of the Swedish coastline. Sweden could not recover against a growing Russian military and naval presence in the Baltic area, which was periodically supported by other powers, including the British Royal Navy.[74] By stages, Sweden was forced to make peace with her enemies, and the war ended in 1721.

The Great Northern War showed that the galley still had a place in shallow littoral waters. In the Mediterranean, both the Morean War (1684–99) and the Venetian-Turkish War (1714–18) showed that mixed galley and sailing warships were still a powerful combination. As in the eastern Baltic, vessels did not need to spend long periods at sea before refreshing, and operations were essentially coastal. Galleys and other small craft which could move easily in shallow waters continued to play an essential part. They were particularly useful in supporting amphibious operations among the islands of the Aegean and eastern Mediterranean.[75]

Global reach: Logistics and bureaucracy, 1713–89

If the wars of 1688–1721 had not demonstrated the decisiveness of the battlefleet, it was, nonetheless, the period in which the decisions and events of nearly twenty years of warfare began to mark out different trajectories of naval power. After the conclusion of the Great Northern War (1701–21), the navies of Sweden and Denmark-Norway showed a gradual decline, while that of Russia, which emerged as the largest in the Baltic, was maintained at a generally higher level than those of her rivals. The War of Spanish Succession was draining upon its main combatants. The land war exhausted France, Spain and the United Provinces, all of which had to sacrifice their naval forces to some degree in order to preserve funding for their armies. Britain was similarly stretched, but, thanks to the establishment of the Bank of England and a system of stable deficit financing developed in conjunction with the state, Britain was able to sustain the expenditure of war more easily.[76] In 1713 the British Royal Navy was the largest battlefleet in Europe, a superiority it extended in the early years of the peace as Holland and France reduced their fleets further and faster than Britain.[77]

However, it was not just in numbers that British naval power began to be distinguished from other European states. Both the tempo of naval war and its geographical spread had changed markedly during the wars. In the third quarter of the seventeenth century, small numbers of warships were sent occasionally to the Americas, but between 1689 and 1713 major operations were conducted in those regions. From 1692, the English ministry considered establishing a permanent naval force in the Mediterranean. This was achieved in 1694. Initially it was supported from Lisbon or Cadiz, but the capture of Gibraltar in 1704 and Minorca in 1708 provided the navy with permanent bases, which were retained after the peace. Gibraltar had serious problems as a main fleet anchorage because of its exposure to southerly gales and the proximity of Spanish forces just across the isthmus. Minorca, on the other hand, had a spacious harbour at Port Mahon and a hinterland to support it.[78]

The ability of the British to sustain large naval forces in distant waters was growing at a faster rate than for any other power, and the development of the infrastructure to support this continued slowly but steadily during the peace.[79] As a logistical network it was far from complete, but it was beginning to mark out British naval investment as different from its rivals. The home yards of Portsmouth and Plymouth were the most developed. The most important installation was the dry dock, in which the hulls of ships could be rapidly repaired and cleaned. All the main yards in England had dry docks by 1700. France had only one and Spain none (until 1754). There were no dry docks outside Europe, except at Bombay (Mumbai) (after 1750), until 1847. Instead, the dangerous alternative of hauling ships down on their sides at careening wharfs had to be employed. There were no facilities in North America capable of repairing large ships of the line until the establishment of Halifax, Nova Scotia, in the 1750s. However, the infrastructures at Minorca, Port Royal in Jamaica (developed further in 1735) and English Harbour in Antigua (established in the 1730s) were adequate for large squadrons of warships. In the Americas only Spain, with its major port cities of Havana and Cartagena de las Indias, had anything comparable to the British.[80]

The British were showing that sustainable global naval power was becoming a reality for Europeans. It was based on investment in infrastructure. This, in turn, relied upon developing fiscal and administrative practices which enabled the Crown to exploit the expanding resources of the maritime economy. This fiscal–administrative–military complex has become a major element in the 'new naval history' of the eighteenth century that developed after 1945. From the early twentieth century there had been an interest in formal administrative structures, particularly in the United States, where the colonial administrative archives shed light on a more complex relationship between Britain and her colonies than the nationalist historiography of the nineteenth century had ever allowed.[81] This interest in structures was shared by British historians who worked on the Admiralty.[82] However, the devastation and massive mobilization of the Second World War had left no one in any doubt that global warfare was, in the words of Martin van Crefeld, a 'war of accountants' and that it was the informal flexibilities that made the difference in organizational systems.[83] Historians who had served in military or administrative capacities during the war, like economists and strategists, now thought more intently on what became known in the 1950s as 'resource-based' explanations for the complete domination of the British Royal Navy over the waters of the western hemisphere by 1763.[84]

In the decades that followed, it was an approach to British naval history that became immensely fruitful, partly owing to its explanatory power, but also to the mass of documentation in the British National Archive at Kew and the National Maritime Museum, Greenwich, which makes such analyses possible.[85]

During the 1970s, the results of doctoral research supervised by this generation of historians began to appear. The work of scholars such as Daniel Baugh, David Syrett, Roger Knight, Patricia Crimmin and Paul Webb began to illuminate the administrative infrastructure of eighteenth-century naval power.[86] These scholars continued their work throughout the rest of the century, and others, such as James Haas, Roger Morriss, Ann Coats, Clive Wilkinson, James Davey and Martin Wilcox, added to these endeavours. Their subject matter has covered the operations of the dockyards and their relationship with the local communities, as well as the subordinate boards of the Admiralty. This work goes on, and has moved to encompass evaluations of the administrative cultures. So far, these studies have focused predominantly on the second half of the eighteenth century, and particularly the period from 1793 to 1815, but together they make up a tremendously valuable branch of scholarship that continues to throw up new questions.[87]

The study of infrastructure and logistics has also attracted the attention of scholars of other navies, and it now dominates much of the current historiography of the sailing navy. The historiographical shift from grand strategic choice to resource and logistical organization is clear, for example, in the work of Professor Christian Buchet, one of the leading French historians of maritime logistics. He sees the development of British naval administration and infrastructure *'sans conteste l'element determinant des success anglais au cours de la guerre de Septs Ans'*.[88]

There are grounds to resist drawing conclusions too soon. Despite deep logistical inequalities, battles still had to be fought and individual decisions made, which could upset resource differentials in any given campaign. The best example of how this administrative, resource-based study has been integrated into the operational history is in the work of Jan Glete. His posthumously published *Swedish Naval Administration, 1521–1721*, stands out as a remarkable study of resources, organization and power.[89] There is not yet the wealth of serious studies like this that will enable a reliable comparative study of naval infrastructures to be undertaken. This is partly due to the loss of many administrative records and the current state of organization and cataloguing in some European archives.

Nevertheless, there have been some great steps forward in linking the logistical administrative analysis of navies to operational performance. Since the nineteenth century, French and Spanish naval historiography has followed a very similar pattern to that in the English-speaking world.

Traditionally, English-speaking historians have seen the Nine Years' War and the War of Spanish Succession as the point of definitive decline for the French navy, at least until the 1760s. By failing to maintain his battlefleet or the logistical infrastructure needed for it, Louis XIV demonstrated that he did not understand naval power and condemned France to long-term, if not permanent, inferiority to Britain.[90]

During the first half of the twentieth century, in the wake of the dominant Mahanian 'navalist' perspective on naval strategy, French historians such as Lacour Gayet, De la Ronciere and Tramond shared this view. It remains an important and powerful interpretation of French naval power. More recently, however, opinion has tended to see the situation of the French fleet by 1713 in far less catastrophic terms than their Anglophone contemporaries. The impact of sea power on French policy was more ambiguous. Barfleur had convinced Louis XIV that defeating both England and the United Provinces at sea was impossible and that diplomatic leverage could only be successfully applied by victory on land. In this, he had been largely successful, despite facing a coalition of the major powers of Europe. Even allied naval attacks on the French coasts were less significant than the attackers hoped.[91] By 1713 a Bourbon was on the throne of Spain, and although, by the Treaty of Utrecht, the Crowns of France and Spain could never be united, the Habsburgs were definitively removed from the Spanish inheritance. The British had also been kept out of the Spanish-American Empire, with the exception of the Asiento contract. After Barfleur, Louis did not let the navy atrophy. Losses were replaced, but by about 1708 the cost of the war and the continental strategy made maintaining a battlefleet that could contest the seas against the allies completely impracticable. Thereafter, France relied increasingly upon privateers to attack enemy trade and colonial possessions and to defend her own trade and communications.[92]

This was enough, from the French perspective, in 1713. The naval situation was not dire. France did not suffer catastrophic defeat anywhere in the world. Although France was unable to contest any seas with the powerful British and Dutch squadrons after 1704, she was able to hold her own against Spanish and Barbary adversaries.[93] Privateers and expeditions caused Britain serious political, economic and diplomatic problems throughout the wars. With the return of peace in 1713, French colonial trade began to recover rapidly, and in due course the state battlefleet could be built up again.[94]

Spanish naval power had also dramatically declined by 1713. There never had been a state or royal navy in the same way as they had emerged in England and France. Naval forces were commissioned for different purposes and financed from different sources. Ship design, financing and organization were not as focused as for other nations. The result was that, at least from the 1670s, Spain was increasingly outdistanced by France, England and the United Provinces in terms of the size of ships, armament, command, organization and distribution. As the Crown was also continually on the verge of bankruptcy and the *Armada* was the most expensive single item in the Spanish defence budget, it was a deficit that the Spanish Crown found impossible to reduce.[95]

The recognition of the new Bourbon monarchy in Spain by the Treaty of Utrecht brought peace, and with it a desire to reorganize Spanish administration along the lines of the French monarchy and a passion within the Spanish court to overturn some of the more irksome provisions of Utrecht, particularly in relation to Italy. Both these factors combined to make a revival of Spanish naval power an urgent matter of policy. Central to the narrative of the reorganization of the Spanish bureaucracy and the rebuilding of the Spanish fleet is José Patiño, the first Intendant of the Marine. Patiño was the initial leading light of the reforming Bourbon administration, but his work was sustained throughout the century by a group of naval administrators and constructors, such as Admiral Antonio Gatazňeta y de Iturribálzaga, the Marques de Ensenada and Romero y Landa. Spain demonstrated a remarkable ability to build, maintain and fight with large numbers of robust and powerful ships, which became the hallmark of the Spanish naval renaissance.[96]

Unlike in France, Spain's eighteenth-century diplomatic–maritime history is not conflated with a contest for predominance as a western and central European land power. Once the Italian dynastic issues had been settled by the death of Philip V in 1746, Spain's American empire was her primary diplomatic consideration. This depended on sea power. There has been less room for ambiguity or contrasting perspectives in Spanish naval historiography. The importance of the Crown's navy in the defence of Spain's essential interests has always been acknowledged. Thus, the difficulties of maintaining that power in the face of limited financial and real maritime resources have been a long-standing interest of historians.

The Dutch administrative system was very different from its contemporaries in that naval forces were organized by five provincial admiralties. Attempts to discover the administrative and logistical workings of the Dutch navy are, therefore, complex and have been further hampered by serious losses of archival materials to fires.[97] Unlike in France and Spain, the revival of the battlefleet has not become an enduring matter of concern for Dutch historians. Until the end of 1780, peaceful coexistence, if not alliance, with Britain was a key policy objective. For both Britain and the United Provinces, the great threat came from French advances by land through the Austrian Netherlands (modern Belgium). Dutch policy had to focus on the preservation of the Flanders Barrier or neutrality in case of a European conflict. The commercial advantage this neutrality gave the United Provinces certainly caused friction with Britain when the latter was at war. The close financial relationship between the two states also placed pressures on them.[98] For the Dutch, the most important maritime objective was the protection of the great trade to the East Indies. Neutrality was, generally, the best guarantee of its security, however much that annoyed the

British, whose traditional policy since 1688 relied on a Dutch Alliance. Thus, so far as naval and maritime history is concerned, most attention has been focused on the history of the Dutch East India Company (VOC), rather than on the structures and systems that underpinned Dutch state naval power.[99]

The United States Navy came into existence a few years after the end of the War of Independence in 1783. For much of the early years of the Republic, the question of the purpose of the navy was contested; concern was not just about the needs of naval defence, but also the potential political danger of raising a navy, with admirals whose position and command gave them the status of a new aristocracy.[100] There was a powerful, ideological clash between the proponents of coastal defence and those of oceanic force. This has provided historians with valuable opportunities to explore how both types of naval force were administered and supported, and provided a particularly interesting case of the organization of naval power.[101]

Other states have not yet had the early modern histories of their navies so fully examined. Jan Glete did a great deal to forward the study of the Nordic navies, and did more than any other scholar to place navies in comparative social contexts. For English-speaking audiences, the early history of the Russian navy is still so closely associated with the heroic story of Peter the Great that it is very difficult to unpick the contribution made by the administrative and logistical infrastructures to the growing power of the Russian fleets in the Baltic and Black Seas. What interest there has been has largely focused upon the British connections with the Russian navy.[102] French audiences have fared little better.[103]

Taken as a whole, the work on naval administration, organization and logistics since 1960 has been tremendous. Our understanding of how and why navies of different states evolved is immeasurably better than it was when Mahan was writing. We are far better informed about how logistical systems influenced policies. We are very much closer to being able to make comparative studies of navies, like those that have informed the history of state-building. So we are much closer to being able to explain the interplay between naval growth and economic, social and political development in the early modern world. Nevertheless, the subject is going to need international collaborations of scholars sharing interests, perspectives and resources to carry out the important comparative studies that will really put the logistical systems into their proper place.

The triumph of sea power, 1739–83: The continental versus maritime war debate and the decisiveness of naval war

The years of intensive warfare between 1689 and 1713 provided states with the pressures and incentives to develop their navies. By 1720, different perspectives of naval power had emerged, and different approaches to investing in, or developing, those navies were becoming very clear. Looking back from the end of the nineteenth century, the decisions made at this point had had a tremendous impact. By 1815, Britain was the undisputed global naval power. A groundwork had been laid, but the decisive clash of arms that confirmed both the significance of those earlier decisions and the importance of sea power happened in the second half of the century. Here, for Mahan, seeing Britain as the archetype, the eternal principles of naval war could be seen most clearly, and here, also, were the warnings for statesmen who did not learn those lessons. Guided by William Pitt the Elder in the Seven Years' War (1756–63), and, to a lesser degree, by his son William during the French Revolutionary and Napoleonic Wars, Britain applied sea power so effectively that France and Spain were inevitably crushed beyond hope of recovery until peace was restored. On the other hand, failure to exploit sea power effectively, as happened under Sir Robert Walpole and the Duke of Newcastle during the War of Austrian Succession (1740–8) or Lord North during the American War (1775–83), led only to national humiliation.

The narrative of the British eighteenth-century naval wars, with their successes and failures, has provided historians ever since with the primary context for understanding and explaining naval power during the 'Age of Sail'. It encapsulated 'navalism'. This was not just a national investment in large naval forces, but the adoption of a philosophy or ideology that allowed the nation's legal, economic and social structures to be shaped by the needs of naval power – the true thalassocracy. State and society created the navy, which, if wielded in a manner consistent with the principles of naval warfare, would end in victory, and that victory would be decisive on the world stage. At the end of the nineteenth century, this belief, mixed with a strong dose of national stereotyping and Social Darwinism, proposed a unique form of courage and leadership within real maritime nations that were real force multipliers. The culmination of this political, economic and social investment was a navy that dominated the world's oceans for over a century. As much as the ships and the logistical infrastructure, disciplined and skilful seamen, led by committed and valiant officers, with a *nonpareil* exemplar in Vice Admiral Horatio Lord Nelson, were the creation of this society. The apotheosis of Nelson with his death at Trafalgar on 21 October 1805 at the point of a massive victory provided the cultural confirmation of the soundness of this navalist ideology.

As has been seen in the previous chapter, naval histories in the first half of the twentieth century were dominated by this narrative. From the 1960s, the detailed examination of administrative and logistical infrastructures across a range of navies has provided more analytical approaches to operational history. The integration of traditional naval history with the more recent work on logistics and administration is most evident for those periods which attract the greatest attention from contemporary scholars – the Royal Navy in the Seven Years' War (1756–63), the War of American Independence

(1775–83), and the French Revolutionary and Napoleonic Wars (1793–15). The period before 1750, and other navies in different regions across the whole century, have not yet attracted as much scrutiny, but, as Jan Glete and David Aldridge have demonstrated, the evidence and the analytical tools are there to be used.[104]

Although Europe had been far from peaceful between 1713 and 1739, very little work has been done on this period in recent decades. The development of the Nordic and Russian navies after 1721 has not attracted much attention. Even the Russo-Swedish War of 1741–3 has barely entered the mainstream of naval history. The Mediterranean was one of the major sources of international tension in this period. As such, traditional diplomatic histories of the period deal substantially with the Italian question and the wars it stimulated (1717–19, 1726–7, 1733–8), but the naval dimension of that diplomacy and warfare is largely ignored.

Only when there was a major battle, for example, off Cape Passaro in August 1718, does the region feature in naval histories.[105] Other aspects of the campaign of the Quadruple Alliance (Britain, France, the United Provinces and Austria) against Spain, for example the British landing at Vigo in September 1719 and operations at the Straits of Gibraltar and in the West Indies, still await their modern historians. Similarly, the Anglo-Spanish conflict of 1726–7 and the manoeuvres of 1731 and 1735–6, which also had an impact in the West Indies and the Atlantic, have had almost no attention other than early narratives that noted their existence.[106] Even the Spanish naval operation to support a Jacobite rising in Scotland in 1719 has been largely ignored. The periodic French and Spanish operations against the Barbary States need more examination, as does the much neglected Venetian-Ottoman War (1714–18).[107]

While the period does not have a well-developed naval historiography, the naval element in international diplomacy has not been entirely neglected. The revival of Spanish naval power in the first half of the eighteenth century could not hide the fact that Spain could not defend her American empire by sea power alone. This has drawn scholars whose principal interests lie in imperial, military and epidemiological history to investigate the defensive system of the Spanish Empire. Historians such as Richard Pares and Gerald Graham carried out essential work linking British naval history to mainstream political and economic history.[108]

The geographical context of the Spanish and French Empires was far more complex than early navalist thinkers assumed. The sea linked the large centres of population, which also relied economically on the littoral. Nevertheless, large land spaces, indigenous populations and tropical diseases caused Spain and France to sustain their imperial positions by the use of fortresses, garrisons and alliances as well as ships.[109] Great strides have been made in exploring the economics of empire and imperial/naval warfare, but a great many gaps still exist in our understanding of the dynamics of the colonial infrastructure. Most of these studies are still largely focused upon the second half of the century. The recent upsurge in 'Atlantic History' has certainly helped in that it has deepened our understanding of the evolving cultural relationships across the ocean. Nevertheless, while the literature is growing, the work on the mechanics of transoceanic warfare and the role of navies within it before 1739 is still underdeveloped.[110]

In October 1739, war between Britain and Spain ushered in a prolonged period of European conflict with a major naval dimension. The diplomatic history of the conflict was researched in the first decades of the twentieth century. In Britain, the political history of the war formed part of a long-established Whig historiographical tradition that saw the conflict principally as a mishandled prelude to the dawning of Britain's true naval destiny during the Seven Years' War. The war was initially over trade in the West Indies. The British were sure that their naval power would soon bring Spain to a satisfactory peace. France was equally determined to prevent Britain from profiting from an attack on the Spanish Indies. France remained neutral, but sent ships to the West Indies to defeat British plans to seize Spanish territories. By the end of 1740, this maritime war had become entangled with a much larger conflict over the Austrian succession (1740–8). This led to British naval operations in the Mediterranean in support of the Austrians, who were under attack in Italy from Spanish forces, supported by the French.

In February 1744, France declared war on Britain. The war had opened with British opinion expecting a quick and decisive victory over Spain. Not only had this failed miserably by the end of 1742, but the following years shook British confidence. The Royal Navy failed to beat a combined Franco-Spanish squadron off Toulon in February 1744. In the same month, the French Brest squadron succeeded in penetrating the Channel as far as Dungeness to cover an invasion from Flanders. Bad weather, rather than the British Channel squadron, forced it to retreat before it could accomplish its mission. The great French fortress of Louisbourg on Cape Breton Island fell to a combined colonial and Royal Navy force in June 1745, but the navy was unable to prevent a French relief force from sailing in 1746. This time the French were defeated by disease rather than the fighting power of the Royal Navy. Only in 1747 did it seem that naval power was beginning to have an impact. French Atlantic commerce was disrupted, and two battles, in May and October 1747 (First and Second Battles of Finisterre), brought the first major victories at sea, as demonstrated by French warships arriving as prizes in British ports.[111]

When the war ended, in October 1748, naval power had not had the decisive impact on the diplomatic settlement that had been expected in Britain. The Austrian succession had generated diplomatic necessities and opportunities that were far beyond the reach of naval power at that time. Even the original Anglo-Spanish dispute remained unresolved. It took another two years of patient diplomacy and a willingness on both sides to compromise to achieve this.

FIGURE 11 *A chase action: first Battle of Finisterre, 3 May 1747 by Samuel Scott.* © *National Maritime Museum. ID BHCO 369.*

Nevertheless, since the beginning of the twentieth century the war has provided scholars with plenty of indicators for the role and importance of sea power. The most important operational narrative of the war is Admiral Sir Herbert Richmond's three volumes, *The Navy in the War of 1739 to 1748*, published in 1920. Although it is still unsurpassed as a narrative, Richmond reflected the assumptions of his times. Richmond was a naval officer deeply concerned about the function and exercise of sea power. He was, and remained, heavily involved in the contemporary debates.[112] His history, while deeply researched, shared the didactic purpose of other navalist scholars and reflected their historical assumptions about the domestic politics and naval power. In 1936, Richard Pares' great study of the importance of the West Indies in the war added depth to both the economic and the geographical context of the fighting. After 1742, the main events of the naval war took place in European waters, but Pares' focus on the Caribbean revived an old seventeenth-century political dispute that had informed thinking on naval strategy at the beginning of the twentieth century and continues today – the apparent dichotomy between engaging in a maritime and a continental commitment.[113]

When William III came to the throne in 1689, he brought with him a diplomatic imperative to defend his Dutch territories. He could not permit his English subjects to stand behind the Channel, disengaged from a Continental war. The Low Countries had always been a primary concern of English policy, but now the security of the United Provinces was allied to this. A political, rhetorical divide, based upon pursuing a continental military strategy or a maritime war, was soon to emerge between the Whigs, who were William's principal supporters, and the Tories, whose Jacobite sympathies resented the use of English resources to defend Dutch interests.

It was a divide that continued when the Hanoverian dynasty succeeded in 1714. Hanover became the *bête noire* of Tory and 'Country' rhetoric, and played into the development of British policy in the 1750s.[114] William Pitt skilfully used this anti-Hanoverian sentiment in building his parliamentary support and developing the political logic for engaging France in North America rather than Germany. The success of the Seven Years' War has embedded the maritime policy deeply in British political assumptions, if not military policy, ever since. At the beginning of the twentieth century, as new naval and land powers began to challenge the British Empire, and new technologies in naval warfare created profound uncertainty for both the creation and the execution of maritime strategy, Sir Julian Corbett, at the Naval War College in Greenwich, tried to synthesize the maritime and continental strategies, using the Anglo-French struggle during the Seven Years' War as his explanatory vehicle.[115] Corbett's history of that war showed that naval power, used in conjunction with diplomatic opportunities, can be used to defeat a powerful continental enemy. French trade was cut off, commerce ruined and finances strangled. Attacking the enemy's overseas territories enriched Britain and provided the fiscal stability for credit and finances by which continental allies were supported, thus preventing France from making any compensatory gains in Hanover or elsewhere. Britain had to engage in the continental war to ensure her allies kept fighting, and the resources to do this were provided by the 'eccentric' maritime strategy.

In 1907, Corbett laid out the process by which maritime war and continental military objectives could and should be reconciled. Pitt was the central hero of the piece, against whom all other ministers could be judged. Richmond's history of the war of 1739–48 provided the evidence that the ministries during this war had not understood maritime war and Britain had consequently failed. Pares reinforced Corbett's analysis with detailed research to demonstrate the importance of economic objectives of warfare. In the 1930s, it was a reinforcement that made perfect sense. During the 1914–18 war, Britain had been threatened with economic disaster by the German U-boat campaigns of 1915 and 1917. Britain had engaged as a major European land force during that war, and the memories of three-quarters of a million dead were very raw. There was very little appetite to renew that engagement, and the 'indirect approach', whose most eloquent exponent was Captain Basil Liddell Hart, was an attractive alternative.[116]

The continental versus maritime war debate, championed by Liddell Hart as a contribution to contemporary politics and strategy and by Pares as an analysis of the eighteenth-century position, has continued to interest historians and strategists. Views have diverged and converged as the historical periods examined have varied and the contemporary concerns have changed. Factors such as the influence of Hanover on British policy from 1714 to 1836, the comparative advantage of Britain in maritime war, or extrapolating the lessons of the Second World War and the Cold War have all contributed to a continuing discussion over British defence policy.[117] In the light of the Second World War and the Cold War, historians have revised their opinions on the Western Front and the practicality of an 'indirect approach' or eccentric strategy upon a continental power. Today, the role of naval warfare in British strategy remains unresolved. It is part of the natural inter-service tussle for public support and has veered dramatically as defence concerns shifted or perceptions of threat altered.[118]

While the operations and policy of the 1739–48 war have been relatively neglected, its contrast with the Seven Years' War has caused scholars to examine some of the phenomena associated with it. Privateering has been extensively covered.[119] Important aspects of naval administration have been explored, but, unfortunately, not all of it has yet been published.[120]

It is with the Seven Years' War that interest in eighteenth-century naval history really begins to flourish. Its scale, decisiveness and consequences for the shaping of the Western world for the next 150 years were evident to historians. To nineteenth-century historians in Britain, Germany and the United States, the war was a watershed in national development. While the survival of Prussia did not immediately presage a fundamental shift in the balance of power in central Europe, British maritime dominance was self-evident to eighteenth-century contemporaries. Although it lay in the middle of a second hundred years' war between Britain and France, it was, nonetheless, the opening of the decisive sixty years, which led through victory, near-catastrophe (1775–83) and struggle for survival (1793–1805) to mastery of the oceans (1805–1900). As the latest historian of the Seven Years' War at sea noted, France, 'the strongest power in Europe', had been comprehensively defeated everywhere in the world.[121] The reasons for Britain's spectacular victory soon became encrusted with myths that were to have major consequences for the self-image of the nation. However, detailed scholarly attention to this conflict over the last half-century has done much to strip away these myths to give us a rich picture of that conflict.

As far as the core Anglo-French dispute over North America was concerned, action on the frontier of Ohio and a small naval action east of Cape Breton reopened that simmering conflict in 1755. Although the war started with no great British advantage, the long-term changes in the British naval infrastructure, recent diplomatic changes and a reconciliation of domestic political conflicts soon began to make the relative strength of British naval power tell on the situation. The Royal Navy was larger, robustly founded on a flourishing maritime economy with powerful political support in Parliament. The diplomatic situation was much improved by the neutrality of Spain, the United Provinces and Austria. Nevertheless, given the experience of the previous war, victory was not a foregone conclusion. Indeed, it was not until the autumn of 1759 that the naval and colonial war turned decisively in favour of Britain.

As with the War of Austrian Succession, the Anglo-French colonial dispute rapidly became entangled with renewed war in Europe between Austria and Prussia. While the war in Europe ultimately ground itself down towards a peace which barely changed the balance of power, the naval war produced unprecedented changes. French naval power was crushed. Weakened within one year by the strains of campaigning, the French navy maintained itself with diminishing effectiveness until defeats at Lagos Bay (August 1759) and Quiberon Bay (November 1759). Naval defeat coincided with the fall of Quebec in September 1759 and fiscal collapse in France. The navy limped on until the end of the war in June 1763, largely unable to have an impact on French policy. With this collapse came the fall of Canada (1759–61) and the loss of Senegal (May 1758), Goree (December 1758), Guadeloupe (May 1759), Dominica (June 1761), Martinique (February 1762), and Grenada, St Lucia and St Vincent (March 1762). The French Empire, and with it French overseas commerce, had been effectively destroyed. In India, the French had more success, but could not prevent the British extending their control of Bengal. A belated attempt by Spain to intervene in order to limit British conquests ended in disaster as Havana and Manila fell to British forces in August and October 1762, respectively. There was now no doubt that naval power, and the power particularly of the battlefleet, had made a decisive impact on European diplomacy. France lost Canada and Spain lost West Florida. Further French losses had only been averted by the French army's stubborn defence of its positions in Westphalia during 1762.[122]

FIGURE 12 *Another chase action: the Battle of Quiberon Bay (or les Cardinaux), 20 November 1759.* © *Trustees of the National Museum of the Royal Navy (Portsmouth).*

The war was brought to an end at the Peace of Paris in January 1763. Although some important British conquests were returned to the Bourbon powers at the peace, it was now clear, as never before, that British naval power had developed into an effective amphibious capability, able to project decisive force on land as well as at sea. It was this combination of naval and military resources that inspired Corbett's description of the 'eccentric strategy'. It has also ensured a steady stream of historical works to the present day.[123]

The strategy that underpinned the war and its impact on Britain's subsequent diplomatic history has also been extensively explored by Daniel Baugh. Baugh and Richard Middleton, among others, have also provided excellent political, organizational histories of the war.[124] However, it remains a contested and developing field. Recently, this naval–Atlantic focus on strategy has caused some historians to re-examine the relative neglect of the European (and specifically Hanoverian) dimension of strategy.[125]

Far more than previous conflicts, the Seven Years' War produced naval commanders, such as Anson, Boscawen, Saunders and particularly Edward Hawke, who became public heroes.[126] The Seven Years' War was fought at a period when, in the literary and cultural domain, biography was diverging from history. The gradual emergence of naval biography took in these heroes of the Seven Years' War, and they became part of a naval pantheon as military biography established itself as a powerful literary genre, which continues to this day. The growing interest in heroes, personalities and their impact on war continued into the twentieth century, making biography as a means of understanding warfare an immensely popular study. Nelson remains the epitome of this phenomenon, and in a very rare case of interest in failure, Admiral Byng, the only British admiral to be shot for not doing his utmost, in March 1757, continues to attract interest.[127]

The war also saw one of the few battles of the century that have continued to attract new scholarship – Hawke's great victory at Quiberon Bay on 20 November 1759.[128] Despite the importance of amphibious operations to the British success in the war, it was only in the second half of the twentieth century that serious attention began to be paid to them. Prior to this, the establishment of control over the sea lines of communication between Europe and America dominated naval histories. The conquests on land, which provided the diplomatic resources with which to negotiate the peace, were seen largely as the inevitable result of sea control. One historian even described Wolfe's force at Quebec as the 'local landing party', giving it and the complexity of its mission scant regard. A new interest in amphibious operations became evident at the end of the Second World War, the experience of which probably stimulated a re-evaluation of this form of warfare. Although we still do not have comprehensive studies of some operations, particularly the coastal raids against France, we now have good modern studies of the amphibious operations at Louisbourg and Quebec,

Havana and Manila, as well as more general narratives of the operations against Guadeloupe and Martinique.[129]

The Seven Years' War marked Britain's rise to pre-eminence as a global naval power, becoming the benchmark for future naval historians. In France, the remarkable collapse of the French navy and the failure of the privateering war, *la guerre de course*, as a viable alternative have presented historians with substantial issues for investigation, which are still in the process of exploration and elaboration. In seeking to understand this collapse, French (and French-Canadian) historians have focused on the lack of skilled mariners in France as a major cause of the rapid deterioration of French naval capacity.[130] They have also identified other significant geographical disadvantages that stood in the way of a sustained development of the French navy. The force was split between the Atlantic (Ponant) and the Mediterranean (Levant). There were few good ports for large warships much further northeast of Brittany, and even Brest had poor landward communications. Once the British had worked out how to sustain a close blockade, supplying Brest with materials was difficult.[131] Most of all, the recurring fiscal weakness of the state, conducting a war across the globe and in Europe, proved fatal. The funding of the navy rested on a knife-edge, and, when news of the fall of Quebec reached Paris in November 1759, finally toppled.[132]

Peace, as usual, has attracted less attention than war. In 1763, Europe was, again, exhausted, but Britain's new status in the world could not be ignored. Between 1763 and 1775, neither of the great continental powers, France and Spain, was able to challenge British diplomatic pressures, backed up as Britain was by a powerful navy. At Newfoundland, the West Indies, West Africa, the Baltic and the Falkland Islands, British naval power effectively dissuaded Bourbon activities. Britain was not always successful. Pressure on Spain to obtain the ransom for Manila and upon France in relation to Dunkirk and the occupation of Corsica all failed. It must be remembered that during these years the key diplomatic issues for France lay in eastern Europe, and conflict with Britain became a lower diplomatic priority. Nevertheless, the primacy that Britain had obtained in the war was resented and a concern for the Bourbon powers.[133]

To Britons after 1763, the Seven Years' War realized the long-held belief that sea power could enable Britain to exert enough force to humiliate her enemies without demanding complicated foreign alliances. Peace would also allow her to reduce the national debt. As part of this process, shifting a greater share of the tax burden onto her American colonies, which had been preserved from French aggression, was thought reasonable and expedient. Resistance in America led to the Royal Navy assuming an unwelcome role, enforcing this more aggressive colonial taxation and trade policy.[134] This is an interesting and important subject, yet there are very few studies relating to the manner in which the navies have assisted the civil power, which is in striking contrast to work done on armies in this function. Given the entrenched idea of a distinction between armies and navies in enforcing the public peace from the seventeenth century, it seems a valuable theme for further development.

The outbreak of rebellion in North America in 1775 was initially viewed as a domestic affair that did not require the mobilization of the fleet. France and Spain had been rebuilding their fleets after 1763, and, gradually, the British began to realize that the revival of these navies posed a threat to their prosecution of the war in America. When France in 1778 and Spain in 1779 joined the American rebels, the Royal Navy was unprepared for this major change in the tempo of the war. The rebuilding of the Bourbon fleets during the decade and a half after 1763 had eliminated Britain's numerical superiority. She was faced with a potential coalition that outnumbered her battlefleet. By the beginning of 1781, Britain was at war with France, Spain and the United Provinces, and faced by a hostile armed neutrality in the Baltic. For the Royal Navy, pitted against the united Bourbon powers, the war was far more difficult than it had been twenty years earlier. The navy failed to score a decisive victory against the French off Ushant in July 1778, and could not prevent a Franco-Spanish invasion force from approaching dangerously close to the British Isles in 1779.[135]

Aside from the constant support given to the rebellious colonies, French and Spanish forces threatened the home islands, Gibraltar, and the West and East Indies. Important victories were won. The victorious actions of Admirals Rodney and Howe against Bourbon forces in European waters did a great deal to preserve Gibraltar and prevent major reinforcements reaching the enemy in the West Indies (Moonlight Battle, 16–17 January 1780, and 13–19 October 1782).[136]

Nevertheless, the Bourbons were able to exert unprecedented pressure on the British. Admiral Edward Hughes' campaign on the Coromandel Coast of India was barely enough to preserve British interests in Bengal and Madras.[137] Spanish forces collaborating with the French in Louisiana succeeded in taking Mobile (14 March 1780) and Pensacola (9 May 1781), undermining the British position in West Florida.[138]

The British in North America were compelled to concentrate their naval forces, which enabled the French to occupy Newport, Rhode Island. This became their naval base in North America. Ultimately, this led to the British naval defeat at the Battle of the Chesapeake (5 September 1781), the surrender of Lord Cornwallis's army at Yorktown and the British decision to end the war. Twenty-two years after the naval victories which underpinned victory in North America, America was lost as a result of a naval battle.[139] While Gibraltar held on under siege, Minorca fell to the Spanish in February 1782. Although the former was a widely celebrated victory in Britain after the war, neither of these campaigns has adequate modern studies.[140]

The war ended in defeat, but in the final years of the war, the British were able to outbuild and then outfight the Bourbons and Dutch at sea.[141] Rodney's victory at the Saintes (12 April 1782) ended any hope of the

Franco-Spanish forces posing a threat to Jamaica or Barbados. The Channel and Gibraltar were secured, but the margin of victory was slight compared with 1763, and the peace was bought with the loss of North America, St Lucia, Tobago, Senegal, Goree, Minorca and West Florida.

This sudden fall from pre-eminence, combined with the resurgence of the Bourbon navies and the birth of the United States, ensured that this war would play an important part in the evolving historiography of international relations. In 1890, Mahan chose to close *The Influence of Sea Power upon History, 1660–1783* with the end of this war. It provided him with the contrast in strategies between the Seven Years' War and the War of Independence, during which Britain abandoned the correct strategy of concentrating naval forces off the naval ports of France and Spain, thus preventing them from having any impact at any point across the globe.[142]

The recovery of the Bourbon navies after 1763 was quite spectacular. Although they may have reached the end of their tether by 1782, their achievements across the globe were unprecedented. For French and Spanish naval historians, it showed how resilient their states were in successfully rebuilding their fleets.[143] The naval contest was in doubt until 1781, and for French historians particularly, it was suggestive of what might have been in store for French sea power if the navy had not been devastated by the Revolution after 1789.[144] For American historians, the war saw the birth of a navy that was to supersede the Royal Navy in the second half of the twentieth century as the world's pre-eminent naval power.[145]

The campaigns have been covered extensively both in traditional narrative form and as an element in naval biographies. There are also some excellent regional studies, although the narrative of the campaign in the Indian Ocean is now very dated and the West Indies have, in general, been neglected. The administration of the Royal Navy, from dockyards to the transport service, has had excellent work devoted to it. The war was full of drama and action, particularly after 1778, which has held the attention of historians as a struggle for supremacy at sea. As with the wars of 1793–1815, the impact of sea power as a means of applying decisive economic or political force upon the enemy has only recently received much attention. Both the British and the Americans could have been badly damaged if the other had managed to tighten a grip on their maritime trade. Richard Buel Jr has shown how the American rhythm of the war was influenced by the British blockade of North American ports. The key ports were never closed, but the blockade constantly limited the ability of the Americans to manage their stores, foodstuffs and specie. On the other hand, American depredations on the British West India trade, and later the Franco-Spanish threat to those islands, disrupted confidence in both Britain and the Caribbean. Understanding more about the economic calculations of the various participants facing this sea power would be a major step towards developing our understanding of sea power in this major conflict.[146]

Personalities, politics, strategy, logistics and tactics have been examined over the two centuries since the peace. More than for earlier wars, technical and organizational changes became a focus of interest for historians. Copper sheathing on hulls, the introduction of the carronade, flintlock firing mechanisms, changes in shipboard life and the relative educations of the officer corps have been examined and assessed as potential factors in the eventual success of the Royal Navy.[147] Another significant factor during these years was that, despite the failure of the war, the Royal Navy emerged as a more globally capable force. After the Seven Years' War, the importance of India in British political thinking began to rise.[148] The campaigns fought in the Indian Ocean between 1780 and 1782 reinforced British positions there, and attention was turning to the Pacific for economic opportunity and naval stores.[149]

The American War reinforced the significance of sea power. It was sea power that enabled the British to shift the centre of gravity of their attacks along the Atlantic seaboard. It enabled them to put constant pressure on the American economy and restrict supplies to the Continental army. It was sea power that prevented the failure in North America from becoming a catastrophic defeat. The failure of the Franco-Spanish invasion attempt in 1779 preserved the home islands. Rodney's victory at the Saintes in April 1782 ensured that a Franco-Spanish invasion of Jamaica was impracticable. Twice, Gibraltar was relieved by naval forces during the long siege of 1780–3. On the other hand, it was French and Spanish sea power

FIGURE 13 *The impact of sea power: the British landing at Kipps Bay, New York Island, 15 September 1776.* © *National Maritime Museum. ID 2891.*

that ultimately won the war. Between 1775 and 1778, low-level, discreet support by provision of arms evaded British attempts to blockade the rebellious colonies. By 1780, Franco-Spanish naval forces stretched British resources across the globe, making it difficult to concentrate without losing an essential supply network that propped up the British-American Empire. French and Spanish ships were also better conducted tactically. The chase actions that had characterized the British successes of the Seven Years' War were replaced by much more equal encounters of well-disciplined squadrons in line of battle. De Grasse's success off the Chesapeake in September 1781 was critical to the eventual surrender of Cornwallis's army at Yorktown on 17 October.

Unlike the Seven Years' War, the Bourbons managed to maintain their battlefleets in action for over four years. The rapid attrition of the 1750s did not reoccur. While their battlefleet remained substantial and at sea, the Royal Navy could not exploit sea control, and ultimately lost it for a brief but critical period off the Virginia Capes in the autumn of 1781.

While the war demonstrated the importance of the battlefleet to the effective seizure of sea power, it also reinforced the importance of amphibious capability in the exploitation of sea power. Riverine and coastal mobility had been a significant feature of operations in North America and had been the dominant feature of the vital campaigns in the West Indies. Whether in the Atlantic, the Caribbean, the Baltic or the Mediterranean, navies had to be balanced forces that could seize command of the sea lanes and exploit that command by projecting force to the enemy ashore. Where this could be done, sea power had a major diplomatic impact. Seizing control was not enough. The tremendous Russian victory at Chesme in 1770 could not be exploited effectively. Throughout the American War, there were many examples of naval power securing the sea space and force being projected ashore. This was particularly so in the West Indies. However, outside the Caribbean, for example at Philadelphia in 1777 and the Carolinas in 1780, the force projected ashore was inadequate to achieve decisive results.

The apogee of naval competition during the Age of Sail, 1763–93

The Seven Years' War was a watershed for naval power in European diplomacy. Britain, with a relatively small standing professional army, had managed to cripple both the French and Spanish overseas empires. No action in Europe seemed capable of restoring the balance. The drama of the conquests, particularly the *annus mirabilis* of 1759, but also every subsequent year to the end of 1762, encouraged a sense of wonder at the power of Britain's naval force and admiration for its guiding hand, William

Pitt. It was a sense of awe that stuck in British political thinking and popular historiography and that resonates to this day. The precise conditions of that success – the blend of diplomacy, balanced naval and military force, domestic political massaging and luck – did not really have serious analyses until the twentieth century.

If the impact of the war remains powerful in the British consciousness, it was no less so for contemporaries in Europe. For at least five years after 1763, French and Spanish diplomacy in relation to Britain was hobbled by the ability of Britain to bring overwhelming naval power to bear upon French maritime, commercial and colonial interests, to which the Bourbons had no countervailing response. Neither France nor Spain could allow this to continue, and the rebuilding of their fleets began in earnest.

The American War demonstrated the wisdom of that investment. Battlefleets could be the arbiters of global power projection. It had also shown that the margins of victory and defeat were so slender that no power could afford to allow its naval strength to diminish without potentially catastrophic consequences, and for the next fifteen years, the maritime powers, including the Ottomans, maintained shipbuilding programmes and reorganized and rebalanced their fleets. A new navy, of the United States, was also emerging. Naval power had been essential for the birth of this republic, but the role of the navy within republican ideology posed problems, and for the first forty years it was dogged by disputes between the navalists, who saw the future linked to powerful naval forces and international trade, and the anti-navalists, who looked more to the underdeveloped interior and believed that naval power should be economical, coastal and defensive.[150]

By 1783, the need to contest the maritime domain was more acute as the Atlantic powers were turning away from central and eastern Europe towards the wider world. Exploration and science, trade and power were closely linked in contemporary thought. Captain James Cook's famous voyages to the Pacific in 1768–71, 1772–5 and 1776–9, under the direction of the Admiralty, were just the most celebrated journeys.[151] In 1766, the Comte de Bougainville embarked on a three-year circumnavigation of the globe, sponsored by the French Crown, that took him round the Falkland Islands, the Solomon Islands and Java. In the same year, Captain Samuel Wallis was instructed by the British Admiralty to make discoveries in the Southern Ocean. Alexandro Malaspina was sent by the Spanish court into the Pacific, including detailed observation of the northwest coast of North America, between 1789 and 1794.[152] Russian and British interest in this region was also growing, and in 1790, caused a major diplomatic crisis between Britain and Spain over Nootka Sound.[153]

While the American War was the clear example of the significance of sea power in international relations, events elsewhere reinforced the point. In the eastern Mediterranean, the Ottoman navy suffered a catastrophic defeat at the hands of the Russians at Chesme in July 1770.

Russia and Turkey had been at war since October 1768, campaigning in Walachia and the Crimea. The Russian Baltic squadron came south into the Mediterranean to stir up revolt among the Sultan's Christian subjects in the Balkans. While it failed to do this, the Russians did catch the Turkish fleet anchored near Chios. The Turks managed to extract themselves from that situation, but were caught again at Chesme and crushed. The victory gave the Russians complete freedom of action in the eastern Mediterranean, and their fleet lay across the sea line of communication for the grain trade between Constantinople and Egypt. The Turks lost heavily at the Peace of Kutchuk Kainardji in 1774. Russia gained major footings along the Black Sea coast. The material impact of the Russian fleet had been less than expected, but the psychological impact on the Ottomans was immense, leading to a determined policy to modernize their navy.[154]

In the Baltic, the Russian navy was also in action against Sweden. After a coup in 1771 that brought Gustavus III to the Swedish throne, there was a revival of the political influence of the Swedish navy. A series of reforms, investment in the ship yard at Karlskrona and the employment of the famous ship constructor Fredric Henrick af Chapman (1721–1808) led to a revival of the Swedish galley, gunboat and sailing forces. In 1780, an ambitious plan to create a navy of twenty-one 60-gun ships of the line, supported by sixteen heavy 40-gun frigates, eventually mounting 24 lb cannon, was initiated. The plan was never completed, but ten of each type were built and performed well.[155] The Swedish attack on Russia by land and sea in the summer of 1788 was indecisive, allowing the Russians to build up their forces. The importance of amphibious operations along the shores of the eastern Baltic required the adversaries to combine their oared and sailing vessels, their ships of the line, frigates and gunboats to project their force inland. Neither side found that it could do this consistently, and the war ended in 1790 with the *status quo ante*.[156]

This naval race in the thirty-five years before the French Revolution was the apogee of naval competition in the 'Age of Sail'. Navies changed their structure and size significantly between 1765 and 1790, reducing British numerical superiority.

However, numbers alone do not make effective sea power. Training, experience, organizational robustness and flexibility are as important, if not more so. Technological changes, such as introduction of the carronade and coppering, as well as improvements in sail plans and hull structures that supported the general growth in the size and burthen of warships, were all important, but there was no technological revolution equivalent to the gunnery 'revolution' of the sixteenth century, the disruptive technologies of steam power and chemical explosives in the nineteenth, or the 'Dreadnought revolution' of the twentieth. Rather, it was a continual pushing of the possibilities of wooden ship design.[157]

Table 1 The Development of Major European Navies, 1765–90

	1765	1770	1775	1780	1785	1790	% +/−
Great Britain							
Line of battle	139	126	117	117	137	130	− 7
Cruisers	91	76	82	111	133	130	42.86
Small ships	36	33	28	58	36	16	− 56
Total	266	235	227	286	306	276	3.76
France							
Line of battle	59	68	59	70	62	73	23.73
Cruisers	23	35	37	58	57	64	178.26
Small ships	21	24	21	34	36	15	− 29
Total	103	127	117	162	155	152	47.57
Spain							
Line of battle	41	55	64	59	61	72	75.61
Cruisers	16	21	28	34	37	46	187.50
Small ships	21	19	23	32	37	7	− 66
Total	78	95	115	125	135	125	60.26
United Provinces							
Line of battle	30	31	26	26	47	48	60.00
Cruisers	29	44	38	40	38	36	24.14
Small ships	0	0	0	0	18	0	
Total	59	75	64	66	103	84	142.37

Source: Harding, R., *Seapower and Naval Warfare, 1650–1830*, 289–92.

Alongside design, the tactical deployment of the ship in the line of battle became a matter of interest to historians of naval tactics for over a century. The line of battle presented a wall of ships broadside on to the enemy. Facing a formidable number of cannons, a commander with similar numbers, technology and seamanship found it difficult to break the line of an enemy or 'double' by going around either end. The great victories of the mid-century, the two battles of Finisterre, Lagos and Quiberon, had been chase actions. At Chesme, the Russians had caught the Turks at anchor and were able to destroy them with fireships. During the American War, with the actions more equal and mostly under sail, breaking through the enemy's line to concentrate fire on, and destroy, an isolated section of it proved difficult. Rodney missed his chance against the French fleet under de Guichen off Martinique in May 1780. He finally achieved it at the Saintes against de Grasse in April 1782, but controversy later mired the success, as doubts were raised as to whether it was an accident, intended by Rodney or prompted by his first captain, Sir Charles Douglas.[158]

By the end of the century, the aim of annihilating the enemy in battle was fully in view, but the means of achieving it was only fleetingly grasped. Whatever the intentions of fleet commanders, their ability to carry them out was severely limited by the mobility of the sailing warship, the signalling systems they possessed and the weather conditions in which they operated. The reality of fleet manoeuvres under sail was more fractured and disorderly than the contemporary paintings of neat lines of warships suggest. Recent work on handling warships under sail has given us a better picture of the difficulties of leading a line into battle.[159]

About the only element over which the commander did have direct control in this complex process was his signals, and the development of the signal book during this period has become an important element in naval history.[160] During the last quarter of the eighteenth century, signalling, like so much else in naval warfare, was evolving.

Between 1789 and 1815, the Revolutionary and Napoleonic Wars violently refocused attention on the European heartland. The seismic shift caused by the French Revolution, which not only shattered the French officer corps but fractured the traditional alliance system, meant that when war did break out, it was not a contest of near equals. The French navy, devoid of support from Spain, was no match for the Royal Navy. However, by then the maritime or naval dimension was so embedded in the economic condition of Europe that it was never far from the calculations of statesmen. This was taken by Mahan and the navalists of the end of the nineteenth century as the natural ordering of affairs, and from it were deduced the immutable principles of naval warfare. They took for granted the economic dependency of the European state on maritime trade. They were less concerned with examining the detail of that dependency. This was left to later generations, for whom naval history provided an entry point into understanding their primary interest – the globalization of the world economy.

CHAPTER THREE

Navies and societies: The widening research agenda

Navies and globalization from the fifteenth to the twenty-first century

Military power has been exercised to accumulate wealth ever since societies were organized. The capacity of military power to destroy wealth is also an ancient fear and a contemporary reality. In so far as the history of international relations is a story of the struggle for control of resources, the role of navies in the accumulation or destruction of economic assets lies at the heart of traditional naval history. By the late seventeenth century, overseas trade, particularly colonial trade, was generating both the financial liquidity and the flexible investment systems for sustained economic growth. All this was protected by naval power. The same naval power was capable of 'noiseless, exhausting pressure' on the enemy's trade. The navalism of the late nineteenth century was predicated on the existence of a global struggle for survival in which the reach of naval power ensured a wider control of resources and markets. So important was this that, according to Mahan, 'the overwhelming seapower of England was the determining factor in European history'.[1] Though open to challenge from many perspectives, this was a claim that seemed logical to those experiencing the aggressive imperialism of the time and to those who could later look back on the effects of the blockade of Germany during the First World War.[2]

If navies played a critical role in the global balance of power, what part do they play in 'globalization'? The term only began to be studied seriously during the 1980s, and there remains some controversy about its precise meaning.[3] It can be defined by at least three levels of exchange. One definition, the most expansive, is that of global economic exchange. This is very broad, and could imply a slow, punctuated growth in international trade since antiquity. It has been refined by limiting it to significant shifts in population, such as the post-1850 migrations.[4] A second definition demands an essential convergence of political power or systems. Finally, a third definition argues that true globalization has only occurred where there has been deep cultural and symbolic exchange or convergence.

Navies have certainly played an important role in the first two levels of exchange. Economic exchange by sea, particularly after the 1450s, was underwritten by state naval power. The sea was always beyond normal legal jurisdictions and hence subject to risk that did not affect land-based commerce. The expansion of oceanic trade required a secure (and profitable) communications network. The work of Frederick C. Lane has been particularly influential in exploring this phenomenon. Lane presented state power (naval power in the global context) as the means of reducing the protection costs for commerce.[5] Navies became, in the words of one historian, 'a maritime protection racket'.[6] It was a 'racket' that was blessed with the intellectual support of the dominant economic theory. Organizing and protecting commerce to maximize the value of maritime trade and ensure positive bullion flows was a basic tenet of mercantilist thinking, and naval power was the essential force to ensure it. Although there is still debate about the effectiveness of the mercantilist policy levers employed by various states, there is a broad consensus concerning the centrality of navies in the inter-European economic rivalries between 1600 and 1815. Mercantilism lost its intellectual grip on policy slowly between the 1770s and the 1840s, and by the time liberal free-trade policies began to dominate international relations, they did so under the protection of British naval hegemony. When that broke down after 1871 in the face of accelerated international economic and naval competition, it brought with it the navalism that dominated the period up to 1914. Today, the fate of the modern integrated economic system relies on global oceanic communications networks which dominate contemporary maritime strategies.

The second definition of globalization, concerning the convergence of power systems, strongly resonates in European colonial and imperial projects and in the development of supranational trade and security bodies after 1945. There is far less consensus on the significance of naval power in relation to the imposition of European power on non-European societies. Controlling the oceanic network was one thing, but being able to impose trade conditions on non-Europeans was entirely another. Colonial expansion, the imposition of unequal treaties and eventually the great imperial surge of 1875–1914 have been ascribed to the technological superiority of gunpowder, guns and ships. They were, no doubt, factors, but this sort of technological determinism is completely inadequate as an explanation, given the complexity of specific situations in both the metropolitan countries and the extra-European world.

Nevertheless, naval power was one important element that influenced the complex processes that spread the political power of some countries across oceans. After 1945, the role of naval power in consensual convergence of national political systems through international bodies is even more obscure. Even in zones of potential conflict, navies carry more weight through public relations than immediate force. When, in August 2007, Russia used two mini submarines to plant a flag on the seabed under the Arctic sea ice, it was announced as 'the start of the revision of the world'. Showing the flag, literally in this case, has always been a diplomatic role of navies, but it met with no serious comment from other members of the UN Convention on the Law of the Sea.[7] It is when and where the international systems for compromise experience strain, such as the disputes over the Spratley Islands and the Senkaku/Daioyu Islands in the South and East China Seas, that navies become an essential diplomatic tool.

The third definition of globalization, which focuses upon the cultural convergence of societies, is more problematic for naval historians. Some recent work on the cultural impact of navies on individual societies has made an important start on this subject. However, so far, too little work has been done to be confident that it forms a reliable base for comparative cultural influence. There are hints that at certain times and in certain contexts navies have played a part in cultural transmission. For example, recent work done on the Imperial Japanese Navy's base at Jinhae in Korea suggests it became a centre for the transfer of ideas on public health and urban planning to Korea.[8] What impact this had on the cultural adaptation of Korea is unknown. Across the centuries, the connections between globally mobile, technically highly developed organizations such as navies and different societies are likely to be greater than we currently know, but confirmation awaits deeper and wider research than has, hitherto, been undertaken.

Maritime economies, industrial revolution and the engine of growth

While the role of navies in globalization is a subject that is very new, debate about their role in relation to economic development goes back at least to the sixteenth century. As far as the economic development of Europe is concerned, recent scholarship continues to emphasize that the exceptional industrialization of Britain in the second half of the eighteenth century was founded on the successful application of a clear mercantilist policy, which defended and promoted overseas trade. While there is a general consensus that naval power was an essential element in the provision of a stable environment for international investment, there is still a need to establish more precisely the significance of navies as part of the wider mercantilist framework.[9]

Most of the studies of the economic impact of navies are focused on the period of intense naval rivalry between Britain and France before 1815. The debate does not revolve around the importance of the navy in protecting Britain, her markets and sources of raw materials – this seems to be axiomatic. Rather, the question is whether this growing oceanic commerce was the cause of accelerating industrialization or a symptom of it.[10] Although it appears causal in Britain's case, there is a danger of slipping into a generalized determinism that naval expansion, or power, caused industrialization. This is still very much open to question, and far more work needs to be done to define any generalized principles that can be sustained across the centuries and societies.[11]

One of the most contentious aspects of the link between naval power and industrialization is the role that the slave trade played in the British Industrial Revolution. After its establishment in the late Middle Ages, the 'slave-sugar complex became the premier institution of European expansion'.[12] West Indian colonies were an important source of wealth in Britain from the 1660s. One of the most important functions of the Royal Navy was the protection of these islands. Eric Williams' *Capitalism and Slavery* (1944) provided the foundation for the modern study of the phenomenon. His contention that slavery caused, or, at the very least, strongly stimulated, the Industrial Revolution provided the ground work for subsequent scholars to develop.[13] At present, the consensus seems to accept the importance of slavery and slave-produced tropical products to European capital accumulation, but the divergence remains between those who put slavery at the very centre of emergent industrialization and those who see its impact as being mediated or reinforced by other important domestic factors that stimulated industrial development in the second half of the eighteenth century.

Whatever the precise contribution of tropical commerce to industrialization, naval power played an important role in determining the distribution of profits from colonial commerce among the European powers. However, the naval contribution to the defence of the slave trade networks remains under-researched. Perhaps too much emphasis is placed upon the role of naval power. Traditionally, the Royal Navy is supposed to have played the crucial role in eliminating piracy in the Atlantic between 1680 and 1720. Piracy did not disappear, nor did smuggling. Only recently has research begun to focus on the nature of the maritime communities, their networks and their resistance to state control.[14] Also, the relationship between naval wars and economic development was not a simple linear extrapolation of the consequences of defeat or victory. As recent French research has shown, naval defeat did not imply economic collapse in colonial commerce. French colonial commerce continued to prosper outside wartime up to the outbreak of the French Revolution.[15] The role of navies in the suppression of the slave trades in both the Atlantic and the Indian Ocean throughout most of the nineteenth century is also something that needs more research.[16]

Science, technology and technological determinism in naval history

The importance of ship design and technology to navies has made this particular aspect one of the most highly developed subjects within naval history. There is a massive literature on ship designs and technology across the entire period, ranging from the highly technical to the very popular. Some of this has been mentioned in the previous chapter, but a search on the Rasor Bibliography gives a good impression of the quantity of writing that is available.

What is more interesting for our present purposes is the role of navies in the wider debates about technology, and its impact on economic development. Navies are highly technological instruments, and the study of the technologies associated with them has been an enduring concern of historians. Most commonly, naval power is measured in the numbers or types of vessels in a fleet compared with its rivals, but it is also measured in terms of the technologies these ships embody. Galleys opposed to broadside square-rigged warships; paddle opposed to screw propulsion; smooth-bore opposed to rifled artillery; dreadnoughts, submarines and aircraft carriers, all have been employed in response to problems. Technological evolution is integrated into international competition and is often thought to be the driver of both that competition and the shape of navies – in other words, the development of navies has been determined by the technology. While this is still a powerful view, the causal power of technological invention or innovation has been questioned.[17] Navies are social organizations that are determined as much by the actors and groups that make up the organization as by the technological possibilities that are open to them. Some technologies assume social significance that goes beyond utilitarian or rational analyses. The longbow, the galley, the sailing warship, and later the battleship, the submarine and the aircraft carrier all carried meanings for societies that were deeper than their value as instruments of warfare. Choices are made and investment or operational trajectories are established based on these social meanings. Technological options are closed or opened as much by these social assumptions as by the intrinsic value of the technologies themselves. Similarly, navies, like all organizations, are influenced by their peers and rivals, and will seek to adopt technologies that appear to confer success or prestige despite the lack of intrinsic value they provide for their own conditions.

Most studies of innovation or adaptation in naval technology are focused on the artefact and its performance. Very few have examined them in the economic and social contexts from which they sprang. Navies were important heavy-purchasing 'early adopters' that could make or break innovation, and the battle for technology adoption was rooted in wider domestic social, political and economic conflicts. The most developed expression of this is the 'military–industrial complex' in the United States after 1945. However, networks of interests between navies, maritime industries and government decision-making are important aspects of history in most societies that have exercised naval power. Recent work by Katherine Epstein on the adoption of the torpedo in the United States and Britain has demonstrated the operation of a military–industrial complex stretching to the late nineteenth century. Similar studies on different technologies in other nations would provide important insight into navies, the innovation process and its impact on naval power.[18] Similarly, technology transfer between states is a subject that is touched upon in numerous studies, but analyses of its operation over time and between different states have yet to be drawn together.[19]

Another aspect of the role of navies is that of exploration and scientific discovery. The great age of exploration and discovery (c.1450–1600) occurred before the formal organization of state navies could have an impact upon it. It was not until the last four decades of the seventeenth century that state naval power could be deployed continuously and purposefully across oceans. Navigation was, however, a state and commercial concern, so navies played an important role.[20] For example, the British Admiralty's Board of Longitude prize, established in 1714, for a means of determining longitude at sea was awarded, after a long delay, to John Harrison for his famous marine chronometer in 1773. During the eighteenth century, most navies played an active role in improving hydrographic information and stimulated the development of cartography. After the end of the Seven Years' War in 1763, European navies became more directly involved in Pacific exploration. The voyages of James Cook and Bougainville are well known, but there were other expeditions that blended science with military reconnaissance.[21] Most naval officers and administrators had to possess a scientific understanding, but they were usually highly pragmatic individuals for whom abstract scientific discovery was not a priority. Nevertheless, throughout the nineteenth century, navies were engaged in the process of discovery and assisting in scientific understanding. There were some famous and significant expeditions, for example the quest for the North-West Passage.[22] The most important, however, was the second voyage of the survey ship HMS *Beagle* between December 1831 and October 1836, which carried Charles Darwin. The public imagination was fired by these events and the results they produced (even if it was twenty-three years between the return of the *Beagle* and the publication of *Origin of Species*). While navies were employed in scientific investigation throughout the nineteenth century, most of this scientific activity still tends to be examined in terms of specific expeditions or experiments. The history of navies as scientific institutions remains to be written.

Navies as complex organizations (structures, systems and expertise)

The study of navies as complex organizations is another thread of research that has evolved fairly recently and is likely to be hotly contested.[23] By

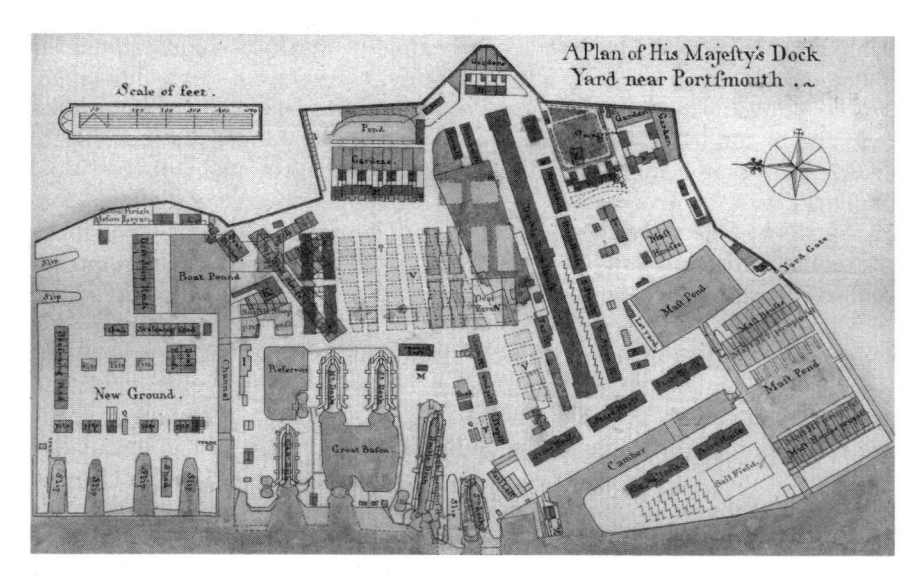

FIGURE 14 *Navies as industrial enterprise: Planned extension to Portsmouth dockyard, 1786.* © Trustees of the National Museum of the Royal Navy (Portsmouth).

the middle of the twentieth century the experience of two world wars had left the old imperial systems shattered and replaced by an international system dominated by the United States and the Soviet Union. Industrialized nations brought unprecedented resources and destructive power to warfare. Understanding the massive mobilization of nations and economies in these struggles brought navies and naval historians far more closely into contact with the concerns of contemporary social scientists. Wars were fought exploiting every possible national resource to the maximum advantage. The key concepts of efficiency (maximum outputs measured against a given set of inputs) and effectiveness (optimum impact on policy objectives measured against a given set of inputs), borrowed from economics and organizational research, were integrated into the military systems far more than ever before, and have subsequently underpinned much of the research in naval history.

The economist, the organizational analyst and the historian do not always share the same assumptions or methods, but the debate between them is fruitful.[24] For both historians and social scientists, the evidence is sacrosanct, and both have to work in situations in which it can be slim or ambiguous. In such cases, assumptions or theoretical constructs provide frameworks for analysis. For social scientists, the need to make explicit *a priori* theoretical positions is important. Indeed, their use of experimental method makes it essential. For historians, whose control over the method of data gathering is limited, the requirement is less pressing. Nevertheless, historians can benefit from the explicit theory and model-building of social scientists. For example, assumptions concerning rational economic behaviour have provided some interesting propositions concerning the behaviour of naval officers, administrators, contractors and politicians.[25] The economist also places far more weight on measurable, quantifiable data than the historian, whose focus can be on a wider range of documentary evidence. The latter might emphasize the personal accounts of an individual involved in a combat situation rather than the metrics of after-action analysis. The role of leadership, training or morale is difficult to quantify compared with cumulative information on investment in technologies or weapons performance data.

An excellent example of how economists and economic historians are engaged in debates in naval history is the issue of the effectiveness of the Royal Navy in the eighteenth century. Analysis of incentive structures provides compelling evidence for micro-economists.[26] On the other hand, macro-economic historians see the foundations of effectiveness in cumulative state investment in naval infrastructure. For example, O'Brien and Duran propose that the economic data of investment in the Royal Navy and trade protection provides a surer explanation of British naval dominance than seamanship, bravery in battle or organizational factors.[27] Unfortunately, the book that expands this argument has not yet appeared, but it promises to produce an interesting debate.

Where clear distinctions between national levels of investment in navies exist, they are strong indicators for performance outcomes. However, the apparent certainty provided by statistical data has many problems. As noted above, the danger of technological determinism is an old one. Performance in modern organizations is too complex to be explained by reference to single sets of data, despite the superficial attractiveness of numbers. Aware of this danger, historians and social scientists have proposed that organizational performance can only be understood in terms of integrated social–technical systems. Here, social, educational, technical and political factors are given parity of significance with fiscal, financial and economic indicators unless proved otherwise.[28]

Navies are organizations created within a state for the execution of national strategy, but they are also organizations which consist of a number of dependent and independent sub-systems. At the same time, they exist as institutions in society which have impacts far beyond the functional requirement to defend the state. The military power of these organizations is at least partly influenced by institutional structures and cultures within the host societies.[29] The performance of navies is, therefore, partly constrained by the way they are structured, how they relate to other institutions and the assumptions of the people who populate them. The theoretical work on this subject has been applied to navies only in a very limited manner, but it supports the empirical interest in naval administration that developed after 1945 and reinforces the interest in the evolution of public administration and professionalization of work roles that occurred in the 1960s.[30]

Although the application of the 'new institutional history' of complex systems is very limited at present, there is now a large body of work on the organizational performance and structure of navies that can be identified as 'New Naval History'. That the British Navy was the starting point of this type of study is no surprise. It was probably the largest and most complex industrial organization in the world during the eighteenth century. In order to put a squadron to sea, it relied upon purchasing, construction, supply and maintenance networks which brought in raw materials from across Britain and Europe, processed them to an acceptable standard and maintained a continuous replenishment to ensure that the squadrons could operate robustly at a great distance from home ports. Its administrative archives were vast, accessible and pertinent to British society after 1945, as it had to come to terms with serious political and economic challenges to maintaining a global navy. It was also important to other countries that sought to explain the historical successes or defeats in terms that extended beyond campaigns at sea.

Effective naval power requires an administrative, social and economic infrastructure to convert labour and raw materials into fighting machinery. This lies at the centre of the debates about state formation and the fiscal-military or fiscal-naval state. It is also critical to the expansion of navies post-1885. The move to coal and then oil fuel imposed new supply chain demands and the development of new robust logistics networks. Once again, British naval administration has been covered quite well, with a steady flow of works on the subject covering the entire period at least up to the 1950s. Other navies have been covered less fully, and those works have tended to be narratives, summaries or case studies rather than analyses of administrative structures and systems as institutions.

One of the foundations of this robust infrastructure was an effective contracting system. This required reliable financing and a robust legal framework.[31] Some of it is currently uncontroversial. However, as more detailed research has been undertaken, some interesting issues have emerged. Clive Wilkinson's study of the financing of the Royal Navy between 1763 and 1775 provides the most detailed investigation of how the Navy Debt was carefully managed to present quite different messages to Parliament and foreign governments.[32] Opinions on efficiency and effectiveness of naval administration also vary. James Haas's *A Management Odyssey: The Royal Dockyards, 1714–1914* (1994) presented the administrative procedures as a march from inefficiency and corruption to modern standards by the end of the nineteenth century. This has been contested by other scholars, notably Roger Morriss and Ann Coats, who have presented naval administrators as being pulled by different priorities and competing concepts of effectiveness.[33] A similar difference of view is evident in the works of Janet Macdonald and Roger Knight and Martin Wilcox concerning the work of the Victualling Board.[34]

One of the key problems in these debates is the lack of good financial data for the early modern state. The historian of the British Navy is fortunate in the survival of state records concerning the navy, but the survival of contractors' records is far more patchy. Historians of the French navy are even less fortunate, but some important work has proved possible concerning individual contractors.[35] A further problem lies in interpreting the financial and contractual documents. It is easy to assume that financial records are accurate in their details and transparent in their purpose. However, accounting was, and is, an intensely political process, and the purposes of administrators, contractors, politicians and service personnel are different and change over time. As Wilkinson demonstrated with the records of the Navy Debt, all reports and accounts have to be used with great care.

The problems of interpretation and analysis did not disappear as modern accounting procedures and the demands of industrial manufacturing led to more and better-structured information. The focus of most of the current studies is on the performance of the administrators, and is heavily reliant on state archives for the purpose. Less attention has been paid to the contractors and manufacturers who played a vital part in the overall effectiveness or efficiency of any given contract. Contractors had their own needs, purposes and environments. These can only be understood if studied from the perspective of the industries, the firms and the individuals. Economic and maritime historians are at work on these subjects, but too seldom are the results of their work fully understood or acknowledged by naval historians. Some historians, such as Katherine Epstein, Gary Weir, Hugh Murphy and Lewis Johnman, deliberately bridge the two, but for most scholars the divide between industries and the service is an acknowledged but unexplored gap.[36]

Another under-researched aspect of the organizational complexity of navies is operational flexibility. Complexity might intuitively suggest a lack of flexibility in rapidly changing conditions – the investment, research and development, and training lead-times alone give a strong hint in this direction. However, a great deal of work has been devoted to the Royal Navy as the archetype of the modern state navy, which has demonstrated an apparently high level of flexibility as conditions changed in its long history. It is not just the long-term flexibility of navies that needs to be understood. Understanding how navies overcome catastrophic defeat, or extinction as a result of political or diplomatic exigencies, is a neglected area of study that needs to go beyond the few works that we have at present.[37] Similarly, the creation of modern navies in societies without a tradition of oceanic power projection is an important subject for historians and contemporary naval thinkers as the balance of economic power shifts decisively to the Pacific Rim.

The officer corps and naval leadership

Navies are made up of the people who serve them: the officers, seamen and administrators. Unsurprisingly, the officer corps has received rather more attention than the seamen. The issue of leadership has played a major part in the evolution of naval history. Professional naval history developed at the end of the nineteenth century as a didactic tool for officer education. They were the people upon whose decisions the military, administrative and political fate of the service ultimately rested. As for any social elite, its records are fuller, more diverse and better preserved than those of the lower orders. Hence, their impact on events, as individuals and groups, is more easily traceable.

Traditionally, the officer corps has been studied through the words of its members – the public and private papers of officers, biography and autobiography. However, this is another aspect of naval history that is receiving more systematic analysis. By the end of the nineteenth century, biography had become an important genre within naval and military historical literature. Classical biography was rare for naval officers in the seventeenth and eighteenth centuries. Reports of their actions were commonly cited as didactic examples, and self-justificatory publication was common, but life stories were unusual.[38] Biographical information inserted in general histories was common by the eighteenth century, and biographical dictionaries were appearing by the third quarter of the century. In the first half of the nineteenth century, history and biography were merging as the sweeping narrative histories were structured around the lives of the great leaders. These included the naval officers, among whom Nelson stands out. Towards the end of the century, there was a growing distinction between history as literature and history as scientific enquiry. Biography was evidently in the former. However, by this time, with growing public literacy, there was a strong demand for biography and autobiography to supplement the output of 'scientific' historians. It is trend that has continued to the present day. Biographies abound, adding colour, information and insight for naval historians, but no thorough analysis of biographical traditions, tropes and purposes has yet been carried out.

During the twentieth century, analyses of the officer corps as social groups have become more important, and some very useful studies have appeared across the decades. The Royal Navy officer corps remains the most fully researched.[39] However, officer corps in general provide a number of threads of interest for historians, which need development. The social origins and professional progress of officers have had some attention. Linked to this is an interest in the social status of officers and how they translated their professional duties into social capital (financial or reputational). There are some excellent social studies of officer corps of France, the United States and Germany, but the overall coverage of the officer corps is still incomplete.[40] For example, apart from some very specific studies and Herwig's work on the Imperial German Navy, the politics of the various officer corps is only sporadically covered, in contrast to the attention that has been given to the politics of army officer corps. Similarly, apart from limited references in generic studies of professionalization, there is still a great deal of work to be done on the evolution of naval service as a profession.

The education of the officer corps is an aspect of their lives that has been well covered. The key function of the officer is to lead, and developing this is the purpose of officer education. Again, the Royal Navy has attracted most attention, but education in the French and United States navies is also well served.[41] The importance of learning in organizations has been recognized for some decades now, and this aspect of naval history is well positioned to be expanded into other navies and contribute to the history of vocational education more generally.

The importance of history as a subject in naval education has also been widely studied. History provided the aspiring officer with role models to emulate and, if he studied deeply enough, an accumulated store of tactical, operational and strategic examples with which to inform current practice. Today, biographies and autobiographies continue to be used to point out the leadership qualities of their subjects. The tradition of presenting exemplars of excellence is alive and well in naval history.[42] The importance of history to the higher education of naval officers today is also evident in the mass of literature that has been produced in the last twenty-five years from publishers as varied as the Naval Institute Press, Frank Cass, Ashgate, Boydell and Brewer, Economica, and the Ministerio de Defensa Madrid. Although naval history has a constant fight to keep its place on the crowded curricula of modern navies, its direct relevance to strategic thinking has ensured a vibrant output directed to this audience.

What is far less well developed at present is the study of leaders in context. Traditional studies of leaders are inevitably *post facto* examinations in which the role of the leader is usually assumed to be a decisive factor. However, contemporary leadership studies have developed methods of studying leadership as a conditional, adaptive, negotiated and distributed social process.[43] The leader is one factor within a dynamic situation, whose influence is variable and needs to be established rather than assumed. Little of this work has, so far, been absorbed into historical studies of naval leadership. The same might be said of that other elite group, the naval administrators. To some extent, their history has suffered more than that of either naval officers or seamen. Professionally distanced from the naval officer as a civilian with an irritating ability to influence events at sea and onshore, he carried neither the prestige nor the drama of a role to attract public attention. Too much part of a fairly anonymous bureaucratic elite, he was of little interest to the social historian focusing on 'history from below'. It was only in the 1950s that interest in administrative history began to grow, and still it has never attracted a broad popular, service or academic audience. Nevertheless, there is now a very solid and growing body of work on naval administration, but much less has been done on the administrators themselves or their lives in the various levels of the systems. This is beginning to change and promises to provide more insights into the linkages between navies and their host societies. Just as we are moving beyond the history of great commanders to understand navies, we are also moving beyond the history of the great administrators, such as Pepys, Colbert or Ensenada, to understand the administrative machinery of navies.

Manpower and navies

In Britain, the social history of seamen has also followed changing historiographical fashion and interest. The growth of social history in the 1960s saw the publication of what are now the standard narratives of life in the Royal Navy.[44] Interest in recovering the lives of working people related to navies has continued ever since. This has been greatly assisted by the mass of official records, such as musters, logs, minutes of committees, enquiries, letters to administrators, records of courts martials or civilian courts, and wills, which have all given historians an insight into the lives of seamen.[45] Much of the interest at present is in the seamen of the Atlantic world in the early modern period. They were not professional naval ratings in the modern sense, but mariners whose work straddled naval and commercial seafaring. As such, they were part of a wider seafaring community, whose history is of great importance to understanding how navies worked.[46]

Before steam, navies depended on human muscle power in almost every aspect of their work, from construction of ships, labouring in dockyards and on deck, to working the sails and guns while at sea. Huge quantities of manpower were needed to work and fight a large sailing warship. For example, in the mid-eighteenth century, the work-horse of the line of battle, the seventy-gun ship, had an establishment of 480 men, the eighty-gun ship 600 men and the 100-gun warship 850 men. Compare this with 674, the anticipated complement of the new British aircraft carrier *Queen Elizabeth*, and the strain imposed by manning a squadron of ships of the line in smaller, pre-industrialized economies becomes quite apparent. Not all these men had to be trained 'topsail men' who could work the sails and yards, but in wartime, with the expansion of fleets, the sheer numbers required to man guns and haul on ropes was daunting.

These men had to be obtained from the maritime communities, where they had alternative employment on merchantmen or privateers, which offered equal or more attractive prospects. Although the popular notion of service on a man-of-war as little more than a floating prison, which offered no advantages, has been demolished by reference to both the numbers of volunteers on warships and comparative studies of their economic benefits, no state could rely entirely on volunteers.[47]

Systems of compulsion were essential. Ensuring an adequate level of acceptability to the local communities and to the political elites was critical for naval administrators and for the overall effectiveness of the systems. Because manpower was so short in wartime, there is a substantial literature on the subject. In Britain, the press gang, which forcibly removed seamen from merchant ships or port towns, is still a deep cultural memory.

Consequently, the press gang and the issue of manning warships has a rich history from many perspectives. Nicholas Rogers has examined it as a social and legal phenomenon. David Starkey and D. Robinson have studied its economic and strategic dimension. Richard Pares explored its impact in the West Indies. Neil Stout and Carl Swanson viewed it from the North American perspective. The administrative and political aspects of seamen's pay and the press have been traced by, among others, Geoffrey Scammell, M. Schoenfeld, Stephen Gradish, Tony Ryan and Gillian Hughes.[48]

Manpower studies of other navies are less full, but the research is continuing and the scope is expanding. As in Britain, the problems were most acute when war imposed intense strain upon navies and the maritime community from which it drew its manpower. The Atlantic powers, France, Spain and the United Provinces, seem to have suffered more in this regard than the less ambitious Baltic or Mediterranean states. The French system of dividing the seafaring population into 'classes', from which the seamen for *La Royale* were drawn, was unpopular, never worked well and was hampered by a fundamental shortage of mariners in the economy.[49] Manning *la Armada* and the Dutch navy were constant problems. Ultimately, no system worked perfectly during the age of the sailing navies. The tensions the manning systems created for administrators, naval commanders, statesmen and the seamen themselves still require more investigation.

Health and medicine in navies

Given the scarcity of manpower, one of the most important functions of the naval officer was to preserve the health of his crew. Since they were confined in small spaces over prolonged periods without access to some essential foodstuffs and often arriving in places where they had no natural immunity to local diseases, this was a difficult task, even after medical knowledge improved in the nineteenth and twentieth centuries. In the early modern period, disability brought on by scurvy went alongside infectious diseases such as dysentery and typhus, which were brought on board by seamen joining a voyage. Diseases such as yellow fever and malaria could be contracted at destinations. In 1741 and 1746, French expeditions to the West Indies and Canada, respectively, were devastated by disease. Expeditions to the West Indies had to be planned with the expectation of mortality quickly diminishing the effectiveness of the force.

Until the latter part of the nineteenth century, medical science had not identified the causes of most diseases and maladies. Remedy had to be sought in administrative action, such as the establishment of hospitals to isolate or quarantine the sick, hygiene procedures and dietary regimes. The fullest account of medical developments in the Royal Navy is still the four-volume study by Lloyd, Keevil and Coulter published between 1957 and 1963. However, a great deal of work has been done since then, and there are now some excellent studies on surgery, administration and the effects of nutrition, exposure and disease in different navies.[50]

The best-known medical problem is scurvy, which provides a good illustration of how the historical treatment of disease is changing and being contested. Traditional histories have presented scurvy as a medical problem, which medical men, such as Thomas Lind, Gilbert Blane and Thomas Trotter, strove to control. The debate has been on the relative merits of each to the task.[51] More recent studies have shifted the emphasis. It is now asserted that it was the naval administrators, rather than the physicians, who, by trials and the effective logistical management of foodstuffs and anti-scorbutics, brought about the reduction of scurvy. The conquest of infectious disease in this period relied more on public hygiene and the disciplinary regimes on board ship than scientific discovery.[52]

The popular view that shipboard life was invariably more disease-ridden and deficient in dietary requirements than for comparable social groups ashore during the eighteenth century is now being challenged. Similarly, surgery in the Royal Navy has a popular image of being little better than butchery, but recent research is showing that the standards of surgery were as high as, or even higher than, a person could expect on shore.[53] Medical history, including psychiatry, and the history of public health is a growing area of study regarding navies.

The sailor at sea and ashore

Seamen were part of complex maritime communities that serviced commercial and naval enterprise. These societies were quite different from that of their land-bound neighbours. Even before uniforms, seaman dressed differently and were easily recognizable. In the early modern world, they were seen as different. The caricatures of Gilray, for example, invoke the landsman's disparaging amusement and fear of this footloose, unpredictable individual roistering ashore. As in any society, seamen lived in hierarchies that affected the lives of their members. Studies are now beginning to shed fascinating light upon the lives of seamen, dockyard workers and their families, as well as their social superiors in the officer and administrative classes. From clothing, to local customs, living space, work opportunities, education and training, sexuality and race barriers, the social mores and boundaries are giving us a richer picture of how navies impacted on the societies they served.[54]

In the early modern world, the sea, where the seamen spent their working lives, was beyond the boundaries of order that existed upon land. It seemed naturally chaotic and lawless. The workings of God and the Devil seemed more dramatic and immediate, and the need for shipboard communities to impose order in their vulnerable little floating societies stimulated both religious and social thinking. The religious practices and beliefs of seamen from the Middle Ages onwards have been studied for many years. How those practices replicated, or differed from, those ashore is an important aspect of understanding how navies were motivated and operated. It added to the religious zeal in the great confrontations between Christianity and Islam in the Mediterranean; gave emphasis to the differences between, largely Presbyterian, sailors and their more radical counterparts in the army during the English Civil War; and provided a point of integration with social change ashore in the Evangelical movement after about 1780.[55] The separation from domestic social hierarchies did not divorce the seaman from social controls and obligations, but it did impose some modifications upon them. Discipline and control were different, but based on the same expectations of obedience and punishment. Maritime communities, and seamen in particular, did have some different expectations of freedoms and traditional loyalties as the centralizing power of the nation-state began to intrude ever more forcefully into the maritime sphere, which led to violence, repression and social change.[56]

Later, as the integration of these communities into more distinct national societies took place during the nineteenth century, the seaman, maritime communities and navies became features of these new imagined social bodies. From fashion to education and public health, navies and maritime culture were significant actors in the wider networks of societies, and this is a story that is at last beginning to be told and understood.[57]

Another aspect of life at sea that needs more work is that of shipboard life. Contemporary narratives of life on the lower decks or the slave benches are now attracting public interest that was once the preserve of biographies of fighting officers – although sometimes modern editing removes important aspects, such as religious conviction, from the author's voice.[58] Modern studies are adding to our understanding of lives spent on warships. Although not specifically naval, sailors' folk art has been studied for a long time, as well as music, dress and manners, but there is still a great deal to be done for most navies across the centuries.[59]

Discipline and social control are other aspects of working life that are beginning to have more serious studies devoted to them. Like the press gang, the popular image of the crew being held to their tasks by brutal discipline is still deeply held. Only recently has work begun on such documents as courts martial records to establish the distortion of this. Already, it is clear that the maintenance of discipline on board ship was more consistent with contemporary norms ashore than had popularly been allowed. However, there are still too few studies across time spans, and particularly across different navies, to draw satisfactory conclusions about this aspect of naval life.[60] Similarly, the breakdown of discipline, and mutiny in particular, needs more work. Mutiny horrified the officer corps and society more widely, so it has a solid and growing literature from a number of perspectives, mostly focused on dramatic events such as the Great Mutiny in the Royal Navy squadrons at the Nore and Portsmouth in 1797 or those on the HMS

Bounty in 1786, HMS *Hermione* in 1797 and the far more famous Russian battleship *Potemkin* in 1905.[61]

Less attention has been paid to how codes of discipline were applied and evolved as expectations of behaviour changed. Work discipline has been a contentious issue among social historians for generations, but it has not penetrated far into naval history, despite the rich records that enable such studies to be undertaken.[62] Frictions created by expectations of social status rather than naval rank, such as between gentlemen or tarpaulins, *rouge* or *bleu*, *plume* or *epée*, have good studies in both the British and French Navies, and this is an area of study ripe for further research.[63]

The change from sail to steam during the middle decades of the nineteenth century brought with it a different demand for seamen. The advent of shell guns and electricity for mechanical power made the changes even starker. The role of the naval seaman was no longer barely distinguishable from that of the merchant seaman. There was a need for professional men-of-war's seamen. In Britain, changes in the economy towards liberal, free-trade global markets also meant that the state had less control over its seafaring labour force. The Royal Navy had difficulty adjusting to these changes between 1815 and 1853, but achieved a continuous service system by the end of this period and became self-sufficient in manpower during peacetime.[64] It would take another fifteen years to improve the system, by which time the expansion of the navy again put it under pressure. Nevertheless, the navy had moved decisively and effectively from impressment to continuous service. In Europe and America, the expansion of navies during the 1890s, combined with growing democratization and popular literacy, almost certainly brought about major changes in institutional relationships. In Britain, recent work by cultural historians has emphasized the fact that over the last decades of the nineteenth century the public perception of the naval seaman gradually changed from a footloose 'Jack Tar' to a respectable symbol of imperial manhood.[65] Similar studies in other societies are needed to establish the extent of a global 'navalist' culture.

At present, the administrative implications of the shift to continuous service are almost completely unexamined. The same is true of changing social relationships in the twentieth century. The mass conscript armies dominate the military-institutional histories of the century. For navies, there are many memoirs and collections of reminiscences from the lower deck, but no systematic analyses from the perspectives of public opinion, governmental bodies or the navies themselves. Since 1945, navies have demanded ever more technically expert specialists in an economic environment in which their resources are strained and the expectations of living standards have been rising. This is a major lacuna, which has attracted little beyond some narratives and anecdotes.[66] The manner in which life in the naval forces is presented and negotiated and differs between forces is potentially a major theme for historical and contemporary analysis. It is a point at which

FIGURE 15 *Naval power as advertising power: Player's cigarettes metal and enamel sign, 1890s. © Trustees of the National Museum of the Royal Navy (Portsmouth).*

traditional naval, social, administrative and cultural history intersect, which has not yet been developed or exploited.

One final aspect of the social life of seamen that is also largely unexplored is related to the time when they cease to be at sea, either through force or through choice. Becoming a prisoner of war was a traumatic experience. The experience of seamen as prisoners of war has only been covered in a limited manner. There is a huge gap in our understanding of how prison systems worked across time and nations, and how the cultures determined the fate of those prisoners. American sailors in British hands during the War of Independence seem to have the best literature devoted to them.[67] Although there has been important work done on the management of prisoners of war in Britain, very little has been done on the experiences of the large numbers of French and Spanish prisoners held in Britain during the eighteenth century, or for the experiences of British seamen held prisoner by their enemies.[68] Most work focuses on the contemporary narratives of suffering rather than analyses that place those experiences into contemporary cultural expectations.

Then there is the home life of the seamen. For the seamen, prior to continuous service there was often little difference between service on a warship and on a merchantman – except that a warship was often on commission far longer than a merchantman on a single voyage, so absences were felt more keenly. Continuous service changed this by marking out the sailor at home as being in the service of the state. How this affected the social standing of individuals and families, their home lives and retirement transitions is another gap in need of serious study.

Navies and cultures

In tune with developments within historical studies generally, the social history of navies is merging into broader cultural-historical studies. Social history has tended to focus on the economic conditions of people in societies. 'New Cultural History' has encompassed the symbolic and ritual aspects of societies that shape so much of how people lived their lives.[69] A key theme is that of identity. Individual identity is bound up with status, stories, artefacts, practices and performances. In this, navies, with their well-documented procedures, hierarchies and symbols, are beginning to provide important points of contact with cultural historians. Along with the physical artefacts of uniform and living space, the Articles of War, codes of behaviour, concepts of honour, and social archetypes in literature and the other art forms have been shown to be worthy of more extensive study.[70]

Beyond the identity of individuals, the study of group cultures is evolving. National cultures have been investigated since the emergence of modern antiquarianism at the beginning of the nineteenth century. Alongside this nationalist project, there are the cultures of regions and localities, which also have a long historiography. Navies and naval events have influenced the creation of national and local identities. To date, this subject, like so much else, has been particularly studied in relation to Britain and the Royal Navy. On the other hand, the revival of local identity, such as in Brittany, can draw on powerful naval and maritime memories.[71] In Britain, the navy, as a symbol of the particular national combination of economic strength, political liberty and imperial power, has featured heavily in national history.[72] It has been an essential national symbol in rituals and the material culture of painting, sculpture, architecture and landscape gardening.[73] In 2005, during the bicentenary of Trafalgar, twenty-seven new woods, named after each of the British ships at that battle, were planted by the Woodland Trust.

The study of the cultural impact of navies on their societies is only just developing. The cultural recognition of Trafalgar is unusual even by British standards. By the early twentieth century, the navy and 'navalism' were becoming institutionally embedded in British society with the campaign to establish a National Maritime Museum (finally achieved in 1937) and societies designed to promote maritime and naval awareness. Ships, particularly the revolutionary *Dreadnought* launched in 1906, were symbols of national identity; the progress and power it represented were readily understood by the public at large.[74] However, it was not to last. After 1918, the iconic status of the ocean liner as a symbol of commercial modernity and luxury developed, and the warship as a symbol of modern power was eclipsed by the aeroplane. Modern warships, like the submarine, had a sinister rather than exciting impact on the public imagination.[75] The weakening of 'navalism' was apparent after 1918, which is a trend that has continued slowly into the twenty-first century. Navies are increasingly invisible. This is partly a physical phenomenon. Stealth is increasingly an essential aspect of naval warfare. Navies are also smaller in size, and thus less intrusive in the lives of the home society. It is also psychological, in that navies and maritime affairs feature far less in the daily lives of the public. There are fewer dockyards. Ports are removed from immediate habitation. Seafaring employs very few people. Services, transferred at the push of a button or delivered between individuals, rather than the production and the movement of goods, dominates employment. Airlines and airports dominate international travel. A person barely needs ever to see the sea to travel the globe. It is the shrinking of navies as factors in national and global culture that will have a huge impact on how navies will be studied in the future. This is a study that is already in need of serious work.

Nevertheless, the legacy of the naval dimension in national culture remains. Navies were, and still are, important elements in the creation of public propaganda through the medium of buildings, sculptures and fine art. The wealth and status of successful naval officers made them potential patrons for the merging of naval themes into the arts and literature, but to date there has been no systematic analysis of this relationship. However, the work carried out by many scholars on the public persona of Nelson and the commemoration of naval heroes in the French Revolutionary and Napoleonic Wars provides an important exception and model for future studies.

Naval themes in twentieth-century popular culture also need far more attention. Naval fiction is a thriving industry, but apart from antiquarian or commemorative collections concerning particular authors, such as C. S. Forrester or Patrick O'Brian, the genre lacks substantial analytical studies.[76] Film has fared rather better, but the subject is only in its infancy. The common inaccuracy of the cinematic portrayal of events is enough to induce apoplexy in many naval historians and cause them to dismiss film with even more disdain than novels. However, it is the medium through which most of the public absorb their perception of what navies are and what they do. Film as propaganda, or as a reflection of the relationship between the service and society, has been studied for over sixty years and is the subject of some important studies. In Britain, the abrupt decline in films featuring maritime or naval subjects after 1960, attributed to a number of factors, is an important aspect of the way in which naval history was written and consumed in the second half of the twentieth century.[77] It is interesting that a recent study on the construction of British national identity though another medium – television – had virtually nothing to say regarding the Royal Navy, sea power or maritime commerce. Indeed, the American series *Victory at Sea*, broadcast in 1952, seemed, to Churchill, to come close to writing the Royal Navy out of recent history.[78] The need for multinational studies of this type of phenomenon is glaringly apparent. How this will continue to evolve as the stock themes of the Second World War and the Cold War fade from the film-goers' direct experience is a matter that is of great importance to those who believe that public understanding of, and interest in, navies and sea power is essential in the modern world.

Modern global digital communications are also changing the way the public views and creates news. This will form part of the historical evidence from which future narratives will be constructed. Individuals who witness dramatic events can film and broadcast them over the internet almost instantaneously, thus helping to create public perceptions of world history. For navies, this raises interesting issues. Few people will ever be able to broadcast directly from naval vessels. Blockade, diplomatic suasion or even ceremonial visits are not the stuff that makes for dramatic visual content. Navies may become even more invisible than they are at present. While this is an important operational objective, it is a serious political danger. How navies will have to adapt to present their value to their political masters is going to be an interesting study for future naval historians.

Conclusion: The future of naval history?

Where does this leave the research agenda for naval history? For many people, naval history is still an exercise in imperial nostalgia, a list of dramatic, but ultimately incomprehensible, sea battles, or a device for training naval officers. Like all history, it has the potential to be little more than romantic stories or uplifting anecdotes, but this study has tried to demonstrate that naval history has, over the last century, evolved into a deeply researched and highly relevant subject. The depth of archival holdings across the world is huge and still has much to reveal. For over 300 years, navies were, and probably still are, the most complex organizations in existence, given their purpose of exerting sea control in three dimensions on a global scale in an environment that is naturally inimical to human life. Naval history has the potential to provide unparalleled perspectives and insights into societies and polities. For decades, naval historians have profited from the research and scholarship of other disciplines, and now it seems that a two-way street is beginning to develop. Naval history is contributing to the development of theory in social and historical science, which can only lead to a further enrichment of all subjects involved.

I started with a concern that the subject had become detached from its audiences. This study suggests there is some truth in this, but to a far lesser degree than I had feared. The debates and perspectives of modern naval history still very much reflect its origins. It emerged from the need for naval officers to understand how the new weaponry and ships of the late nineteenth century should be used. The requirement was to have a clear understanding of the principles underpinning sea power. Detailed historical studies of operational performance were needed. From that time to the present day, scholars of many nationalities and backgrounds have produced a remarkable output of operational studies. Naval history now has a rich, varied and growing operational historiography meeting the needs and interests of professional, scholarly and popular audiences. It continues to provoke important debates and stimulate new insights as navies continually reorientate their missions and materials to new conditions.

On the other hand, the world has changed in another way. At the beginning of the twentieth century, navies did not need to worry about the public comprehension of their role. Between 1880 and 1914, 'navalism' was strongly embedded in the political cultures of those societies engaged in active naval development. Today, this is not the case. Public understanding of naval power, how it is constructed, maintained and used, is not strong. Detailed understanding of sea power may never have been strong, as ideology stood in for detailed reasoning, but the ideological axioms that were accepted then have now all but disappeared. The disappearance of these public assumptions has not been replaced by cogent expression of the realities of sea power. Navies are not particularly good at explaining to the public the importance of maritime security or the constraints within which long-term security operates. Navies and sea power operate invisibly for most of the time, and it is easy for the public to forget that they actually exist. Navies can be seen as a collection of more or less impressive hardware with ambiguous usefulness. The operational studies that now dominate naval history are overwhelmingly concentrated on the struggle for sea control. Far less attention is given to the exercise of sea power in the maritime commons, which was and is the founding rationale for navies. Histories of the latter do not have the drama of battles or direct operational lessons, but without them, societies are unlikely to comprehend the significance of sea power in the past and present. Without this understanding, the links between navies and their host societies will be limited and the discourse between societies and their navies will be impoverished, making the negotiation of sustainable and effective roles more difficult. The need for high-quality naval history exploring the application of sea power is as important now as understanding the operational deployment of navies was at the beginning of the twentieth century. If this is so, widening of the research effort seems to be imperative.

The wider academic community has also played an important part in the production and consumption of naval history. To an extent, they have provided a link between the public and navies, stimulating a public engagement with navies as social entities. Operational histories have, generally, been of limited interest, but the importance of navies to politics, diplomacy, economics, social relations, regions and cultures has led to a steady stream of work. The size of naval archives and the breadth of contact that navies have had with all these aspects of society have helped give naval history a presence in so many different types of study. Naval history is not divorced from this academic and public audience, but has a different focus. Navies are often tangential to the main subjects under examination, but they provide insights and, in turn, are enriched by the research effort. As has been evident throughout this work, the effort and the conclusions are at present partial. There is a massive amount still to be done, and this can only be good for the future of naval history as a subject.

What seems very clear is that naval history must become more comparative, international and linked to the interests of the public at large. Massive strides have been made over the last fifty years in generating research in many nations. Conferences have been held and views exchanged. Perspectives from different nations have enriched our understanding. Continuing to explore apparent differences between navies can only add to public comprehension of the development, role and structure of naval power.

Thus, naval history is not disconnected from its audiences. In quality, quantity and variety, it has probably never been stronger. What constitutes naval history is expanding as scholars with other research agendas are using naval archives and commenting on navies. There are still very important gaps that need filling and debates to encourage from a range of perspectives. As long as the world retains an interest in globalized economics, a pattern of diplomatic engagement based on the nation-state, and a need for large-scale organizations to deliver both economic and diplomatic results, navies will remain an essential aspect of historical scholarship.

NOTES

Introduction

1. Saul, N. 'The Russian Navy, 1682-1854: Some Suggestions for Future Study'. In *New Aspects of Naval History*, edited by C. L. Symonds, 131–9, especially 132. Annapolis: US Naval Institute Press, 1981.
2. Erhman, J. *The Navy in the War of William III, 1689-1697: Its State and Direction*, xxii. Cambridge: Cambridge University Press, 1953.
3. Broeze, F., ed. *History at the Crossroads: A Critical Review of Recent Historiography*. St John's, Newfoundland: International Maritime Economic History Association, 1995; Harding, R. 'The Society for Nautical Research: Where are we now and where are we going?' *The Mariner's Mirror* 97 (2011): 10–21.
4. Hattendorf, J., ed. *The Oxford Encyclopaedia of Maritime History*. 4 vols. New York: Oxford University Press, 2007.
5. I am grateful to Professors Roger Knight and Eugene Rasor and Dr Peter Van Der Merwe for information on this point.
6. This started with the publication of Menzies, G. *1421: The Year China Discovered the World*. London: Bantam, 2003. The response was a devastating rebuttal by scholars of the subject, but this has not discouraged a continuing public appetite for such ideas, which has expanded into a supposed visit by a Chinese fleet to Venice in 1434 and a worldwide search for facts to support the hypothesis. For examples of the response, see Finlay, R. 'How Not to (Re)Write World History: Gavin Menzies and the Chinese Discovery of America'. *Journal of World History* 15, no. 2 (2004): 229–42; Prazniak, R. 'Menzies and the New Chinoiserie: Is Sinocentrism the Answer to Eurocentrism in Studies of Modernity?' *The Medieval History Journal* 13, no.1 (April 2010): 115–30.
7. Henige, D. 'The Alchemy of Turning Fiction into Truth'. *Journal of Scholarly Publishing* 39, no. 4 (2008): 354–72; Melleuish, G., K. Sheiko and S. Brown. 'Pseudo History/Weird History: Nationalism and the Internet'. *History Compass* 7, no. 6 (2009): 1484–95.
8. International Maritime Organization. http://www.imo.org/OurWork/Environment/Pages/Default.aspx (accessed 17 May 2015).
9. UNCTAD Review of Maritime Transport 2013, 6–7. (http://unctad.org/en/PublicationsLibrary/rmt2013_en.pdf. Accessed 17 May 2015).
10. Monkkenon, E. H., ed. *Engaging the Past: The Uses of History across the Social Sciences*. Durham, NC: Duke University Press, 1994: Broeze, F., ed., *History at the Crossroads*; Cannadine, D., ed. *Empire: The Sea and Global*

History; Britain's Maritime World, C.1760 – C1840. London: Palgrave, 2007; O'Hara, G. '"The Sea Is Swinging into View": Modern British Maritime History in a Globalised World'. *English Historical Review* 124, no. 510 (2009): 1109–34.

11 Black, J. *Rethinking Military History.* London: Routledge, 2004; Black, J. *Beyond the Military Revolution.* London: Palgrave, 2011.

12 Kagan, D. 'Athenian Strategy in the Peloponnesian War'. Chap. 2 In *The Making of Strategy: Rulers, States and War,* edited by Williamson Murray, Knox MacGregor and Alvin Bernstein, 24–55. Cambridge, 1994.

13 Miller, C. A. *Ship of State: The Nautical Metaphors of Thomas Jefferson,* 6–30. Lanham: University of America Press, 2003.

14 Scott, J. *When the Waves Ruled Britainnia: Geography and Political Identities, 1500-1800.* Cambridge: Cambridge University Press, 2011.

15 Gray, C. S. 'History for Strategists: British Seapower as a Relevant Past'. *Journal of Strategic Studies* 17 (1994): 7–32.

16 Wormell, D. *Sir John Seeley and the Uses of History.* Cambridge: Cambridge University Press, 2008; Kenyon, J. *The History Men.* London: Weidenfeld and Nicholson, 1983.

17 Mahan, A. T. *The Influence of Sea Power upon History, 1660-1783,* Boston: Little Brown, 1890; Mahan, A. T. *The Influence of Sea Power upon the French Revolution and Empire, 1793-1812.* 2 vols. Boston: Little Brown, 1892; Corbett, J. S. 'The Teaching of Naval and Military History'. *History* 1 (1916), 12–19; Schurman, D. *The Education of a Navy: The Development of British Naval Strategic Thought, 1867-1914.* London: Cassell, 1965; Lambert, A. *The Foundations of Naval History: John Knox Laughton, the Royal Navy and the Historical Profession.* London: Chatham Publishing, 1998; Sumida, J. *Inventing Grand Strategy and Teaching Command: The Classic Works of Alfred Thayer Mahan Reconsidered.* Baltimore: Johns Hopkins University Press, 1997.

18 Hamilton, W. M. *The Nation and the Navy: Methods and Organization of British Navalist Propaganda, 1889-1914.* New York: Garland, 1986.

19 Chickering, R. 'Patriotic Societies and German Foreign Policy, 1890-1914'. *International History Review* 1 (1979): 470–89; Ruger, J. *The Great Naval Game: Britain and Germany in the Age of Empire.* Cambridge: Cambridge University Press, 2007.

20 Murphy, H. and D. Oddy. *The Mirror of the Seas: A Centenary History of the Society for Nautical Research.* London: Society for Nautical Research, 2010.

21 Schurman, D. M. 'Historians and Britain's Imperial Strategic Stance in 1914'. In *Perspectives of Empire,* edited by J. E. Flint and G. Williams, 172–88. London, 1973.

22 Rose, J. H. *Naval History and National History.* Cambridge: Cambridge University Press, 1919; Hattendorf, J. B. 'The Study of War History at Oxford 1862-1990'. In *The Limitations of Military Power: Essays Presented to Professor Norman Gibbs on His 80th Birthday,* edited by J. B. Hattendorf and M. Murfett, 3–61. London: Macmillan, 1990.

23 Redford, D. and P. D. Grove. *The Royal Navy: A History since 1900.* London: I. B. Tauris, 2014.

24 Evans, F. 'History Versus the Rivet Counters'. *Times Higher Education Supplement* 14 (February 1986): 11.

25 Reynolds, C. G. *Command of the Sea: The History and Strategy of Maritime Empires*. New York: Morrow, 1974.

26 The classic thalassocratic thesis forms the basis of Peter Padfield's trilogy, *Maritime Supremacy and the Opening of the Western Mind: Naval Campaigns That Shaped the Modern World, 1588-1782*. London: John Murray, 1999; *Maritime Power and the Struggle for Freedom, 1788-1851*. London: John Murray, 2003; *Maritime Dominion and the Triumph of the Free World: Naval Campaigns That Shaped the Modern World, 1852-2001*. London: Murray, 2009. For a more critical perspective see Black, J. 'Naval Capability in the Early Modern Period: An Introduction', *The Mariner's Mirror* 97, no. 2 (2011): 21–32; Black, J. *Naval Power: A History of Warfare and the Sea from 1500*. London: Palgrave, 2009.

27 Erickson, A. S., L. J. Golstein and C. Lord, eds. *China Goes to Sea: Maritime Transformation in Comparative Historical Perspective*. Annapolis: Naval Institute Press, 2009.

28 Till, G. *Seapower: A Guide for the Twenty-First Century*. 3rd edn, 1–44. London: Routledge, 2013; Hattendorf, J. B. 'The United States Navy in the Twenty-First Century: Thoughts on Naval Theory, Strategic Constraints and Opportunities'. *The Mariner's Mirror* 97 (2011): 285–97; Grove, E. 'The Royal Navy in the Twenty-First Century: Does it have a Role beyond the Defence of Britain's Seas?' *The Mariner's Mirror* 97 (2010): 298–313.

29 See, for example, Callender, G. *Bibliography of Naval History*. London: Historical Association, 1924 and 1925; Manwaring, G. E. *Bibliography of British Naval History: A Biographical and Historical Guide to Printed and Manuscript Sources*. London: Routledge, 1930 (rpt. 1970): Morriss, R. *Guide to British Naval Papers in North America*. London: Mansell, 1994; Albion, R. G. *Naval and Maritime History: An Annotated Bibliography*. 4th edn. Newton Abbot: David and Charles, 1973. After Albion's death in 1983, a supplement was produced: Labaree, B. W. *A Supplement (1971-1986) to Robert G. Albion's Naval and Maritime History: An Annotated Bibliography*. Mystic: Mystic Seaport Museum, 1988. For an appreciation of Albion and the condition of public maritime history in the 1970s, see Kemble, J. H. 'Maritime History in the Age of Albion'. In *The Atlantic World of Robert G. Albion*, edited by B. W. Labaree, 3–17. Middleton: Wesleyan University Press, 1975. See also Adams, T. R. and D. W. Waters. *English Maritime Books Printed before 1801*. London: National Maritime Museum, 1995.

30 See, for example, Cock, R. and N. A. M. Rodger, eds. *A Guide to the Naval Records in the National Archives of the UK*. London: Institute of Historical Research and National Archives, 2006; Thomas, G. *Records of the Royal Marines*. London: PRO Publications, 1994.

31 For some excellent examples see the bibliographies and research guides maintained by the US Naval History and Heritage Command (http://www.history.navy.mil/search.html?q=Bibliographies. Accessed 17 May 2015); the Rasor Bibliography, hosted by the Centre for Maritime Historical Studies at the University of Exeter (http://centres.exeter.ac.uk/cmhs/rasor/index.htm. Accessed 22 April 2012). This website is highly recommended

to any researcher. Museums, national libraries, defence institutions and journals are increasingly posting indices of their own holdings or publications. However, the current estimate of the average life of a web page is approximately seventy-five days. See, for example, http://blogs.loc.gov/digitalpreservation/2011/11/the-average-lifespan-of-a-webpage/ (accessed 17 May 2015). I am grateful to Prof. Derek Law for this latter point. For an excellent example of how the web is enabling researchers to access easily previously diffuse sources of information, see The Naval Biographical Database, which provides access to details of commissioned, warrant and dockyard officers serving in the Royal Navy between 1660 and c. 1870. See http://www.navylist.org. (accessed 6 June 2015).

32 Doenhoff, R. A. von, ed. *Versatile Guardian: Research in Naval History*. Washington, DC: Howard University Press, 1979; Hattendorf, J. B., ed. *The Influence of History on Mahan*. Newport: Naval War College Press, 1991: Hattendorf, J. B. and J. Goldrick, eds. *Mahan Is Not Enough: The Proceedings of a Conference on the Works of Sir Julian Corbett and Admiral Sir Herbert Richmond*. Vol. 10, Historical Monographs Series. Newport: Naval War College Press, 1993.

33 Hattendorf, J. B., ed. *Ubi Sumus? The State of Naval and Maritime History*. Newport: Naval War College Press, 1994.

34 Hattendorf, J. B., ed. *Doing Naval History: Essays Towards Improvement*. Newport: Naval War College Press, 1995.

35 Morillo, S. and M. F. Pavkovic. *What Is Military History?* Cambridge: Polity, 2006; Biddle, T. D. and R. M. Citino. 'The Role of Military History in the Contemporary Academy'. *Society for Military History*, 2015. http://www.smh-hq.org/docs/SMHWhitePaper.pdf (accessed 17 May 2015).

Chapter 1

1 Harper, L. A. *The English Navigation Laws*. New York: Columbia University Press, 1939.

2 Seeley, J. *The Expansion of England*, 1–19. London: Macmillan, 1907; Burroughs, P. 'John Robbert Seeley and British Imperial History'. *Journal of Imperial and Commonwealth History* 1 (1973): 191–211; Wormell, D. *Sir John Seeley and the Uses of History*. Cambridge: Cambridge University Press, 2008.

3 Seeley, *Expansion*, 153–63.

4 Even Halford Mackinder, who saw the future dominated by continental power blocks rather than trading networks, recognized that the British imperial network might eventually convert the 'British navy' into the 'Navy of the Britains' and preserve its position among the great powers. See Mackinder, H. J. *Britain and the British Seas*, 358. London: William Heinemann, 1902.

5 Semmel, B. *Liberalism and Naval Strategy: Ideology, Interest, and Sea Power During the Pax Britannica*. London: Allen and Unwin, 1986; Kennedy, P. *Strategy and Diplomacy, 1870-1945*, 43–85. London: Fontana, 1984.

6 Mahan, A. T. *The Influence of Sea Power Upon the French Revolution and Empire, 1793-1812*. 2 vols. Boston: Little Brown, 1892.

7 Mahan, A. T. *The Influence of Sea Power Upon History, 1660-1763*, 209. Boston: Little Brown, 1890.

8 Webb, P. L. C. 'The Rebuilding and Repair of the Fleet 1783-1793'. *Bulletin of the Institute of Hisorical Research* 50 (1977): 194–209.

9 Acerra, M. and A. Zysberg. *L'essor des Marines de Guerres Europennes (Vers 1680 – Vers 1790)*. Paris: SEDES, 1997; Acerra, M. and J. Meyer, eds. *Marines et Revolution*. Rennes: Editions Ouest-France, 1988.

10 Cormack, W. S. *Revolution and Political Conflict in the French Navy, 1789-1794*. Cambridge: Cambridge University Press, 1995.

11 Knight, R. *Britain against Napoleon: The Organization of Victory, 1793-1815*. London: Allen Lane, 2013.

12 Emsley, C. *British Society and the French Wars, 1793-1815*. London: Macmillan, 1979; Colley, L. 'The Reach of the State the Appeal of the Nation: Mass Arming and Political Culture in the Napoleonic Wars'. In *An Imperial State at War: Britain from 1689 to 1815*, edited by L. Stone, 165–84. London: Routledge, 1994.

13 Lambert, A. 'The Magic of Trafalgar: The Nineteenth Century Legacy'. In *Trafalgar in History: A Battle and Its Afterlife*, edited by D. Cannadine, 155–74. Basingstoke: Palgrave, 2006; Lambert, A. D. 'The Construction of Naval History 1815–1914'. *The Mariner's Mirror* 97, no. 1 (2011): 207–24.

14 Ronald, D. A. B. 'The Symbolic Power of Youth as Represented in the *Naval Chronicle* (1799-1818)'. Unpublished PhD, University of Exeter, 2011.

15 James, W. *The Naval History of Great Britain during the French Revolutionary and Napoleonic Wars*. 6 vols. London: Conway Maritime Press (reprint 1990).

16 Arthur, B. *How Britain Won the War of 1812: The Royal Navy's Blockade of the United States, 1812-1815*. Woodbridge: Boydell Press, 2011.

17 Holland-Rose, J. *Naval History and National History*. Cambridge: Cambridge University Press, 1919; Breemer, J. S. 'The Burden of Trafalgar: Decisive Battle and Naval Strategic Expectations on the Eve of World War I'. *Journal of Strategic Studies* 17 (1994): 33–62.

18 Duffy, M. *Soldiers, Sugar and Seapower: The British Expeditions to the West Indies and the War against Revolutionary France*. Oxford: Clarendon Press, 1987.

19 Warner, O. *The Glorious First of June*. London: Batsford, 1961; Willis, S. B. A. *The Glorious First of June: The First Battle in the Reign of Terror*. London: Quercus, 2012.

20 Saxby, R. 'The Blockade of Brest in the French Revolutionary War'. *The Mariner's Mirror* 78, no. 1 (1992): 25–35; Morriss, R. and D. Saxby, eds. *The Channel Fleet and the Blockade of Brest, 1793-1801*. London: Navy Records Society, 2001.

21 Lloyd, C. *St Vincent and Camperdown*. London: Batsford, 1963; Mackesy, P. *Statesmen at War: The Strategy of Overthrow, 1798-1799*, 200–2. London: Longman, 1974.

22 Warner, O. *Nelson's Battles*, 27–102. Newton Abbot: David and Charles, 1971; Lavery, B. *Nelson and the Nile: The Naval War against Bonaparte 1798*. London: Chatham Publishing, 1998.

23 Mackesy, P. *British Victory in Egypt 1801: The End of Napoleon's Conquest*. London: Routledge, 1995.

24 Desbriere, E. *1793-1805: Projets Et Tentatives De Debarquement Aux Iles Brittaniques*. 4 vols. Paris: R. Chapelot, 1900–2.

25 Feldbaek, O. *The Battle of Copenhagen, 1801*. Barnsley: Leo Cooper, 2002.

26 Martel, G. 'The Meaning of Power: Rethinking the Decline and Fall of Great Britain'. *The International History Review* 13, no. 4 (1991): 662–94.

27 Sanderson, M. W. B. 'English Naval Strategy and Maritime Trade in the Caribbean 1793-1802'. PhD, London, 1968; Mackesy, P. *War without Victory; the Downfall of Pitt, 1799-1802*. Oxford: Clarendon Press, 1984; Duffy, *Soldiers, Sugar and Seapower*.

28 Ingram, E. 'The Failure of British Sea Power in the War of the Second Coalition, 1798-1801'. In *In Defence of British India: Great Britain and the Middle East, 1775-1842*, edited by E. Ingram, 67–77. London: Frank Cass, 1984; Ingram, E. 'Illusions of Victory: The Nile, Copenhagen and Trafalgar Revisited'. *Military Affairs* 48, no. 3 (1984): 140–3.

29 Mahan, *The Influence of Seapower on History*, 209.

30 Beerbuhl, M. S. 'Supplying the Belligerent Countries: Transnational Trading Networks during the Napoleonic Wars'. In *The Contractor State and Its Implications, 1659-1815*, edited by R. Harding and S. Sobles Ferri, 21–34. Las Palmas: Universidad de las Palmas de Gran Canaria, 2012.

31 Mackesy, P. *The War in the Mediterranean, 1803-1810*. London: Longman Green, 1957.

32 Parkinson, C. N. *War in the Eastern Seas, 1793-1815*. London: George Allen and Unwin, 1954; Taylor, S. *Storm and Conquest: The Battle for the Indian Ocean, 1809*. London: Faber and Faber, 2007; Ward, P. *British Naval Power in the East, 1794-1805: The Command of Admiral Peter Rainier*. Woodbridge: Boydell Press, 2013.

33 Ryan, A. N. 'The Defence of British Trade with the Baltic, 1808-1813'. *The English Historical Review* 74, no. 292 (1959): 443–66; Ryan, A. N. 'Trade with the Enemy in the Scandanavian and Baltic Ports During the Napoleonic War: For and Against'. *Transactions of the Royal Historical Society* 12 (1961): 123–40; Voelcker, T. *Admiral Saumarez Versus Napoleon: The Baltic, 1807-1812*. Woodbridge: Boydell Press, 2009; Davey, J. *The Transformation of British Naval Strategy: Seapower and Supply in Northern Europe, 1808-1812*. Woodbridge: Boydell Press, 2012.

34 Crouzet, F. 'War, Blockade and Economic Change in Europe, 1792-1815'. *Journal of Economic History* 24 (1964): 567–90.

35 Mahan, A. T. *The Influence of Sea Power Upon the French Revolution and Empire*, ii. 179.

36 Coutau-Bégarie, H. 'France'. In *Ubi Sumus? The State of Naval and Maritime History*, edited by J. B. Hattendorf, 115–136, especially 115–16. Newport, RI: Naval War College Press, 1994.

37 Crowhurst, P. *The Defence of British Trade, 1689-1815*. Folkstone: Dawson, 1977; Crowhurst, P. *The French War on Trade: Privateering, 1793-1815*. Aldershot: Scholar Press, 1989; Tracy, N., ed. *Sea Power and the Control of Trade: Belligerent Rights from the Russian War to the Beira Patrol, 1854-1970*. Vol. 149. London: Navy Records Society, 2005.

38 Ryan, A. N. 'The Navy at Copenhagen in 1807'. *The Mariner's Mirror* 39 (1953), no. 3: 201–10; Munch-Petersen, T. *Defying Napoleon: How Britain Bombarded Copenhagen and Seized the Danish Fleet in 1807*. Stroud: Sutton Publishing, 2007.

39 Bond, G. C. *The Grand Expedition: The British Invasion of Holland in 1809*. Athens, Georgia: University of Georgia Press, 1979.

40 Sondhaus, L. 'Napoleon's Shipbuilding Programme at Venice and the Struggle for Mastery in the Adriatic, 1806-1814'. *Journal of Military History* 53 (1989): 349–62; Masson, P. and J. Muracciole. *Napoleon et La Marine*, 296–306. Paris: J. Peyronnet & Cie, 1968; Gillet, J-C. *La Marine Imperiale; Le Grand Reve De Napoleon*. St Denis la Plaine: Bernard Giovanangeli, 2010.

41 Hall, C. D. *Wellington's Navy: Sea Power and the Peninsula War, 1807-1814*. London: Chatham Publishing, 2004.

42 Mahan, A. T. *Sea Power in Its Relations to the War of 1812*. 2 vols, i, 275. London: Sampson, Low, Marston, 1905.

43 Flayhart, W. H. *Counterpoint to Trafalgar: The Anglo-Russian Invasion of Naples, 1805-1806*. Columbia: University of South Carolina Press, 1992; Mackesy, P. *British Victory in Egypt 1801;* Hall, *Wellington's Navy;* Ward, P. *British Naval Power in the East, 1794-1805*.

44 Fletcher, I. *The Waters of Oblivion: The British Invasion of the Rio De La Plata, 1806-7*. Tunbridge Wells: Spellmount, 1991; Grainger, J. D., ed. *The Royal Navy in the River Plate, 1806-1807*. London: Navy Records Society, 1996.

45 Palmer, M. A. *Stoddert's War: Naval Operations During the Quasi-War with France, 1798-1801*. Columbia: University of South Carolina Press, 1987.

46 Symonds, C. L. *Navalists and Antinavalists: The Naval Policy Debate in the United States, 1785-1827*, 155–68. Newark: University of Delaware Press, 1980; Tucker, S. C. and T. R. Frank. *Injured Honor: The Chesapeake-Leopard Affair June 22, 1807*. Annapolis: Naval Institute Press, 1996.

47 Bickham, T. *The Weight of Vengeance: The United States, the British Empire and the War of 1812*. Oxford: Oxford University Press, 2012.

48 Chapelle, H. I. *The History of the American Sailing Navy: Their Ships and Their Development*, 243–311. New York: W. W. Norton, 1949; Valle, J. E. 'The Navy's Battle Doctrine in the War of 1812'. *American Neptune* 44 (1984): 171–8; Malcomson, R. *Warships of the Great Lakes, 1754-1834*, 63–133. London: Chatham Publishing, 2001; Canney, D. L. *Sailing Warships of the US Navy*. London: Chatham, 2001; McCranie, K. D. *Utmost Gallantry: The US and Royal Navies at Sea in the War of 1812*. Annapolis: Naval Institute Press, 2011.

49 Arthur, B. *How Britain Won the War of 1812: The Royal Navy's Blockade of the United States, 1812-1815*. Woodbridge: Boydell Press, 2011; Lambert, A.

The Challenge: Britain against America in the Naval War of 1812. London: Faber, 2012.

50   Tucker, S. C. *The Jeffersonian Gunboat Navy*. Columbia: University of South Carolina Press, 1993, 171–8.

51   Shoemaker, R. L. 'Diplomacy from the Quarterdeck: The US Navy in the Caribbean, 1815-1830'. In *Changing Interpretations and New Sources in Naval History*, edited by R. W. Love, 169–79. New York: Garland, 1980.

52   Symonds, *Navalists and Antinavalists*, 235; Schroeder, J. H. *Shaping a Maritime Empire: The Commercial and Diplomatic Role of the American Navy, 1829-1861*. Westport, CT: Greenwood, 1985.

53   Sherwig, J. M. *Guineas and Gunpowder: British Foreign Aid in the Wars with France, 1793-1815*, 315–44. Cambridge, MA: Harvard University Press, 1969.

54   Gorshkov, S. G. *The Sea Power of the State*, 1–16. Malabar, FL: Robert E. Krieger, 1983; Erickson, A. S. and L. J. Goldstein. 'Chinese Perspectives on Maritime Transformation'. In *China Goes to Sea: Maritime Transformation in Comparative Historical Perspective*, edited by A. S. Erickson, L. J. Goldstein and C. Lord, xiii–xxviii, Annapolis: Naval Institute Press, 2009

55   Jenks, T. *Naval Engagements: Patriotism, Cultural Politics and the Royal Navy, 1793-1815*. Oxford: Oxford University Press, 2006; Hamilton, C. I. 'Naval Hagiography and the Victorian Hero'. *The Historical Journal* 23, no. 2 (1980): 381–98.

56   Cowie, L. W. *Lord Nelson, 1758-1805: A Bibliography*. London: Meckler, 1990.

57   Some of the best are White, C. *Nelson: The Admiral*. Stroud: Sutton, 2005; Lambert, A. *Nelson: Britannia's God of War*. London: Faber, 2004; Knight, R. *The Pursuit of Victory: The Life and Achievement of Horatio Nelson*. London: Allen Lane, 2005; Coleman, T. *Nelson: The Man and the Legend*. London: Bloomsbury, 2002.

58   Czisnik, M. 'Nelson and the Nile: The Creation of Admiral Nelson's Public Image', *The Mariner's Mirror* 88 (2002): 41–60; Jenks, J. 'Contesting the Hero: The Funeral of Admiral Lord Nelson'. *Journal of British Studies* 39 (2000): 423–53; Yarrington, A. 'Nelson the Citizen Hero: State and Public Patronage of Monumental Sculpture'. *Art History* 6 (1983): 315–29. See also *The Trafalgar Chronicle: Yearbook of the 1805 Club* 15 (2005); *The Nelson Despatch*, December 2005; Cannadine, D., ed. *Admiral Lord Nelson: Context and Legacy*. London: Palgrave, 2005.

59   The first substantial collection being N. Nicholas's *The Despatches and Letters of Lord Nelson*. 6 vols. London: Colburn, 1844–7, republished by Chatham Publishing in 2005. Other collections have appeared periodically since then. A major project was carried out leading up to the bicentenary to find and publish other previously unpublished letters. See White, C., ed. *Nelson: The New Letters*. Woodbridge: Boydell Press, 2005.

60   Dashing commanders have been a particular favourite, particularly Cochrane (the model for Forester's Hornblower and O'Brian's Aubrey). Grimble, I. *The Sea Wolf: The Life of Admiral Cochrane*. London: Blond and Briggs, 1978; Thomas, D. *Cochrane: Britannia's Sea Wolf*. London: Cassell, 1978; Harvey, R. *Cochrane: The Life and Exploits of a Fighting Captain*. London:

Constable, 2000; Vale, B. *The Audacious Admiral Cochrane: The True Life of a Naval Legend*. London: Brassey, 2004. Others include Wareham, T. *Frigate Commander*. Barnsley: Pen and Sword, 2004. This is a study of Graham Moore, one of the star frigate captains; Shankland, P. *Beware of Heroes: Admiral Sir Sidney Smith's War against Napoleon*. London: William Kimber, 1975; Padfield, P. *Broke and the Shannon*. London: Hodder and Stoughton, 1968; Krajeski, P. C. *In the Shadow of Nelson: The Naval Leadership of Admiral Sir Charles Cotton, 1753-1812*. Westport: Greenwood Press, 2000; McCranie, K. D. *Admiral Lord Keith and the Naval War against Napoleon*. Gainsville: University of Florida Press, 2006; Gordon, I. *Admiral of the Blue: The Life and Times of Admiral John Child Purvis, 1747-1825*. Barnsley: Pen and Sword, 2005. Short biographies of a range of officers appear in Le Fevre, P. and R. Harding. *British Admirals of the Napoleonic Wars: The Contemporaries of Nelson*. London: Chatham Publishing, 2005. Frigate captains particularly attracted public attention. The demographic details of the British frigate captains are analysed in Wareham, T. *The Star Captains: Frigate Command in the Napoleonic Wars*. London: Chatham Publishing, 2001. There are biographical studies of officers in other navies, which include Dupont, M. *L'Amiral Willaumez*. Paris: Tallandier, 1987; Guimerá, A. 'Gravina and the Naval Leadership of his Day'. *Journal for Maritime Research* 7 (2005): 44–69; Monaque, R. 'Latouche-Tréville: The Admiral Who Defied Nelson'. *The Mariner's Mirror* 86, no. 3 (2000): 272–84.

61 Cannadine, D., ed. *Trafalgar in History: A Battle and Its Afterlife*. Basingstoke: Palgrave Macmillan, 2006; Hattendorf, J. B. 'Whither with Nelson and Trafalgar? A Review Article on the Bicentenary Scholarship of the Nelson Era'. *Journal for Maritime Research* 9, no. 1 (2007): 37–66; Quirk, R. J. *Literature as Introspection: Spain Confronts Trafalgar*. New York: Peter Lang, 1998.

62 Corbett, J. S. *The Campaign of Trafalgar*. 2 vols. London: Longman Green, 1919.

63 Board of Admiralty. *Report of a Committee Appointed by the Admiralty to Examine & Consider the Evidence Relating to the Tactics Employed by Nelson at the Battle of Trafalgar*. London: HMSO, 1913 (reprint 2006).

64 Clayton, T. and P. Craig. *Trafalgar: The Men, the Battle and the Storm*. London: Hodder and Stoughton, 2004; Warwick, P. *Voices from the Battle of Trafalgar*. Newton Abbot: David and Charles, 2005; Nicholson, A. *Men of Honour: Trafalgar and the Making of the English Hero*. London: Harper Collins, 2005. See also Blake, N. *Steering to Glory: A Day in the Life of a Ship of the Line*. London: Chatham Publishing, 2005.

65 Saul, N. E. 'The Impact of the Napoleonic Wars upon Russian Priorities on Naval Development'. In *New Interpretations in Naval History*, edited by W. B. Cogar, 45–60. Shewsbury: Tri-Service Press, 1989; Saul, N. *Russia and the Mediterranean, 1797-1807*. Chicago: University of Chicago Press, 1970; Daly, J. C. K. *Russian Seapower and 'The Eastern Question, 1827-41'*. London: Macmillan, 1991. Anglo-Dutch naval relations post-1815 are briefly covered in van Sas, N. 'Between the Devil and the Deep Blue Sea: The Logic of Neutrality'. In *Colonial Empires Compared: Britain and the Netherlands, 1750-1850*, edited by B. Moore and H. van Nierop, 33–44. Aldershot: Ashgate,

2003. Aspects of Anglo-French naval diplomacy in this period can be found in some of the essays in Freeman, E., ed. *Les Empires en Guerre et Paix, 1793-1860*. Vincennes: Service Historique de la Marine, 1990; Haudrere, P. 'Francais Et Anglais Aux Mascareignes Apres Le Traite De Paris, 1814-1823'. In *Les Empires En Guerre Et Paix, 1793-1860: II*es *Journees Franco-Anglaises D'histoire de la Marine*, edited by E. Freeman, 59–69. Vincennes: Service Historique de la Marine, 1990; Crimmin, P. K. 'Great Britain and France in the Levant, 1793-1827: From Naval Conflict to Co-Operation'. In *Les Empires En Guerre et Paix, 1793-1860: IIes Journees Franco-Anglaises de la Marine*, edited by E. Freeman, 71–84. Vincennes: Service Historique de la Marine, 1990. The revival and development of the Neapolitan navy can be followed in Radogna, L. *Storia della Marina Militare delle Due Sicilie*, 78–144. Milan: Muria, 1978.

66 Bartlett, C. J. *Great Britain and Sea Power, 1815-1853*. Oxford: Oxford University Press, 1963.

67 The most accessible overview of the naval affairs in Latin America is Scheina, R. L. *Latin America: A Naval History, 1810-1987*. Annapolis: Naval Institute Press, 1987, but see also the works of Brian Vale, especially Vale, B. *A War Betwixt Englishmen: Brazil against Argentina on the River Plate, 1825-1830*. London: I. B. Tauris, 2000.

68 Cable, J. *Navies in a Violent Peace*. London: Macmillan, 1989; Cable, J. *Gunboat Diplomacy, 1919-1991*. Studies in International Security. 3rd edn. London, 1994. See also Murfett, M. H. 'Gunboat Diplomacy: Outmoded or Back in Vogue?' In *The Changing Face of Maritime Power*, edited by A. Dorman, M. L. Smith and M. R. H. Uttley, 81–93. Basingstoke: Macmillan, 1999.

69 Matzke, R. B. *Deterrence through Strength: British Naval Power and Foreign Policy under Pax Britannica*. Lincoln, Nebraska: University of Nebraska Press, 2011. The broadest overview of the connection between British diplomacy and naval power in the first half of the nineteenth century is still Bartlett's *Great Britain and Sea Power, 1815-1853*. However, other interesting studies are: Hattendorf, J. B. 'The Bombardment of Acre, 1840: A Case Study in the Use of Naval Force for Deterrence'. In *Les Empires En Guerre Et Paix, 1793-1860: II*es *Journees Franco-Anglaises D'histoire de la Marine*, edited by E. Freeman, 205–26. Vincennes: Service Historique de la Marine, 1990; Lambert, A. 'The Royal Navy, 1856-1914: Deterrence and the Strategy of World Power'. In *Navies and Global Defense: Theories and Strategy*, edited by N. Keith and E. J. Errington, 69–92. Westport, CT: Praeger, 1995. See also Lambert, A. *The Last Sailing Battlefleet: Maintaining Naval Mastery, 1815-1850*, 1–12. London: Conway, 1991.

70 Freedman, L. *Deterrence*, 26–31. Cambridge: Polity, 2004.

71 Bartlett, *Great Britain and Sea Power*, 104–25.

72 Hamilton, C. I. *Anglo-French Naval Rivalry, 1840-1870*. Oxford: Clarendon Press, 1993.

73 Sondhaus, L. *Naval Warfare, 1815-1914*, 18–23. London: Routledge, 2001.

74 Battesti, M. *La Marine de Napoleon III: Une Politique Navale*. 2 vols, i, 24. Vincennes: Service Historique de la Marine, 1997. This essential study of the

French imperial navy covers the pre-history, technology, administration and operations between 1850 and 1871.

75 Sondhaus, *Naval Warfare, 1815-1914*, 32–45.

76 Greenhill, B. and A. Giffard. *Steam, Politics and Patronage: The Transformation of the Royal Navy, 1815-54*, 101–31. London: Conway Maritime Press, 1994; Clowes, W. L., ed. *The Royal Navy: A History from the Earliest Times to 1900*. 7 vols, vii, 157–74. London: Sampson, Low, Marston, 1898.

77 Battesti, *La Marine de Napoleon III*, i, 25.

78 Lambert, A. 'Responding to the Nineteenth Century: The Royal Navy and the Introduction of the Screw Propeller'. *History of Technology* 21 (1997): 1–28.

79 Tredrea, J. and E. Sozaev. *Russian Warships of the Age of Sail, 1696-1860: Design, Construction, Careers and Fates*, 17. Barnsley: Seaforth Publishing, 2010; Lambert, A., ed. *Steam, Steel and Shellfire: The Steam Warship, 1815-1905*, 50–5. London: Conway Maritime Press, 1992.

80 For an excellent collection of essays devoted to the decisive technological shift from sail to steam, see the transactions of *The First International Colloquium in Naval History, 24th-28th August 1987*. Athens: International Commission of Military History, 1988.

81 In 1898, F. T. Jane produced the first edition of *All the World's Fighting Ships* as a compendium on contemporary navies. *Jane's Fighting Ships*, along with other publications on defence technology from that publisher, have now become a standard reference point to support contemporary naval strategists and an essential source for naval historians. Since the 1970s, publishers like Conway and, later, Seaforth have provided high-quality reference works for a more popular audience. See, for example, Lambert, A. *Battleships in Transition: The Creation of the Steam Battlefleet, 1815-1860*. London: Conway Maritime Press, 1984.

82 Lambert, A. D., ed. *Steam, Steel and Shellfire: The Steam Warship, 1815-1905*, 47–60. London: Conway Maritime Press, 1992.

83 Beeler, J. F. *Birth of the Battleship: British Capital Ship Design, 1870-1881*, 65–86. London: Chatham Publishing, 2001.

84 Lyon, D. 'Underwater Warfare and the Torpedo Boat'. In *Steam, Steel and Shellfire: The Steam Warship, 1815-1905*, edited by R. Gardiner, 134–45. London: Conway Maritime Press, 1992; Lyon, D. *The First Destroyers*. London: Chatham Publishing, 1996; Briggs, M. 'Innovation and the Mid-Victorian Royal Navy: The Case of the Whitehead Torpedo'. *The Mariner's Mirror* 88, no. 4 (2002): 447–55.

85 Friedman, N. *Submarine: Design and Development*. London: Conway, 1984 gives the overarching principles of submarine development in historical context. For the introduction of the submarine, see Wilson, M. 'Early Submarines'. In R. Gardiner, *Steam, Steel and Shellfire*, 147–57. See also Masson, H. Le. *Les Sous-Marins Francais des Origins (1863) à Nos Jours*. Paris: Editions de la Cité, 1980; Rössler, E. *The U Boat*. London: Arms and Armour Press, 1981; Alden, J. D. *The Fleet Submarines of the US Navy: A*

Design and Construction History. London: Arms and Armour Press, 1979; Lambert, N. *The Submarine Service, 1900-1918*. London: Navy Records Society, 2001.

86 Lambert, A. *The Crimean War: British Grand Strategy, 1853-1856*. 1st edn, 230–44. Manchester: Manchester University Press, 1990; Lambert, A. 'The Crimean War Blockade: 1854-56'. In *Naval Blockades and Seapower: Strategies and Counter-Strategies, 1805-2005*, edited by B. A. Elleman and S. C. M. Paine, 46–59. London: Routledge, 2006: Merrill, J. M. 'British-French Amphibious Operations in the Sea of Azov, 1855'. *Military Affairs* 20, no. 1 (1956): 16–27; Preston, A. and J. Major. *Send a Gunboat: The Victorian Navy and Supremacy at Sea, 1854-1904*. 2nd edn, 18–35. London: Conway Maritime Press, 2007.

87 Manuele, P. *Il Piemonte Sul Mare: La Marina Sabauda dal Mediovvo All'unita D'italia*, 207–20. Cueno: L'Arciere, 1997; Battesti, *La Marine de Napoleon III*, ii, 798–812.

88 Sondhaus, L. *The Habsburg Empire and the Sea: Austrian Naval Policy, 1799-1866*, 254–5. West Lafayette, IN: Purdue University Press, 1989.

89 Hough, R. *Admirals in Collision*. London: White Lion, 1959.

90 The fullest narrative is still Jones, V.C. *The Civil War at Sea*. 3 vols. New York: Holt, 1960–2. However, for modern analyses see McPherson, J. M. *War on the Waters: The Union and Confederate Navies, 1861-1865*. Chapel Hill: The University of North Carolina Press, 2012; Symonds, C. L. *The Civil War at Sea*. New York: Oxford University Press, 2012. See also Canney, D. L. *Lincoln's Navy: The Ships, Men and Organization, 1861-65*. London: Conway Maritime Press, 1998; Still, W. N. Jr. *The Confederate Navy: The Ships, Men and Organization, 1861-65*. London: Conway Maritime Press, 1997; Luraghi, R. *A History of the Confederate Navy*, translated by P. E. Coletta. Annapolis: Naval Institute Press, 1996.

91 Stoker, D. *The Grand Design: Strategy and the US Civil War*, 36–43. New York: Oxford University Press, 2010.

92 Davis, W. C. *Duel between the First Ironclads*. New York: Doubleday, 1975; Roberts, W. H. *Civil War Ironclads: The US Navy and Industrial Mobilisation*. Baltimore: Johns Hopkins University Press, 2002.

93 Wise, S. R. *Lifeline of the Confederacy: Blockade Running During the Civil War*. Columbia: University of South Carolina Press, 1989.

94 Lemnitzer, J. M. *Power, Law and the End of Privateering*, 115–72. London: Palgrave Macmillan, 2014.

95 Hearn, C. H. *Gray Raiders of the Sea: How Eight Confederate Warships Destroyed the Union's High Seas Commerce*, xv. Camden, ME: International Maritime Publishing, 1992.

96 Olivier, D. H. *German Naval Strategy 1856-1888: Forerunners of Tirpitz*, 2. London: Frank Cass, 2004.

97 Baer, G. W. *One Hundred Years of Sea Power: The U.S. Navy, 1890-1990*, 10. Stanford: Stanford University Press, 1994.

98 Perry, M. F. *Infernal Machines: The Story of Confederate Submarine and Mine Warfare*, 4, 199–201. Baton Rouge: Louisiana State University Press, 1965.

99 Taaffe, S. *Commanding Lincoln's Navy: Union Naval Leadership During the Civil War*, 91–117, 197–210. Annapolis: Naval Institute Press, 2009.

100 Fuller, H. J. *Clad in Iron: The American Civil War and the Challenge of British Naval Power*. Westport, CT: Praeger, 2008.

101 Luvaas, J. *The Military Legacy of the Civil War: The European Inheritance*. 2nd edn, 40–1, 67–8. Lawrence, KS: University Press Kansas, 1988.

102 Carroll, F. M. 'Diplomats and the Civil War at Sea'. *Canadian Review of American Studies* 40 (2010): 117–30; Meril, F. J. *Great Britain and the Confederate Navy, 1861-1865*. Bloomington: Indiana University Press, 1970; Meril, F. J. *The Alabama, British Neutrality and the American Civil War*. Bloomington: Indiana University Press, 2004; Bernath, S. L. *Squall Across the Atlantic: American Civil War Prize Cases and Diplomacy*. Berkeley: University of California Press, 1970; Lambert, A. 'Australia, the Trent crisis of 1861 and the strategy of imperial defence'. In *Southern Trident: Strategy, History and the Rise of Australian Naval Power*, edited by D. Stevens and J. Reeve, 99–118. Crow's Nest, NSW: Allen and Unwin, 2001. For a view that explores the balance between economic and political reasons for British neutrality, putting the issue of slavery at the centre, see Steele, B. J. 'Ontological Security and the Power of Self-Identity: British Neutrality and the American Civil War'. *Review of International Studies* 31 (2005): 519–40.

103 Aston, G. G. *Letters on Amphibious Wars*, 1–86. London: Murray, 1911.

104 Sondhaus, L. *Navies in Modern World History*, 141–70. London: Reaktion Books, 2004.

105 Clayton, G. D. *Britain and the Eastern Question: Missolonghi to Gallipoli*, 114–15. London: University of London Press, 1971.

106 Sondhaus, *Naval Warfare, 1815-1914*, 122–6; Langensiepen, B. and A. Güleryüz. *The Ottoman Steam Navy, 1828-1923*, translated by J. Cooper, 5–7. Annapolis: Naval Institute Press, 1995.

107 Allen, M. 'The British Mediterranean Squadron during the Great Eastern Crisis of 1876-9'. *The Mariner's Mirror* 85, no. 1 (1999): 53–67.

108 Mitchell, D. W. *A History of Russian and Soviet Sea Power*, 190. London: Andre Deutsch, 1974.

109 The development of the Russian fleet still needs to be explored more fully, particularly the political decision-making and the administrative infrastructure. Most works focus on the ships. Apart from Donald Mitchell, accessible introductions include Watts, A. J. *The Imperial Russian Navy*. London: Arms and Armour Press, 1990.

110 Callwell, C. E. *The Effect of Maritime Command on Land Operations since Waterloo*, 199, 205. Edinburgh: Blackwood, 1907.

111 Wright, R. N. J. *The Chinese Steam Navy 1862-1945*, 33–84. London: Chatham Publishing, 2000; Evans, D. C. and M. R. Peattie. *Kaigun: Strategy,*

Tactics and Technology in the Imperial Japanese Navy, 1887-1941, 1–31. Annapolis: Naval Institute Press, 1997.

112 Lone, S. *Japan's First Modern War: Army and Society in the Conflict with China, 1894-95*. Basingstoke: Macmillan, 1994; Elleman, B. A. 'Naval Warfare and the Refraction of China's Self-Strengthening Reforms into Scientific and Technological Failure, 1865-1895'. *Modern Asian Studies* 38 (2004): 283–326.

113 Wright, *The Chinese Steam Navy*, 85–105; Evans and Peattie, *Kaigun*, 33–51.

114 Rodriguez Gonzalez, A. R. *El Desastre Naval de 1898*, 22. Madrid: Arco/Libros, 1997.

115 Rodriguez Gonzalez, A. R. *Politica Naval de la Restauracion (1875-1898)*, 149–215. Madrid: Editorial San Martin, 1988; Pérez-Llorca, J. *1898: La Estrategia Del Desastre*. Madrid: SILEX, 1998.

116 Rentfrow, J. A. *Home Squadron: The U.S. Navy on the North Atlantic Station*, 136–47. Annapolis: Naval Institute Press, 2014.

117 Rodriguez Gonzalez, *El Desastre Naval de 1898*.

118 Evans and Peattie, *Kaigun*, 91–132; Kowner, R. 'The Impact of the War on Naval Warfare'. In *The Impact of the Russo-Japanese War*, edited by R. Kowner, 269–89. London: Routledge, 2007; Towle, P. 'The Evaluation of the Experience of the Russo-Japanese War'. In *Technical Change and British Naval Policy, 1860-1939*, edited by B. Ranft, 65–79. London: Hodder and Stoughton, 1977.

119 Lambert, 'The Royal Navy, 1856-1914'.

120 Lambert, A. D. 'Politics, Technology and Policy Making 1859-1865: Palmerston, Gladstone and the Management of the Ironclad Naval Race'. *Northern Mariner* 8, no. 3 (1998): 9–38.

121 The best study of naval power ashore in this period is Brookes, R. *The Long Arm of Empire: Naval Brigades from the Crimea to the Boxer Rebellion*. London: Constable, 1999. See also Bleby, A. *The Victorian Naval Brigades*. Caithness: Whittles Publishing, 2006. For a longer chronological perspective, see Hore, P., ed. *Seapower Ashore: 200 Years of Royal Navy Operations on land*. London: Chatham Publishing, 2001. The role of French naval power in her imperial expansion is presented in Battesti, M. *La Marine au XIXe Siècle: Interventions extérieures et colonies*. Paris: Du May, 1993. See also a short, well-illustrated narrative: Olender, P. *Sino-French Naval War, 1884-1885*. Petersfield: Mushroom Model Publications, 2012.

122 Lambert, A. 'The Royal Navy, 1856-1914: Deterrence and the Strategy of World Power'. In *Navies and Global Defense: Theories and Strategy*, edited by N. Keith and E. J. Errington, 69–92. Westport, CT: Praeger, 1995; Beeler, J. 'A One Power Standard? Great Britain and the Balance of Naval Power, 1860-1880'. *Journal of Strategic Studies* 15 (1992): 548–72.

123 The most accessible narrative of the period in English is still T. Ropp. *The Development of a Modern Navy: French Naval Policy, 1871-1904*, edited by S. S. Roberts. Annapolis: Naval Institute Press, 1987. The work originates in

a doctoral thesis of 1937. However, Walser, R. *France's Search for a Battle Fleet: Naval Policy and Naval Power, 1898-1914*. New York: Garland, 1992 provides a much more detailed analysis of the politics underpinning naval policy as the credibility of the *Jeune Ecole* disintegrated. See also Masson, P. 'La Pensée Navale Française de 1871 à 1940'. *Revue Historique des Armées* (1982): 42–51; Halpern, P. 'The French Navy, 1880-1914'. In *Technology and Naval Combat in the Twentieth Century and Beyond*, edited by P. P. O'Brien, 36–52. Abingdon: Routledge, 2001.

124   The fullest modern account is Motte, M. *Une education géostratégique: La pensée navale française de la jeune école à 1914*. Paris: Economica, 2004.

125   Marder, A. J. *The Anatomy of British Sea Power: A History of British Naval Policy*; Parkinson, R. *The Late Victorian Navy: The Pre-Dreadnought Era and the Origins of the First World War*. Woodbridge: Boydell Press, 2008.

126   Evans, D. C. 'Japanese Naval Construction, 1878-1918'. In *Technology and Naval Combat in the Twentieth Century and Beyond*, edited by P. P. O'Brien, 22–35. Abingdon: Routledge, 2001; Schencking, C. J. *Making Waves: Politics, Propaganda and the Emergence of the Imperial Japanese Navy, 1868-1922*. Stanford: Stanford University Press, 2005.

127   Sullivan, B. R. 'Italian Warship Construction and Maritime Strategy, 1873-1915'. In *Technology and Naval Combat in the Twentieth Century and Beyond*, edited by P. P. O'Brien, 3–12. London: Cass, 2001; Ferrante, E. 'The Impact of the *Jeune Ecole* on the Way of Thinking of the Italian Navy'. In *Marine Et Technique Au Xixe Siecle*, 517–25. Vincennes: Service historique de la Marine, 1995.

128   Sondhaus, L. *The Naval Policy of Austria-Hungary, 1867-1918: Navalism, Industrial Development and the Politics of Dualism*. West Lafayette, IN: Purdue University Press, 1994; Vego, M. N. *Austro-Hungarian Naval Policy, 1904-1914*, 1–34. London: Frank Cass, 1996.

129   For a contemporary view, see Klado, N. *The Russian Navy in the Russo-Japanese War*. London: George Bell and Sons, 1905. See also Mitchell, *A History of Russian and Soviet Sea Power*, 192–7; Papastratigakis, N. *Russian Imperialism and Naval Power: Military Strategy and the Build-up to the Russo-Japanese War*. London: I. B. Tauris, 2011.

130   Baer, *One Hundred Years of Sea Power*, 9–26; Hagan, *This People's Navy: The Making of American Sea Power*. New York: Free Press, 1991.

131   Sondhaus, L. *Preparing for Weltpolitik: German Sea Power before the Tirpitz Era*. Annapolis: Naval Institute Press, 1997; Olivier, D. H. *German Naval Strategy 1856-1888: Forerunners of Tirpitz*. London: Frank Cass, 2004; Epkenhans, M. *Tirpitz; Architect of the German High Seas Fleet*. Washington, DC: Potomac Books, 2008; Holger. H. *'Luxury Fleet': The Imperial German Navy, 1888-1918*. New York: Humanity Books, 1987. See also Lambi, I. N. *The Navy in German Power Politics, 1862-1914*. London: Allen and Unwin, 1984; Epkenhans, M. 'Technology, Shipbuilding and Future Combat in Germany, 1880-1914'. In *Technology and Naval Combat in the Twentieth Century and Beyond*, edited by P. P. O'Brien, 53–68. London: Cass, 2001.

132 Early examples include Westcott, A. *Mahan on Naval Warfare*. Boston: Sampson Low, 1919; Pulseton, W. D. *Mahan*, London: Cape, 1939. See also J. B. Hattendorf, ed. *The Influence of History on Mahan*. Newport: US Naval War College Press, 1991; Sumida, J. T. *Inventing Grand Strategy and Teaching Command: The Classic Works of Alfred Thayer Mahan Reconsidered*. Baltimore: Johns Hopkins University Press, 1997.

133 Beeler, J. F. *British Naval Policy in the Gladstone-Disraeli Era, 1866-1880*. Stanford: Stanford University Press, 1997; Schurman, D. M. *Imperial Defence, 1868-1887*. London: Cass, 2000.

134 For the context of growing British naval insecurity, see Parkinson, *The Late Victorian Navy*, particularly 44–80. See also Marder, *The Anatomy of British Sea Power*, 44–61; Kennedy, P. M. *The Rise and Fall of British Naval Mastery*, 205–37. London: Macmillan, 1976; Kennedy, P. M. *Strategy and Diplomacy, 1870-1945*, 15–85. London: Allen and Unwin, 1983; Kennedy, P. M. *The Realities behind Diplomacy: Background Influences on British External Policy, 1865-1980*, 17–117. London: Fontana, 1981; Yerxa, D. A. *Admirals and Empire: The United States Navy and the Caribbean, 1898-1945*. Columbia: University of South Carolina Press, 1991; Nish, I. *The Anglo-Japanese Alliance: The Diplomacy of Two Island Empires, 1894-1907*. London: Athlone Press, 1965; Morris, A. J. A. *The Scaremongers: The Advocacy of War and Rearmament, 1896-1914*. London: Routledge, 1984.

135 Rodriguez Gonzalez, A. R. *La Reconstruccion De La Escuadra: Planes Navales Espanoles, 1898-1920*, 79–138. Madrid: Galland Books, 2009.

136 Herwig, H. H. 'The German Reaction to the Dreadnought Revolution'. *The International History Review* 13, no. 2 (1991): 273–83; Brown, D. K. *Warrior to Dreadnought: Warship Development, 1860-1905*. London: Chatham Publishing, 1997; Sumrall, R. F. 'The Battleship and Battlecruiser'. In *The Eclipse of the Big Gun: The Warship, 1906-45*, edited by R. Gardiner, 14–24. London: Conway, 1992; Roberts, J. *Battlecruisers*, 7–45. London: Chatham Publishing, 1997.

137 The most accessible narrative of the war is currently Halpern, P. *A Naval History of World War I*. London: UCL Press, 1994.

138 Schurman, D. M. *Julian S. Corbett, 1854-1922*, 183–7. London: Royal Historical Society, 1981.

139 Marder, A. *From Dreadnought to Scapa Flow: The Royal Navy in the Fisher Era, 1904-1919*. 5 vols. Oxford: Oxford University Press, 1961–70.

140 For an excellent example of this pre-war writing, see Woodward, E. L. *Great Britain and the German Navy*. Oxford: Clarendon Press, 1935; Herwig, H. and D. F. Trask. 'The Failure of Imperial Germany's Undersea Offensive against World Shipping, February 1917–October 1918'. *Historian* 33, no. 4 (1971): 611–31; Herwig, H. 'Admirals versus Generals: The War Aims of the Imperial German Navy, 1914-1918'. *Central European History* 5, no. September (1972): 208–33; Herwig, *'Luxury Fleet'*; Epkenhans, M. *Tirpitz: Architect of the German High Seas Fleet*. Washington, DC: Potomac Books, 2008; Seligmann, M. S., F. Nagler and M. Epkenhans, eds. *The Naval Route to the Abyss: The Anglo-German Naval Race 1895-1914*. London: Navy Records Society, 2014.

141 Sumida, J. T. *In Defence of Naval Supremacy: Finance, Technology and British Naval Policy, 1889-1914*. Boston: Unwin Hyman, 1989.

142 Lambert, N. *Sir John Fisher's Naval Revolution*. Columbia: University of South Carolina Press, 1999.

143 Brookes, J. *Dreadnought Gunnery and the Battle of Jutland: The Question of Fire Control*. London: Routledge, 2005.

144 Seligmann, M. S. 'New Weapons for New Targets: Sir John Fisher, the Threat from Germany, and the Building of HMS Dreadnought and HMS Invincible, 1902–1907'. *The International History Review* 30, no. 2 (2008): 303–31; Seligmann, M. S. 'A Prelude to the Reforms of Admiral Sir John Fisher: The Creation of the Home Fleet, 1902–3'. *Historical Research* 83, no. 221 (2010): 506–19; Bell, C. M. 'Sir John Fisher's Naval Revolution Reconsidered: Winston Churchill at the Admiralty, 1911-1914', *War in History* 18 (2011): 333–56.

145 Podsoblyaev, E. F., F. King and J. Biggart. 'The Russian Naval General Staff and the Evolution of Naval Policy, 1904-1914'. *Journal of Military History* 66, no. 1 (2002): 37–69.

146 Black, N. *The British Naval Staff in the First World War*. Woodbridge: Boydell Press, 2009.

147 Gordon, A. *The Rules of the Game: Jutland and British Naval Command*. London: John Murray, 1996.

148 Ranft, B. 'The Protection of British Seaborne Trade and the Development of Systematic Planning for War, 1860-1906'. In *Technical Change and British Naval Policy, 1860-1939*, edited by B. Ranft, 1–2. London: Hodder and Stoughton, 1977; McKillip, R. W. 'Undermining Technology by Strategy: Resolving the Trade Protection Dilemma of 1917', *Naval War College Review* 44, no. 3 (1991): 18–37. The U-boat campaign can be followed in Tarrant, V. E. *The U-Boat Offensive, 1914-1945*, 7–76. London: Cassell, 1989; Terraine, J. *Business in Great Waters: The U Boat Wars, 1916-1945*, 17–140. London: Leo Cooper, 1985.

149 Lambert, N. A. *Planning for Armageddon: British Economic Warfare and the First World War*, 497–503. Cambridge, MA: Harvard University Press, 2012; Vincent, C. P. *The Politics of Hunger: The Allied Blockade of Germany, 1915-1919*. Athens, OH: Ohio University Press, 1985. The legal and operational issues related to an economic blockade of Germany are discussed in Tracy, N. *Sea Power and the Control of Trade: Belligerent Rights from the Russian War to the Beira Patrol, 1854-1970*, xv–xxi. London: Navy Records Society, 2005; Offer, 'Morality and Admiralty'; Fisher, J. 'Economic Warfare and the Laws of War'. *Journal of Contemporary History* 23 (1997): 99–118.

150 Halpern, P. *The Naval War in the Mediterranean, 1914-1918*. London: Allen and Unwin, 1987.

151 Philpott, M. *Air and Sea Power in World War I*. London: I. B. Tauris, 2012; Layman, R. D. *Naval Aviation in the First World War*. London: Chatham Publishing, 1996. The significance of the aerial campaign over the English Channel can be followed in Karau, M. D. *Wielding the Dagger: The MarineKorps Flandern and the German War Effort, 1914-1918*. Westport:

Praeger, 2003. See also Till, G. *Air Power and the Royal Navy*. London: Jane's, 1979. For the inter-service rivalry in Britain over the control of air forces during this period, see Cooper, M. *The Birth of Independent Air Power*. London: Allen and Unwin, 1986, especially 42–53.

152 Wester-Wemyss, L. *The Navy in the Dardanelles Campaign*. London: Hodder and Stoughton, 1919.

153 Wiest, A. 'Haig's Abortive Amphibious Assault on Belgium, 1917'. *The Historian* 54, no. 4 (Summer 1992): 669–82. The Royal Navy's contribution to the campaign on the Western Front is covered in Wiest, A. A. *Passchendaele and the Royal Navy*. Westport: Greenwood Press, 1995.

154 For a modern, concise recapitulation of this argument, see White, C. 'The Navy and Naval War Considered'. In *Home Fires and Foreign Fields*, edited by P. Liddle, 115–34. London: Brassey, 1985.

155 Hagan, *This People's Navy*, 252–8. The development of the Anglo-American naval relationship after 1900 is explored in an interesting collection of essays: Hattendorf, J. B. and R. S. Jordan, eds. *Maritime Strategy and the Balance of Power: Britain and America in the Twentieth Century*. Basingstoke: Macmillan, 1989.

156 Corbett, J. S. and H. Newbolt. *History of the Great War: Naval Operations*. 5 vols. London: Longmans and Company, 1920–31. The writing and significance of these official histories of the naval war is an interesting subject in its own right, and is in need of detailed examination.

157 Green, A. *Writing the Great War: Sir James Edmonds and the Official Histories, 1915-1948*. London: Cass, 2003.

158 Herwig, *Luxury Fleet*, 294.

159 Ufficio Storico dell Regina Marina. *La Marina Italiana Nella Grande Guerra*. 8 vols. Florence: Vallecchi, 1935–42.

160 Jellicoe, J. *The Grand Fleet, 1914-16: Its Creation, Development and Work*. London: Cassell, 1919; Bacon, R. *The Dover Patrol, 1915–1917*. 2 vols. London: Hutchinson, 1919; Von Tirpitz, A. *My Memoirs*. 2 vols. London: Hurst and Blackett, 1919; Sims, W. *Victory at Sea*. Garden City: Doubleday, 1920.

161 Fisher, J. *Memoirs*. London: Hodder and Stoughton, 1919; Fisher, J. *Records*. London: Hodder and Stoughton, 1919.

162 Churchill, W. S. *The World Crisis, 1915*. London: Butterworth, 1923. For a reaction to this, see Dewar, A. 'Winston Churchill and the Dardanelles'. *Naval Review* 12, no. 1 (1924): 25–39.

163 Bacon, R. *The Jutland Scandal*. London: Hutchinson, 1924; Bacon, R. *The Life of John Rushworth, Earl Jellicoe*. London: Cassell, 1936.

164 Keyes, R. *The Naval Memoirs of Admiral of the Fleet Sir Roger Keyes*. 2 vols. London: Butterworth, 1934–5.

165 Murray, W. and A. R. Millett. *Calculation: Net Assessment and the Coming of World War II*, 1–18. New York: Free Press, 1992.

166 Nish, I. *Japanese Foreign Policy 1869-1942: Kasumigaseki to Miyakezaka*, 139–45. London: Routledge, 1977.

167 Richmond, H. W. *Sea Power in the Modern World*. London: G. Bell and Sons, 1934; Hunt, B. D. *Sailor-Scholar: Admiral Sir Herbert Richmond, 1871-1946*. Ontario: Wilfred Laurier University Press, 1982; Till, G., ed. *The Development of British Naval Thinking: Essays in Memory of Bryan Ranft*. Abingdon: Routledge, 2006.

168 Gordon, G. A. H. *British Seapower and Procurement between the Wars: A Reappraisal of Rearmament*. London: Macmillan, 1988; Roskill, S. *Naval Policy Between the Wars*. 2 vols. London: Collins, 1968 and 1976; Bell, C. M. *The Royal Navy, Seapower and Strategy between the Wars*. London: Palgrave, 2000; Baugh, D. A. 'Confusions and Constraints: The Navy and British Defence Planning, 1919-1939'. In *Naval Power in the Twentieth Century*, edited by N. A. M. Rodger, 120–33. London: Macmillan, 1996; Gordon, A. 'The Admiralty and Imperial Overstretch, 1902-1941'. *Journal of Strategic Studies* XX (1994): 63–85. For the United States Navy, Baer, *One Hundred Years of Sea Power*, 83–145; for the Japanese reaction, see Evans and Peattie, Kaigun, 171–298.

169 Sprout, H. and M. Sprout. *Towards a New Order of Sea Power: American Naval Policy and the World Scene, 1918-1922*. Westport, CT: Greenwood, 1976.

170 Jordan, J. *Warships after Washington: The Development of the Five Major Fleets, 1922-1930*. Barnsley: Seaforth, 2011; Baer, *One Hundred Years of Sea Power*, 93–103; Ford, D. 'US Naval Intelligence and the Imperial Japanese Fleet during the Washington Treaty Era, C.1922–36'. *The Mariner's Mirror* 93, no. 3 (2007): 281–306.

171 Holland Rose, J. 'The Indecisiveness of Modern Naval War'. In *The Indecisiveness of Modern War and Other Essays*, 1–28. London: Bell, 1927.

172 Bagnasco, E. *Submarines of World War Two*, 24–8. London: Arms and Armour Press, 1977.

173 Sadao, A. 'The Japanese Navy and the United States'. In *Pearl Harbor as History: Japanese-American Relations, 1931-1941*, edited by D. Borg and S. Okamoto, 225–59. New York: Columbia University Press, 1973; Heinrichs, Jr., W. H. 'The Role of the United States Navy'. In *Pearl Harbor as History: Japanese-American Relations, 1931-1941*, edited by D. Borg and S. Okamoto, 203–9. New York: Columbia University Press, 1973; Nish, *Japanese Foreign Policy 1977*, 203–9. See also Ishimaru, T. *Japan Must Fight Britain*, London: Hurst & Blackett, 1936.

174 Perett, W. G. 'French Naval Policy and Foreign Affairs, 1930-39'. PhD, Stanford University, 1977. For a concise background, see also Halpern, P. 'French and Italian Naval Policy in the Mediterranean, 1898-1945'. In *Naval Policy and Strategy in the Mediterranean: Past, Present and Future*, edited by J. B. Hattendorf, 78–107. London: Cass, 2000. See also Salerno, R. M. 'The French Navy and the Appeasement of Italy, 1937-9'. *English Historical Review* 112 (1997): 67–104; Pratt, L. R. *East of Malta, West of Suez: Britain's Mediterranean Crisis, 1936-1939*. Cambridge: Cambridge University Press, 1975; Brescia, M. *Mussolini's Navy: A Reference Guide to the Regina Marina, 1930-1945*, 18–21. Barnsley: Seaforth Publishing, 2012. For the German navy, see also Rahn, W. 'German Naval Strategy and Armaments,

1919-1939'. In *Technology and Naval Combat in the Twentieth Century and Beyond*, edited by P. P. O'Brien, 109–28, 123–53. London: Cass, 2001.

175 Thomas, C. S. *The German Navy in the Nazi Era*, 95–8. London: Routledge, 1990; Berg, M. W. 'Admiral William H. Stanley and the Second London Naval Treaty, 1934-1936'. *The Historian* 33, no. February (1971): 215–36.

176 For excellent explorations of how the Royal Navy grappled with technologies (including the delivery of chemical weapons) and its attempts to blend them into the operational capability of the battlefleet, see Moretz, J. *The Royal Navy and the Capital Ship in the Interwar Period: An Operational Perspective*. London: Cass, 2002; Franklin, G. D. 'A Breakdown in Communication: Britain's over Estimation of Asdic's Capabilities in the 1930s'. *The Mariner's Mirror* 84, no. 2 (1998): 204–14. For a good overview of the interaction of technology, strategy and tactics, see Sumida, J. T. 'British Naval Procurement and Technological Change'. In *Technology and Naval Combat in the Twentieth Century and Beyond*, edited by P. P. O'Brien, 128–47. London: Cass, 2001; Murfett, M. *Naval Warfare, 1919-1945: An Operational History of a Volatile War at Sea*. London: Routledge, 2008.

177 Buckley, J. *Air Power in the Age of Total War*, 99–124. London: UCL Press, 1999, especially 109; Till, G. *Air Power and the Royal Navy, 1914-1945: A Historical Survey*, 117–31. London: Jane's, 1979; Hezlet, A. *Aircraft and Sea Power*, 104–38. London: Davies, 1970.

178 Isby, D., ed. *The Luftwaffe and the War at Sea, 1939-45: As Seen by Officers of the Kriegsmarine and Luftwaffe*. London: Chatham, 2005.

179 Weir, G. *Building American Submarines, 1914-1940*. Washington, DC: Naval Historical Center, 1991; Henry, D. 'British Submarine Policy, 1918-1939'. In *Technological Change and British Naval Policy, 1860-1939*, edited by B. Ranft, 80–107. London: Hodder and Stoughton, 2003; Franklin, G. *Britain's Anti-Submarine Capability, 1919-1939*. London: Cass, 2003.

180 Stokesbury, J. L. 'British Concepts and Practice of Amphibious Warfare, 1867-1916'. Durham: Duke University, 1968.

181 Harding, R. 'Learning from the War: The Development of British Amphibious Capability, 1919–29'. *The Mariner's Mirror* 86, no. 2 (2000): 173–85; Clifford, K. J. *Amphibious Warfare Development in Britain and America from 1920-1940*. Laurens and New York: Edgewood, 1983; Millett, A. R. 'Assault from the Sea: The Development of Amphibious Warfare between the Wars'. In *Military Innovation in the Inter-War Period*, edited by W. Murray and A. R. Millett, 50–95. Cambridge: Cambridge University Press, 199; Massam, D. R. 'British Maritime Strategy and Amphibious Capability, 1900-1940'. Oxford: D.Phil, 1995.

182 Roskill, *Naval Policy*, vol. 1; Bell, *The Royal Navy*, 49–58. The bibliography in this last book gives excellent additional reading: Cowan, I. *Dominion or Decline: Anglo-American Naval Relations in the Pacific, 1937-1941*. Oxford: Berg, 1996. US–Japanese naval relations can be found in Miller, E. S. *War Plan Orange: The US Strategy to Defeat Japan, 1897-1945*. Annapolis: Naval Institute Press, 1991; Baer, *One Hundred Years of Sea Power*, 119–80. Anglo-German relations are best followed in Maiolo, J. A. *The Royal Navy and Nazi Germany, 1933-1939: A Study in Appeasement and the Origins of*

the Second World War. London: Palgrave, 1998. See also Till, G. 'Richmond and the Faith Reaffirmed: British Naval Thinking between the Wars'. In *The Development of British Naval Thinking: Essays in Memory of Bryan Ranft*, edited by G. Till, 103–33. London: Cass, 2006.

183 The story of Anglo-Japanese relations can be found in Marder, A. *Old Friends, New Enemies: The Royal Navy and the Imperial Japanese Navy:Strategic Illusions, 1936-1941*. Oxford: Oxford University Press, 1981; Field, A. *Royal Navy Strategy in the Far East, 1919-1939: Preparing for War against Japan*. London: Frank Cass, 2004; Haggie, P. *Britannia at Bay: The Defence of the British Empire against Japan, 1931-1941*. Oxford: Oxford University Press, 1981; McIntyre, W. D. *The Rise and Fall of the Singapore Naval Base*. London: Macmillan, 1979. See also Neilson, K. 'Unbroken Thread: Japan. Maritime Power and British Imperial Defence, 1920-1932'. In *British Naval Strategy East of Suez, 1900-2000: Influences and Actions*, edited by G. Kennedy, 62–89. London: Cass, 2005. Pratt, L. R. East of Malta, West of Suez: Britain's Mediterranean Crisis, 1936-1939. Cambridge: Cambridge University Press, 1975.

184 See Mallett, R. *The Italian Navy and Fascist Expansionism, 1935-1940*. London: Cass, 1998. The bibliography of this work is an excellent starting point for further reading. See also Sadkovich, J. J. *The Italian Navy in World War II*. Westport: Greenwood Press, 1994; Gooch, J. *Mussolini and his Generals: The Armed Forces and Fascist Foreign Policy, 1922-1940*. Cambridge: Cambridge University Press, 2007. Sadkovich, J. J. 'The Indispensable Navy: Italy as a Great Power, 1911-1943'. In *Naval Power in the Twentieth Century*, edited by N. A. M. Rodger, 88–100. London: Macmillan, 1996.

185 French naval policy can be traced in Perett, W. G. 'French Naval Policy and Foreign Affairs, 1930-39'. PhD, Stanford University, 1977, and Salerno, R. M. 'The French Navy and the Appeasement of Italy, 1937-9'. *English Historical Review* 112 (1997): 67–104.

186 Rahn, W. 'German Naval Strategy and Armaments, 1919-1939'. In *Technology and Naval Combat in the Twentieth Century and Beyond*, edited by P. P. O'Brien, 109–28. London: Cass, 2001; Dulffer, J. 'Determinants of German Naval Policy 1920-1939.' In *The German Military in the Age of Total War*, edited by W. Deist, 152–70. Oxford: Berg, 1985; Thomas, C. S. *The Germany Navy in the Nazi Era*. London: Routledge, 1990.

187 Keegan, J. *The Battle for History: Re-Fighting World War II*. London: Pimlico, 1997.

188 Frankland, N. *History at War*. London: Giles de la Mare, 1998; Gough, B. *Historical Dreadnoughts: Arthur Marder, Stephen Roskill and the Battles for Naval History*, 134–71. Barnsley: Seaforth, 2010.

189 Liddell Hart Military Archive, King's College London, Liddell Hart Papers, Tedder to Liddell Hart, 7 March 1963. See also Reynolds, D. *In Command of History: Churchill Fighting and Writing the Second World War*. London: Allen Lane, 2004.

190 A good narrative starting point is Blair, C. *Hitler's U Boat War: The Hunters, 1939-1942*. London: Random House, 1996; Blair, C. *Hitler's U Boat War:*

The Hunted, 1942-1945. London: Random House, 1998. An excellent concise account is in Milner, M. *The Battle of the Atlantic*. Stroud: Tempus, 2005. For the technical history of the U-boat, see Rössler, E. *The U Boat: The Evolution and Technical History of German Submarines*. London: Cassell, 2002. The final phase of the campaign is well presented in Tarrant, V. E. *The Last Year of the Kriegsmarine, May 1944-May 1945*. London: Arms and Armour Press, 1994; White, J. *Endgame: The U Boat Inshore Campaign, 1944-1945*. London: The History Press, 1998. See also Syrett, D. *The Defeat of the German U-Boats: The Battle of the Atlantic*. Columbia: University of South Carolina Press, 1994; Showell, J. M. *U-Boat Command and the Battle of the Atlantic*. London: Conway, 1989; Grove, E., ed. *The Defeat of the Enemy Attack on Shipping, 1939-1945*. London: Navy Records Society, 1997; Franklin, G. D. *Britain's Anti-Submarine Capability, 1919-1939*. London: Cass, 2003; Llewellyn-Jones, M. *The Royal Navy and Anti-Submarine Warfare, 1917-1949*. London: Cass, 2005.

191 Price, A. *Aircraft Versus Submarines in Two World Wars*, 221–3. Barnsley: Pen and Sword, 2004; Redford, D. *A History of the Royal Navy: World War II*, 77–85. London: I. B. Tauris, 2014.

192 The best study of the role of ULTRA in this campaign is Gardner, W. *Decoding History: The Battle of the Atlantic and Ultra*. Basingstoke: Macmillan, 1999.

193 Kahn, D. *Seizing the Enigma: The Race to Break the German U-Boat Codes, 1939-1943*. London: Faber, 1998.

194 Cumming, A. J. *The Royal Navy and the Battle of Britain*. Annapolis: Naval Institute Press, 2010.

195 Parshall, J., and A. Tully. *Shattered Sword: The Untold Story of the Battle of Midway*. Dulles: Potomac, 2005.

196 Willmott, H. *The Battle of Leyte Gulf: The Last Fleet Action*. Bloomington: University of Indiana Press, 2005.

197 Tully, A.P. *Battle of Surigao Strait*. Bloomington: University of Indiana Press, 2009.

198 Tillman, Barrett. *Clash of Carriers: The True Story of the Marianas Turkey Shoot of World War II*. New York: NAL Caliber, 2005.

199 The outlines of the campaigns are best followed in Morison and in the official histories of the USMC. More recent work includes the thorough re-examination of the Battle of Midway, using Japanese sources, Parshall, J., and A. Tully. *Shattered Sword: The Untold Story of the Battle of Midway*. Dulles: Potomac, 2005. Other recent reinterpretations include Zimm, A. D. *Attack on Pearl Harbor: Strategy, Combat, Myths, Deception*. Philadelphia: Casemate, 2011; The battles can also be followed from the perspectives of the biographers of participants in many cases.

200 Excellent starting points include the following. Evans, D. C. and M. R. Peattie. *Kaigun* provides an excellent technical and operational history. The technological development of the aircraft carrier, and many other types of warship, has been traced in the works of Norman Friedman. In this context, his *US Carriers: An Illustrated Design History*. Annapolis: United States Naval Institute Press, 1983; *Carrier Air Power*. New York: Routledge, 1981; and

British Carrier Aviation: The Evolution of the Ships and their Aircraft. London: Conway, 1988 are the best introductions. Also useful is Brown, D. K. *Carrier Operations in World War II*. 2 vols. London: Ian Allen, 1968 and 1974.

201 Coox, A. *Japan: The Final Agony*, 56. London: Macdonald, 1970.

202 A large narrative history, full of detail and interesting anecdote but unfortunately without footnotes, is Blair, C. *The Silent Victory: The US Submarine Victory against Japan*. Annapolis: United States Naval Institute Press, 2001. The technical side of the submarine force is covered in Alden, J. D. *The Fleet Submarine in the US Navy: A Design and Construction History*. London: Arms and Armour Press, 1979.

203 The official history of the USMC, published between 1958 and 1971, provides a detailed narrative of all the Pacific operations. A more accessible history (still under the official eye) is Isley, J. A. and P. A. Crowl. *The US Marines and Amphibious War: Its Theory and its Practice in the Pacific*. Princeton: Princeton University Press, 1951. For broader histories, see Moskin, J. R. *The Story of the US Marine Corps*. New York: McGraw-Hill, 1979; Clifford, K. J. *Progress and Purpose: A Developmental History of the United States Marine Corps 1900-1970*. Washington, DC: USMC History and Museums Division HQ, 1973. Among the many histories of the battles, the following are useful: Frank, R. B. *Guadalcanal: The Definitive Account of the Landmark Battle*. New York: Random House, 1990; Gailey, H. *The Liberation of Guam: 21st July-10th August 1944*. Novato: Presidio, 1988; Feifer, F. *Okinawa 1945: The Stalingrad of the Pacific*. Stroud: Tempus, 2005; Barbey, D. E. *MacArthur's Amphibious Navy: Seventh Amphibious Force Operations, 1943-1945*. Annapolis: Naval Institute Press, 1969. Among the many popular histories, there is a series of very short, but well-illustrated, narratives written by Gordon Rottman. The volumes also have short, but helpful, bibliographies. For example, Rottman, G. L. *Saipan and Tinian: Piercing the Japanese Empire*. London: Osprey, 2004; *The Marshall Islands: Operation Flintlock, the Capture of Kwajalein and Eniwetok*. London: Osprey, 2004; Moran, J. and G. Rottman. *Peleliu, 1944: The Forgotten Corner of Hell*. London: Osprey, 2002.

204 Wright, D. *The Battle for Iwo Jima 1945*, 97. Frome: Sutton, 1999.

205 The history of logistics across the Pacific did get some early attention; for example, Carter, W. R. *Beans, Bullets and Black Oil: The Story of Fleet Logistics Afloat in the Pacific during World War II*. Washington: US Government Printing Office, 1953 presents a clear narrative. McGee, W. L. and S. McGee, eds. *Pacific Express: The Critical Role of Military Logistics in World War*. Tiburon, CA: BMC, 2009 is a useful compilation, edited from various important printed sources, but does not add a great deal to assist analysis. A broader treatment of one aspect of the problem is covered very well in Nash, P. V. *Development of Mobile Logistics Support in Anglo-American Naval Policy, 1900-1953*. Gainsville: University of Florida Press, 2009.

206 For examples, see Clifford, K. J. *Amphibious Warfare Development in Britain and America from 1920 to 1940*. New York: Edgewood, 1983; Millett, A. R. 'Assault from the Sea: The Development of Amphibious Warfare between the Wars'. In *Military Innovation in the Inter-War Period*, edited by

W. Murray and A. R. Millett, 50–95. Cambridge: Cambridge University Press, 1996; Harding, R. 'Learning from the War: The Development of British Amphibious Capability, 1919-1929'. *The Mariner's Mirror* 86 (2000): 173–85; Harding, R. 'Amphibious Warfare, 1930-1939'. In *The Royal Navy 1930-2000: Innovation and Defence*, edited by R. Harding, 42–68. London: Cass, 2005. See also the unpublished theses of Stokesbury, J. L. 'British Concepts and Practice of Amphibious Warfare, 1867-1916'. PhD, Duke University, 1968 and Massam, R. 'British Maritime Strategy and Amphibious Capability, 1900-1940'. D.Phil., University of Oxford, 1995. Some useful short essays can be found in Bartlett, M. L., ed. *Assault from the Sea: Essays on the History of Amphibious Warfare*. Annapolis: Naval Institute Press, 1983 and Lovering, T., ed. *Amphibious Assault: Manoeuvre from the Sea*. Woodbridge: Seafarer, 2007. A useful general study is Speller, I. and C. Tuck. *Amphibious Warfare: The Theory and Practice of Amphibious Operations in the 20th Century*. Staplehurst: Spellmount, 2001. A history of the creation of British amphibious method and capability written by participants can be found in Maund, L. E. H. *Assault from the Sea*. London: Methuen, 1949; Fergusson, B. *The Watery Maze: The Story of Combined Operations*. London: Collins, 1961. See also Ladd, J. *Assault from the Sea 1939-45: The Craft, the Landings, the Men*. Newton Abbot: David and Charles, 1976.

207 An early history of *Operation Neptune* was Edwards, K. *Operation Neptune*. London: Collins, 1946. This was added to by another participant in 1974: Schofield, B. B. *Operation Neptune: The Inside Story of Naval Operations for the Normandy Landings 1944*. London: Ian Allen, 1974. Renewed attention to this would be interesting. The official battle summaries of the invasion plans, which were prepared in 1952, were published in 1994. Good examples of modern research include Lewis, A. R. *Omaha Beach: A Flawed Victory*. Chapel Hill: University of North Carolina Press, 2001; Howcroft, I. 'The role of the Royal Navy in the amphibious assaults in the Second World War'. PhD, University of Exeter, 2003. Useful histories of other important operations have tended to focus on the military, rather than the naval, side of events. See, for example, D'Este, C. *Bitter Victory: The Battle for Sicily, July-August 1943*. London: Fontana, 1989; D'Este, C. *Fatal Decision: Anzio and the Battle for Rome*. London: Harper Collins, 1991; Moulton, J. L. *Battle for Antwerp: Liberation of the City and the Opening of the Scheldt, 1944*. London: Ian Allen, 1978; Beale, P. *The Great Mistake: The Battle for Antwerp and the Beveland Peninsula, September 1944*. Stroud: Sutton, 2004. Anglo-American friction over the priorities and planning of the Mediterranean campaign is well known, but relations between the two navies in this theatre could do with new research. Samuel Morison noted how Vice Admiral Hewitt's Eighth US Fleet in the Mediterranean was essentially an amphibious navy that depended on the British Mediterranean Fleet for support by battleship, carrier and heavy cruiser (*History of US Naval Operations*, volume 9, x). See Stoler, M. A. 'The American Perception of British Mediterranean Strategy, 1941–1945'. In *New Aspects of Naval History*, edited by W. Cogar and C.L. Symonds, 325–39. Annapolis: United States Naval Institute Press, 1981.

208 Field, C. *Britain's Sea Soldiers*. 2 vols. Liverpool: Lyceum Press, 1924, i preface. The best general history of the RM during this period is Ladd, J. *The Royal Marines, 1919-1980: An Authorised History*. London: Jane's, 1980.

209 Gatchel, T. L. *At the Water's Edge: Defending against the Modern Amphibious Assault*. Annapolis: Naval Institute Press, 1996.

210 Scott, P. *The Battle of the Narrow Seas: A History of the Light Coastal Forces in the Channel and North Sea, 1939-1945*. London: Country Life, 1945. Other popular histories are Cooper, B. *The Buccaneers*. London: Macdonald, 1970; Cooper, B. *The Battle of the Torpedo Boats*. London: Pan, 1970.

211 At present, the best works remain Leighton, R. M. and R. W. Coakley. *Global Logistics and Strategy, vol. 1 (1940-1943); vol. 2 (1943-1945)*. Washington, DC: Department of the Army, 1955 and 1968; Carter, W. R. and E. E. Duval. *Ships, Salvage and the Sinews of War: The Story of Fleet Logistics Afloat in Atlantic and Mediterranean Waters during World War II*. Washington, DC: Department of the Navy, 1954; Ballantine, D. *U.S. Naval Logistics in the Second World War*. Princeton: University of Princeton, 1947.

212 An excellent study, which provides both detailed analytical study of intentions and chronology, is Willmott, H. P. *Grave of a Dozen Schemes: British Naval Planning and the War against Japan, 1943-1945*. Annapolis: Naval Institute Press, 1996. The story of the British Pacific Fleet operations can be found in Smith, P. *Task Force 57*. London: William Kimber, 1969; Hobbs, D. *The British Pacific Fleet: The Royal Navy's Most Powerful Strike Force*. Barnsley: Seaforth, 2011.

213 Madsen, C. *The Royal Navy and German Naval Disarmament, 1942-1947*. London: Frank Cass, 1998.

214 For the Russian navy, see Rohwer, J. and M. S. Monakov. *Stalin's Ocean-Going Fleet: Soviet Naval Strategy and Shipbuilding Programmes, 1935-1953*. London: Cass, 2006. The period 1917–36 is covered in Herrick, R. W. *Soviet Naval Theory and Policy: Gorshkov's Inheritance*. Newport, RI: US Naval War College, 1988. For the Italian navy, see Greene J. and A. Massignani. *The Naval War in the Mediterranean, 1940-1943*. Barnsley: Frontline, 2011. The bibliography in this last work provides an excellent basis for further study of the Italian perspective.

215 Cathcart, B. *Test of Greatness: Britain's Struggle for the Atom Bomb*, 7–21. London: John Murray, 1994.

216 Roskill, S. W. *The Strategy of Sea Power: Its Development and Application*. Lees-Knowles Lectures. Cambridge: Cambridge University Press, 1962; Gretton, P. *Maritime Strategy: A Study of British Defence Problems*. London: Cassell, 1965; Schurman, D. M. 'An Historian and the Sublime Aspects of the Naval Profession'. In *Dreadnought to Polaris: Maritime Strategy since Mahan* edited by A. M. J. Hyatt, 1–11. Annapolis: Naval Institute Press, 1973; Luttwak, E. N., ed. *The Political Uses of Sea Power*. Baltimore: Johns Hopkins University Press, 1974; Hill, J. R. *Maritime Strategy for Medium Powers*. London: Croom Helm, 1986; Modelski, G. and W. R. Thompson. *Seapower in Global Politics, 1494-1993*. Seattle: University of Washington Press, 1988; Speller, I. 'The Royal Navy, Expeditionary Operations and the End of Empire, 1956-75'. In *British Naval Strategy East of Suez, 1900 – 2000: Influences and Actions*, edited by G. Kennedy, 178–98. Abingdon: Cass, 2005; Booth, K. *Navies and Foreign Policy*. London: Croom Helm, 1977; Alford, J., ed. *Sea Power and Influence: Old Issues and New Challenges*. Farnborough: Gower, 1980; Moinville, H. *Naval Warfare Today*

        and Tomorrow. London: Blackwell, 1983; Gray, C. and R. W. Barnett, eds. *Seapower and Strategy*. Annapolis: Naval Institute Press, 1989; Grove, E. *The Future of Seapower*. London: Routledge, 1990; Watson, B. W. *The Changing Face of the World's Navies 1945 to the Present*. London: Arms and Armour Press, 1991.

217 Hattendorf, J. B. 'Rear Admiral Henry E. Eccles and the "Lessons of Suez", 1956-1968'. In *Talking About Naval History: A Collection of Essays*, edited by J. B. Hattendorf, 291–303. Newport: Naval War College Press, 2012.

218 Gough, B. *Historical Dreadnoughts: Arthur Marder, Stephen Roskill and the Battles for Naval History*, 137–41. Barnsley: Seaforth, 2010.

219 Compared with the Second World War, the role of the United Nations navies in the Korean War is under-researched. There are many accounts of ships, aircraft and personal memoirs, but overviews of the campaign from the perspective of the various United Nations are still very thin. The USMC official history of the Korean War appeared in five volumes in 1957. The United States Navy's role in Vietnam up to 1965 is in Hooper, E. B., D. C. Allard and O. P. Fitzgerald. *The United States Navy and the Vietnam Conflict: Setting the Stage to 1959*. Washington, DC: Naval Historical Center, 1976 and Marolda, E. J. and O. P. Fitzgerald. *The United States Navy and the Vietnam Conflict: From Military Assistance to Combat, 1959-1965*. Washington, DC: Naval Historical Center, 1976. The history of the USMC in Vietnam was published in nine volumes between 1977 and 1997. See also the United States Naval Historical Center, http://www.history.navy.mil/biblio/biblio6.htm and the USMC website at http://www.tecom.usmc.mil/HD/General/Publications.htm#2001 (both accessed 19 March 2012).

220 Farrar-Hockley, A., ed. *A Distant Obligation: The British Part in the Korean War. An Official History. Volume 1*. London: HMSO, 1990; Farrar-Hockley, A. *An Honorable Discharge: The British Part in the Korean War. An Official History. Volume 2*. London: HMSO, 1995; Freedman, L. *Official History of the Falklands Campaign: War and Diplomacy*. 2 vols. Vol. 2. London: Taylor and Francis, 2007. See also Edwards, M. *The Korean War: An Annotated Bibliography*. Westport: Greenwood, 1998; Rasor, E. L. *The Falklands/Malvinas Campaign: A Bibliography*. Westport, CT: Greenwood, 2002.

221 Malony, S. M. *Securing Command of the Sea: Nato Naval Planning, 1948-1954*. Annapolis: Naval Institute Press, 1995.

222 See, for example, Kane, T. M. *Chinese Grand Strategy and Maritime Power*, 139–45. London: Cass, 2002; Hattendorf, J. B., ed. *The Influence of History on Mahan*. Newport: Naval War College Press, 1991; Baer, G. 'Alfred Thayer Mahan and the Utility of US Naval Forces Today'. In *The Changing Face of Maritime Power*, edited by A. Dorman, M. L. Smith and M. R. H. Uttley, 14–18. London: Macmillan, 1999; Till, G. 'Sir Julian Corbett and the Twenty-First Century: Ten Maritime Commandments'. In Dorman, Smith and Uttley, eds. *The Changing Face of Maritime Power*, 19–32; Gray, C. S. 'History for Strategists: British Seapower as a Relevant Past'. *Journal of Strategic Studies* 17 (1994): 7–32; Till, G. *Seapower: A Guide for the Twenty-First Century*.

223 Kane, T. *Chinese Grand Strategy and Maritime Power*, 139–45. London: Frank Cass, 2002.

224 The Falklands War (1982) took place at a critical juncture in British defence decision-making. The future of the Royal Navy as a medium force was in the balance. It was very much a naval campaign and rapidly generated work reflecting both the success of the campaign and the fragility of British sea power. See, for example, Preston, A. *Sea Combat off the Falklands: The Lessons that must be Learned*. London: Willow, 1982; Villar, R. *Merchant Ships at War: The Falklands Experience*. London: Conway, 1984; Thompson, J. *No Picnic: 3 Commando Brigade in the South Atlantic*. London: Leo Cooper, 1985; Brown, D. *The Royal Navy and the Falklands War*. London: Leo Cooper, 1987. Later important works include: Woodward, S. and P. Robinson. *One Hundred Days*. London; Harper Collins, 1992; Clapp, M. and E. Southby-Tailyour. *Amphibious Assault Falklands: The Battle for San Carlos Water*. London: Leo Cooper, 1996; Puddefoot, G. *No Sea Too Rough: The Royal Fleet Auxiliary in the Falklands War; The Untold Story*. London: Chatham Publishing, 2007; Ponting, C. *The Right to Know: The Inside Story of the Belgrano Affair*. London: Sphere, 1986; Rice, D. and A. Garvshon. The Sinking of the Belgrano. London: Secker and Warburg, 1984; Rossiter, M. *Sink the Belgrano*. London: Bantam Press, 2007.

225 Scammell, C. 'Anglo-American Strategic Co-operation: The Role of Carrier Aviation in Western Strategy, 1945-1955'. PhD, King's College London, 2001; Benbow, T. *The Impact of Air Power on Navies: The United Kingdom, 1945-1957*. D.Phil., University of Oxford, 1999; Alexander, J. H. and M. L. Bartlett. *Sea Soldiers in the Cold War: Amphibious Warfare 1945-1991*. Annapolis: Naval Institute Press, 1995.

226 Palmer, M. A. *Origins of the Maritime Strategy: American Naval Strategy in the First Postwar Decade*. Washington, DC: Naval Historical Center, 1988; Hattendorf, J. B. *The Evolution of the U.S. Navy's Maritime Strategy, 1977-1986*. Newport: Naval War College, 2004; Gray, C. S. 'Sea Power for Containment: The U.S. Navy in the Cold War'. In *Navies and Global Defense: Theories and Strategy*, edited by K. Neilson and E. J. Errington, 181–208. Westport: Praeger, 1995; Friedman, N. *The US Maritime Strategy*. Annapolis: Naval Institute Press, 1988; Till, G., *The Future of British Sea Power*. Annapolis: Naval Institute Press, 1984. A useful general bibliography related to British strategy can be found in Overdale, R. *British Defence Policy since 1945*. Manchester: Manchester University Press, 1994; Grove, E. *The Future of Seapower*. London: Routledge, 1990. For a valuable collection of essays that go beyond Anglo-American experience after 1945, see Rodger, N. A. M., ed. *Naval Power in the Twentieth Century*. London: Macmillan, 1996.

227 See, for example, Herrick, R. W. *Soviet Naval Strategy: Fifty Years of Theory and Practice*. Annapolis: Naval Institute Press, 1968; Grove, E. J. 'The Superpowers and Secondary Navies in Northern Waters during the Cold War'. In *Navies in Northern Waters, 1721-2000*, edited by R. Hobson and T. Kristiansen, 211–21. London: Cass, 2004; Tamnes, R. 'Major Coastal State – Small Naval Power: Norway's Cold War Policy and Strategy'. In *Navies in Northern Waters*, edited by R. Hobson and T. Kristiansen, 222–48.

London: Cass, 2004; Brouwer, J. W. L. 'Dutch Naval Policy in the Cold War Period'. In *Strategy and Response in the Twentieth Century Maritime World*, edited by J. R. Bruijn, A. M. C. van Dissel, G. Jackson and P. C. van Royen, 42–50. Amsterdam: Batavian Lion International, 2001; Auer, J. E. *The Postwar Rearmament of Japanese Maritime Forces, 1945-71*. New York: Praeger, 1973; Wooley, P. J. *Japan's Navy: Politics and Paradox, 1971-2000*. Boulder: Lynne Rienner, 2000; Monte, P. 'Die Rolle der Marine der Bundesrepublik Deutschland in der Verteidigungsplanung für Mittel- und Nordeuropa von den 50er Jahren bis zur Wende 1989/90'. In *Deutsche Marinen im Wandel*, edited by W. Rahn, 565–98. Munchen: R. Oldenbourg, 2005; K. Eckstein, 'Die Volksmarine im Kalten Krieg'. In *Deutsche Marinen im Wandel*, edited by W. Rahn, 615–31. Munchen: R. Oldenbourg, 2005; Hiranandani, G. M. *Transition to Triumph: The Indian Navy 1965-1975*. New Delhi: Lancer, 2000; Hiranandani, G. M. Transition to Eminence: The Indian Navy 1976-1990. New Delhi: Lancer, 2005.

228 Modelski and Thompson, *Seapower in Global Politics*, 13.

229 Cable, J. *Gunboat Diplomacy, 1919-1991*. Studies in International Security. 3 ed. vol. 16, London, 1994; Cable, J. *Navies in a Violent Peace*. London: Palgrave, 1989; Coutau-Bégerie, H. *Le Meilleur des Ambassadeurs: Théorie et Practique de la Diplomatie Navale*. Paris: Economica, 2010; Murffett, M. 'Gunboat Diplomacy: Outmoded or Back in Vogue?' In Dorman, Smith and Uttley, *The Changing Face of Maritime Power*, 81–93. See also Elleman, B. A. and S. C. M. Paine. *Naval Blockades and Seapower: Strategies and Counter-Strategies, 1805-2005*. London: Routledge, 2006.

230 Erikson, A. S., L. J. Goldstein and C. Lord, eds. *China Goes to Sea*; Bussert, J. C. and B. A. Elleman. *People's Liberation Army Navy: Combat Systems Technology, 1949-2010*. Annapolis: Naval Institute Press, 2011. Much of the emerging literature on the PLAN and the evolving maritime situation in the Indian Ocean and Pacific is to be found in the professional service journals, such as the *Naval War College Review* (see https://www.usnwc.edu/Publications/Naval-War-College-Review/IndexPages/Index-by-Subject.aspx, accessed 16 June 2012) and the *Journal of the Royal United Services Institution*.

231 Pant, H. V., ed. *The Rise of the Indian Navy: Internal Vulnerabilities, External Challenges*. Abingdon: Gower, 2012. See also Hiranandani, G. M. *Transition to Guardianship: The Indian Navy, 1991-2000*. New Delhi: Lancer, 2009; Goldrick, J. 'Imperial Jetsam or National Guardians? The Navies of the Indian Sub-Continent'. In *Naval Power in the Twentieth Century*, edited by N. A. M. Rodger, 200–14. London: Macmillan, 1996; Woolley, J. *Japan's Navy: Politics and Paradox, 1971-2000*. London: Lynne Rienner, 2000.

232 Murray, W. and M. Knox. 'Thinking About Revolutions in Warfare'. In *The Dynamics of Military Revolution, 1300-2050*, edited by M. Knox and W. Murray, 1–14. Cambridge: Cambridge University Press, 2001.

233 For example, see Friedman, N. *Network-Centric Warfare: How Navies Learned to Fight Smarter through Three World Wars*. Annapolis: Naval Institute Press, 2009; Friedman, N. *Seapower and Space: From the Dawn of the Missile Age to Net-Centric Warfare Development*. London: Conway, 1984; Friedman, N. *Modern Warship Design and Development*. London:

Conway, 1979; Friedman, N. *The Postwar Naval Revolution*. London: Conway, 1986. The size and structure of navies in the period to 1982 can be followed in Gardiner, R., ed. *All the World's Fighting Ships 1947-1982: Part 1 The Western Powers*. London, Conway, 1983; *Part 2: The Warsaw Pact and Non-Aligned Nations*. London, Conway, 1983. The importance of understanding contemporary technology in some form of historical context is evident from some of the ten volumes in the Brassey's 'Seapower: Naval Vessels, Weapons Systems and Technology Series' published in the mid-1990s.

234 The Royal Navy features heavily in the works of Norman Friedman outlined above, who has also produced specific works on the subject. See Friedman, N. *British Destroyers and Frigates: The Second World War and After*. Barnsley: Seaforth, 2008. See also Brown, D. K. and G. Moore. *Rebuilding the Royal Navy: Warship Design since 1945*. London: Chatham Publishing, 2003. The most significant technological changes involved the adoption of nuclear power and weaponry, both of which, ultimately, enabled the Royal Navy to take over the custodianship of Britain's nuclear deterrent from the Royal Air Force. See Moore, R. *The Royal Navy and Nuclear Weapons*. London: Cass, 2001; Nailor, P. *The Nassau Connection: The Organization and Management of the British Polaris Project*. London: HMSO, 1988. For a brief introduction, see Brown and Moore, *Rebuilding the Royal Navy*, 120–9; Friedman, N. 'Nuclear Weapons and Navies'. In *Navies in the Nuclear Age*, edited by R. Gardiner, 133–41. London: Conway, 1993.

235 Sumida, J. T. 'Reimagining the History of Twentieth Century Navies'. In *Maritime History as World History*, edited by D. Finamore, 167–82. Tallahassee: University of Florida Press, 2004; Elleman, B. A. and S. C. M. Paine, eds. *Naval Coalition Warfare: From the Napoleonic War to Operation Iraqi Freedom*. Abingdon: Cass, 2008; Till, G. 'The Return to Globalism: The Royal Navy East of Suez, 1975-2003'. In *British Naval Strategy East of Suez, 1900–2000: Influences and Actions*, edited by G. Kennedy, 244–68. London: Routledge, 2005.

236 Speller, I. *The Role of Amphibious Warfare in British Defence Policy, 1945-56*. London: Palgrave, 2001; Lovering, T., ed. *Amphibious Assault: Manoeuvre from the Sea*. Woodbridge: Seafarer, 2007; Evans, M. H. H. *Amphibious Operations: The Projection of Sea Power Ashore*. London: Brassey, 1990; Alexander, J. H. and M. L. Bartlett. *Sea Soldiers in the Cold War: Amphibious Warfare, 1945-1991*. Annapolis: Naval Institute Press, 1995.

237 See, for example, Sontag, S. and C. Drew. *Blind Man's Buff: The Untold Story of Cold War Submarine Espionage*. London: Routledge, 1999. The classic studies of British naval intelligence are Beesley, P. *Room 40: British Naval Intelligence, 1914-1918*. London: Hamish Hamilton, 1982; Beesley, P. *Very Special Intelligence: The Story of the Admiralty's Operational Intelligence Centre War, 1939-1945*. London: Hamish Hamilton, 1977. For a post-war example of the potential intelligence impact on a naval campaign, see West, N. *The Secret War for the Falklands: The SAS, MI6 and the War Whitehall nearly Lost*. Boston: Little Brown, 1997. Interest in intelligence gathering is now showing results in other periods. See, for example, Maffeo, S. E. *Most Secret and Confidential: Intelligence in the Age of Nelson*. London: Chatham

Publishing, 2000; Knight, J. 'Nelson and the Eastern Mediterranean, 1803-1805'. *The Mariner's Mirror* 91 (2005): 195–215.

238 The best overview of the financial problem remains the work of Philip Pugh. See Pugh, P. *The Cost of Seapower: The Influence of Money on Naval Affairs from 1815 to the Present Day*. London: Conway Maritime Press, 1986. See also Grove, E. *Vanguard to Trident: British Naval Policy since World War II*. London: Bodley Head, 1987; Till, G., ed. *The Future of British Sea Power*, 171–212. Annapolis: Naval Institute Press, 1984. The importance of the navy to the emergence of the US 'military–industrial complex' is demonstrated in Cooling, B. F. *Gray Steel and Blue Water Navy: The Formative Years of America's Military-Industrial Complex, 1881-1917*. Hamden: Archon Books, 1979; Epstein, K. C. *Torpedo: Inventing the Military-Industrial Complex in the United States and Great Britain*. Cambridge, MA: Harvard University Press, 2014; Weir, G. *Forged in War: The Naval-Industrial Complex and American Submarine Construction, 1940-1961*. Washington, DC: Naval Historical Center, 1993.

239 MacKenzie, D. 'Missile Accuracy: A Case Study in the Social Processes of Technological Change'. In *The Social Construction of Technological Systems: New Directions in the Sociology and History of Technology*, edited by W. E. Bijker, T. P. Hughes and T. J. Pinch, 195–222. Cambridge, MA: MIT Press, 1987; MacKenzie, D. *Inventing Accuracy: A Historical Sociology of Nuclear Missile Guidance*. Cambridge, MA: MIT Press, 2000; Spinardi, G. *From Polaris to Trident: The Development of US Fleet Ballistic Missile Technology*. Cambridge: Cambridge University Press, 1994.

Chapter 2

1 Bentley, M. *Modernizing England's Past: English Historiography in the Age of Modernism, 1870-1970*, 73. Cambridge: Cambridge University Press, 2005.

2 Kenyon, J. *The History Men*, 177. London: Weidenfeld and Nicholson, 1983.

3 Wilson, K., ed. *A New Imperial History: Culture, Identity and Modernity in Britain and the Empire, 1660-1840*. Cambridge: Cambridge University Press, 2004.

4 Wilson, A. R. 'The Maritime Transformation of Ming China'. In *China Goes to Sea: Maritime Transformation in Comparative Historical Perspective*, edited by A. S. Erickson, L. J. Goldstein and C. Lord, 238–85. Annapolis: Naval Institute Press, 2009.

5 Rose, S. *Medieval Naval Warfare, 1000-1500*. London: Routledge, 2002.

6 Glete, J. *Warfare at Sea, 1500-1650: Maritime Conflicts and the Transformation of Europe*. London: Routledge, 2000.

7 Glamann, K. 'European Trade 1500-1700'. In *The Fontana Economic History of Europe: The Sixteenth and Seventeenth Centuries*, edited by C. M. Cipolla, 427–527. London: Fontana, 1974.

8 Rose, *Medieval Naval Warfare, 1000-1500*, 109–16.

9 Trim, D. J. B. and M. C. Fissel, eds. *Amphibious Warfare, 1000-1700: Commerce, State Formation and European Expansion*. Leiden: Brill, 2006.

10 Parrott, D. *The Business of War: Military Entreprise and Military Revolution in Early Modern Europe*. Cambridge: Cambridge University Press, 2012.

11 Parry, J. H. *The Age of Reconnaissance: Discovery, Exploration and Settlement, 1450-1650*. London: Weidenfeld and Nicholson, 1963; Parry, J. H. *The Spanish Seaborne Empire*. London: Hutchinson, 1966; Boxer, C. R. *The Portuguese Seaborne Empire, 1415-1825*. London: Hutchinson, 1969; Boxer, C. R. *The Dutch Seaborne Empire, 1600-1800*. London: Hutchinson, 1965.

12 Cipolla, C. M. *Guns, Sails and Empires: Technological Innovation and the Early Phases of European Expansion, 1400-1700*. Mahatten, KS: Sunflower University Press, 1985; Raudzens, G. *Empires, Europe and Globalization, 1492-1788*. Stroud: Sutton, 1999.

13 Scammell, G. V. *The First Imperial Age: European Overseas Expansion, C1400-1715*, 71–6. London: Routledge, 1989.

14 Schurz, W. L. 'Mexico, Peru, and the Manila Galleon'. *Hispanic American Historical Review* 1, no. 4 (1918): 389–402.

15 Froude, J. A. *English Seamen in the 16th Century*. London: Longmans Green, 1895. See also Brady, C. *James Anthony Froude: An Intellectual Biography of a Victorian Prophet*. Oxford: Oxford University Press, 2013; Quinn, D. B. and A. N. Ryan. *England's Sea Empire, 1550-1642*. London: Allen and Unwin, 1983; Martin, C. and G. Parker. *The Spanish Armada*. 2nd edn. 1999 ed. London: Hamish Hamilton, 1988; Bicheno, H. *Elizabeth's Sea Dogs: How the English Became the Scourge of the Seas*. London: Conway, 2012.

16 Williamson, J. A. *The Ocean in English History*, 203–4. Oxford: Clarendon Press, 1941.

17 Sicking, L. *Neptune and the Netherlands: State, Economy and the War at Sea in the Renaissance*. History of Warfare, edited by K. Devries. Leiden: Brill, 2004; Israel, J. I. *Dutch Primacy in World Trade, 1585-1740*. Oxford: Clarendon Press, 1989; Haley, K. H. D. *The Dutch in the Seventeenth Century*. Library of European Civilization. Barraclough. London: Thames and Hudson, 1972.

18 Scott, J. *When the Waves Ruled Britannia: Geography and Political Identities, 1500-1800*. Cambridge: Cambridge University Press, 2011.

19 Levine, P. *The Amateur and the Professional: Antiquarians, Historians an Archaeologists in Victorian England, 1838-1886*. Cambridge: Cambridge University Press, 1986.

20 See, for example, Glasgow, T. 'The Navy in Philip and Mary's War, 1557–1558'. *The Mariner's Mirror* 53, no. 4 (1967): 321–42; Glasgow, T. 'The Navy in the French Wars of Mary and Elizabeth I'. *The Mariner's Mirror* 54, no. 3 (1968): 281–96; Glasgow, T. 'Maturing of Naval Administration, 1556-1564'. *The Mariner's Mirror* 56 (1970): 3–56; Parker, G. 'The Dreadnought Revolution of Tudor England'. *The Mariner's Mirror* 82 (1996): 269–300; Andrews, K. R. *Trade, Plunder and Settlement: Maritime Enterprise and the Genesis of the British Empire, 1480-1630*. Cambridge: Cambridge University Press, 1984; Adams, S. 'The Gran Armada 1988 and After'. *History* 76, no. 347 (1991), 238–49; Fernandez-Armesto, F. *The Spanish Armada: The*

Experience of War in 1588. Oxford: Oxford University Press, 1989; Loades, D. *The Tudor Navy: An Administrative, Political and Military History*. Studies in Naval History. Aldershot: Scholar Press, 1992; Loades, D. *The Making of the Elizabethan Navy, 1540-1590: From the Solent to the Armada*. Woodbridge: Boydell Press, 2009.

21 This is now available online at http://www.armada.mde.es/ArmadaPortal/page/Portal/ArmadaEspannola/ciencia_ihcn/01_a-cesareo-fernandez-duro (accessed 30 April 2014).

22 Rodriguez Salgado, M. J. 'The Spanish Story of the 1588 Armada Reassessed'. *Historical Journal* 33, no. 2 (1990): 461–78; Pierson, P. 'The Development of Spanish Naval Strategy and Tactics in the Sixteenth Century'. In *Politics, Religion and Diplomacy in Early Modern Europe: Essays in Honor of De Lemar Jensen*, edited by M. R. Thorp and A. J. Slavin, 191–218. Kirksville, MO: Sixteenth Century Journal Publishers Inc., 1994; Llano, J. Alcala Zamora y Quelpo de. *Espana, Flandres y el Mar del Norte (1618-1639)*. Barcelona: Planeta, 1975; Serrano-Mangas, F. *Los Galeones De La Carrera De Indias, 1650-1700*. Seville: Escuela de Estudios Hispano-Americanos de Sevilla, 1985; Phillips, C. R. *Six Galleons for the King of Spain: Imperial Defence in the Early Seventeenth Century*. Baltimore: Johns Hopkins University Press, 1986; Stradling, R. A. *The Armada of Flanders: Spanish Maritime Policy and European War, 1568-1668*. Cambridge: Cambridge University Press, 1992; Goodman, D. *Spanish Naval Power, 1589-1665: Reconstruction and Defeat*. Cambridge: Cambridge University Press, 1997. See also Marchena Giménez, J. M. *La Marina De Guerra de los Austurias; Una Approxima Bibliografica*. Madrid: Ministerio de defensa, 2010.

23 Tramond, J. *Manuel D'histoire de La Marine de La France Des Origines a 1815*. Paris: Clio, 1947; Masson, P. *Histoire de La Marine*: Vol. 1: L'Ere de la voile, Paris, 1981; Meyer, J. 'La Marine Française de 1545 á 1715'. In *Histoire Militaire de La France (Des Orgines À 1715)*, edited by P. Contamine and A. Corvisier, 486–526. Paris: Presses Universitaires de France, 1992; James, A. *Navy and Government in Early Modern France, 1572-1661*. Studies in History. Woodbridge: Boydell and Brewer, 2004.

24 The fullest account of the Mediterranean naval forces of this period is Olesa-Munido, F-F. *La Organizacion Naval de los Estados Mediterraneos y en especial de Espana durante Los Siglos XVI y XVII*. 2 vols. Madrid: Editorial Naval, 1968. Olesa-Munido does not deal with the Knights of St Stephen, but their history can be found in Guarnieri, G. *I Cavalieri Di Santo Stefano Nella Storia Della Marina Italiana (1562-1859)*. Pisa: Nistri-Lischi, 1960. For recent studies on the galley, see Guilmartin, J. F. *Gunpowder and Galleys: Changing Technology and Mediterranean Warfare at Sea in the Sixteenth Century*. Cambridge: Cambridge University Press, 1974; Pryor, J. H. 'The Geographical Conditions of Galley Navigation in the Mediterranean'. In *The Age of the Galley: Mediterranean Oared Vessels since Pre-Classical Times*, edited by R. Gardiner, 206–16. London: Conway, 1995; Dotson, J. E. 'Economics and Logistics of Galley Warfare'. In *The Age of the Galley: Mediterranean Oared Vessels since Pre-Classical Times*, 217–23. London: Conway, 1995.

25 Bicheno, H. *Crescent and Cross: The Battle of Lepanto 1571*, 146–8. London: Cassell, 2003.

26 Bamford, P. W. *Fighting Ships and Prisons: The Mediterranean Galleys of France in the Age of Louis XIV.* Minneapolis: University of Minnesota Press, 1973; Pike, R. *Penal Servitude in Early Modern Spain*, 3–26, 66–87. Madison: University of Wisconsin Press, 1983; for the role of domestic political considerations in the organization and structure of French naval forces, particularly the galley fleet, James, A. *Navy and Government in Early Modern France, 1572-1661.* Studies in History, 92–107. Woodbridge: Boydell and Brewer, 2004; Marteillhe, J. *Galley Slave.* Barnsley: Seaforth, 2010.

27 Hocker, F. *Vasa: A Swedish Ship.* Stockholm: Medstroms Bokforlag, 2011.

28 Glete, J. 'Bridge and Bulwark: The Swedish Navy and the Baltic 1500-1809'. In *In Quest of Trade and Security: The Baltic in Power Politics, 1500-1900*, edited by G. Rystad, K-R. Bohme and W. N. Carlgren, 9–60. Lund: Lund University Press, 1994.

29 Teitler, G. *The Genesis of the Professional Officers Corps.* London: Sage, 1977. This volume provides a wide-ranging generalized sociological approach to the emergence of professional officer corps at sea and on land. The stated preconditions of professionalization and the conclusions could do with detailed comparative studies.

30 Glete, *Warfare at Sea, 1500-1650*, 165–85.

31 Lavery, B. *The Ship of the Line. Vol. 1: The Development of the Battlefleet, 1650-1850*, 22–3. London: Conway Maritime Press, 1983.

32 Murphy, E. *Ireland and the War at Sea, 1641-1653*, 54–61. Woodbridge: Boydell and Brewer, 2012.

33 Thrush, A. 'In Pursuit of the Frigate, 1603-40'. *Historical Journal* 64 (1991): 29–45.

34 Maltby, W. 'Politics, Professionalism and the Evolution of Sailing Ship Tactics, 1650-1714'. In *The Tools of War: Instruments, Ideas and Institutions of Warfare, 1445-1871*, edited by J. A. Lynn, 56–73. Urbana: University of Illinois Press, 1990.

35 Corbett, J. S. *Fighting Instructions, 1530-1816.* London: Navy Records Society, 1905; Mainwaring, G. E., ed. *The Life and Works of Sir Henry Mainwaring.* 2 vols. London: Navy Records Society, 1920–1; Powell, J. R. and E. K. Timings, eds. *Documents Relating to the Civil War, 1642-1648.* London: Navy Records Society, 1963; Tanner, J. R., ed. *Two Discourse on the Navy, 1638 and 1659.* London: Navy Records Society, 1896; Oppenheim, M., ed. *The Naval Tracts of Sir William Monson.* Vols 1–4. London: Navy Records Society, 1902–13; Perrin, W. G., ed. *The Autobiography of Phineas Pett.* London: Navy Records Society, 1917; McGowan, A. P., ed. *The Jacobean Commissions of Enquiry, 1608 and 1618.* London: Navy Records Society, 1971. Other important works include Andrews, K. R. *Ships, Money and Politics: Seafaring and Naval Enterprise in the Reign of Charles I.* Cambridge, Cambridge University Press, 1991. Theses that have important contributions include McGowan, A. P. 'The Royal Navy under the First Duke of Buckingham, Lord High Admiral, 1618-28'. PhD, London, 1967; Appleby, J. C. 'English Privateering during the French and Spanish Wars, 1625-1630'. PhD, Hull, 1983; Hebb, D. D. 'The English Government and the Problem of Piracy, 1616-1642'. PhD, London,

1985; Thrush, A. 'The Navy under Charles I, 1635-1640'. PhD, London, 1991; Clayton, N. 'Naval Administration, 1603-1628'. PhD, Leeds, 1935.

36 Powell, J. R. *The Navy in the English Civil War*. London: Archon Books, 1962. See also Hebb, D. D. *Piracy and the English Government, 1616-1642*. Aldershot: Scholar Press, 1994.

37 See, for example, Powell, J. R. *Robert Blake: General-at-Sea*. London: Collins, 1972; Baumber, M. *General-at-Sea: Robert Blake and the Seventeenth Century Revolution in Naval Warfare*. London: John Murray, 1989; Anderson, R. C. 'The Royalists at Sea, 1648'. *The Mariner's Mirror* 9, no. 2 (1923): 34–46; Anderson, R. C. 'The Royalists at Sea in 1650'. *The Mariner's Mirror* 17, no. 2 (1931): 135–68.

38 Wilson, C. *Profit and Power: A Study of England and the Dutch Wars*. London: Longman Green and Co., 1957; Peck, L. L. *Court Patronage and Corruption in Early Stuart England*. London: Routledge, 1991; Young, M. B. *Servility and Service: The Life and Work of Sir John Coke*. Woodbridge: Royal Historical Society, 1986.

39 Capp, B. *Cromwell's Navy: The Fleet and the English Revolution, 1648-1660*, 15–41. Cambridge: Cambridge University Press, 1989.

40 Tilly, C., ed. *The Formation of National States in Western Europe*. Princeton: Princeton University Press, 1975; Tilly, C. *Coercion, Capital and European States*. Oxford: Oxford University Press, 1990.

41 Storrs, C., ed. *The Fiscal-Military State in Eighteenth Century Europe: Essays in Honour of P.G.M. Dickson*. Aldershot: Ashgate, 2009.

42 Downing, B. M. *The Military Revolution and Political Change: Origins of Democracy and Autocracy in Early Modern Europe*. Princeton: University of Princeton Press, 1992.

43 Meyers, A. R. *Parliaments and Estates in Europe to 1789*. London: Thames and Hudson, 1975; Miller, J., ed. *Absolutism in Seventeenth Century Europe*. London: Macmillan, 1990.

44 Brewer, J. *The Sinews of Power: War, Money and the English State, 1688-1783*. London: Unwin Hyman, 1989.

45 Knight, R. and M. Wilcox. 'War, Government and the Market: The Direction of the Debate on the British Contractor State, c.1740-1815'. In *The Contractor State and Its Implications, 1659-1815*, edited by R. Harding and S. Solbes Ferri, 175–98. Las Palmas: Universidad de las Palmas de Gran Canaria, 2012.

46 Glete, *Warfare at Sea, 1500-1650*, 60–9; Glete, J. *War and the State in Early Modern Europe: Spain, the Dutch Republic and Sweden as Fiscal-Military States, 1500-1660*. London: Routledge, 2002.

47 Wheeler, J. S. *The Making of a World Power: War and the Military Revolution in Seventeenth Century England*. Stroud: Sutton Publishing, 1999.

48 Brenner, R. *Merchants and Revolution: Commercial Change, Political Conflict and London's Oveseas Traders, 1550-1653*. Cambridge: Cambridge University Press, 1993.

49 Conway, S. and R. Torres Sanchez, eds. *The Spending of States: Military Expenditure During the Long Eighteenth Century: Patterns, Organisation and Consequences*. Saarbrucken: VDM Verlag Dr Muller, 2011.

NOTES

50 North, D. C. 'Institutions'. *Journal of Economic Perspectives* 5, no. 1 (1991): 97–112.

51 Prestwich, M. 'Diplomacy and Trade in the Protectorate'. *Journal of Modern History* 22 (1950): 103–21; Howat, G. M. D. *Stuart and Cromwellian Foreign Policy*, 74–93. London: Black, 1974; Conquest, R. 'The State and Commercial Expansion in England in the Years 1642-1688'. *Journal of European Economic History* 14 (1985): 155–72.

52 Taylor, S. A. G. *The Western Design: An Account of Cromwell's Expedition to the Caribbean*. Kingston: Solstice, 1969.

53 Webb, S. S. *1676: The End of American Independence*. New York: Alfred A. Knopf, 1984.

54 Bruijn, J. R. *The Dutch Navy in the Seventeenth and Eighteenth Centuries*. Columbia: University of South Carolina Press, 1993.

55 Pincus, S. *Ideologies and the Making of English Foreign Policy, 1650-1668*. Cambridge: Cambridge University Press, 1996.

56 Harding, R. *The Evolution of the Sailing Navy, 1509-1815*. British History in Perspective, 69–84. Basingstoke: Macmillan, 1995.

57 The three-deck ship had a chequered history, falling in and out of favour, as the size and displacements of warships and weight of guns carried generally expanded. See Lavery, B. *The Ship of the Line*, vol. 1, 30–75. London: Conway, 1983; Lavery, B. 'The Ship of the Line'. In *The Line of Battle: The Sailing Warship, 1650-1840*, edited by R. Gardiner, 11–26. London: Conway, 1992.

58 Harding, R. *Seapower and Naval Warfare, 1650-1830*, 13–36. London: UCL Press, 1999.

59 Glete, J. *Navies and Nations; Warships, Navies and State Building in Europe and America, 1500-1860*, vol. 1, 187–92; vol. 2, 550–1, 574, 639. Stockholm: Almqvist and Wiksell, 1993.

60 This assumption has been challenged in Davies, J. D. 'Introduction'. In *Dutch Warships in the Age of Sail, 1600-1714*, edited by J. Bender, 17–44, especially 26–7. Barnsley: Seaforth, 2014.

61 Meyer, J. *Colbert*, 260–95. Paris: Hachette, 1981; Taillemitte, E. 'Colbert et la Marine.' In. *Un Nouveau Colbert*, edited by R. Mousnier, 216–28. Paris: SEDIE, 1985.

62 An excellent collection of essays, representing the origins and the state of the debate in the mid-1990s, is Rogers, C. J., ed. *The Military Revolution Debate: Readings on the Military Transformation of Early Modern Europe*. Boulder: Westview, 1995. A good recapitulation of the position, illustrating how the geographical dimension has played into the debate, is Black, J. *Beyond the Military Revolution: War in the Seventeenth Century World*. London: Palgrave, 2011. Also important is the December 2011 issue of the *Journal for Maritime Research* 13 (2011), which is devoted to the Military Revolution debate and how it relates to naval affairs.

63 Guilmartin, J. F. 'The Military Revolution: Origins and First Tests Abroad'. In *The Military Revolution Debate: Readings in the Military Transformation of Early Modern Europe*, edited by C. Rogers, 299–333. Boulder, 1995; Black, *Beyond the Military Revolution*.

64 Raudzens, G. 'Military Revolution or Maritime Evolution? Military Superiorites or Transport Advantges as Main Causes of European Colonial Conquests to 1788'. *Journal of Military History* 63, no. 3 (1999): 631–41.

65 Glete, *Navies and Nations*, vol. 2, 501–18, 706–9.

66 Ware, C. *The Bomb Vessel: Shore Bombardment Ships of the Age of Sail*. London: Conway, 1994.

67 Fox, F. *Great Ships: The Battlefleet of King Charles II*. London: Conway Maritime Press, 1980; Harding, R. 'Contractors, Warships of the Royal Navy and Sea Power, 1739-1748'. In *The Contractor State and Its Implications, 1659-1815*, edited by R. Harding and S. Solbes Ferri, 159–74. Las Palmas: Universidad de Las Palmas de Gran Canaria, 2012; Knight, R. 'Devil bolts and deception? Wartime naval shipbuilding in private shipyards, 1739–1815'. *Journal for Maritime Research* 5 (2003): 34–51.

68 Work has been done on most periods from the early sixteenth century until the demise of that form of warfare in the second half of the nineteenth century. A wide selection of essays on the history of privateering can be found in Mollat, M., ed. *Course et Piraterie*. Paris: Centre National de la Recherche Scientifique, 1975. Of particular interest for the matter in hand are Delumeau, J. 'La Guerre de Course Francaise sous L'Ancien Regime'. In *Course et Piraterie*, edited by M. Mollat, 271–91. Other important works include Bruijn, J. R. 'Dutch Privateering during the Second and Third Dutch Wars'. *Acta Historicae Neerlandicae* 11 (1977): 79–93. The extensive work of John Bromley, primarily on French privateering, is helpfully collected into a single volume: Bromley, J. S. *Corsairs and Navies, 1660-1760*. London: Hambledon Press, 1987. The standard work on British privateering is Starkey, D. J. *British Privateering Enterprise in the Eighteenth Century*. Exeter: University of Exeter Press, 1990. For an earlier period, see Meyer, W. 'English Privateering in the War of 1688-1697'. *The Mariner's Mirror* 67 (1981): 259–72 and Meyer, W. 'English Privateering in the War of Spanish Succession, 1702-1713'. *The Mariner's Mirror* 69 (1983): 435–46. For the war against maritime commerce more generally, see Tracy, N. *Attack on Maritime Trade*. London: Macmillan, 1991. See also *Revue historique de Dunkerque et du Littoral* (Colloque Jean Bart et son Temps), 37 (January 2004).

69 Jones, D. W. *War and Economy in the Age of William III and Marlborough*. Oxford: Blackwell, 1988. For the debates over strategy, see Johnston, J. A. 'Parliament and the Navy, 1688-1714'. PhD, Cambridge, 1968; Denman, T. J. 'The Political Debate over Strategy, 1689-1712'. PhD, Cambridge, 1985; Hattendorf, J. H. *England in the War of Spanish Succession: A Study of the English View and Conduct of Grand Strategy, 1702-1712*. New York: Garland, 1987.

70 Otero Lana, E. *Los Cosarios Españoles durante la Decadencia de los Austrias. El Corso Español del Atlantico peninsular en el siglo xvii(1621-1697)* Madrid: Editorial Naval, 1992; De la Ronciere, C. *Histoire de la Marine Française*. Paris: E. Plon, Nouritt et cie, 1932. 6 vols. vi (Le Crépuscule du Grand Régne l'Apogé de la Guerre de Course), 406–8.

71 Powley, E. B. *The Naval Side of King William's War*, 146–8. London: John Baker, 1972; Aubrey, P. *The Defeat of James Stuart's Armada, 1692*, 51–8,

133–48. Leicester: University of Leicester Press, 1979; Villiers, P. 'Marine de Colbert ou Marine de Seignelay: Victoire de Barfleur et Progess Technique'. In *Guerres Maritime (1688-1713)*, 173–92. Vincennes: Service Historique de la Marine, 1996. The naval side of the War of Spanish Succession is in need of modern research. Standard works are still Bourne, R. *Queen Anne's Navy in the West Indies*. New Haven: Yale University Press, 1939; Owen, J. H. *War at Sea under Queen Anne, 1702-1708*. Cambridge: Cambridge University Press, 1938.

72 Buchet, C. *La Lutte pour l'Espace Caribe et la Façade Atlantique de l'Amérique Centrale du Sud (1672-1763)*. 2 vols. i, 26–9, 197–203. Paris: Editeur, 1991. For the French expedition to Cartagena, see Nerzic, J. Y. and C. Buchet. *Marins et Flibustiers du Roi Soleil: Carthagène 1697*. Paris: Pyrégraph, 2002. For the expeditions to Canada, see Graham, G., ed. *The Walker Expedition to Quebec, 1711*. London: Navy Records Society, 1953; Harding, R. 'The Expeditions to Quebec, 1690 and 1711: The Evolution of British Trans-Atlantic Amphibious Power'. In *Guerres Maritimes (1688-1713)*, 197–212. Vincennes: Service Historique de la Marine, 1992. The development of English amphibious capability is covered in McClay, K. 'Combined Operations: British Naval and Military Co-operation in the Wars of 1688-1713'. PhD, Glasgow, 2003.

73 Bromley, J. 'The North Sea in Wartime, 1688-1713'. *Bijdragen en Mededelingen Befreffende de Geschiedenis der Nederlanden* 92 (1977): 270–99.

74 Anderson, R. C. *Naval Wars in the Baltic*, 128–207. For the Russian fleet, see Tredrea, J. and E. Sozaev. *Russian Warships in the Age of Sail, 1696-1860: Design, Construction, Careers and Fates*. Barnsley: Seaforth, 2010.

75 The best overview of these wars is still Anderson, R. C. *Naval Wars in the Levant, 1559-1853*, 185–236, 243–69. Liverpool: Liverpool University Press, 1952. See also Anderson, R. C. 'The Sicilian War of 1674-1678'. *The Mariner's Mirror* 57 (1971): L 239–65. The best overview of early amphibious operations is Trim, D. J. B. and M. C. Fissel, eds. *Amphibious Warfare, 1000-1700: Commerce, State Formation and European Expansion*. Leiden: Brill, 2006.

76 Jones, D. W. *War and Economy in the Age of William III and Marlborough*, 198–226. Oxford: Blackwell, 1988.

77 Glete, *Nations and Navies*, i, 226. The term 'British' rather than 'English' fleet is employed hereafter, as the Union with Scotland in 1707 changed the status of the Crown's naval resources.

78 Corbett, J. S. *England in the Mediterranean: A Study of the Role and Influence of British Power within the Straits, 1603-1714*. 2 vols, ii, 142–78. London: Longman, 1904. John Ehrman traces the decision further back than Corbett, to 1692: Ehrman, J. *The Navy in the War of William III, 1689-1697: Its State and Direction*, 495–7. Cambridge: Cambridge University Press, 1953; Davies, J. D. 'Gibraltar in Naval Strategy, c1600-1783'. *Transactions of the Naval Dockyards Society* 2 (December 2006): 9–18; Le Fevre, P. 'Gibraltar, Tangier and the English Mediterranean Fleet, 1680-1690'. *Transactions of the Naval Dockyards Society* 2 (December 2006): 19–30.

79 Coad, J. *The Royal Dockyards, 1690-1850: Architecture and Engineering Works of the Sailing Navy*. Aldershot: Scolar Press, 1989.

80 McNeill, J. R. *Atlantic Empires of France and Spain: Louisbourg and Havana, 1700-1750*. Chapel Hill: University of North Carolina Press, 1985.

81 Ubbelohde, C. *The American Colonies and the British Empire, 1607-1763*, 1–8. London: Routledge, 1968; Paulin, C. O. *Paulin's History of Naval Administration, 1775-1911*. Annapolis: Naval Institute Press, 1968. The latter is a reprinting of a collection of essays written between 1905 and 1914.

82 Oppenheim, M. *A History of the Administration of the Royal Navy and of the Merchant Shipping in Relation to the Navy from 1509 to 1660 with an Introduction Treating of the Preceding Period*. London: Bodley Head, 1896. See, particularly, O. A. R. Murray's ten-part, posthumous, unfinished history 'The Admiralty', *The Mariner's Mirror* 23 (1937): 13–35, 129–47, 316–31; 24 (1938):101–4, 204–25, 329–52, 458–75; 25 (1939): 89–111, 216–28, 328–38. Murray had served in the Admiralty for his whole professional life, and was Secretary to the Board of Admiralty from 1917 until his death in 1936. See also Lady M. *The Making of a Civil Servant: Sir Oswyn Murray GCB, Secretary of the Admiralty, 1917-1936*. London: Methuen, 1940; James, G. F. and J. J. Sutherland Shaw. 'Admiralty Administration and Personnel, 1619-1714'. *Bulletin of the Institute of Historical Research* 14 (1936–7): 10–24, 166–83.

83 The phrase is used by van Crefeld in relation to the campaign in northwest Europe, 1944–5, but applies equally, if not more so, to the Pacific Campaign, 1941–5. See van Crefeld, M. *Supplying War: Logistics from Wallenstein to Patton*, 203–30. Cambridge: Cambridge University Press, 1977.

84 Penrose, E. *The Theory of the Growth of the Firm*. Oxford: Blackwell, 1959.

85 Knight, R. 'Changing the Agenda: The New Naval History of the British Sailing Navy'. *The Mariner's Mirror* 97 (2011): 225–42. As Knight's article makes clear, this interest was not limited to naval historians.

86 Baugh, D. *British Naval Administration in the Age of Walpole*. Princeton: Princeton University Press, 1965; Baugh, D. *Naval Administration, 1715-1750*. London: Navy Records Society, 1977; Syrett, D. *Shipping and the American War, 1775-83: A Study of British Transport Organization*. London: University of London Press, 1970. Syrett continued to work on the eighteenth-century administration of shipping organization until the end of his life. See his posthumously published *Shipping and Military Power in the Seven Years War*. Exeter: University of Exeter Press, 2008; Knight, R. J. B. 'Civilians and the Navy, 1660-1832'. In *Sea Studies: Essays in Honour of Basil Greenhill*, ed. Basil Greenhill, 63–70. London: National Maritime Museum, 1983; Knight, R. J. B. 'The performance of the Royal Dockyards in England during the American War of Independence'. *Proceedings of the 14th Conference of the International Commission for Maritime History*. London, 1974; Knight, R. J. B. 'The Building and Maintenance of the British Fleet during the Anglo-French Wars, 1688-1815'. In *Les Marines de Guerre Européennes XVII-XVIIIe siècles*, edited by M. Acerra, J. Merino and J. Meyer, 35–43. Paris: Presses de l'Université de Paris-Sorbonne, 1985; Crimmin, P. K. 'Admiralty Relations with the Treasury, 1783-1806: The Preparation of Estimates and the Beginnings of Treasury Control'. *The Mariner's Mirror* 53 (1969): 63–72; Crimmin, P. K. 'The Sick and Hurt Board and the Health of Seamen, c1700-1806'. *Journal*

for Maritime Research 1(1999): 48–65; Webb, P. 'The Rebuilding and Repair of the Fleet, 1783-1793'. *Bulletin of the Institute of Historical Research* 50 (1977): 194–209; Webb, P. 'Construction, Repair and Maintenance of the Royal Navy, 1793-1815'. In *The British Navy and the Uses of Naval Power*, edited by J. Black and P. Woodfine, 207–19. Leicester: University of Leicester Press, 1989.

87 Morriss, R. *The Royal Dockyards during the Revolutionary and Napoleonic Wars*. Leicester: University of Leicester Press, 1983; Morriss, R. *Naval Power and British Culture, 1760-1850: Public Trust and Government Ideology*. Aldershot: Ashgate, 2004; Morriss, R. *The Foundations of British Maritime Ascendency: Resources, Logistics and the State, 1755-1815*. Cambridge: Cambridge University Press, 2011; Haas, J. M. 'The Royal Dockyards: The Earliest Visitations and Reform, 1749-1778'. *Historical Journal* 13 (1970): 191–215. Haas subsequently chronologically expanded his study of the dockyards in *A Management Odyssey: The Royal Dockyards, 1714-1914*. New York: University Press of America, 1994; Coats, A. 'Efficiency in Dockyard Administration 1660-1800: A Reassessment'. In *The Age of Sail. The International Annual of the Historic Sailing Ship*, edited by N. Tracy, 116–32. London: Conway, 2002; Wilkinson, C. *The British Navy and the State in the Eighteenth Century*. Woodbridge: Boydell Press, 2004; Davey, J. 'War, Naval Logistics and the British State: Supplying the Baltic Fleet, 1808-1812'. PhD, Greenwich, 2009; Knight, R. and M. Wilcox. *Sustaining the Fleet, 1793-1815: War, the British Navy and the Contractor State*. Woodbridge: Boydell Press, 2010; MacDonald, J. *The British Navy's Victualling Board, 1793-1815: Management Competence and Incompetence*. Woodbridge: Boydell Press, 2010.

88 Buchet, C. *Marine, Économie et Société: Une Exemple d'interaction: l'avitaillement de la Royal Navy Durant la guerre de sept ans*. Paris: Honoré Champion Not Editeur, 1999, 19.

89 Glete, J. *Swedish Naval Administration, 1521-1721: Resource Flows and Organizational Capabilities*. Leiden: Brill, 2010.

90 Mahan, *The Influence of Sea Power Upon History*, 158–9, 225–7; Bourne, R. *Queen Anne's Navy in the West Indies*, 262–4. New Haven: Yale University Press, 1939; Jenkins, E. H. *A History of the French Navy*, 105. London: Macdonald and Jane, 1973; Symcox, G. *The Crisis of French Seapower 1688-1697: From the Guerre d'Escadre to the Gurerre de Course*. Hague: Nijhoff, 1974. For an excellent overview of the Anglo-French naval conflict, see Dull, J. R. *The Age of the Ship of the Line: The British and French Navies, 1650-1815*. Barnsley: Seaforth Publishing, 2009. See Lacour-Gayet, G. *La Marine Militaire de la France sous la Règne de Louis XV*, 9–17. Paris: Champion, 1902 (2nd edn. 1910); Tramond, J. *Manuel d'Histoire Maritime de la France (des Origines à 1815)*, 311–33, 369. Paris: Société d'éditions géographiques, maritimes et coloniales, 1937; De la Ronciere, *Histoire de la Marine Française*, vi, 588–90; Symcox, G. 'The Navy of Louis XIV'. In *The Reign of Louis XIV: Essays in Celebration of Andrew Lossky*, edited by P. Sonnino, 127–42. New Jersey, 1990; Dessert, D. *La Royale: Vaisseaux et Marine de Louis XIV*. Paris: Fayard, 1996.

91 Paoletti, C. 'Prince Eugene of Savoy, the Toulon Expedition and the English Historians: A Dissenting View'. *Journal of Military History* 70, no. 4 (2006): 939–62.

92 Taillemite, E. 'Une Marine pour quoi faire? La Strategie Navale de Louis XIV'. In *Guerres Maritimes (1688-1713)*, 93–102. Vincennes: Service Historique de la Marine, 1996. On the replacements for losses at Barfleur, see Acerra, M. 'Les Forces Navales Française au début de la Guerre de la Ligue d'Augsbourg'. In *Guerres Maritimes (1688-1713)*, 15–24. Vincenne: Service Historique de la Marine s, 1996; Meyer, J. 'La Marine Française de 1545 à 1715'. In *Histoire Militaire de la France (Des Orgines à 1715)*, edited by P. Contamine, 486–526, especially 513–26. Paris: Presses Universitaires de France, 1992; Pilgrim, D. G. 'The Uses and Limitations of French Naval Power in the Reign of Louis XIV: The Administration of the Marquis de Seignelay, 1683-1690'. PhD, Brown University, 1969.

93 Bourland, R. D. 'Maurepas and his Administration of the French Navy on the Eve of the War of Austrian Succession (1737-1742)', 137–50. PhD, Notre Dame, 1978.

94 Acerra, M. and A. Zysberg *L'Essor des Marines de Guerres Europeennes (vers 1680 vers 1790)*. Paris: SEDES, 1997; Acerra, M. 'L'Arsenal, Pivot de la Puissance Maritime?' In *La Puissance Maritime*, edited by C. Buchet, J. Meyer and J-P. Poussou. Paris: Presses de l'Université Paris-Sorbonne, 2004.

95 Storrs, C. *The Resilience of the Spanish Monarchy, 1665*-1700, 63–105. Oxford: Oxford University Press, 2006; Glete, *Nations and Navies*, i, 241.

96 Fernández Duro, *Armada española*, vi, 209–21. See also de Béthencourt y Massieu, A. *Patiño en la Politica Internacional de Felipe V*. Valladolid: CSIC, 1954. The best study of the Spanish Navy in the eighteenth century is Merino Navarro, J. P. *La Armada Española en el Siglo XVIII*. Madrid: Fundación Universitária Española, 1981. See also Harbron, J. D. *Trafalgar and the Spanish Navy*, 11–39. London: Conway, 1988. For the changing Spanish administrative system, see also Domínguez Ortez, A. *Sociedad y Estado en el Siglo XVIII Español*. Barcelona: Ariel, 1976.

97 Bruijn, J. R. *The Dutch Navy in the Seventeenth and Eighteenth Centuries*, xiii. Columbia: University of South Carolina Press, 1993. Bruijn, J. R. 'De Admiraliteit van Friesland an Amsterdam in de Eerste Helft van de Achttiende Eeuw'. *Jaarboek van het Fries Scheepvaart Museum in Oudheidkamer* (1966): 33–7; Bruijn, J. R. 'A Little Incident in 1707: The Demise of a Once Glorious Dutch Naval Organization'. In A. M. Forsberg et al., *Organizing History*, 110–22.

98 For Anglo-Dutch friction over the latter's commercial advantages, both when these nations were allies and when the Dutch were neutral, see Clark, G. N. *The Dutch Alliance and the War against French Trade, 1688-1697*, 63–119. Manchester: Manchester University Press, 1923; Pares, R. *Colonial Blockade and Neutral Rights, 1739-1763*, 231–54. Oxford: Oxford University Press, 1938. For the diplomatic problems of the Dutch Republic and those associated with its close financial relationship with Britain, see Carter, A. C. *The Dutch Republic in the Seven Years War*. London: Macmillan, 1971; Wilson, C. *Anglo-Dutch Commerce and Finance in the Eighteenth Century*.

Cambridge: Cambridge University Press, 1941; 't Hart, M. 'Mobilising Resources for War: The Dutch and British Financial Revolutions Compared'. In *War, State and Development. Fiscal-Military States in the Eighteenth Century*, edited by R. T. Sánchez, 179–200. Barañáin, EUNSA, 2007; van Sas, N. 'Between the Devil and the Deep Blue Sea: The Logic of Neutrality'. In *Colonial Empires Compared: Britain and the Netherlands, 1750-1850*, edited by B. Moore and H. van Neirop, 33–44. Aldershot: Ashgate, 2003.

99 For a very useful collection of essays that reflects the historiographical emphases in the scholarship of the Anglo-Dutch relationship, see Raven, G. J. A. and N. A. M. Rodger, eds. *Navies and Armies: The Anglo-Dutch Relationship in War and Peace*. Edinburgh: Donald, 1990. See also Raven, G. J. A. 'A Summary of the Development of Netherlands Naval Organization'. *Revue Internationale d'Histoire Militaire* 58 (1984): 155–65. See also the leading Dutch-language journal, *Tijdschrift voor Zegeschiedenis*.

100 Symonds, *Navalists and Anti-Navalists*; Smith, G. A. 'A Means to an End: Gunboats and Thomas Jefferson's Theory of Defense'. *American Neptune* 55 (1994): 111–21; Smelser, M. *Congress Founds Navy, 1787-1798*. Notre Dame: University of Notre Dame Press, 1959; McKee, C. *A Gentlemanly and Honorable Profession: The Creation of the U.S. Naval Officer Corps, 1794-1815*, 43–50. Annapolis: Naval Institute Press, 1991. See also Hagan, K. J. *This People's Navy: The Making of American Sea Power*. New York: Free Press, 1991.

101 Nuxoll, E. M. 'The American Navy, the "War of Finance"', and the Quest for Specie'. In *New Interpretations in Naval History*, edited by W. B. Cogar, 28–44. Shrewsbury: Tri-Service Press, 1989; Long, D. F. 'The Navy under the Board of Navy Commissioners, 1815-1842'. In *In War and Peace: Interpretations of American Naval History*, edited by K. J. Hagen, 62–78. Westport: Greenwood, 1984.

102 See, for example, Bridge, C. A. G., ed. *History of the Russian Fleet during the Reign of Peter the Great by a Contemporary Englishman (1724)*. London: Navy Records Society, 1899; Anderson, *Naval Wars in the Baltic, 1522-1850*; Anderson, R. C. 'British and American Officers in the Russian Navy'. *The Mariner's Mirror* 33, no. 1 (1947): 17–27; Anderson, M. S. 'Great Britain and the Russian Fleet, 1769-1770'. *Slavonic and East European Studies Review*, no. December (1952): 148–64; Christie, I. R. 'Samuel Bentham and the Russian Dniepre Flotilla, 1787-1788'. *Slavonic and East European Studies Review* 50 (1972): 173–96; Clendenning, P. H. 'Admiral Sir Charles Knowles and Russia, 1771–1774.' *The Mariner's Mirror* 61, no. 1 (1975): 39–49. A regional balance is now much better since the publication of Phillips, E. J. *The Founding of Russia's Navy: Peter the Great and the Azov Fleet, 1688-1714*. Westport: Greenwood, 1995. The history of the ships themselves is covered with short contextual essays in J. Tredrea and E. Sozaev, *Russian Warships in the Age of Sail*.

103 Monasterev, A. and S. Terestchenko. *Histoire de las Marine Russe*. Paris: Payot, 1932.

104 Aldridge, D. D. *Admiral Sir John Norris and the British Naval Expeditions to the Baltic Sea, 1715-1726*. Lund: Nordic Academic Press, 2009.

105 Hattendorf, J. B. 'Admiral Sir George Byng and the Cape Passaro Incident, 1718: A Case Study in the use of the Royal Navy as a Deterrent'. In *Guerres et Paix*, 19–38. Vincennes: Service Historique de la Marine, 1987. For an account of the campaign, see Cranmer-Byng, J. L., ed. *Pattee Byng's Journal, 1718-1720*. London: Navy Records Society, 1950.

106 Clowes, W. L. *The Royal Navy: A History from the Earliest Times to 1900*, iii, 29–39, 261–5. London: Sampson, Low, Maston, 1898; Harding, R. 'Gibraltar: A Tale of Two Sieges, 1726-7 and 1779-83'. *Transactions of the Naval Dockyards Society* 2 (2006): 31–46.

107 Anderson, *Naval Wars in the Levant*, 243–69.

108 Pares, R. *War, Trade and the West Indies, 1739-1763*. Oxford: Oxford University Press, 1936; Graham, G. S. *Empire of the North Atlantic: The Maritime Struggle for North America*. Toronto: University of Toronto Press, 1950; Graham, G. S. *The Politics of Naval Supremacy: Studies in British Maritime Ascendancy*. Cambridge: Cambridge University Press, 196; Satsuma, S. *Britain and Colonial Maritime War in the Early Eighteenth Century: Silver, Seapower and the Atlantic*. Woodbridge: Boydell Press, 2013.

109 McNeill, J. R. *Atlantic Empires of France and Spain: Louisbourg and Havana, 1700-1763*. Chapel Hill: University of North Carolina Press, 1985; Sanders, G. E. 'The Spanish Defense of America, 1700-1763'. PhD, Southern California, 1973; McNeill, J. R. 'The Ecological Basis of Warfare in the Caribbean, 1700-1804'. In *Adapting to Conditions: War and Society in the Eighteenth Century*, edited by M. Ultee, 26–42. Tuscaloosa: University of Alabama Press, 1986; Zapatero, J. M. *Historia de las Fortificaciones de Cartagena de Indias*. Madrid: Centro Iberoamericano de cooperacion, 1979; Zapatero, J. M. 'La Fortificación y la Defensa del Islmo Centralamericano en la Contienda Angloespañola del Siglo XVIII'. *Revista ASINTO* 7, no. 25 (1960): 5–30; Fernández, J. M. *Oficiales y Soldados en la Ejercito de America*. Seville: CSIC, 1983; de Zuletta, J. 'Health and Military Factors in Vernon's Failure at Cartagena'. *The Mariner's Mirrror* 78 (1992): 127–41.

110 For an introduction to Atlantic history, see Bailyn, B. *Atlantic History: Concept and Contours*. Cambridge, MA: Harvard University Press, 2005. For a strongly economic perspective, reflecting the historiographical focus of the times, see Davies, K. G. *The North Atlantic World in the Seventeenth Century*. Oxford: Oxford University Press, 1974. Ian Steele places the communication network at the centre of an English Atlantic world, and, by extension, the role of naval power in maintaining this network: see Steele's *The English Atlantic, 1675-1740*. Oxford: Oxford University Press, 1986. War and maritime defence run as a thread through the essays in McCusker. J. J. and Morgan, K., eds. *The Early Modern Atlantic Economy*. Cambridge: Cambridge University Press, 2000; see also Canny, N. and P. Morgan. *The Oxford Handbook of the Atlantic World, 1450-1850*. Oxford: Oxford University Press, 2011.

111 For an operational history of this war, see Richmond, H. W. *The Navy in the War of 1739-48*. 3 vols. Cambridge: Cambridge University Press, 1920. For the naval war in the wider context, see Harding, R. *The Emergence of Britain's Global Naval Supremacy: The War of 1739-1748*. Woodbridge: Boydell and Brewer, 2010.

112 Marder, A. J. *Portrait of an Admiral: The Life and Papers of Herbert Richmond*. Cambridge, MA: University of Harvard Press, 1952; Hunt, B. D. *Sailor-Scholar: Admiral Sir Herbert Richmond, 1871-1946*. Ontario: Wilfred Laurier University Press, 1982.

113 Pares, R. 'American Versus Continental Warfare, 1739-1763'. *English Historical Review* 51, no. July (1936): 429–65.

114 Rodger, N. A. M. 'Queen Elizabeth and the Myth of Sea Power in English History'. *Transactions of the Royal Historical Society* (6th series) 14 (2004): 153–74.

115 Corbett, J. S. *England and the Seven Years War: A Study of Combined Strategy*. 2 vols. London: Longman, 1907. See also Callwell, C. E. *Military Operations and Maritime Preponderance: Their Relations and Interdependence*. Edinburgh: Blackwood, 1905.

116 Liddell Hart, B. *The British Way in Warfare*. London: Faber and Faber, 1932; Liddell Hart, B. *The Strategy of the Indirect Approach*. London: Faber and Faber, 1941. See also Bond, B. *Liddell Hart: A Study of his Military Thought*, 37–87. London; Cassell, 1976; Danchev, A. *Alchemist of War: The Life of Basil Liddell Hart*, 156–83. London: Weidenfeld and Nicholson, 1998.

117 Terraine, J. 'History and the Indirect Approach'. *Journal of the United Services Institution* 116 (1971): 44–9; Black, J. *The Continental Commitment: Britain, Hanover and Interventionism, 1714-1793*. London: Routledge, 2005; Peters, M. 'Early Hanoverian Consciousness: Europe or Empire'. *English Historical Review* 122 (2007): 632–68; Rodger, N. A. M. 'The Continental Commitment in the Eighteenth Century'. In *War, Strategy and International Politics: Essays in Honour of Sir Michael Howard*, edited by L. Freedman, P. Hayes and R. O'Neill, 39–55. Oxford: Oxford University Press, 1992.

118 Self, R. *British Foreign and Defence Policy since 1945: Challenges and Dilemmas in a Changing World*. Basingstoke: Palgrave Macmillan, 2010.

119 Starkey, *British Privateering Enterprise*, 117–60; Swanson, C. A. *Predators and Prizes: American Privateering and Imperial Warfare, 1739-1748*. Columbia: University of South Carolina Press, 1991; Villiers, P. *Marine Royale, Corsaires et Trafic dans l'Atlantique de Louis XIV a Louis XVI*. 2 vols, i, 272–92. Dunkerque: SDHA, 1991; Bromley, J. S. *Corsairs and Navies, 1660-1760*. London: Hambledon, 1987. For the shift in French strategy in 1745, see Taillemite, E. 'Une bataille de l'Atalantique au XVIIIe siècle: la Guerre de Succession e'Autriche, 1744-1748'. In *Guerres et Paix*, 131–48. Vincennes: Service Historique de la Marine, 1987.

120 Morgan, G. W. 'The Impact of War on the Administration of the Army, Navy and Ordnance in Britain, 1739-1748'. PhD, Leicester, 1977; Bourland, R. D. 'Maurepas and his Administration of the French Navy on the Eve of the War of Austrian Succession, 1732-1742'. PhD, Notre Dame, 1978; Ibáñez, I. R. 'Mobilising Resources for War: The British and Spanish Intelligence Systems during the War of Jenkins' Ear (1739-1744)'. PhD, London, 2009; Crewe, D. G. *Yellow Jack and the Worm: British Naval Administration in the West Indies, 1739-1748*. Liverpool: University of Liverpool Press, 1993.

121 Baugh, D. A. *The Global Seven Years War, 1754-1763*, 621. London: Pearson, 2011.

122 Dull, J. R. *The French Navy and the Seven Years War*, 227–8. Lincoln: University of Nebraska Press, 2005.

123 Rodger, N. A. M. *The Wooden World: An Anatomy of the Georgian Navy*. London: Collins, 1986; Syrett, D. *Shipping and Military Power in the Seven Years War: The Sails of Victory*. Exeter: University of Exeter Press, 2008; Syrett, D. 'The Methodology of British Amphibious Operations in the Seven Years War'. *The Mariner's Mirror* 58 (1972): 269–80; Middleton, C. R. 'The Administration of Newcastle and Pitt: The Departments of State and the Conduct of the Seven Years War'. PhD, Exeter, 1968; Gradish, S. *The Manning of the British Navy during the Seven Years War*. London: Royal Historical Society, 1980; Buchet, Christian. *Marine, Économie et Société: Un Exemple D'interaction L'avitaillement de la Royal Navy Durant la Guerre de Sept Ans*. Paris: Honore Champion, 1999.

124 Baugh, D. 'Great Britain's "Blue Water" Policy, 1689-1815'. *International History Review* 10 (1988): 33–58; Baugh, D. 'Maritime Strength and Atlantic Commerce: The Uses of a "Grand Maritime Empire"'. In *An Imperial State at War: Britain from 1689 to 1815*, edited by L. Stone, 185–213. London: Routledge, 1994; Baugh, D. 'Withdrawing from Europe: Anglo-French Maritime Geopolitics, 1750-1800'. *International History Review* 20 (1998): 1–32; Baugh, D. 'Naval Power: What gave the British Navy Superiority?' In *Exceptionalism and Industrialization: Britain and its European Rivals, 1688-1815*, edited by L. Pardos de la Escoura, 235–57. Cambridge: Cambridge University Press, 2004; Baugh, *The Global Seven Years War, 1754-1763*, 8–16, 62–8. Middleton, C. R. *The Bells of Victory; The Pitt-Newcastle Ministry and the Conduct of the Seven Years War, 1757-1762*. Cambridge: Cambridge University Press, 1985; Middleton, C. R. 'British Naval Strategy, 1755-1762: The Western Squadron'. *The Mariner's Mirror* 75 (1989): 349–67. See also Viner, J. 'Power versus Plenty as Objectives of Foreign Policy in the Seventeenth and Eighteenth Centuries'. In *Trade in the Pre-Modern Era II*, edited by D. Irwin, 303–31. Cheltenham: Edward Elgar, 1996. There is a huge literature on the Seven Years' War. Even that which focuses on the Anglo-French struggle in North America would be too large to reference here. Attention has been restricted to those works that highlight the naval and maritime dimension of the war.

125 Black, J. *America or Europe?: British Foreign Policy, 1739-1763*. London: UCL Press, 1998; Black, J. 'Hanover and British Foreign Policy, 1714-60'. *English Historical Review* 220 (2005): 309–39; Conway, S. 'Continental Connections: Britain and Europe in the Eighteenth Century'. *History* 90 (2005): 353–74; Harding, R. 'British Maritime Strategy and Hanover, 1714–1763'. In *The Hanoverian Dimension in British History, 1714-1837*, edited by B. Sims and T. Riotte, 252–74. Cambridge: Cambridge University Press, 2007.

126 Cardwell, M. J. *Arts and Arms: Literature, Politics and Patriotism During the Seven Years War*. Manchester: Manchester University Press, 2004.

127 Tunstall, B. *Admiral Byng and the Loss of Minorca*. London: Philip Allan, 1928; Pope, D. *At Twelve Mr Byng was Shot*. London: Secker and Warburg,

1962; Ware, C. *Admiral Byng: His Rise and Execution*. Barnsley: Pen and Sword, 2009.

128 Marcus, G. *Quiberon Bay*. London: Hollis and Carter, 1960; Mackay, R. *Admiral Hawke*. Oxford: Clarendon Press, 1965; Le Moing, G. *La Bataille Navale des 'Cardinaux'(20 Novembre 1759)*. Paris: Economica, 2003; Mackay, R. and M. Duffy. *Hawke and Nelson and British Naval Leadership, 1747-1805*. Woodbridge: Boydell Press, 2009; Tracy, N. *The Battle of Quiberon Bay 1759: Hawke and the Defeat of the French Invasion*. London: Pen and Sword, 2010.

129 For examples of the centrality of the navy's control of the sea lines of communication to the narrative of the colonial war, see Wood, *The Logs of the Conquest of Canada*. Toronto: Champlain Society, 1909. Wood describes Wolfe's landing at Quebec as the 'local landing party' (x). See also Little, C. H. *The Influence of Sea Power on the Conquest of Quebec*. Halifax: Maritime Museum of Canada, 1958. Revived interest in amphibious operations can be seen in Creswell, J. *Generals and Admirals: The Story of Amphibious Command*. London: Longman, 1952 and Vagts, A. *Landing Operations Strategy, Psychology, Tactics, Politics, from Antiquity to 1945*. Harrisburg: Military Service Publishing, 1946. For amphibious operations in the Seven Years' War, see Boscawen, H. *The Capture of Louisbourg 1758*. Norman: University of Oklahoma Press, 2011; Smelser, M. *The Campaign for the Sugar Islands, 1759; A Study of Amphibious Warfare*. Chapel Hill: University of North Carolina Press, 1955; Syrett, D. 'The British Landing at Havana: An Example of an Eighteenth Century Combined Operation'. *The Mariner's Mirror* 55 (1969): 325–31; Syrett, D. *The Siege and Capture of Havana 1762*. London: Navy Records Society, 1970; Marley, D. '"A Fearful Gift": The Spanish Naval Build-Up in the West Indies, 1759-1762'. *The Mariner's Mirror* 80 (1994): 403–17; Marley, D. 'Havana Surprised: Prelude to the British Invasion, 1762'. *The Mariner's Mirror* 78 (1992): 293–305; Tracy, N. *Manila Ransomed: The British Assault on Manila in the Seven Years War*. Exeter: University of Exeter Press, 1995. The literature on Quebec is too large to reference. The classic modern study is by Stacy, C. P. *Quebec 1759: The Siege and the Battle*. Toronto: Macmillan, 1959, but there have been a number of recent studies. A good example is Ward, M. C. *The Battle for Quebec 1759*. Stroud: Tempus, 2005. The raids on the coast of France have not had such full treatment in published work. The best overall account, still unpublished, is Hackman, W. K. 'British Expeditions to the Coast of France, 1757-1761'. PhD, Michigan, 1969.

130 Le Goff, T. J. A. 'Problèmes de recrutement de la marine française pendent la Guerre de Septs Ans'. *Revue Historique*, 283 (1990): 205–33; Le Goff, T. J. A. 'Les gens de mer devant le système des classes (1755-1763)'. In *Les Hommes et la Mer dans l'Europe du Nord-Ouest de l'Antiquité à nos Jours*, edited by A. Lottin, J-C. Hocquet and S. Lebecq, 463–79. Paris: Revue du Nord, 1986.

131 Dull, *The French Navy and the Seven Years War*; Pritchard, J. *Louis XV's Navy 1748-1762: A Study of Organization and Administration*. Montreal: McGill-Queen's University Press, 1987; Acerra, M. and A. Zysberg. *L'Essor des Marines de Guerre Europeenes (vers 1680-1790)*. Paris: SEDES, 1997.

132 Bosher, J. 'Financing the French Navy in the Seven Years War: Beaujon Goossens et Compagnie in 1759'. *Business History* 28 (1986): 115–33.

133 Tracy, N. *Navies, Deterrence and American Independence: Britain and Seapower in the 1760s and 1770s*. Vancouver: University of British Columbia Press, 1988.

134 Stout, N. R. *The Royal Navy in America, 1760-1775: A Study of Enforcement of British Colonial Policy in the Era of the American Revolution*. Annapolis: Naval Institute Press, 1973. For the other side of the story in one seaport, see Truvas, T. M. *Defying Empire: Trading with the Enemy in Colonial New York*. New Haven: Yale University Press, 2008.

135 Temple Patterson, A. *The Other Armada: The Franco-Spanish Attempt to Invade Britain in 1779*. Manchester: Manchester University Press, 1960.

136 Spinney, D. Rodney, 296–316. London: Allen and Unwin, 1969. London: Allen and Unwin, 1969; Syrett, D. *Admiral Lord Howe: A Biography*, 100–6. Annapolis: Naval Institute Press, 2006.

137 The best study of this campaign is still Richmond, H. W. *The Navy in India 1763-1783*. London: Ernest Benn, 1931.

138 Rush, N. O. *Spain's Final Triumph over Great Britain in the Gulf of Mexico: The Battle of Pensacola, March 9 to May 8, 1781*. Florida State University Studies. Tallahassee: The Florida State University, 1966.

139 For a study of the battle in its diplomatic context, see Larrabee, H. A. *Decision at the Chesapeake*. London: Kimber, 1965. See also Middleton, R. 'Naval Resources and the British Defeat at Yorktown, 1781'. *The Mariner's Mirror* 100, no. 1 (2014): 29–43.

140 The standard British account of the siege is still McGuffie, T. H. *The Siege of Gibraltar, 1779-1783*. London: Batsford, 1965, but by current standards it is entirely deficient regarding the Spanish side of the campaign. The overall context of the Minorca campaign can be found in Desmond, G. *Minorca: The Illusory Prize. A History of the British Occupation of Minorca, 1708-1802*. Rutherford: Fairleigh Dickinson University Press, 1990. See also Villiers, P. 'Deux Opérations Amphibies Contre L'île de Minorque: Les Débarquements De 1756 Et De 1781/82'. *Neptunia* 266, no. Juin (2012).

141 Baugh, D. A. 'Why did Britain lose Command of the Sea during the War for America?' In *The British Navy and the Use of Naval Power in the Eighteenth Century*, edited by J. Black and P. Woodfine, 149–70. Leicester University Press, 1988.

142 Mahan, *Influence of Sea Power*, 523–35.

143 Vergé-Franceschi, M. *La Marine Française au XVIIIe Siècle: Guerre-Administration-Exploration*, edited by 138–60. Paris: SEDES, 1996; Scott, H. M. 'The Importance of Bourbon Naval Reconstruction to the Strategy of Choiseul after the Seven Years War'. *International History Review* 1 (1979): 17–35; Merino-Navarro, *La Armada Española*; Tracy, N. 'British Assessments of French and Spanish Naval Construction, 1763-176'. *The Mariner's Mirror* 61 (1974): 73–85; Singh, R. J. *French Diplomacy in the Caribbean and the American Revolution*. New York: Exposition Press, 1977.

144 Acerra, M., J. Merino and J. Meyer, eds. *Les Marines de Guerre Europeenes, Xvii^e-Xviii^e Siecles*. Paris: PUP, 1985; Acerra, M. and A. Zysberg. *L'essor Des*

Marines De Guerres Europennes (Vers 1680 - Vers 1790). Paris: SEDES, 1997; Vergé-Francheschi, M. *La Marine Francaise au XVIIIe Siecle*. Paris: SEDES, 1996; Chaline, O., P. Bonnichon and C.-P. de Vergennes, eds. *Les Marines De La Guerre D'indpendence Americaine (1763-1783)*. Paris: PUPS, 2013.

145 Fowler, Jr., W. M. *Rebels under Sail*. New York: Charles Scribner's Sons, 1976; Chapelle, H. I. *The History of the American Sailing Navy: The Ships and their Development*. New York: W. W. Norton. 1949. For a recent controversy, see Dull, J. 'Was the Continental Navy a Mistake?' *American Neptune* 34 (1984): 167–70; Dudley, W. S. and M. A. Palmer. 'No Mistake about It: A Response to Jonathan R. Dull'. *American Neptune* 35 (1985): 244–8.

146 Tilley, A. *The British Navy and the American Revolution*. Columbia: University of South Carolina Press, 1987. A good, illustrated overview is provided in Gardiner, R., ed. *Navies and the American Revolution, 1775-1783*. London: Chatham Publishing, 1996. Excellent regional studies are Syrett, D. *The Royal Navy in American Waters, 1775-1783*. Aldershot: Scholar Press, 1989; Syrett, D. *The Royal Navy in European Waters during the American Revolutionary War*. Columbia: University of South Carolina Press, 1998; Richmond, H. W. *The Navy in India, 1763-1783*. London: Ernest Benn, 1931. Apart from Richmond, the war in the Indian Ocean has been rather neglected. However, Suffren has recent biographies from Caron, F. *Le Mythe de Suffren*. Vincennes: Service Historique de la Marine, 1996; Cavaliero, R. *Admiral Satan: The Life and Campaigns of Suffren*. London: Tauris, 1994. The transport of troops and stores to America has been covered extensively by David Syrett in a number of articles and *Shipping and the American War, 1775-1783*. London: University of London Press, 1970. The work of the dockyards during the war can be traced in Knight, R. J. B. 'The Royal Dockyards in England at the Time of the American War of Independence'. PhD, London, 1972. The French side of the naval campaign can be found in Dull, J. R. *The French Navy and American Independence: A Study of Arms and Diplomacy, 1774-1787*. Princeton: Princeton University Press, 1975. The economic impact of the Royal Navy on the American economy is found in Buel Jr, R. *In Irons: Britain's Naval Supremacy and the American Revolutionary Economy*. New Haven: Yale University Press, 1998. The war in the West Indies is not covered so well. A. G. Jamieson's 'The War in the Leeward Islands, 1775-1783'. D.Phil., Oxford, 1981 is the best narrative, but sadly unpublished. The economic impact of the war in the region can be followed in O'Shaughnessy, A. J. *An Empire Divided: The American Revolution and the British Caribbean*. Philadelphia: University of Pennsylvania Press, 2000. Details of campaigns there can also be found in the biographies of Rodney and the papers of Barrington, Rodney and Sandwich printed by the Navy Records Society. The naval war also benefits from the twelve volumes of printed documents edited by Clark, W. B. and M. J. Crawford. *Naval Documents of the American Revolution*. Washington: Naval History Center, 1964–2005, which are now available online from the US Naval History and Heritage Command at http://www.history.navy.mil/research/publications/naval-documents-of-the-american-revolution.html (accessed 29 January 2015). Piers Mackesy puts the war at sea into the overall context of operations in North America in Mackesy, P. *The War for*

America, 1775-1783. London: Longman, 1964. Apart from Merino Navarro and Bruijn, respectively, the Spanish and Dutch participation in the war is not well covered. However, see Fernandez-Shaw, C. 'Participación de la armada española en la Guerra de la Independencia de los Estados Unidos'. *Revista de Historia Naval* 3 (1985): 75–80; Coker, W. S. and R. R. Rea, eds. *Anglo-Spanish Confrontation on the Gulf Coast during the American Revolution*. Pensacola: Gulf Coast History, 1982. The British privateering war can be followed in Starkey. Starkey, David J.*British Privateering Enterprise in the Eighteenth Century*. Exeter: University of Exeter Press, 1990. The French reaction is in Villiers, P. 'La Lutte contra la Course Anglaise en Atlantique pendant la Guerre d'Indépendance des Etats Unis d'Amerique, 1778-1783'. In *Course et Piraterie*, edited by M. Mollat, 572–83. Paris: ECNRS, 1975. The American privateering is covered in Morgan, W. J. 'American Privateering in America's War for Independence, 1775-1783'. In *Course et Piraterie*, 556–71. Paris: ECNRS, 1975. For the Dutch, see Van Zijverden, J. 'The Risky Alternative: Dutch Privateering during the Fourth Anglo-Dutch War, 1780-1783'. In *Pirates and Privateers: New Perspectives on the War on Trade in the Eighteenth and Nineteenth Centuries*, edited by D. Starkey, E. S. van Eyck van Heslinga and J. A. de Moor, 186–205. Exeter: University of Exeter Press, 1997.

147 Knight, R. J. B. 'The Performance of the Royal Dockyards in England during the American War of Independence'. *The American Revolution and the Sea*. London: National Maritime Museum, 1974; *The American Revolution at Sea* is a set of conference proceedings. The contributions are often quite short, but they are very interesting in that they illustrate the wide variety of work that was being done on navies during this period and the move away from battle narratives towards organizational and economic analyses of naval power. See also Knight, R. 'The Introduction of Copper Sheathing into the Royal Navy'. *The Mariner's Mirror* 59 (1973): 299–309.

148 Marshall, P. J. *The Making and Unmaking of Empires: Britain, India and America, 1750-1783*. Oxford: Oxford University Press, 2005.

149 Frost, A. *The Global Reach of Empire: Britain's Maritime Expansion in the Indian and Pacific Oceans, 1764-1815*. Carlton: Miegunyah Press, 2003; Gough, B. M. *The Royal Navy and the Northwest Coast of North America*. Vancouver: University of British Columbia Press, 1974.

150 Symonds, *Navalist and Anti-Navalists*; Smelser, *Congress Founds a Navy, 1787-1798*; Smith. 'A Means to an End'; Tucker, S. 'The Jeffersonian Gunboats in Service, 1804-1825'. *American Neptune* 35 (1995): 97–110; Sharrer, G. Terry. 'The Search for a Naval Policy 1783-1812.' Chap. 2 In *In Peace and War: Interpretations of American Naval History, 1775-1978*, edited by Kenneth J. Hagan, 27–45. Westport: Greenwood Press, 1984.

151 Frost, A. and G. Williams 'The Beginnings of Britain's Exploration of the Pacific Ocean in the Eighteenth Century'. *The Mariner's Mirror* 83, no. 4 (1997): 410–18.

152 Hulme, P. 'The Malaspina Expedition'. *Studies in Travel Writing* 10, no. 1 (2006): 71–81.

153 Webb, P. 'The Naval Aspects of the Nootka Sound Crisis'. *The Mariner's Mirror* 61, no. 2 (1975): 133–54.

154 The Russian navy is still in need of solid archival work on its organization, resources and leadership. See Saul, N. 'The Russian Navy, 1682-1854: Some Suggestions for Future Study'. In *New Aspects of Naval History*, edited by C. L. Symonds, 131–9. Annapolis: Naval Institute Press, 1981. Little has changed since this article was published. The Anglo-centric analysis of the Russian fleet remains dominant. The most accessible narrative remains Anderson, *Naval Wars in the Baltic,* but see also Chapman, W. C. 'Prelude to Chesme'. *The Mariner's Mirror* 52 (1966): 61–76; Anderson, M. S. 'Great Britain and the Russian Fleet, 1769-1770'. *Slavonic and East European Review*, no. December (1952): 148–63; Anderson, M. S. 'Great Britain and the Russo-Turkish War, 1768-1774'. *English Historical Review* 49 (1954): 39–58; Anderson, M. S. 'Russia and the Mediterranean, 1788-1791: A Little Known Chapter in the History of Naval Warfare and Privateering'. *The Mariner's Mirror* 45 (1959): 25–35; Menning, B. 'Russian Military Innovation in the Second Half of the Eighteenth Century'. *War and Society* 2 (1984): 23–41. Work on the Ottoman navy is becoming more widely accessible in English. For this period, see Stanford Shaw, J. 'Selem III and the Ottoman Navy'. *Turcica* 1 (1969): 212–41; Zorlu, T. *Innovation and Empire in Turkey: Sultan Selim III and the Modernisation of the Ottoman Navy.* London: Tauris, 2008.

155 Harris, D. G. 'Admiral Frederic Af Chapman's Auxiliary Vessels for the Swedish Inshore Fleet'. *The Mariner's Mirror* 75, no. 3 (1989): 211–29.

156 Glete, J. 'The Foreign Policy of Gustavus III and the Navy as an Instrument of Policy'. In *The War of King Gustavus III and the Naval Battles of Ruotsinsalmi*, 5–42. Kotka: Museum of Kymenlaaksa, 1993; Nordman, C. 'L'essor de la flotte de Guerre Suedo-Finlandais' au xviiie siécle'. In *Les Hommes de La Mer dans l'Europe du Nord-Quest*, edited by A. Lottin, J-C. Hocquet and S. Lebecq, 343–68. Paris: Revue de Nord, 1986.

157 Lavery, B. *The Ship of the Line.* 2 vols. London: Conway, 1983 and 1984 and Gardiner, R., ed. *The Line of Battle: The Sailing Warship, 1650-1840.* London: Conway, 1992 are excellent contributions to the subject. A valuable book that looks at the relationship between developing scientific knowledge and naval architecture is Ferreiro, L. D. *Ships and Science: The Birth of Naval Architecture in the Scientific Revolution, 1600-1800.* Cambridge, MA: MIT Press, 2007.

158 Spinney, *Rodney,* 427–9.

159 Rodger, N. A. M. 'Image and Reality in Eighteenth Century Naval Tactics'. *The Mariner's Mirror* 89 (2003): 280–97; Willis, S. *Fighting at Sea in the Eighteenth Century: The Art of Sailing Warfare.* Woodbridge: Boydell Press, 2008; Willis, S. 'Fleet Performance and Capability in the Eighteenth Century Royal Navy'. *War in History* 11 (2004): 373–92.

160 The most accessible study is Tunstall, B. *Naval Warfare in the Age of Sail: The Evolution of Fighting Tactics, 1650-1815*, edited by N. Tracy. London: Conway, 1990. Tunstall built on the work of his father-in-law Sir Julian S. Corbett's *Fighting Instructions.* London: Navy Records Society, 1905, to include French and Spanish instructions. For a wider discussion of the matter of naval tactics, see Coutau-Bégarie, H., ed. *L'Evolution de la Pensée Navale.*

3 vols. Paris: Fondation pour les Etudes de Defense Nationale, 1990, 1992 and 1995. See also Tracy, N. *Nelson's Battles: The Art of Victory in the Age of Sail*. London: Chatham, 1996.

Chapter 3

1. Mahan, *Influence of Sea Power*, 209.
2. Fayle, C. E. 'Deflection of Strategy by Commerce in Eigtheenth Century'. *Journal of the Royal United Services Institution* (1923): 281–94.
3. Waters, M. *Globalization: Key Ideas*. London: Routledge, 1995; Sklair, L. 'Competing Conceptions of Globalization'. *Journal of World-Systems Research* 5, no. 2 (1999): 143–63.
4. Daunton, M. 'Britain and Globalisation since 1850: I. Creating a Global Order, 1850-1914'. *Transactions of the Royal Historical Society* 16 (2006): 1–38.
5. Lane, F. C. *Profit from Power: Readings in Protection Rent and Violence-Controlling Enterprises*. Albany: SUNY Press, 1979.
6. Raudzens, G. *Empires, Europe and Globalization, 1492-1788*, 35. Stroud: Sutton, 1999.
7. Shaffer, B. *Energy Politics*, 78. Philadelphia: University of Pennsylvania Press, 2009.
8. Kyo-Ryul, R. 'The Establishment of Naval Port Jinhae and the Imperial Japanese Navy'. Conference paper at *Naval Expertise and the Making of the Modern World*. Wolfson College, Oxford, 2013.
9. Buchet, C. 'Le Marine, moteur du développement économique'. In *La Puissance Maritime*, edited by C. Buchet, J. Meyer and J-P. Poussou, 509–14. Paris: Presses de l'université Paris-Sorbonne, 2004; Mather, I. R. *The Role of the Royal Navy in the English Atlantic Empire, 1660-1720*. D.Phil., Oxford, 1995; O'Brien, P. K. and X. Duran 'Total Factor Productivity for the Royal Navy from Victory at the Texel(1653) to Triumph at Trafalgar(1805)'. In *Shipping and Economic Growth, 1350-1850*, edited by R. W. Unger, 307. Leiden: Brill, 2011; Reitan, E. *Politics, War and Empire: The Rise of Britain to a World Power, 1688-1792*. Arlington Heights: Harlan Davidson, 1994. For a call to develop the study of mercantilist framework or policy levers, see Coats, A. W. Bob. 'Mercantilism, Economic Ideas, History and Policy'. In *Trade in the Pre-Modern Era, 1400-1700*, edited by D. A. Irwin, ii, 350–69. Cheltenham: Edward Edgar, 1996; Irwin, D. A. 'Strategic Trade Policy and Mercantilist Trade Rivalries'. In Irwin, *Trade in the Pre-Modern Era*, ii, 407–12; John, A. H. 'War and the English Economy, 1700-1763'. *Economic Historical Review* 7(1955): 329–44. For a view that places the naval influence on industrial development into the wider French domestic context see Crouzet, F. 'Angleterre et France au XVIIIe Siécle: Essai d'analyse comparée de deux croissances economique'. *Annales: Economies, Societies et Civilizations* 21 (1996): 254–91; Crouzet, F. 'War, Blockade and Economic Change in Europe, 1792-1815'. *Journal of Economic History* 24 (1964): 567–90.

10 O'Brien, P. K. and S. L. Engerman. 'Exports and the Growth of the British Economy from the Glorious Revolution to the Peace of Amiens'. In *Slavery and the Rise of the Atlantic System*, edited by B. L. Solow, 177–209. Cambridge: Cambridge University Press, 1991.

11 O'Brien, P. 'The Nature and Historical Evolution of an Exceptional Fiscal State and Its Possible Significance for the Precocious Commercialization and Industrialization of the British Economy from Cromwell to Nelson'. *The Economic History Review* 64, no. 2 (2011): 408–46; O'Brien, P. K. 'Fiscal and Financial Preconditions for the Formation of Developmental States in the West and the East from the Conquest of Ceuta (1415) to the Opium War (1839).' *Journal of World History* 23, no. 3 (2012): 513–33.

12 Solow, B. L. 'Capitalism and Slavery'. In *British Capitalism and Caribbean Slavery: The Legacy of Eric Williams*, edited by B. L. Solow and S. L. Engerman, 51–78. Quotation 55. Cambridge: Cambridge University Press, 1987.

13 For the debate over the role of the slave trade and British industrialization, see Richardson, D. 'The Slave Trade, Sugar and British Economic Growth'. In *British Capitalism and Caribbean Slavery: The Legacy of Eric Williams*, edited by B. L. Solow and S. L. Engerman, 103–33. Cambridge: Cambridge University Press, 1987. See also Solow, B. L., ed. *Slavery and the Rise of the Atlantic System*. Cambridge: Cambridge University Press, 1991; Inikori, J. E. 'Slavery and the Development of Industrial Capitalism'. In Solow and Engerman. *British Capitalism and Caribbean Slavery*, 79–102; Morgan, K. *Slavery, Atlantic Trade and the British Economy, 1660-1800*. Cambridge: Cambridge University Press, 2000.

14 Chet, G. *The Ocean Is a Wilderness: Atlantic Piracy and the Limits of Governmental Legitimacy in the Early-Modern State, 1688-1856*. Boston: University of Massachusetts Press, 2014.

15 Stein, R. 'Measuring the French Slave Trade, 1713-1792'. *Journal of African Studies* 19 (1978): 515–21; Stein, R. 'The State of French Colonial Commerce on the Eve of the French Revolution'. *Journal of European Economic History* 12 (1983): 105–17; Boulle, P. 'Patterns of French Colonial Trade and the Seven Years War'. *Histoire Sociale – Social History* 7(1974): 48–86; Doeflinger, T. M. 'The Antilles Trade and the Old Regime: A Statistical Overview'. *Journal of Interdisciplinary Studies* 3 (1976): 397–415.

16 Given the depth of scholarship on slavery and the slave trade, relatively little work has been done on the mechanics of abolition. On the suppression of the trade on the East African coast, see Howell, R. *The Royal Navy and the Slave Trade*. London: Croom Helm, 1987; Lloyd, C. C. *The Navy and the Slave Trade: The Suppression of the African Slave Trade in the Nineteenth Century*. London: Longmans, 1949; Canney, D. L. *Africa Squadron: The U.S. Navy and the Slave Trade, 1843-1861*. Washington: Potomac, 2006; Hunter, Mark C. Policing the Seas: Anglo-American Relations and the Equatorial Atlantic, 1819-1865. Research in Maritime History, edited by Lewis Fischer, Vol. 36, St John's: International Maritime Economic History Association, 2008.

17 Smith, M. R. and L. Marx. *Does Technology Drive History?: The Dilemma of Technological Determinism*. Cambridge, MA: MIT Press, 1994.

18 Epstein, K. C. *Torpedo: Inventing the Military-Industrial Complex in the United States and Great Britain*. Navies as users of industrial technologies are also examined in Pebbles, R. H. 'Navy Shipbuilders "Discover" Welding'. In *Naval History: The Sixth Symposium of the US Naval Academy*, edited by D. M. Masterson, 157–66. Wilmington: Scholarly Resources, 1987; Johnman, L. and H. Murphy. 'Welding and the British Shipbuilding Industry'. In *The Royal Navy 1930-2000: Innovation and Defence*, edited by R. Harding, 89–116. London: Cass, 2005; Friedman, N. 'Electronics and the Royal Navy'. In Harding, *The Royal Navy 1930-2000*, 246–85; Briggs, M. 'Innovation and the Mid-Victorian Royal Navy: The Case of the Whitehead Torpedo'. *The Mariner's Mirror* 88, no. 4 (2002): 447–55; Musson, A. E. 'Technological Change and Manpower'. *History* 67 (1982): 237–51, especially 240–1.

19 Discussion of late-eighteenth-century technology transfer to the Ottoman Empire can be found in Zorlu, T. *Innovation and Empire in Turkey*. Shipbuilding technology transfer to Spain can be found in Scheybeler, C. 'A Study of Spanish Naval Policy during the Reign of Ferdinand VI', 42–109. PhD, London, 2014. Naval technology transfer to Russia is in Cross, A. *By the Banks of the Neva: Chapters from the Lives and Careers of the British in Eighteenth Century Russia*. Cambridge: Cambridge University Press, 1997, especially 159–223; Morriss, R. *Science, Utility and Maritime Power: Samuel Bentham in Russia, 1779-91*. Abingdon: Ashgate, 2015.

20 There is an excellent series of essays on navigation and exploration c.1740–1815 with a clear linkage to naval objectives in J. B. Hattendorf, ed. *Maritime History: The Eighteenth Century and the Classic Age of Sail*. Malabar, Florida: Krieger, 1997. See also Williams, G. '"To Make Discoveries of Countries Hitherto Unknown": The Admiralty and Pacific Exploration in the Eighteenth Century'. *The Mariner's Mirror* 82 (1996): 14–27; Frost, A. and Samson, J., eds. *Pacific Empires: Essays in Honour of Glyndwr Williams*. Vancouver: University of British Columbia Press, 1999; Lincoln, M., ed. *Science and Exploration in the Pacific: European Voyages to the Southern Ocean in the Eighteenth Century*. Woodbridge: Boydell Press, 1998; van der Merwe, P., ed. *Science and the French and British Navies, 1700-1850*. London: National Maritime Museum, 2003. For a useful overview, see Whitfield, P. *The Charting of the Oceans: Ten Centuries of Maritime Maps*. London: British Library, 1996, 91 et seq.

21 Fontillana, E. R. 'Carlos III ye el Control des Estrecho de Magalleaneo: La Expedicion del Captan de Navio Don Antonio de Cordoba (1785-1786). In *Temas Historica Militar*. 1 vol, 103–12. Madrid: 2nd Congress de Historia Militar, 1988; de la Peñera y Rivas, A. 'Los Marinos Salvador de Medina y Vincente Doz en la Observation de Venus desde California en el año 1769'. *Temas de Historia Militar* 1 (1988): 87–99; David, A. C. F. 'Alexander Dalrymple and the Emergence of the Admiralty Chart'. In *Five Hundred Years of Nautical Science, 1400-1900*, edited by D. Howse, 153–66. London: National Maritime Museum, 1981; Terrill, C. 'Captain Columbine, Alexander Dalrymple and the Troubled Birth of the British Admiralty Hydrographic Service'. In *Guerres et Paix*, edited by 245–57. Vincennes: Service Historique de la Marine, 1987.

22 Savours, A. *The Search for the North West Passage*. London: Chatham Publishing, 1999; Lambert, A. *Franklin: Tragic Hero of Polar Navigation*. London: Faber, 2009. See also Day, A. E. *Search for the Northwest Passage: An Annotated Bibliography*. New York: Garland, 1986.

23 Weick, K. E. and K. H. Roberts. 'Collective Mind in Organizations: Heedful Interrelating on Flight Decks'. *Administrative Science Quarterly* 38 (1993): 357–81; Perrow, C. *Complex Organizations: A Critical Essay*. 3rd edn. New York: McGraw Hill, 1986; Lansing, J. S. 'Complex Adaptive Systems'. *Annual Review of Anthropology* 32, no. 1 (2003): 183–204.

24 Hyde, F E. 'Economic Theory and Business History: A Comment on the Theory of Profit Maximisation'. *Business History* 5 (1962): 1–10.

25 Karpoff, J. M. 'Public Versus Private Initiatives in Arctic Exploration: The Effects of Incentives and Organizational Structure'. *Journal of Political Economy* 100, no. 11 (2001): 38–78.

26 Allen, Douglas 'The British Navy Rules: Monitoring and Incompatible Incentives in the Age of Fighting Sail'. *Explorations in Economic History* 39 (2002): 204–31; Benjamin, D. K. and C. F. Thornberg. 'Comment: Rules, Monitoring and Incentives in the Age of Sail'. *Explorations in Economic History* 40 (2003): 195–211; Benjamin, D. K. and C. F. Thornberg. 'Organization and Incentives in the Age of Sail'. *Explorations in Economic History* 44 (2007): 317–41. See also Allen's reply to Benjamin and Thornberg in Allen, Douglas, 'Rules and Rewards in the Age of Sail: A Reply', *Explorations in Economic History* 40 (2003): 212–20.

27 O'Brien, P. K. and X. Duran. 'Total Factor Productivity for the Royal Navy from Victory at the Texel (1653) to Triumph at Trafalgar (1805)'. In *Shipping and Economic Growth, 1350-1850*, edited by R. W. Unger, 279–307. Leiden: Brill, 2011.

28 Mayntz, R. and T. P. Hughes, eds. *The Development of Large Technical Systems*. Boulder: Westview, 1988; Edgerton, D. *The Shock of the Old: Technology and Global History since 1900*. Oxford: Oxford University Press, 2007.

29 North, D. C. 'Institutions'. *Journal of Economic Perspectives* 5, no. 1 (1991): 97–112; North, D. C. and B. R. Weingast. 'Constitutions and Commitment: The Evolution of Institutions Governing Public Choice in Seventeenth-Century England'. *Journal of Economic History* 4 (1989): 803–32.

30 Parris, H. *Constitutional Bureaucracy*. London: Allen and Unwin, 1969; Sutherland, G., ed. *Studies in the Growth of Nineteenth Century Government*. London: Routledge, 1972; Macleod, R., ed. *Government and Expertise: Specialists, Administrators and Professionals*. Cambridge: Cambridge University Press, 1988.

31 A basic narrative of contracting by the British Navy Board can be found in Pool, B. *Navy Board Contracts, 1660-1832*. London: Longman, 1966.

32 Wilkinson, C. *The British Navy and the State in the Eighteenth Century*. Woodbridge: Boydell Press, 2004..

33 Haas, J. *A Management Odyssey: The Royal Dockyards, 1714-1914*. New York: University Press of America, 1994; Morriss, R. *Naval Power and British*

Culture, 1760-1850: Public Trust and Government Ideology. Aldershot: Gower, 2004; Morriss, R. *The Foundations of British Maritime Ascendency: Resources, Logistics and the State, 1755-1815*. Cambridge: Cambridge University Press, 2010; Coats, A. 'Efficiency in Dockyard Administration 1660-1800: A Reassessment'. In *The Age of Sail. The International Annual of the Historic Sailing Ship*, edited by N. Tracy, 116–32. London: Conway, 2002.

34 Knight, R. and M. Wilcox. *Sustaining the Fleet, 1793-1815: War, the British Navy and the Contractor State*. Woodbridge: Boydell Press, 2010; Macdonald, J. *The British Navy's Victualling Board, 1793-1815: Management Competence and Incompetence*. Woodbridge: Boydell Press, 2010.

35 Bosher, J. F. 'Financing the French Navy in the Seven Years War: Beaujon, Goosens et Compagnie in 1759'. *Business History* 28 (1986): 115–33.

36 Johnman, L. and H. Murphy. 'The Rationalisation of Warship Building in the United Kingdom, 1945-2000'. *Journal of Strategic Studies* 24 (2001):107–27; Johnman, L. and H. Murphy. *British Shipbuilding and the State since 1918*. Exeter: Exeter University Press, 2002.

37 The study of national trauma and its impact on navies is very limited at present, but see Knight, R. J. B. 'The Royal Navy's Recovery after the Early Phase of the American Revolutionary War'. In *The Aftermath of Defeat: Societies, Armed Forces and the Challenge of Recovery*, edited by G. J. Andreopoulos and H. E. Selsky, 10–25. New Haven: Yale University Press, 1994; Horten, D. 'Errfahrungen Im Deutschen Einigungsprozess. Die Auflösung Der Volksmarine 1990/91'. In *Deutsche Marinen Im Wandal: Von Symbol Nationaler Einheit Zum Instrument Internationaler Sicherheit*, edited by W. Rahn, 657–72. München: R. Oldenbourg, 2005.

38 Stauffer, D. A. *The Art of Biography in Eighteenth Century England*. Princeton: Princeton University Press, 1941. Van Reine, R. P. 'Michiel Adriaenzoon De Ruyter and His Biographer Gerard Brandt'. In *De Ruyter: Dutch Admiral*, edited by J. R. Bruijn, R. Prud'homme van Reine and R. van Hövell tot Westerflier, 37–55. Rotterdam: Karwansaray, 2011.

39 For example, see Lewis, M. *England's Sea Officers: The Story of the Naval Profession*. London: Allen and Unwin, 1939; Teiller, G. *The Genesis of the Professional Officers Corps*. London: Sage, 1977; Capp, B. *Cromwell's Navy: The Fleet and the English Revolution, 1648-1660*. Oxford: Oxford University Press, 1989, especially 155–211; Davies, J. D. *Gentlemen and Tarpaulins: The Officers and Men of the Restoration Navy*. Oxford: Oxford University Press, 1991; Davison, R. L. *The Challenges of Command: The Royal Navy's Executive Branch Officers, 1880-1919*. Farnham: Ashgate, 2011; Rodger, N. A. M. 'Commissioned Officers' Careers in the Royal Navy, 1690-1815'. *Journal for Maritime Research* 3 (2001): 85–129; Consolvo, C. 'The Prospects and Promotion of British Naval Officers, 1793-1815'. *The Mariner's Mirror* 91 (2005): 137–59; McLeod, A. B. *British Naval Captains of the Seven Years War: The View from the Quarterdeck*. Woodbridge: Boydell Press, 2012.

40 Vergè-Franceschi, M. 'Officiers Généraux de la Marine Royale (1669-1774)'. *Revue Historique* 278 (1987): 335–59; Vergè-Franceschi, M. *Les Officiers Généraux de la Marine Royale, 1715-1774*. 7 vols. Paris: Libraire de l'Inde, 1990; Aman, J. *Les Officiers Blues dans la Marine Française au XVIIIe Siecle*.

Geneva: Centre de Recherches d'Histoire et de Philologie, 1976; McKee, C. *A Gentlemanly and Honorable Profession: The Creation of the US Naval Officers Corps, 1794-1815;* Herwig, H. H. *The German Naval Officer Corps: A Social and Political History, 1890-1918.* Oxford: Oxford University Press, 1973; Karsten, P. *The Naval Aristocracy: The Golden Age of Annapolis and the Emergence of Modern American Navalism.* New York: Free Press, 1972; Karsten, P. 'The "Naval Aristocracy" and the "Young Turks" of the "Fin De Siècle": A Dotting of the "I"S and Crossing of the "T"S'. *The Journal of Military History* 66, no. 4 (10 January 2002): 1177–80; Symonds, C. L. *Lincoln and His Admirals: Abraham Lincoln, the U.S. Navy, and the Civil War.* Oxford: Oxford University Press, 2008.

41 Naval education can be followed in Dickinson, H. W. *Educating the Royal Navy: Eighteenth and Nineteenth Century Education for Officers.* London: Cass, 2007; Schurman, D. M. *The Education of a Navy: The Development of British Naval Strategic Thought, 1867-1914.* London: Cassell, 1965; Rodger, N. A. M. 'Officers, Gentlemen and their Education, 1793-1860'. In *Les Empires en Guerre et Paix, 1793-1860*, edited by E. Freeman, 139–54. Vincennes: Service Historique de la Marine, 1990; Sumida, J. T. *Inventing Grand Strategy and Teaching Command: The Classic Works of Alfred Thayer Mahan Reconsidered.* Baltimore: Johns Hopkins University Press, 1997; Sullivan, F. B. 'The Origins and Development of Education in the Royal Navy from 1702 to 1902'. PhD, Reading, 1975; Richmond, H. W. *Command and Discipline.* London: Stanford, 1927; Richmond, H. W. *Naval Training.* Oxford: Oxford University Press, 1933; Anonymous, *Science and the British Officer: The Early Days of the Royal United Services Institute for Defence Studies (1829-1869).* London: RUSI, 1998. The link between history and naval education is strong in the above works. The following addresses the subject directly: Schurman, D. M. *Julian S. Corbett, 1854-1922.* Woodbridge: Royal Historical Society, 1981; Lambert, A. *The Foundations of Naval History: John Knox Laughton, the Royal Navy and the Historical Profession.* London: Chatham Publishing, 1998; Spector, R. *Professors of War: The Naval War College and the Development of the Naval Profession.* Newport: Naval War College Press, 1977. See also Gough, *Historical Dreadnoughts;* Downes, C. *Special Trust and Confidence: The Making of an Officer.* London: Cass, 1991 has some information on twentieth-century British naval officer recruitment.

42 Roskill, S. *The Art of Leadership.* London: Collins, 1964; Sweetman, J. *The Great Admirals: Command at Sea, 1587-1945.* Annapolis: Naval Institute Press, 1997; Palmer, M. A. *Command at Sea: Naval Command and Control since the Sixteenth Century.* Cambridge, MA: Harvard University Press, 2005; Lambert, A. *Admirals: Naval Commanders who made Britain Great.* London: Faber, 2008.

43 Grint, K. *Leadership: A Very Short Introduction.* Oxford: Oxford University Press, 2010.

44 Lewis, M. *A Social History of the Navy, 1793-1815.* London: Allen and Unwin, 1960; Lewis, M. *The Navy in Transition: A Social History 1814-1864.* London: Hodder and Stoughton, 1965; Lloyd, C. *The British Seaman 1200-1860.* London: Collins, 1968. See also Langley, H. D. *Social Reform in the United States Navy*, Chicago: Illinois University Press, 1967.

45 Clayton, T. *Tars: The Men who made Britain rule the Waves*. London: Hodder and Stoughton, 2007; Adkins, R. L. *Jack Tar: The Extraordinary Lives of Ordinary Seamen in Nelson's Navy*. London: Little Brown, 2008. See also Earle, P. *Sailors: English Merchant Seamen, 1650-1775*. London: Methuen, 1998; Ronald, D. A. B. *Young Nelsons: Boy Sailors During the Napoleonic Wars*. Oxford: Osprey, 2009; Pietsch, R. *The Real Jim Hawkins: Ships' Boys in the Georgian Navy*. Barnsley: Seaforth Publishing, 2010.

46 Fury, C. A., ed. *The Social History of English Seamen, 1649-1815*. Woodbridge: Boydell and Brewer, 2014; Fury, C. A., ed. *The Social History of the English Seamen, 1485-1649*. Woodbridge: Boydell Press, 2012; Rediker, M. *Between the Devil and the Deep Blue Sea: Merchant Seamen, Pirates and the Anglo-American Maritime World, 1700-1750*. Cambridge: Cambridge University Press, 1987; Linebaugh, P. and R. Marcus. 'The Many-Headed Hydra: Sailors, Slaves and the Atltantic Working-Class in the Eighteenth Century'. In *Jack Tar in History: Essays in the History of Maritime Life*, edited by C. Howell and R. J. Twomey, 11–36. Fredericton: Arcadiensis Press, 1991.

47 Rodger, *The Wooden World*, 153–82; Dancy, J. Ross. *The Myth of the Press Gang: Volunteers, Impressment and the Naval Manpower Problem of the Late Eigtheenth Century*. Woodbridge: Boydell Press, 2015.

48 Rogers, N. *The Press Gang: Naval Impressment and its Opponents in Georgian Britain*. London: Continuum, 2007; Rogers, N. 'Impressment and the Law in Eighteenth Century Britain'. In *Law, Crime and English Society, 1660-1830*, edited by N. Landau, 71–94. Cambridge: Cambridge University Press, 2002; Robinson, D. E. 'Secret of British Power in the Age of Sail: Admiralty Records of the Coasting Fleet'. *American Neptune* 48 (1988): 5–21; Starkey, D. J. 'War and the Market for Seafarers in Britain'. In *Shipping and Trade, 1750-1950: Essays in International Maritime Economic History*, edited by L. R. Fischer and H. W. Nordvik, 25–42. Pontefract: Lofthouse, 1990; Pares, R. 'The Manning of the Navy in the West Indies, 1702-1763'. *Transactions of the Royal Historical Society* 19 (1937): 31–60; Swanson, Carl E. 'The Competition for American Seamen during the War of 1739-1748.' Man and Nature/ L'homme et la nature 1 (1982): 119-29.; Stout, N. R. 'Manning the Royal Navy in North America, 1763-1775'. *American Neptune* 23 (1963): 174–85; Scammell, G. V. 'The Sinews of War: Manning and Provisioning English Fighting Ships, c.1550-1650'. *The Mariner's Mirror* 73 (1987): 351–67; Schoenfeld, M. P. 'The Restoration Seaman and his Wages'. *American Neptune* 25 (1965): 278–87; Gradish, S. *The Manning of the Navy in the Seven Years War*. London: Royal Historical Society, 1980. The idea of a register of seamen from which individuals would be called in an orderly way appeared at various points in the eighteenth century, but got little political support. See Lloyd, *The British Seaman, 1200-1860*, 174–89; Hughes, G. 'The Act for the Increase and Encouragement of Seamen, 1696-1710: Could it have solved the Royal Navy's Manning Problem?' In *Guerres Maritimes (1688-1713)*, 25–34. Vincennes: Service Historique de la Marine, 1996; Ryan, A. N. 'An Act of Parliament cannot make men: The Quota Acts of 1795-1796'. In *Les Empires en Guerre et Paix, 1793-1860*, 103–6. Vincennes: Service Historique de la Marine, 1990. See also Bromley, J. S., ed. *The Manning of the Royal Navy: Selected Public Pamphlets, 1693-1873*. London: Navy Records Society, 1974. The reactions of

seamen to these forms of compulsion have been discussed in Linebaugh, P. and M. Rediker. *The Many-Headed Hydra* and in Rediker, M. *Between the Devil and the Deep Blue Sea*.

49 Phillips, C. R. '"The Life Blood of the Navy": Recruiting Sailors in Eighteenth Century Spain'. *The Mariner's Mirror* 87 (2001): 420–45; Raven, G. J. A. 'That Expensive Asset: A Short History of Netherlands Naval Personnel'. *Revue Internationale d'Histoire Militaire* 58 (1984): 167–85; Meyer, J. 'Gens de Mer en Mediterranee au xviiie Siecle: La France et L'Espagne, essai de comparison'. In *Le Genti del Mare Mediterraneo*. 2 vols, edited by R. Ragosta, ii, 905–36. Naples: Pironti, 1981; Asher, E. L. *The Resistance to the Maritime Classes: The Survival of Feudalism in the France of Colbert*. Berkeley: University of California Press, 1960; Le Goff, T. J. A. 'Problèmes de Recrutement de la Marine Française pendent la Guerre de Sept Ans'. *Revue Historique* 283 (1990): 208–33; Le Goff, T. J. A. 'Les gens de mer devant le système des classes (1755-1763)'. In Lottin et al., *Les Hommes et la mer dans l'Europe du Nord-Ouest de l'antiquité à nos jours: actes du colloque de Boulogne-sur-Mer, 15-17 juin 1984*. Revue du Nord, 463–79 (Spécial Hors Série 1 1986); Taillemite, E. 'Les Problèmes de la Marine de Guerre au XVIIe'. *XVIIe Siecle* 86 (1970): 21–37, especially 28–9; Bromley, J. S. 'Quelques Reflexions sur le Fonctionnement des Classes Maritimes en France, 1689-1713'. In *Corsairs and Navies, 1660-1760*, 121–38. London: Hambledon, 1987; Lijo, J. M. V. *La Matricula De Mar En La Espana Del Siglo XVIII: Registro, Inspeccion Y Evolution De Las Classes De Marineria Y Maestranza*. Madrid: Ministerio de Defensa, 2006. Context is, of course, vital to the effectiveness of any system. Denmark, with more constrained naval forces, had a relatively effective manning system.

50 Lloyd, C. C., J. Keevil and J. L. S. Coulter, *Medicine and the Navy, 1200-1900*. 4 vols. Edinburgh: Livingstone, 1957–62. An excellent series of essays on the effects of nutrition and exposure in different navies can be found in *Starving Sailors: The Influence of Nutrition upon Naval and Maritime History*. London: National Maritime Museum, 1981. Another excellent collection is Buchet, C., ed. *L' Homme, La Santé et la Mer*. Paris: Honoré Champion, 1997. The impact of disease on operations can be seen in McNeill, J. R. 'The Ecological Basis of Warfare in the Caribbean, 1700-1804'. In *Adapting to Conditions: War and Society in the Eighteenth Century*, edited by M. Ultee, 26–42. Tuscaloosa: University of Alabama Press, 1986; de Zulueta, J. 'Health and Military Factors in Vernon's Failure at Cartagena'. *The Mariner's Mirror* 78 (1992): 137–41; Jones, E. 'Royal Naval Psychiatry: Organisation, Methods and Outcomes, 1900-1945'. *The Mariner's Mirror* 92, no. 2 (2006): 190–203; Langley, H. D. *A History of Medicine in the Early US Navy*. Baltimore: Johns Hopkins University, 1995.

51 McBride, W. M. 'Normal Medicine, Science and the British Treatment of Sea Scurvy, 1753-75'. *Journal of the History of Medicine and Allied Sciences* 46 (1991): 157–77.

52 Morriss, R. 'Practicality and Prejudice: The Blockade Strategy and Naval Medicine during the French Revolutionary Wars, 1793-1801'. In *Science and the French and British Navies, 1700-1850*, edited by P. van der Merve, 77–87. London: National Maritime Museum, 2003; Bowden-Dann, J. 'Dirt, Diet and

Discipline: Medical Developments in Nelson's Navy'. *The Mariner's Mirror* 90 (2004): 260–72; Vale, B. 'The Conquest of Scurvy in the Royal Navy 1793-1800: A Challenge to the Current Orthodoxy'. *The Mariner's Mirror* 94 (2008): 160–75; Buchet, C. 'Santé et expeditions géo-stratégiques au temps de la marine à voile'. In *Marine et Technique au XIX ^{e} Siecle*, 141–62. Vincennes: Service Historique de la Marine, 1995; Nerzic, J-Y. 'Le Service de Santé de la Marine du Roi au temps de la Guerre de la Ligue d'Augsbourg'. *Chronique d'Histoire Maritime* 55 (2004): 44–59; Penn, C. 'The Medical Staffing of the Royal Navy in the Russian War, 1854–6'. *The Mariner's Mirror* 89, no. 1 (2003): 51–8; Poirier, J-L. 'Questions sanitaires pendant la Guerre de Crimée'. In *Les Empires En Guerre Et Paix*, edited by E. Freeman, 245–66. Vincennes: Service Historique de la Marine, 1989. See also Riley, J. C. *The Eighteenth Century Campaign to Avoid Disease*. London: Macmillan, 1987; Crimmin, P. K. 'The sick and hurt board and the health of seamen c.1700–1806'. *Journal for Maritime Research* 1 (1999): 48–65; Harland, K. 'The Royal Naval Hospital at Minorca, 1711: An example of an Admiral's Involvement in the Expansion of Naval Medical Care'. *The Mariner's Mirror* 94 (2008): 36–47.

53 Watt, J. 'Surgeons of the Mary Rose: The Practice of Surgery in Tudor England'. *The Mariner's Mirror* 69, no. 1 (1983): 3–19; Watt, J. 'The Health of Seamen in Anti-Slavery Squadrons'. *The Mariner's Mirror* 88, no. 1 (2002): 69–78; Watt, J. 'Surgery at Trafalgar'. *The Mariner's Mirror* 91 (2005): 266-283.

54 Coats, A. V. *The Oeconomy of the Navy and Portsmouth: A Discourse between the Civilian Naval Administration of Portsmouth Dockyard and the Surrounding Communities, 1650-1800*. D.Phil., Sussex, 1999. After the abolition of the French galley squadron in 1748, penal service in the galleys was replaced by service in the arsenals until 1873. See Henwood, P. *Bagnards à Brest*. Rennes: Ouest France, 1986; Lincoln, M. *Naval Wives and Mistresses*. London: National Maritime Museum, 2007; Romans, E. 'The Internal Economy of the Royal Navy in the Twentieth Century'. *The Mariner's Mirror* 94 (2008): 79–88; Haxhaj, E. 'More Bang for a Bob: The Decision to "Go Nuclear" and its Impact on Chatham Dockyard'. *The Mariner's Mirror* 91 (2005): 554–71; Mort, M. *Building the Trident Network: A Study of the Enrolment of People, Knowledge and Machines*. Cambridge, MA: MIT Press, 2002; Lunn, K. and A. Day, eds. *History of Work Labour Relations in the Royal Dockyards*. London: Mansell, 1999.

55 Blake, R. *Evangelicals in the Royal Navy, 1775-1815*. Woodbridge: Boydell and Brewer, 2008; Blake, R. *Religion in the British Navy, 1815-1879: Piety and Professionalism*. Woodbridge: Boydell and Brewer, 2014.

56 Chet, G. *The Ocean Is a Wilderness: Atlantic Piracy and the Limits of Governmental Legitimacy in the Early-Modern State, 1688-1856*. Boston: University of Massachusetts Press, 2014.

57 The value of naval records for social historians is evident in McLean, D. *Education and Empire: Naval Tradition and English Elite Schooling*. London: I. B. Tauris, 1998; McLean, D. *Public Health and Politics in the Age of Reform: Cholera, the State and the Royal Navy in Victorian Britain*. London: I. B. Tauris, 2006. See also Fox, C. *The Arts of Industry in the Age of the*

Enlightement. New Haven: Yale University Press, 2009, especially 46–69, 116–21, 138–41; Rose, C. 'The Meanings of the Late Victorian Sailor Suit'. *Journal for Maritime Research* 11 (2009): 24–50.

58 Spavens, W. *The Narrative of William Spavens: A Chatham Pensioner by Himself*. London: Chatham Publishing, 1998; Marteille, J. *Galley Slave*. Barnsley: Seaforth, 2010; Baynham, H. *From the Lower Deck: The Navy, 1700-1840*. London: Arrow, 1969.

59 Rose, K. 'Nostalgia and Imagination in Nineteenth-Century Sea Shanties'. *The Mariner's Mirror* 98, no. 2 (2012): 147–60.

60 Byrn, J. D. Jr. *Crime and Punishment in the Royal Navy: Discipline on the Leeward Islands Station, 1784-1812*. Aldershot: Scholar Press, 1989. Rodger, N. A. M. 'Officers and Men'. In *Maritime History: The Eighteenth Century and the Classic Age of Sail*, edited by J. B. Hattendorf, 137–44. Malabar, FL: Krieger, 1997; Eder, M. *Crime and Punishment in the Royal Navy of the Seven Years War, 1755-1763*. Aldershot: Gower, 2004.

61 Pope, D. *The Black Ship*. London: Weidenfeld and Nicholson, 1963; Coats, A. V. and P. McDougall. *The Naval Mutinies of 1797*. Woodbridge: Boydell Press, 2011; Dening, G. *Mr Bligh's Bad Language: Passion, Power and Theatre on the Bounty*. Cambridge: Cambridge University Press, 1992; Alexander, C. *The Bounty: The True Story of the Mutiny on the Bounty*. London: Harper Perennial, 2004; Woodman, R. *A Brief History of Mutiny*. London: Robinson, 2005.

62 Walton, O. '"A Great Improvement in the Sailor's Feeling Towards the Naval Service": Recruiting Seamen for the Royal Navy, 1815–1853'. *Journal for Maritime Research* 12 (2010): 27–57; Walton, O. 'New Kinds of Discipline: The Royal Navy in the Second Half of the Nineteenth Century'. Chapter 9 in *Naval Leadership and Management, 1650-1950*, edited by H. Doe and R. Harding, 143–56. Woodbridge: Boydell and Brewer, 2012.

63 Davies, *Gentlemen and Tarpaulins*; Aman, *Les Officiers Bleus Dans La Marine Francaise*; Verge-Franceschi, *La Marine Francaise au XVIIIe Siecle*, 177–215; Cavell, S. A. 'Social Politics and the Midshipmen's Mutiny, Portsmouth 1791'. *The Mariner's Mirror* 98, no. 1 (2012): 30–42.

64 Lewis, *The Navy in Transition*; Rasor, E. *Reform in the Royal Navy*. Hamden: Archon, 1976; Rasor, E. L. 'The Manning Question in the Royal Navy in the Early Ironclad Era'. In *Changing Interpretations and New Sources in Naval History*, edited by R. W. Love, 208–15. New York: Garland, 1980; Miller, G. A. 'From Jack Tar to Bluejacket: Impressment, Manning and the Development of Continuous Service in the Royal Navy, 1815-1853'. PhD, London, 2011.

65 Conley, M. *From Jack Tar to Union Jack: Representing Naval Manhood in the British Empire, 1870-1918*. Manchester: Manchester University Press, 2009. On the subject of public representation of the navy, see Lincoln, M. 'Origins of Public Maritime History'. *Journal for Maritime Research* 4 (2002): 52–66.

66 Spector, R. *At Sea at War: Sailors and Naval Warfare in the Twentieth Century*. London: Allen Lane, 2001.

67 Cohen, S. S. *Yankee Sailors in British Gaols: Prisoners of War at Forton and Mill*. Newark: University of Delaware Press, 1995; Bowman, L. G. *Captive*

American Prisoners during the American Revolution. Athens, OH: Ohio University Press, 1976.

68 Abell, F. *Prisoners of War in Britain, 1756-1815.* Oxford: Humphrey Milford, 1914; Shaw, J. J. S. 'The Commission of Sick and Wounded and Prisoners, 1664–1667'. *The Mariner's Mirror* 25, no. 3 (1939): 306–27; Anderson, O. 'The Treatment of Prisoners of War in Britain During the American Revolution'. *Bulletin of the Institute of Hisorical Research* 28, no. January (1955): 63–83; Anderson, O. 'Establishment of British Supremacy at Sea and the Exchange of Naval Prisoners of War'. *English Historical Review* 75, no. 294 (1960): 77–89.

69 The best introduction to this subject is Burke, P. *What is Cultural History?* Cambridge: Polity, 2004.

70 Lincoln, M. *Representing the Royal Navy: British Sea Power, 1750-1815.* Aldershot: Ashgate, 2002; Ronald, *The Symbolic Power of Youth*; Glass, R. E. 'The Image of the Sea Officer in English Literature, 1660-1710'. *Albion* 26 (1994): 583–99; Rodger, N. A. M. 'Honour and Duty at Sea, 1660-1815'. *Historical Research* 75 (2002): 427–47; Nicholson, A. *Men of Honour: Trafalgar and the Making of the English Hero.* London: Harper Collins, 2005; Colville, Q. 'Jack Tar and the Gentleman Officer: The Role of Uniform in Shaping the Class- and Gender-Related Identities of British Naval Personnel, 1930-1939'. *Transactions of the Royal Historical Society*, 6th Series, 13 (2003): 105–30; Rose, 'The Meanings of the Late Victorian Sailor Suit'; Miller, A. *Dressed to Kill: British Naval Uniform, Masculinity and Contemporary Fashions, 1748-1857.* London: National Maritime Museum, 2007; Wathen, B. *Sir Francis Drake: The Construction of a Hero.* Woodbridge: Boydell and Brewer, 2009.

71 Lagadec, Y, and D. Hopkin. *La Bataille De Saint-Cast (Bretagne, 11 Septembre 1758) Entre Histoire Et Memoire.* Rennes: Presses Universitaires de Rennes, 2009. I am grateful to Dr David Hopkin for alerting me to this work.

72 Scott, *When the Waves Ruled Britannia*; Wilson, K. 'Empire, Trade and Popular Politics in Mid-Hanoverian Britain; the Case of Admiral Vernon'. *Past and Present* 121 (1988): 74–109; Jordan, G. and N. Rogers. 'Admirals as Heroes: Patriotism and Liberty in Hanoverian England'. *Journal of British Studies* 28 (1989): 201–24.

73 Pratt, L. 'Naval Contemplation: Poetry, Patriotism and the Navy, 1797-99'. *Journal for Maritime Research* 2 (2000): 84–105; Jenks, T. *Naval Engagements: Patriotism, Cultural Politics and the Royal Navy, 1793-1815.* Oxford: Oxford University Press, 2006; Quilley, G., ed. *Art for the Nation: The Oil Paintings Collections of the National Maritime Museum.* London: National Maritime Museum, 2006; Craske, M. 'Making National Heroes? A Survey of the Social and Political Functions and Meanings of Major British Funeral Monuments to Naval and Military Figures, 1730-70'. In *Conflicting Visions: War and Visual Culture in Britain and France c1700-1850*, edited by J. Bonehill and G. Quilley, 41–60. Aldershot: Ashgate, 2005; Yarrington, A. W. 'The Commemoration of the Hero, 1804-1864: Monuments to the British Victors of the Napoleonic Wars'. PhD, Cambridge, 1980; Yarrington, A. W. 'Nelson the Citizen Hero: State and Public Patronage of Monumental

Sculpture'. *Art History* 6 (1983): 315–29; Eyres, P., ed. 'Hearts of Oak: Commerce, Empire and the Landscape Garden'. *New Arcadian Journal* 35, no. 6 (1993); Eyres, P., ed. 'Sons of the Sea'. *New Arcadian Journal* 37, no. 8 (1994). Also see Hattendorf, J. B. *Faces of the College: An Illustrated Catalogue of the US Naval War College's Collection of Portrait Paintings and Busts.* Newport: USNWC, 2009; De Beer, G. 'Painting'. In *The Oxford Encyclopedia of Maritime History.* 4 vols, edited by J. B. Hattendorf, vol. 3, 247–62. New York: Oxford University Press, 2007; Schokkenbroek, J. C. A. 'Portraits: Celebrities'. In Hattendorf, *The Oxford Encyclopedia of Maritime History,* vol. 3, 311–19.

74 Blyth, R., A. Lambert and J. Rüger, eds. *The Dreadnought and the Edwardian Age.* Farnham: Ashgate, 2011; Thomas, R. D. 'Empire Naval Pageantry and Public Spectacles – the Launch of HMS Iron Duke'. *The Mariner's Mirror* 88 (2002): 202–12. The German navalist movement is explored in the context of wider cultural and political changes in Rüger, J. *The Great Naval Game: Britain and Germany in the Age of Empire.* Cambridge: Cambridge University Press, 2007. See also Chickering, R. 'Patriotic Societies and German Foreign Policy, 1890-1914'. *International History Review* 1 (1979): 470–89.

75 Smith, A. W. 'The Sinister Submarine as a Motif in Contemporary Legend and Popular Imagination'. *Contemporary Legend* 3 (2000): 64–82; Redford, D. *The Submarine: A Cultural History from the Great War to Nuclear Combat.* London: I. B. Tauris, 2010.

76 Hartelie, O. 'Notes from Naval Novels'. *The Mariner's Mirror* 6, no. 11 (1920): 339–43; Anderson, R. C. 'Naval Warfare in Fiction'. *The Mariner's Mirror* 51, no. 3 (1965): 243–52; Cunningham, A. E. *Patrick O'Brian: Critical Appreciations and a Bibliography.* Boston Spa: British Library, 1994; Parrill, S. *Nelson's Navy in Fiction and Film: Depictions of British Sea Power in the Napoleonic Era.* Jefferson, NC: McFarland and Company, 2009.

77 Rayner, J. *The Naval War Film: Genre, History and National Cinema.* Manchester: Manchester University Press, 2007; Suid, L. *Sailing on the Silver Screen: Hollywood and the US Navy.* Annapolis: Naval Institute Press, 1996; Smith, A. 'Mountbatten goes to the Movies: Promoting the Heroic Myth through Cinema'. *Historical Journal of Film, Radio and Television* 26 (2006): 395–416; Carolan, V. 'British Maritime History, National Identity and Film, 1900-1960'. PhD, London, 2012; Burgoyne, R. The Hollywood Historical Film. Oxford: Blackwell, 2008;

78 Dillon, R. *History on Television: Constructing Nation, Nationality and Collective Memory,* 246–47. Manchester: Manchester University Press, 2012.

SELECT BIBLIOGRAPHY

A work attempting to cover such a broad subject must limit the bibliography. This bibliography is largely confined to those works cited in the text.

Abell, F. *Prisoners of War in Britain, 1756 to 1815. A Record of Their Lives, Their Romance and Their Sufferings.* London: Humphry Milford, 1914.
Acerra, M. 'L'Arsenal, Pivot de la Puissance Maritime?'. In *La Puissance Maritime*, edited by C. Buchet, J. Meyer and J. P. Poussou. Paris: Presses de l'Université Paris-Sorbonne, 2004.
Acerra, M. 'Les Forces Navales Française Au Début de la Guerre de la Ligue D'augsbourg'. In *Guerres Maritimes (1688–1713)*, 15–24. Vincennes: Service Historique de la Marine, 1996.
Acerra, M., and A. Zysberg. *L'essor des Marines de Guerres Européennes (Vers 1680 – Vers 1790).* Paris: SEDES, 1997.
Acerra, M., and J. Meyer, eds. *Marines et Revolution.* Rennes: Editions Ouest-France, 1988.
Acerra, M., J. Merino and J. Meyer, eds. *Les Marines de Guerre Europeenes, XVIIe–XVIIIe Siecles.* Paris: PUP, 1985.
Adams, T. R. and D. W. Waters. *English Maritime Books Printed before 1801.* London: National Maritime Museum, 1995.
Adkins, R., and L. Adkins. *Jack Tar: The Extraordinary Lives of Ordinary Seamen in Nelson's Navy.* London: Little Brown, 2008.
Admiralty, Board of. *Report of a Committee Appointed by the Admiralty to Examine & Consider the Evidence Relating to the Tactics Employed by Nelson at the Battle of Trafalgar.* London: HMSO, 1913 (reprint 2006).
Albion, R. G. *Naval and Maritime History: An Annotated Bibliography*, 4th edn, Newton Abbot: David and Charles, 1973.
Alcala-Zamora, J. *España, Flandres y el Mar del Norte (1618–1639): La Ultima Offensiva Europea de los Austrias Madrilenos.* Barcelona: Planeta, 1975.
Alden, J. D. *The Fleet Submarine in the U.S. Navy: A Design and Construction History.* London: Arms and Armour Press, 1979.
Aldridge, D. D. *Admiral Sir John Norris.* Lund: Nordic Academic Press, 2009.
Aldridge, D. D. 'Victualing the British Expeditions to the Baltic 1715–1727'. *Scandinavian Economic History Review* 12, no. 1 (1964): 1–25.
Alexander, C. *The Bounty: The True Story of the Mutiny on the Bounty.* London: Harper Perennial, 2004.
Alexander, J. H., and M. L. Bartlett. *Sea Soldiers in the Cold War: Amphibious Warfare 1945–1991.* Annapolis: Naval Institute Press, 1995.
Alford, J., ed. *Sea Power and Influence: Old Issues and New Challenges*, International Institute for Strategic Studies. Farnborough: Gower, 1980.

Allen, D. W. 'The British Navy Rules: Monitoring and Incompatible Incentives in the Age of Fighting Sail'. *Explorations in Economic History* 39, no. 2 (2002): 204–31.

Allen, D. W. 'Rules and Rewards in the Age of Sail: A Reply'. *Explorations in Economic History* 40 (2003): 212–20.

Allen, M. 'The British Mediterranean Squadron during the Great Eastern Crisis of 1876-9'. *Mariner's Mirror* 85, no. 1 (1999): 53–67.

Allen, M. 'The Deployment of Untried Technology: British Naval Tactics in the Ironclad Era'. *War in History* 15, no. 3 (2008): 269–93.

Allen, M. 'The Foreign Intelligence Committee and the Origins of the Naval Intelligence Department of the Admiralty'. *The Mariner's Mirror* 81, no. 1 (1995): 65–78.

Aman, J. *Les Officiers Bleus Dans La Marine Francaise*. Geneva: Centre de Recherches d'Histoire et de Philologie, 1976.

Anderson, O. 'The Establishment of British Supremacy at Sea and the Exchange of Naval Prisoners of War, 1689–1783'. *English Historical Review* 75, no. January (1960): 77–89.

Anderson, O. 'The Treatment of Prisoners of War in Britain During the American Revolution'. *Bulletin of the Institute of Hisorical Research* 28, no. January (1955): 63–83.

Anderson, M. S. 'Great Britain and the Russian Fleet, 1769–1770'. *Slavonic and East European Studies Review* 31, no. 76 (1952): 148–63.

Anderson, M. S. 'Great Britain and the Russo-Turkish War of 1768–1774'. *English Historical Review* 69, no. 270 (1954): 39–58.

Anderson, M. S. 'Russia in the Mediterranean, 1788–1791: A Little-Known Chapter in the History of Naval Warfare and Privateering'. *The Mariner's Mirror* 45, no. 1 (1959): 25–35.

Anderson, R. C. 'British and American Officers in the Russian Navy'. *The Mariner's Mirror* 33, no. 1 (1947): 17–27.

Anderson, R. C. 'Denmark and the First Anglo-Dutch War'. *The Mariner's Mirror* 53, no. 1 (1967): 55–62.

Anderson, R. C. 'The English Fleet at the Battle of Portland'. *The Mariner's Mirror* 39, no. 3 (1953): 171–7.

Anderson, R. C. 'Naval Warfare in Fiction'. *The Mariner's Mirror* 51, no. 3 (1965): 243–52.

Anderson, R. C. *Naval Wars in the Baltic, 1522–1850*. London: Gilbert-Wood, 1910.

Anderson, R. C. *Naval Wars in the Levant, 1559–1853*. Liverpool: Liverpool University Press, 1952.

Anderson, R. C. 'The Royalists at Sea in 1650'. *The Mariner's Mirror* 17, no. 2 (1931): 135–68.

Anderson, R. C. 'The Royalists at Sea, 1648'. *The Mariner's Mirror* 9, no. 2 (1923): 34–46.

Anderson, R. C. 'The Royalists at Sea, 1651–1653'. *The Mariner's Mirror* 21, no. 1 (1935): 61–90.

Anderson, R. C. 'The Sicilian War of 1674–1678'. *The Mariner's Mirror* 57, no. 3 (1971): 239–65.

Anderson, R. C. 'The Thirty Year's War in the Mediterranean'. *The Mariner's Mirror* 55, no. 4 (1969): 435–51.

SELECT BIBLIOGRAPHY

Anderson, R. C. 'The Thirty Year's War in the Mediterranean'. *The Mariner's Mirror* 56, no. 1 (1970): 41–57.
Andrews, C. M. 'Colonial Commerce'. *American Historical Review* 20, no. 1 (1914): 43–63.
Andrews, K. R. 'The Aims of Drake's Expedition, 1577-80'. *American Historical Review* 73 (1968): 724–42.
Andrews, K. R. 'Caribbean Rivalry and the Anglo-Spanish Peace of 1604'. *History* 59 (1974): 1–17.
Andrews, K. R. *Drake's Voyages: A Reappraisal of Their Place in Elizabethan Maritime Expansion.* London: Wiedenfeld and Nicholson, 1967.
Andrews, K. R. 'The Elizabethan Seaman', *The Mariner's Mirror* 68, no. 3 (1982): 245–62.
Andrews, K. R. *Elizabethan Privateering.* Cambridge: Cambridge University Press, 1964.
Andrews, K. R. *English Privateering Voyages to the West Indies, 1588–1595*, vol. 111, London: Hakluyt Society, 1959.
Andrews, K. R. *Ship Money and Politics: Seafaring and Naval Enterprise in the Reign of Charles I.* Cambridge: Cambridge University Press, 1991.
Andrews, K. R. 'Sir Robert Cecil and Mediterranean Plunder'. *English Historical Review* 87 (1972): 513–32.
Andrews, K. R. *The Spanish Caribbean: Trade and Plunder, 1530–1630.* New Haven: Yale University Press, 1978.
Andrews, K. R. *Trade, Plunder and Settlement: Maritime Enterprise and the Genesis of the British Empire, 1480–1630.* Cambridge: Cambridge University Press, 1984.
Appleby, J. C. 'English Privateering during the French and Spanish Wars, 1625–1630'. Hull: University of Hull, 1983.
Arthur, B. *How Britain Won the War of 1812: The Royal Navy's Blockade of the United States, 1812–1815.* Woodbridge: Boydell Press, 2011.
Asher, E. L. *The Resistance of the Maritime Classes: The Survival of Feudalism in the France of Colbert.* Berkeley and Los Angeles: University of California Press, 1960.
Aston, G. G. *Letters on Amphibious Wars.* London: John Murray, 1911.
Aubrey, P. *The Defeat of James Stuart's Armada.* Leicester: Leicester University Press, 1979.
Auer, J. E. *The Postwar Rearmament of Japanese Maritime Forces, 1945-71.* New York: Praeger, 1973.
Bacon, R. *The Dover Patrol, 1915–1917.* 2 vols. London: Hutchinson, 1919.
Bacon, R. *The Jutland Scandal.* London: Hutchinson, 1924.
Bacon, R. *The Life of John Rushworth, Earl Jellicoe.* London: Cassell, 1936.
Baer, G. W. 'Alfred Thayer Mahan and the Utility of US Naval Forces Today'. In *The Changing Face of Maritime Power*, edited by A. Dorman, M. L. Smith and M. R. H. Uttley, 14–18. London: Macmillan, 1999.
Baer, G. W. *One Hundred Years of Sea Power: The U.S. Navy, 1890–1990.* Stanford: Stanford University Press, 1994.
Bagnasco, E. *Submarines of World War Two.* London: Arms and Armour Press, 1977.
Bailyn, B. *Atlantic History: Concept and Contours.* Cambridge, MA: Harvard University Press, 2005.

Ballantine, D. *U.S. Naval Logistics in the Second World War*. Princeton: University of Princeton Press, 1947.
Bamford, P. W. *Fighting Ships and Prisons: The Mediterranean Galleys of France in the Age of Louis XIV*. Minneapolis: University of Minnesota Press, 1973.
Barbey, D. E. *Macarthur's Amphibious Navy: Seventh Amphibious Force Operations, 1943–1945*. Annapolis: Naval Institute Press, 1969.
Bartlett, C. J. *Great Britain and Sea Power, 1815–1853*. Oxford: Oxford University Press, 1963.
Bartlett, M. L., ed. *Assault from the Sea: Essays on Amphibious Warfare*. Annapolis: Naval Institute Press, 1983.
Battesti, M. *La Marine Au XIXe Siècle: Interventions Extérieures Et Colonies*. Paris: Du May, 1993.
Battesti, M. *La Marine de Napoleon III: Une Politique Navale*. 2 vols. Vincennes: Service Historique de la Marine, 1997.
Baugh, D. *The Global Seven Years War, 1754–1763*. Harlow: Longman, 2011.
Baugh, D. 'Great Britain's "Blue Water" Policy, 1689–1815'. *International History Review* 10 (1988): 33–58.
Baugh, D. 'Maritime Strength and Atlantic Commerce: The Uses of a "Grand Maritime Empire"'. In *An Imperial State at War: Britain from 1689 to 1815*, edited by L. Stone, 185–213. London: Routledge, 1994.
Baugh, D., ed. *Naval Administration, 1715–1750*. London: Navy Records Society, 1977.
Baugh, D. 'Naval Power: What Gave the British Navy Superiority?' In *Exceptionalism and Industrialization: Britain and Its European Rivals, 1688–1815*, edited by L. Pardos de la Escoura, 235–57. Cambridge: Cambridge University Press, 2004.
Baugh, D. 'Withdrawing from Europe: Anglo-French Maritime Geopolitics, 1750–1800'. *International History Review* 20 (1998): 1–32.
Baugh, D. A. *British Naval Administration in the Age of Walpole*. Princeton: Princeton University Press, 1965.
Baugh, D. A. 'British Strategy during the First World War in the Context of Four Centuries: Blue Water versus Continental Commitment'. In *Naval History: The Sixth Symposium of the U.S. Naval Academy*, edited by Daniel Masterson, 83–110. Wilmington: Scholarly Resources Inc., 1987.
Baugh, D. A. 'Confusions and Constraints: The Navy and British Defence Planning, 1919–1939'. In *Naval Power in the Twentieth Century*, edited by N. A. M. Rodger, 120–33. London: Macmillan, 1996.
Baugh, D. A. *The Global Seven Years War, 1754–1763*. London: Pearson, 2011.
Baugh, D. A. 'Why Did Britain Lose Command of the Sea during the War for America?' Chapter 7 in *The British Navy and the Uses of Naval Power in the Eighteenth Century*, edited by Jeremy Black and Philip Woodfine, 149–70. Leicester: Leicester University Press, 1988.
Baumber, M. *General-at-Sea: Robert Blake and the Seventeenth Century Revolution in Naval Warfare*. London: John Murray, 1989.
Baumber, M. L. 'The Navy and the Civil War in Ireland, 1641–1643'. *The Mariner's Mirror* 57, no. 4 (1971): 85–97.
Baumber, M. L. 'The Navy and the Civil War in Ireland, 1643–46'. *The Mariner's Mirror* 75, no. 3 (1989): 255–68.

Baumber, M. L. 'Parliamentary Naval Politics, 1641-49'. *The Mariner's Mirror* 82, no. 4 (1996): 398–408.
Baynham, H. *From the Lower Deck: The Navy, 1700–1840*. London: Arrow, 1969.
Beeler, J. F. *Birth of the Battleship: British Capital Ship Design, 1870–1881*. London: Chatham Publishing, 2001.
Beeler, J. F. *British Naval Policy in the Gladstone-Disraeli Era, 1866–1880*. Stanford: Stanford University Press, 1997.
Beeler, J. F. 'A One Power Standard? Great Britain and the Balance of Naval Power 1860–1880'. *Journal of Strategic Studies* 15 (1992): 548–92 (fn. 122).
Beeler, J. F. 'Steam, Strategy and Schurman Imperial Defence in the Post Crimea Era 1856–1905'. In *Far Flung Lines: Essays on Imperial Defence in Honour of Donald Mackenzie Schurman*, edited by K. Neilson and G. Kennedy, 27–54. London: Frank Cass, 1997.
Beerbuhl, M. S. 'Supplying the Belligerent Countries: Transnational Trading Networks During the Napoleonic Wars'. In *The Contractor State and Its Implications, 1659–1815*, edited by R. Harding and S. Sobles Ferri, 21–34. Las Palmas: Universidad de las Palmas de Gran Canaria, 2012.
Beesley, P. *Room 40: British Naval Intelligence, 1914–1918*. London: Hamish Hamilton, 1982.
Beesley, P. *Very Special Intelligence: The Story of the Admiralty's Operational Intelligence Centre War, 1939–1945*. London: Hamish Hamilton, 1977.
Bell, C. *The Royal Navy, Seapower and Strategy between the Wars*. London: Palgrave, 2000.
Bell, C. M. 'Sir John Fisher's Naval Revolution Reconsidered: Winston Churchill at the Admiralty, 1911–1914'. *War in History* 18, no. 3 (2011): 333–56.
Benbow, T. 'The Impact of Air Power on Navies: The United Kingdom, 1945–1957'. D.Phil. Oxford, 1999.
Bender, J. *Dutch Warships in the Age of Sail, 1600–1714: Design, Construction, Careers and Fates*. Barnsley: Seaforth, 2014.
Benjamin, D. K. and C. F. Thornberg. 'Comment: Rules, Monitoring and Incentives in the Age of Sail'. *Explorations in Economic History* 40 (2003): 195–211.
Benjamin, D. K. and C. F. Thornberg. 'Organization and Incentives in the Age of Sail'. *Explorations in Economic History* 44 (2007): 317–41.
Bentley, M. *Modernizing England's Past: English Historiography in the Age of Modernism, 1870–1970*. Cambridge: Cambridge University Press, 2005.
Berg, M. W. 'Admiral William H. Stanley and the Second London Naval Treaty, 1934–1936'. *The Historian* 33, no. February (1971): 215–36.
Bernath, S. L. *Squall across the Atlantic: American Civil War Prize Cases and Diplomacy*. Berkeley: University of California Press, 1970.
Béthencourt y Massieu, A. de. *Patiño en la Politica Internacional De Felipe V*. Valladolid: CSIC, 1954.
Bicheno, H. *Crescent and Cross: The Battle of Lepanto 1571*. London: Cassell, 2003.
Bicheno, H. *Elizabeth's Sea Dogs: How the English Became the Scourge of the Seas*. London: Conway, 2012.
Bickham, T. *The Weight of Vengeance: The United States, the British Empire and the War of 1812*. Oxford: Oxford University Press, 2012.

Biddle, T. D and R. M. Citino. 'The Role of Military History in the Contemporary Academy'. Society for Military History White Paper, http://www.smh-hq.org/docs/SMHWhitePaper.pdf (accessed 17 May 2015).
Black, J. *America or Europe?: British Foreign Policy, 1739–1763*. London: UCL Press, 1998.
Black, J. *Beyond the Military Revolution*. London: Palgrave, 2011.
Black, J. *The Continental Commitment: Britain, Hanover and Interventionism, 1714–1793*. Abingdon: Routledge, 2005.
Black, J. 'Naval Capability in the Early Modern Period: An Introduction'. *Mariner's Mirror* 97, no. 2 (2011): 21–31.
Black, J. *Naval Power: A History of Warfare and the Sea from 1550*. London: Palgrave, 2009.
Black, J. 'Hanover and British Foreign Policy, 1714-60'. *English Historical Review* 220 (2005): 309–39.
Black, J. *Rethinking Military History*. London: Routledge, 2004.
Black, N. *The British Naval Staff in the First World War*. Woodbridge: Boydell Press, 2009.
Blair, C. *Hitler's U Boat War: The Hunters, 1939–1942*. London: Random House, 1996.
Blair, C. *The Silent Victory: The US Submarine Victory against Japan*. Annapolis: Naval Institute Press, 2001.
Blair, C. *U Boat War: The Hunted, 1942–1945*. London: Random House, 1998.
Blake, N. *Steering to Glory: A Day in the Life of a Ship of the Line*. London: Chatham Publishing, 2005.
Blake, R. *Evangelicals in the Royal Navy, 1775–1815*. Woodbridge: Boydell and Brewer, 2008.
Blake, R. *Religion in the British Navy, 1815–1879: Piety and Professionalism*. Woodbridge: Boydell and Brewer, 2014.
Bleby, A. *The Victorian Naval Brigades*. Caithness: Whittles Publishing, 2006.
Blyth, R., A. Lambert, and J. Rüger, eds. *The Dreadnought and the Edwardian Age*. Farnham: Ashgate, 2011.
Bond, B. *Liddell Hart: A Study of His Military Thought*. London: Cassell, 1976.
Bond, G. C. *The Grand Expedition: The British Invasion of Holland in 1809*. Athens, Georgia: University of Georgia Press, 1979.
Booth, K. *Navies and Foreign Policy*. London: Croom Helm, 1977.
Boruwer, J. W. L. 'Dutch Naval Policy in the Cold War Period'. In *Strategy and Response in the Twentieth Century Maritime World*, edited by J. R. Bruijn, A. M. C. van Dissel, G. Jackson and P. C. van Royen, 42–50. Amsterdam: Batavian Lion International, 2001.
Boscawen, H. *The Capture of Louisbourg, 1758*. Norman: University of Oklahoma Press, 2011.
Bosher, J. F. 'Financing the French Navy in the Seven Years War: Beaujon, Goosens Et Compagnie in 1759'. *Business History* 28, no. 3, July (1986): 115–33.
Boulle, P. H. 'Patterns of French Colonial Trade and the Seven Years War'. *Histoire Sociale – Social History* 7 (1974): 48–86.
Boulle, P. H. 'Slave Trade, Commercial Organization and Industrial Growth in Eighteenth Century Nantes'. *Revue Francaise d'Histoire d'Outre-Mer* 59, no. 214 (1972): 70–112.

Bourland, R. D. 'Maurepas and His Administration of the French Navy on the Eve of the War of Austrian Succession (1737–1742)'. Ph.D, Notre Dame University, 1978.
Bourne, R. *Queen Anne's Navy in the West Indies*. New Haven: Yale University Press, 1939.
Bowden-Dan, J. 'Diet, Dirt and Discipline: Medical Developments in Nelson's Navy. Dr John Snipe's Contribution'. *The Mariner's Mirror* 90, no. 3 (1 January 2004): 260–72.
Bowman, L. G. *Captive Americans: Prisoners during the American Revolution*. Athens, OH: Ohio University Press, 1976.
Boxer, C. R. *The Dutch Seaborne Empire, 1600–1800*. London: Hutchinson, 1965.
Boxer, C. R. *The Portuguese Seaborne Empire, 1415–1825*. London: Hutchinson, 1969.
Brady, C. *James Anthony Froude: An Intellectual Biography of a Victorian Prophet*. Oxford: Oxford University Press, 2013.
Breemer, J. S. 'The Burden of Trafalgar: Decisive Battle and Naval Strategic Expectations on the Eve of World War I'. *Journal of Strategic Studies* 17 (1994): 33–62.
Brenner, R. 'The Civil War Politics of London's Merchant Community'. *Past & Present* 58 (1973): 53–107.
Brenner, R. *Merchants and Revolution: Commercial Change, Political Conflict and London's Overseas Traders, 1550–1653*. Cambridge: Cambridge University Press, 1993.
Brescia, M. *Mussolini's Navy: A Reference Guide to the Regina Marina, 1930–1945*. Barnsley: Seaforth Publishing, 2012.
Brewer, J. *The Sinews of Power: War, Money and the English State, 1688–1783*. London: Unwin Hyman, 1989.
Bridge, C., ed. *History of the Russian Fleet During the Reign of Peter the Great by a Contemporary Englishman (1724)*. London: Navy Records Society, 1899.
Briggs, M. 'Innovation and the Mid-Victorian Royal Navy: The Case of the Whitehead Torpedo'. *The Mariner's Mirror* 88, no. 4 (2002): 447–55.
Broeze, F., ed. *Maritime History at the Crossroads: A Critical Review of Recent Historiography*, edited by Lewis Fischer, R., Research in Maritime History, vol. 9. St John's, Newfoundland: International Maritime Economic History Association, 1995.
Bromley, J. S., ed. *Corsairs and Navies, 1660–1760*. London: Hambledon Press, 1987.
Bromley, J. S., ed. *The Manning of the Royal Navy: Selected Public Pamphlets, 1693–1873*. London: Navy Records Society, 1974.
Bromley, J. S. 'The North Sea in Wartime, 1688–1713'. *Bijdragen en Mededelingen Befreffende de Geschiedenis der Nederlanden* 92 (1977): 270–99.
Bromley, J. S. 'Quelques Reflexions sur le Fonctionnement des Classes Maritimes En France, 1689–1713'. In *Corsairs and Navies*, edited by J. S Bromley, 121–38. London: Hambledon, 1987.
Brookes, J. *Dreadnought Gunnery and the Battle of Jutland: The Question of Fire Control*. London: Routledge, 2005.
Brookes, R. *The Long Arm of Empire: Naval Brigades from the Crimea to the Boxer Rebellion*. London: Constable, 1999.

Brouwer, J. W. L. 'Dutch Naval Policy in the Cold War Period'. In *In Strategy and Response in the Twentieth Century Maritime World*, edited by J. R. Bruijn, A. M. C. van Dissel, G. Jackson and P. C. van Royen, 42–50. Amsterdam: Batavian Lion International, 2001.

Brown, D. *The Royal Navy and the Falklands War*. London: Leo Cooper, 1987.

Brown, D. K. *Carrier Operations in World War II, Volume 1*. London: Ian Allen, 1968.

Brown, D. K. *Carrier Operations in World War II: Volume 2*. London: Ian Allen, 1974.

Brown, D. K. *Warrior to Dreadnought: Warship Development, 1860–1905*. London: Chatham Publishing, 1997.

Brown, D. K., and G. Moore. *Rebuilding the Royal Navy: Warship Design since 1945*. London: Chatham Publishing, 2003.

Bruijn, J. R. 'Commandanten Van Oost-Indievaarders in De Achttiende Eeuw'. *Tijdschrift voor Zeegeschiedenis* 20, no. 1 (2001): 4–14.

Bruijn, J. R. 'De Admiraliteit Van Friesland En Amsterdam'. *Jaarboek van het Fries Schepvaart Museum en Oudheitkamer* (1966): 33–7.

Bruijn, J. R. 'The Dutch Navy Goes Overseas c1750-c1850'. *Tijdschrift voor Zeegeschiedenis* 20, no. 2 (2001): 163–74.

Bruijn, J. R. *The Dutch Navy in the Seventeenth and Eighteenth Centuries*. Columbia: University of South Carolina Press, 1993.

Bruijn, J. R. 'Dutch Privateering during the Second and Third Anglo-Dutch Wars'. *Acta Historicae Neerlandicaas* 11 (1977): 79–93.

Bruijn, J. R. 'A Little Incident in 1707: The Demise of a once Glorious Dutch Naval Organisation'. Chapter 5 in *Organizing History: Studies in Honour of Jan Glete*, edited by A. M. Forsberg, M. Hallenberg, O. Husz and J. Nordin, 110–22. Lund: Nordic Academic Press, 2011.

Bruijn, J. R. 'The Long Life of Treaties the Dutch Republic and Great Britain in the Eighteenth Century'. Chapter 2 In *Navies and Northern Waters*, edited by R. Hobson and T. Kristiansen, 41–58. London: Frank Cass, 2004.

Bruijn, J. R. 'William III and His Two Navies'. *Notes and Records of the Royal Society of London* 43, no. 2 (1989): 117–32.

Bruijn, J. R., R. Prud'homme van Reine, and R. van Hovell tot Westerflier, eds. *De Ruyter: Dutch Admiral*. Rotterdam: Karawansaray Publishers, 2011.

Bryn, J. D. *Crime and Punishment in the Royal Navy: Discipline on the Leeward Islands Station, 1784–1812*. Aldershot: Scholar Press, 1989.

Buchet, C. *The British Navy, Economy and Society in the Seven Years War*. Woodbridge: Boydell Press, 2013.

Buchet, C., ed. *L' Homme, La Santé et la Mer*. Paris: Honoré Champion, 1997.

Buchet, Christian. *La Lutte Pour L'espace Caraibe et la Facade Atlantique de l'amerique Centrale Du Sud (1672–1763)*. 2 vols. Vol. 1, Paris: Libraire de l'Inde, Editeur, 1991.

Buchet, C. *La Lutte Pour L'espace Caraibe et la Facade Atlantique de l'Amerique Centrale Du Sud (1672–1763)*. 2 vols. Vol. 2. Paris: Libraire de l'Inde, Editeur, 1994.

Buchet, C. 'Le Marine, Moteur du Développement Économique'. In *La Puissance Maritime*, edited by C. Buchet, J. Meyer and J-P. Poussou, 509–14. Paris: Presses de l'université Paris-Sorbonne, 2004.

Buchet, C. *Marine, Economie et Societe: Un Exemple D'interaction L'avitaillement de la Royal Navy Durant la Guerre de Sept Ans*. Paris: Honore Champion, 1999.

Buchet, C. 'Sante Et Expeditions Geo-Strategiques Au Temps De La Marine a Voile'. In *Marine Et Technique*, 141–66. Vincennes: Service historique de la Marine, 1995.

Buckley, J. *Air Power in the Age of Total War*. Warfare in History. edited by Black Jeremy London: UCL Press, 1999.

Buel, R. *In Irons: Britain's' Naval Supremacy and the American Revolutionary Economy*. New Haven: Yale University Press, 1998.

Burgoyne, R. *The Hollywood Historical Film*. Malden, MA: Blackwell Publishing, 2008.

Burke, P. *What Is Cultural History?* Cambridge: Polity Press, 2004.

Burrell, R. S. 'Breaking the Cycle of Iwo Jima Mythology: A Strategic Study of Operation Detachment'. *Journal of Military History* 68, no. 4 (2004): 1143–86.

Burroughs, P. 'John Robert Seeley and British Imperial History'. *Journal of Imperial and Commonwealth History* 1 (1973): 192–211.

Bussert, J. C. and B. A. Elleman. *Plan: People's Liberation Army Navy: Combat Systems Technology, 1949–2010*. Annapolis: Naval Institute Press, 2011.

Byrn, J. D. jnr. *Crime and Punishment in the Royal Navy: Discipline on the Leeward Islands Station, 1784–1812*. Aldershot: Scholar Press, 1989.

Cable, Sir J. *Britain's Naval Future*. London: Macmillan, 1983.

Cable, Sir J. *Gunboat Diplomacy, 1919–1991*. Studies in International Security, 3rd edn, vol. 16. London, 1994.

Cable, Sir J. *Navies in a Violent Peace*. London: Macmillan, 1989.

Callender, G. *Bibliography of Naval History*. London: Historical Association, 1924/1925.

Callwell, C. E. *The Effect of Maritime Command on Land Operations since Waterloo*. Edinburgh: Blackwood, 1907.

Callwell, C. E. *Military Operations and Maritime Preponderance: Their Relations and Interdependence*. Edinburgh: Blackwood, 1905.

Callyea, S. C. 'Bridging History and Future Security Policy'. In *Naval Policy and Strategy in the Mediterranean; Past, Present and Future*, edited by J. B. Hattendorf, 261–300. London: Cass, 2000.

Cannadine, D., ed. *Admiral Lord Nelson: Context and Legacy*. Basingstoke: Palgrave Macmillan, 2005.

Cannadine, D., ed. *Trafalgar in History: A Battle and Its Afterlife*. Basingstoke: Palgrave Macmillan, 2006.

Cannadine, D., ed. *Empire: The Sea and Global History; Britain's Maritime World, C.1760 – C1840*. London: Palgrave, 2007.

Canney, D. L. *Africa Squadron: The U.S. Navy and the Slave Trade, 1843–1861*. Washington: Potomac, 2006.

Canney, D. L. *Lincoln's Navy: The Ships, Men and Organization, 1861-65*. London: Conway Maritime Press, 1998.

Canney, D. L. *Sailing Warships of the US Navy*. London: Chatham, 2001.

Canny, N., and P. Morgan, eds. *The Oxford Handbook of the Atlantic World, 1450–1850*. Oxford: Oxford University Press, 2011.

Capp, B. *Cromwell's Navy: The Fleet and the English Revolution, 1648–1660*. Oxford: Oxford University Press, 1989.

Cardwell, M. J. *Arts and Arms: Literature, Politics and Patriotism During the Seven Years War*. Manchester: Manchester University Press, 2004.
Carolan, V. D. 'British Maritime History, National Identity and Film, 1900–1960'. PhD, Queen Mary, 2012.
Caron, F. *Le Mythe De Suffren*. Vincennes: Service Historique de la Marine, 1996.
Carroll, F. M. 'Diplomats and the Civil War at Sea'. *Canadian Review of American Studies* 40 (2010): 117–30.
Carter, A. C. *The Dutch Republic in Europe in the Seven Years War*. London: Macmillan, 1971.
Carter, W. R. *Beans, Bullets and Black Oil: The Story of Fleet Logistics Afloat in the Pacific during World War II*. Washington: US Government Printing Office, 1953.
Carter, W. R. and E. E. Duval. *Ships, Salvage and the Sinews of War: The Story of Fleet Logistics Afloat in Atlantic and Mediterranean Waters During World War II*. Washington, DC: Department of the Navy, 1954.
Cathcart, B. *Test of Greatness: Britain's Struggle for the Atom Bomb*. London: John Murray, 1994.
Cavaliero, R. *Admiral Satan: The Life and Campaigns of Suffren*. London: I. B. Tauris, 1994.
Cavell, S. A. *Midshipmen and Quarterdeck Boys in the British Navy, 1771–1831*. Woodbridge: Boydell Press, 2012.
Cavell, S. A. 'Social Politics and the Midshipmen's Mutiny, Portsmouth 1791'. *The Mariner's Mirror* 98, no. 1 (2012): 30–42.
Chaline, O., P. Bonnichon, and C.-P. de Vergennes, eds. *Les Marines De La Guerre d'indpendence Americaine (1763–1783)*. Paris: PUPS, 2013.
Chapelle, H. I. *The History of the American Sailing Navy: Their Ships and Their Development*. New York: W. W. Norton, 1949.
Chapman, W. C. 'Prelude to Chesme'. *Mariner's Mirror* 52 (1966): 61–76.
Chet, G. *The Ocean Is a Wilderness: Atlantic Piracy and the Limits of Governmental Legitimacy in the Early-Modern State, 1688–1856*. Boston: University of Massachusetts Press, 2014.
Chickering, R. 'Patriotic Societies and German Foreign Policy, 1890–1914'. *International History Review* 1, no. 4 (1979): 470–89.
Christie, I. R. 'Samuel Bentham and the Russian Dniepre Flotilla, 1787–1788'. *Slavonic and East European Studies Review* 50 (1972): 173–96.
Churchill, W. S. *The World Crisis*. Vol. 2, London: Thornton Butterworth, 1923.
Cipolla, C. M. *Guns, Sails and Empires: Technological Innovation and the Early Phases of European Expansion, 1400–1700*. Mahatten, KS: Sunflower University Press, 1985.
Clapp, M., and E. Southby-Tailyour. *Amphibious Assault Falklands: The Battle for San Carlos Water*. London: Leo Cooper, 1996.
Clark, G. N. *The Dutch Alliance and the War against French Trade, 1688–1697*. Manchester: Manchester University Press, 1923.
Clark, W. B. and M. J. Crawford, eds. *Naval Documents of the American Revolution*. Washington, DC: Naval History Center, 1964–2005.
Clayton, G. D. *Britain and the Eastern Question: Missolonghi to Gallipoli*. London History Studies, edited by R. Ben Jones. London: University of London Press, 1971.
Clayton, N. 'Naval Administration, 1603–1628'. PhD, Leeds, 1935.

Clayton, T. *Tars: The Men Who Made Britain Rule the Waves.* London: Hodder and Stoughton, 2007.
Clayton, T. and P. Craig. *Trafalgar: The Men, the Battle, the Storm.* London: Hodder and Stoughton, 2004.
Clendenning, P. H. 'Admiral Sir Charles Knowles and Russia, 1771–1774'. *The Mariner's Mirror* 61, no. 1 (1975): 39–49.
Clifford, K. J. *Amphibious Warfare Development in Britain and America from 1920–1940.* Laurens, New York: Edgewood, 1983.
Clifford, K. J. *Progress and Purpose: A Developmental History of the United States Marine Corps, 1900–1970.* Washington, DC: United States Marine Corps History and Museums Division HQ, 1973.
Clowes, W. L., ed. *The Royal Navy: A History from the Earliest Times to 1900.* 7 vols. London: Sampson, Low, Maston, 1898.
Coad, J. *The Royal Dockyards, 1690–1850: Architecture and Engineering Works of the Sailing Navy.* Aldershot: Scolar Press, 1989.
Coats, A. 'Efficiency in Dockyard Administration 1660–1800: A Reassessment'. In *The Age of Sail. The International Annual of the Historic Sailing Ship*, edited by N. Tracy, 116–32. London: Conway, 2002.
Coats, A. 'The Oeconomy of the Navy and Portsmouth: A Discourse between the Civilian Naval Administration of Portsmouth Dockyard and the Surrounding Communities, 1650–1800'. PhD, Sussex, 1999.
Coats, Bob A. W. 'Mercantilism, Economic Ideas, History and Policy'. In *Trade in the Pre-Modern Era, 1400–1700*, edited by D. A. Irwin, 350–67. Cheltenham, 1996.
Coats, A. V. and P. McDougall, eds. *The Naval Mutinies of 1797: Unity and Perseverance.* Woodbridge: Boydell Press, 2011.
Cock, R. and N. A. M. Rodger, eds. *A Guide to the Naval Records in the National Archives of the UK.* London: Institute of Historical Research and National Archives, 2006.
Cohen, S. S. *Yankee Sailors in British Gaols: Prisoners of War at Forton and Mill, 1775–1783.* Newark: University of Delaware Press, 1995.
Coker, W. S., and R. R. Rea, eds. *Anglo-Spanish Confrontation on the Gulf Coast during the American Revolution.* Pensacola: Gulf Coast History, 1982.
Coleman, T. *Nelson: The Man and the Legend.* London: Bloomsbury, 2002.
Coles, P. *The Ottoman Impact on Europe.* Library of European Civilisation, edited by G. Barraclough. London: Thames and Hudson, 1968.
Colley, L. *Britons: Forging the Nation, 1707–1837.* New Haven: Yale University Press, 1992.
Colley, L. 'The Reach of the State the Appeal of the Nation: Mass Arming and Political Culture in the Napoleonic Wars'. In *An Imperial State at War: Britain from 1689 to 1815*, edited by L. Stone, 165–84. London: Routledge, 1994.
Colville, Q. 'Jack Tar and the Gentleman Officer: The Role of Uniform in Shaping Class- and Gender-Related Identities of British Naval Personnel, 1930–1939'. *Transactions of the Royal Historical Society* 13 (2003): 105–29.
Conley, M. A. *From Jack Tar to Union Jack: Representing Naval Manhood in the British Empire, 1870–1918.* Manchester: Manchester University Press, 2009.
Conquest, R. 'The State and Commercial Expansion: England in the Years 1642–1688'. *Journal of European Economic History* 14 (1985): 155–72.

Consolvo, C. 'The Prospects and Promotion of British Naval Officers 1793–1815'. *The Mariner's Mirror* 91, no. 2 (2005): 137–59.
Conway, S. 'Continental Connections: Britain and Europe in the Eighteenth Century'. *History* 90 (2005): 353–74.
Conway, S., and R. Torres Sanchez, eds. *The Spending of States: Military Expenditure during the Long Eighteenth Century: Patterns, Organisation and Consequences*. Saarbrucken: VDM Verlag Dr Muller, 2011.
Cooling, B. F. *Gray Steel and Blue Water: The Formative Years of America's Military-Industrial Complex, 1881–1917*. Hamden, CT: Archon Books, 1979.
Cooper, B. *The Battle of the Torpedo Boats*. London: Pan, 1970.
Cooper, B. *The Buccaneers*. London: Macdonald, 1970.
Cooper, M. *The Birth of Independent Air Power*. London: Allen and Unwin, 1986.
Coox, A. *Japan: The Final Agony*. London: Macdonald, 1970.
Corbett, J. S. *The Campaign of Trafalgar*. 2 vols. London: Longman Green, 1919.
Corbett, J. S. *England and the Seven Years War: A Study of Combined Strategy*. 2 vols. London: Longman, 1907.
Corbett, J. S. *England in the Mediterranean: A Study of the Role and Influence of British Power within the Straits, 1603–1714*. 2 vols. London: Longman, 1904.
Corbett, J. S. *Fighting Instructions, 1530–1816*. Lightning Source UK edn. Vol. 29. London: Navy Records Society, 1905.
Corbett, J. S., ed. *Signals and Instructions, 1776–1794*. London: Navy Records Society, 1908.
Corbett, J. S. 'The Teaching of Naval and Military History'. *History* 1, April (1916): 12–19.
Corbett, J. S., and H. Newbolt. *History of the Great War: Naval Operations*. 5 vols. London: Longmans, 1920–1931.
Corfield, P. *Power and the Professions in Britain, 1700–1850*. London: Routledge, 1995.
Cormack, W. S. *Revolution and Political Conflict in the French Navy, 1789–1794*. Cambridge: Cambridge University Press, 1995.
Coudre, A. 'Predecesseurs Et Collegues De Castex Les Cours De Strategie Et De Tactique De L'ecole De Guerre Navale De 1920 a 1930'. In *L'evolution De La Pensee Navale VIII*, edited by H. Coutau-Begarie, 215–50. Paris: Economica, 2007.
Coutau-Bégarie, H. 'France'. Chapter 11 in *Ubi Sumus? The State of Naval and Maritime History*, edited by J. B. Hattendorf. Historical Monograph Series, 115–36. Newport, Rhode Island: Naval War College Press, 1994.
Coutau-Bégarie, H. *La Puisance Maritime: Castex Et La Strategie Navale*. Paris: Fayard, 1985.
Coutau-Bégarie, H. *L'evolution De La Pensee Navale I*. Paris: Fondation pour les Etudes de Defense Nationale, 1990.
Coutau-Begarie, H. *L'evolution De La Pensee Navale III*. Paris: Fondation pour les Etudes de Defense Nationale, 1993.
Coutau-Bégarie, H. *L'evolution De La Pensee Navale VIII*. Paris: Economica, 2007.
Coutau-Bégarie, H. *Le Meilleur Des Ambassadeurs: Théorie Et Practique De La Diplomatie Navale*. Paris: Economica, 2010.
Cowan, I. *Dominion or Decline: Anglo-American Naval Relations in the Pacific, 1937–1941*. Oxford: Berg, 1996.
Cowie, L. W. *Lord Nelson, 1758–1805: A Bibliography*. London: Meckler, 1990.

Cranmer-Byng, J. L., ed. *Pattee Byng's Journal, 1718–1720*. London: Navy Records Society, 1950.
Craske, M. 'Making National Heroes? A Survey of the Social and Political Functions and Meanings of Major British Funeral Monuments to Naval and Military Figures, 1730-70'. In *Conflicting Visions: War and Visual Culture in Britain and France C.1700–1830*, edited by G. Quilley and J. Bonehill, 41–60. Aldershot: Ashgate, 2005.
Crefeld, M. van. *Supplying War: Logistics from Wallenstein to Patton*. Cambridge: Cambridge University Press, 1977.
Creswell, J. *Generals and Admirals: The Story of Amphibious Command*. London: Longmans Green, 1952.
Crewe, D. G. *Yellow Jack and the Worm: British Naval Administration in the West Indies, 1739–1748*. Liverpool: University of Liverpool Press, 1993.
Crimmin, P. 'The Sick and Hurt Board and the Problem of Scurvy'. *Journal for Maritime Research* 15, no. 1 (2013): 47–53.
Crimmin, P. K. 'Admiralty Relations with the Treasury, 1783–1806: The Preparation of Estimates and the Beginnings of Treasury Control'. *Mariner's Mirror* 53 (1969): 63–72.
Crimmin, P. K. 'Great Britain and France in the Levant, 1793–1827: From Naval Conflict to Co-Operation'. In *Les Empires En Guerre Et Paix, 1793–1860: II*es *Journees Franco-Anglaises de la Marine*, edited by E. Freeman, 71–84. Vincennes: Service Historique de la Marine, 1990.
Crimmin, P. K. 'The Sick and Hurt Board and the Health of Seamen C1700–1806'. *Journal of Maritime Research* 1 (1999): 48–65.
Cross, A. *By the Banks of the Neva: Chapters from the Lives and Careers of the British in Eighteenth Century Russia*. Cambridge: Cambridge University Press, 1997.
Crouzet, F. 'Angleterre Et France Au XVIIIe Siécle: Essai D'analyse Comparée De Deux Croissances Economique'. *Annales: Economies, Societes et Civilizations* 21 (1996): 254–91.
Crouzet, F. 'War, Blockade and Economic Change in Europe, 1792–1815'. *Journal of Economic History* 24 (1964): 567–90.
Crowhurst, P. *The Defence of British Trade, 1689–1815*. Folkstone: Dawson, 1977.
Crowhurst, P. 'The French War on Trade 1793–1801: Commercial Venture or Patriotic Endeavour?' Chapter 16 in *Britain and the Northern Seas*, edited by W. E. Minchinton, 139–48. Pontefract: Lofthouse Publications, 1988.
Crowhurst, P. *The French War on Trade: Privateering , 1793–1815*. Aldershot: Scholar Press, 1989.
Crowhurst, R. P. 'The Admiralty and the Convoy System in the Seven Years War'. *The Mariner's Mirror* 57, no. 2 (1971): 163–73.
Crowson, P. S. *Tudor Foreign Policy*. London: Black, 1973.
Cumming, A. J. *The Royal Navy and the Battle of Britain*. Annapolis: Naval Institute Press, 2010.
Cunningham, A. E. *Patrick O'Brian: Critical Appreciations and a Bibliography*. Boston Spa: British Library, 1994.
Czisnik, M. 'Nelson and the Nile: The Creation of Admiral Nelson's Public Image'. *The Mariner's Mirror* 88, no. 1 (2002): 41–60.
Daly, J. C. K. *Russian Seapower and 'the Eastern Question,' 1827-41*. London: Macmillan, 1991.

Danchev, A. *Alchemist of War: The Life of Basil Liddell Hart*. London: Weidenfeld and Nicholson, 1998.
Dancy, J. R. *The Myth of the Press Gang: Volunteers, Impressment and the Naval Manpower Problem of the Late Eighteenth Century*. Woodbridge: Boydell Press, 2015.
Daunton, M. 'Britain and Globalisation since 1850: I. Creating a Global Order, 1850–1914'. *Transactions of the Royal Historical Society* 16 (2006): 1–38.
Davey, J. *The Transformation of British Naval Strategy: Seapower and Supply in Northern Europe, 1808–1812*. Woodbridge: Boydell Press, 2012.
Davey, J. 'War, Naval Logistics and the British State Supplying the Baltic Fleet 1808–1812'. PhD, Greenwich, 2009.
David, A. C. F. 'Alexander Dalrymple and the Emergence of the Admiralty Chart'. In *Five Hundred Years of Nautical Science, 1400–1900*, edited by D. Howse, 153–66. London: National Maritime Museum, 1981.
Davies, J. D. *Gentlemen and Tarpaulins: The Officers and Men of the Restoration Navy*. Oxford: Oxford University Press, 1991.
Davies, J. D. 'Gibraltar in Naval Strategy, c1600–1783'. *Transactions of the Naval Dockyards Society* 2, no. December (2006): 9–18.
Davies, J. D. 'Introduction'. In *Dutch Warships in the Age of Sail, 1600–1714*, edited by J. Bender, 17–44. Barnsley: Seaforth, 2014.
Davies, K. G. *The North Atlantic World in the Seventeenth Century*. Oxford: Oxford University Press, 1974.
Davis, W. C. *Duel between the First Ironclads*. New York: Doubleday, 1975.
Davison, R. L. *The Challenges of Command: The Royal Navy's Executive Branch Officers, 1880–1919*. Farnham: Ashgate, 2011.
Day, A. E. *Search for the Northwest Passage: An Annotated Bibliography*. New York: Garland, 1986.
de Zulueta, J. 'Health and Military Factors in Vernon's Failure at Cartagena'. *Mariner's Mirror* 78 (1992): 127–41.
D'Este, C. *Bitter Victory: The Battle for Sicily, 1943*. New York: Dutton, 1988.
D'Este, C. *Fatal Decision: Anzio and the Battle for Rome*. London: Harper Collins, 1991.
De Beer, G. 'Painting'. In *The Oxford Encyclopedia of Maritime History*, edited by J. B. Hattendorf, 247–62. New York: Oxford University Press, 2007.
Delumeau, J. 'La Guerre De Course Francaise Sous L'Ancien Regime'. In *Course Et Piraterie*, edited by M. Mollat, 271–91. Paris: Centre National de la Recherche Scientifique, 1975.
Dening, G. *Mr Bligh's Bad Language: Passion, Power and Theatre on the Bounty*. Cambridge: Cambridge University Press, 1992.
Denman, T. J. 'The Political Debate over Strategy, 1689–1712'. PhD, Cambridge, 1985.
Depeyre, M. *Entre Vent Et Eau: Un Siecle D'hesitations Tactiques Et Strategiques, 1790–1890*. Paris: Institut de Strategie Comparee, 2005.
Depeyre, M. 'John Clerk of Eldin Un Penseur Naval Conteste'. In *L'evolution De La Pensee Navale*, edited by H. Coutau-Begarie, 55–85. Paris: Centre d'Analyse Politique Comparee, 1992.
Desbriere, E. *1793–1805: Projets Et Tentatives De Debarquement Aux Iles Brittaniques*. 4 vols Paris: R. Chapelot, 1900–2.
Dessert, D. *La Royale: Vaisseaux Et Marine Du Roi-Soleil*. Paris: Fayard, 1996.

Dewar, A. 'Winston Churchill and the Dardanelles'. *Naval Review*, no. 1 (1924): 25–39.
Dickens, A. G. *The Counter Reformation*. Library of European Civilisation, edited by G. Barraclough. London: Thames and Hudson, 1968.
Dickinson, H. *Wisdom and War: The Royal Naval College Greenwich, 1873–1998*. Farnham: Ashgate, 2012.
Dickinson, H. W. 'Educational Provision for Officers of the Royal Navy 1857–1877'. PhD, London, 1994.
Dickinson, H. W. 'Her Majesty's Inspectors in Admiralty Schools, 1839–1864'. *The Mariner's Mirror* 93, no. 4 (1 January 2007): 469–81.
Dickinson, H. W. 'The Portsmouth Academy, 1733–1806'. *The Mariner's Mirror* 89, no. 1 (2003): 17–30.
Dillon, R. *History on Television: Constructing Nation, Nationality and Collective Memory*. Studies in Popular Culture, edited by J. Richards. Manchester: Manchester University Press, 2012.
Doeflinger, T. M. 'The Antilles Trade and the Old Regime: A Statistical Overview'. *Journal of Interdisciplinary Studies* 3 (1976): 397–415.
Doenhoff, R. A. von, ed. *Versatile Guardian: Research in Naval History*. Washington, DC: Howard University Press, 1979.
Domínguez Ortez, A. *Sociedad Y Estado En El Siglo Xviii Español*. Barcelona: Ariel, 1976.
Dotson, J. E. 'Economics and Logistics of Galley Warfare'. In *The Age of the Galley: Mediterranean Oared Vessels since Pre-Classical Times*, edited by R. Gardiner, 217–23. London: Conway, 1995.
Douglas, W. A. B. 'Canadian Naval Historiography'. *Mariner's Mirror* 70, no. 4 (1984): 349–62.
Douglas, W. A. B. 'The Prospects for Naval History'. *Northern Mariner* 1, no. 4 (1994): 19–26.
Downes, C. *Special Trust and Confidence: The Making of an Officer*. London: Frank Cass, 1991.
Downing, B. M. *The Military Revolution and Political Change: Origins of Democracy and Autocracy in Early Modern Europe*. Princeton: University of Princeton Press, 1992.
Dudley, W. S., and M. A. Palmer. 'No Mistake About It: A Response to Jonathan R. Dull'. *American Neptune* 35 (1985): 244–8.
Duffy, M. '"... All Was Hushed Up": The Hidden Trafalgar'. *The Mariner's Mirror* 91, no. 2 (2005): 216–40.
Duffy, M. *Soldiers, Sugar and Seapower: The British Expeditions to the West Indies and the War against Revolutionary France*. Oxford: Claredon Press, 1987.
Dulffer, J. 'Determinants of German Naval Policy 1920–1939'. In *The German Military in the Age of Total War*, edited by Wilhelm Deist, 152–70. Oxford: Berg, 1985.
Dull, J. *The Age of the Ship of the Line: The British and French Navies, 1650–1815*. Barnsley: Seaforth Publishing, 2009.
Dull, J. *The French Navy and American Independence*. Princeton: Princeton University Press, 1975.
Dull, J. *The French Navy and the Seven Years War*. Lincoln: University of Nebraska Press, 2005.

Dull, J. R. 'Was the Continental Navy a Mistake?' *American Neptune* 44 (1984): 167–70.
Dull, J. R. 'Why Did the French Revolutionary Navy Fail?' *Proceedings of the Consortium on Revolutionary Europe XVIII* 2 (1989): 121–37.
Dupont, M. *L'amiral Willaumez*. Paris: Tallandier, 1987.
Duro, Cesaro Fernandez. *Armada Española Desde La Union De Los Reinos De Castilla Y De Aragon*. 9 vols. Madrid: Est. tipográfico 'Sucesores de Rivadeneyra', 1894–1902.
Earle, P. *Sailors: English Merchant Seamen, 1650–1775*. London: Methuen, 1998.
Eckstein, K. 'Die Volksmarine Im Kalten Krieg'. In *Deutsche Marinen Im Wandel: Vom Symbol Nationaler Einhiet Zum Instrument Internationaler Sicherheit*, edited by W. Rahn, 615–31. Munchen: R. Oldenbourg, 2005.
Eder, M. *Crime and Punishment in the Royal Navy of the Seven Years War, 1755–1763*. Aldershot: Gower, 2004.
Edgerton, D. *The Shock of the Old: Technology and Global History since 1900*. Oxford: Oxford University Press, 2007.
Edgerton, D. *Warfare State: Britain, 1920–1970*. Cambridge: Cambridge University Press, 2006.
Edwards, K. *Operation Neptune*. London: Collins, 1946.
Edwards, P. M. *The Korean War: An Annotated Bibliography*. Westport, CT: Greenwood, 1998.
Ehrman, J. *The Navy in the War of William III, 1689–1697: Its State and Direction*. Cambridge: Cambridge University Press, 1953.
Elleman, B. A. 'Naval Warfare and the Refraction of China's Self-Strengthening Reforms into Scientific and Technological Failure, 1865–1895'. *Modern Asian Studies* 38 (2004): 283–326.
Elleman, B. A., and S. C. M. Paine, eds. *Naval Blockade and Seapower: Strategies and Counter-Strategies, 1805–2005*. London: Routledge, 2006.
Elleman, B. A., and S. C. M. Paine, eds. *Naval Coalition Warfare: From the Napoleonic War to Operation Iraqi Freedom*. London: Cass Routledge, 2008.
Emsley, C. *British Society and the French Wars, 1793–1815*. London: Macmillan, 1979.
Epkenhans, M. 'Technology, Shipbuilding and Future Combat in Germany, 1880–1914'. In *Technology and Naval Combat in the Twentieth Century and Beyond*, edited by Phillips Payson O'Brien, 53–68. Abingdon: Routedge, 2001.
Epkenhans, M. *Tirpitz: Architect of the German High Seas Fleet*. Washington, DC: Potomac Books, 2008.
Epstein, K. C. *Torpedo: Inventing the Military-Industrial Complex in the United States and Great Britain*. Cambridge, MA: Harvard University Press, 2014.
Erickson, A. S., and L. J. Goldstein. 'Chinese Perspectives on Maritime Transformation'. In *China Goes to Sea: Maritime Transformation in Comparative Historical Perspective*, edited by A. S. Erickson, L. J. Goldstein and C. Lord, xiii–xxviii. Annapolis: Naval Institute Press, 2009.
Erikson, A. S., L. J. Goldstein and C. Lord, eds. *China Goes to Sea: Maritime Transformation in Comparative Historical Perspective*. Annapolis: Naval Institute Press, 2009.
Evans, D. C. 'Japanese Naval Construction, 1878–1918'. In *Technology and Naval Combat in the Twentieth Century and Beyond*, edited by Phillips Payson O'Brien, 22–35. Abingdon: Routledge, 2001.

Evans, D. C., and M. R. Peattie. *Kaigun: Strategy, Tactics and Technology in the Imperial Japanese Navy, 1887–1941*. Annapolis: Naval Institute Press, 1997.
Evans, F. 'History versus the Rivet Counters'. *Times Higher Education Supplement* 14, no. February (1986): 11.
Evans, M. H. H. *Amphibious Operations: The Projection of Sea Power Ashore*. London: Brassey, 1990.
Eyres, P. 'Hearts of Oak: Commerce, Empire and the Landscape Garden'. *New Arcadian Journal* 35, no. 6 (1993).
Eyres, P. 'Sons of the Sea'. *New Arcadian Journal* 37, no. 8 (1994).
Farrar-Hockley, A., ed. *A Distant Obligation: The British Part in the Korean War. An Official History. Volume 1*. 2 vols. Vol. 1. London: HMSO, 1990.
Farrar-Hockley, A., ed. *An Honorable Discharge: The British Part in the Korean War. An Official History. Volume 2*. 2 vols. Vol. 2, London: HMSO, 1995.
Fayle, C. E. 'Deflection of Strategy by Commerce in Eighteenth Century'. *Journal of the Royal United Services Institution* 68, no. 470 (1923): 281–94.
Feifer, G. *Okinawa 1945: The Stalingrad of the Pacific*. Stroud: Tempus, 2005.
Feldbaek, O. *The Battle of Copenhagen, 1801*. Barnsley: Leo Cooper, 2002.
Fergusson, B. *The Watery Maze: The Story of Combined Operations*. London: Collins, 1961.
Fernández, J. M. *Oficiales Y Soldades En La Ejercito De America*. Seville: CSIC, 1983.
Fernandez-Armesto, F. *The Spanish Armada: The Experience of War in 1588*. Oxford: Oxford University Press, 1989.
Fernandez-Shaw, C. 'Participación De La Armada Española En La Guerra De La Independencia De Los Estados Unidos'. *Revista de Historia Naval* 3 (1985): 75–80.
Ferrante, E. 'The Impact of the Jeune Ecole on the Way of Thinking of the Italian Navy'. In *Marine Et Technique Au Xixe Siecle*, 517–25. Vincennes: Service Historique de la Marine, 1995.
Ferreiro, L. D. *Ships and Science: The Birth of Naval Architecture in the Scientific Revolution, 1600–1800*. Cambridge, MA: MIT Press, 2007.
Field, C. *Britain's Sea Soldiers*. 2 vols. Liverpool: Lyceum Press, 1924.
Field, A. *Royal Navy Strategy in the Far East, 1919–1939: Preparing for War against Japan*. London: Frank Cass, 2004.
Finlay, R. 'How Not to (Re)Write World History: Gavin Menzies and the Chinese Discovery of America'. *Journal of World History* 15, no. 2 (2004): 229–42.
Fisher, J. 'Economic Warfare and the Laws of War'. *Journal of Contemporary History* 23 (1997): 99–118.
Fisher, J. *Memories*. London: Hodder and Stoughton, 1919.
Fisher, J. *Records*. London: Hodder and Stoughton, 1919.
Flayhart, W. H. *Counterpoint to Trafalgar: The Anglo-Russian Invasion of Naples, 1805–1806*. Columbia: University of South Carolina Press, 1992.
Fletcher, I. *The Waters of Oblivion: The British Invasion of the Rio De La Plata, 1806–7*. Tunbridge Wells: Spellmount, 1991.
Fontillana, E. R. 'Carlos III Ye El Control Des Estrecho De Magalleaneo: La Expedicion Del Captan De Navio Don Antonio De Cordoba (1785–1786)'. In *Temas Historica Militar*, 103–12. Madrid: 2nd Congress de Historia Militar, 1988.

Ford, D. 'US Naval Intelligence and the Imperial Japanese Fleet during the Washington Treaty Era, C.1922–36'. *The Mariner's Mirror* 93, no. 3 (2007): 281–306.
Fowler, jnr, W. M. *Rebels under Sail: The American Navy During the Revolution.* New York: Charles Scribener's, 1976.
Fox, C. *The Arts of Industry in the Age of the Enlightenment.* New Haven: Yale University Press, 2009.
Fox, F. *Great Ships: The Battlefleet of King Charles Ii.* London: Conway Maritime Press, 1980.
Frangakis-Syrett, E. *Commerce of Smyrna in Eighteenth Century (1700–1820).* Athens: Bibliotheca Asiae Minoris Historica, 1992.
Frank, R. B. *Guadalcanal: The Definitive Account of the Landmark Battle.* New York: Random House, 1990.
Frankland, N. *History at War.* London: Giles de la Mare, 1998.
Franklin, G. *Britain's Anti-Submarine Capability, 1919–1939.* London: Cass, 2003.
Franklin, G. D. 'A Breakdown in Communication: Britain's over Estimation of Asdic's Capabilities in the 1930s'. *The Mariner's Mirror* 84, no. 2 (1998): 204–14.
Freedman, L. *Deterrence.* Cambridge: Polity, 2004.
Freedman, L. *The Official History of the Falklands Campaign: The Origins of the Falklands War.* 2 vols. Vol. 1. London: Taylor and Francis, 2007.
Freedman, L. *Official History of the Falklands Campaign: War and Diplomacy.* 2 vols. Vol. 2. London: Taylor and Francis, 2007.
Fremantle, S. R. *My Naval Career, 1880–1928.* London: Hutchinson, no date.
French, D. *The British Way in Warfare, 1688–2000.* London: Unwin, 1990.
Friedman, N. *British Carrier Aviation: The Evolution of the Ships and Their Aircraft.* London: Conway, 1988.
Friedman, N. *British Destroyers and Frigates: The Second World War and After.* Barnsley: Seaforth, 2008.
Friedman, N. *Carrier Air Power.* New York: Routledge, 1981.
Friedman, N. 'Electronics and the Royal Navy' In *The Royal Navy 1930–2000: Innovation and Defence,* edited by R. Harding, 246–85. London: Frank Cass, 2005.
Friedman, N. *Modern Warship Design and Development.* London: Conway Maritime Press, 1979.
Friedman, N. *Network-Centric Warfare: How Navies Learned to Fight Smarter through Three World Wars.* Annapolis: Naval Institute Press, 2009.
Friedman, N. 'Nuclear Weapons and Navies'. In *Navies in a Nuclear Age,* edited by R. Gardiner, 133–41. London: Conway, 1993.
Friedman, N. *The Postwar Naval Revolution.* London: Conway Maritime Press, 1986.
Friedman, N. *Seapower and Space: From the Dawn of the Missile Age to Net-Centric Warfare Development.* London: Conway Publishing, 2000.
Friedman, N. *Submarine Design and Development.* London: Conway Maritime Press, 1984.
Friedman, N. *US Carriers: An Illustrated Design History.* Annapolis: Naval Institute Press, 1983.
Friedman, N. *The US Maritime Strategy.* Annapolis: Naval Institute Press, 1988.
Frost, A. *The Global Reach of Empire: Britain's Maritime Expansion in the Indian and Pacific Oceans, 1764–1815.* Carlton: Miegunyah Press, 2003.

Frost, A., and J. Samson, eds. *Pacific Empires: Essays in Honour of Glynwdr Williams*. Vancouver: University of British Columbia Press, 1999.
Frost, A., and G. Williams. 'The Beginnings of Britain's Exploration of the Pacific Ocean in the Eighteenth Century'. *The Mariner's Mirror* 83, no. 4 (1997): 410–18.
Froude, J. A. *English Seamen in the 16th Century*. New edn. London: Longmans Green, 1895.
Fuller, H. J. *Clad in Iron: The American Civil War and the Challenge of British Naval Power*. Westport, CT: Praeger, 2008.
Fuller, H. J. '"This Country Now Occupies the Vantage Ground": Understanding John Ericsson's Monitors and the American Union's War against British Naval Supremacy'. *American Neptune* 62 (2002): 91–111.
Fury, C. A. *Tides in the Affairs of Men: The Social History of Elizabethan Seamen, 1580–1603*. Westport, CT: Greenwood, 2002.
Fury, C. A., ed. *The Social History of the English Seamen, 1485–1649*. Woodbridge: Boydell Press, 2012.
Fury, C. A., ed. *The Social History of English Seamen, 1649–1815*. Woodbridge: Boydell and Brewer, 2014.
Gailey, H. *The Liberation of Guam: 21st July–10th August 1944*. Novato: Presidio, 1988.
Garcia Sanchez, J. M. 'Exploring the Genre: Spanish Discoveries in the Pacific Northwest at the End of the Eighteenth Century'. *Tiempos Modernas* 17 (2008): 1–11.
Gardiner, R., ed. *All the World's Fighting Ships 1947–1982: Part 1 The Western Powers*. London: Conway, 1983.
Gardiner, R., ed. *All the World's Fighting Ships 1947–1982: Part 2: The Warsaw Pact and Non-Aligned Nations*. London: Conway, 1983.
Gardiner, R., ed. *The Line of Battle: The Sailing Warship, 1650–1840*. edited by Robert Gardiner, Conway's History of the Ship. London: Conway Maritime Press, 1992.
Gardiner, R., ed. *Navies and the American Revolution*. London: Conway Maritime Press, 1996.
Gardner, W. J. R. *Decoding History: The Battle of the Atlantic*. London: Macmillan, 1999.
Gatchel, T. L. *At the Water's Edge: Defending against the Modern Amphibious Assault*. Annapolis: Naval Institute Press, 1996.
Gillet, J.-C. *La Marine Imperiale; Le Grand Reve De Napoleon*. St Denis la Plaine: Bernard Giovanangeli, 2010.
Gino, G. *I Cavalieri Di Santo Stefano Nella Storia Della Marina Italiana (1562–1859)*. Pisa: Nistri-Lischi, 1960.
Glamann, K. 'European Trade 1500–1700'. In *The Fontana Economic History of Europe: The Sixteenth and Seventeenth Centuries*, edited by C. M. Cipolla, 427–527. London: Fontana, 1974.
Glasgow, T. 'Maturing of Naval Administration, 1556–1564'. *Mariner's Mirror* 56 (1970): 3–56.
Glasgow, T. 'The Navy in Philip and Mary's War, 1557–1558'. *Mariner's Mirror* 53 (1967): 321–42.
Glasgow, T. 'The Navy in the First Elizabethan Undeclared War, 1559–1560'. *The Mariner's Mirror* 54, no. 1 (1968): 23–37.

Glasgow, T. 'The Navy in the French Wars of Mary and Elizabeth I'. *The Mariner's Mirror* 54, no. 3 (1968): 281–96.
Glass, R. A. 'The Image of the Sea Officer in English Literature, 1660–1710'. *Albion* 26 (1994): 583–99.
Glete, J. 'Bridge and Bulwark: The Swedish Navy and the Baltic 1500–1809'. In *In Quest of Trade and Security: The Baltic in Power Politics, 1500–1900*, edited by Goran Rystad, Klaus-R. Bohme and Wilhelm N. Carlgren, 9–60. Lund: Lund University Press, 1994.
Glete, J. 'The Foreign Policy of Gustavus III and the Navy as an Instrument of Policy'. In *The War of King Gustavus III and the Naval Battles of Ruotsinsalmi*, 5–42. Kotka: Museum of Kymenlaaksa, 1993.
Glete, J. *Navies and Nations: Warships, Navies and State Building in Europe and America, 1500–1860*. 2 vols. Stockholm: Probus, 1993.
Glete, J. *Warfare at Sea, 1500–1650: Maritime Conflicts and the Transformation of Europe*. Warfare and History, edited by J. Black. London: Routledge, 2000.
Goff, T. J. A. Le. 'Problemes De Recrutement De La Marines Francais'. *Revue Historique* 283, no. 574 (1990): 205–33.
Gooch, J. *Mussolini and His Generals: The Armed Forces and Fascist Foreign Policy, 1922–1940*. Cambridge: Cambridge University Press, 2007.
Goodman, D. *Spanish Naval Power, 1589–1665: Reconstruction and Defeat*. Cambridge: Cambridge University Press, 1997.
Gordon, A. 'The Admiralty and Imperial Overstretch, 1902–1941'. *Journal of Strategic Studies* 20 (1994): 63–85.
Gordon, G. A. H. *British Seapower and Procurement between the Wars: A Reappraisal of Rearmament*. London: Macmillan, 1988.
Gordon, I. *Admiral of the Blue: The Life and Times of Admiral John Child Purvis, 1747–1825*. Barnsley: Pen and Sword, 2005.
Gorshkov, S. G. *The Sea Power of the State*. Malabar, FL: Robert E. Krieger, 1983.
Gough, B. M. *Historical Dreadnoughts: Arthur Marder, Stephen Roskill and the Battles for Naval History*. Barnsley: Seaforth, 2010.
Gough, B. M. *The Royal Navy and the Northwest Coast of North America*. Vancouver: University of British Columbia Press, 1974.
Gradish, S. *The Manning of the British Navy during the Seven Years War*. London: Royal Historical Society, 1980.
Graham, G. S. *Empire of the North Atlantic: The Maritime Struggle for North America*. Toronto: University of Toronto Press, 1950.
Graham, G. S. *The Politics of Naval Supremacy: Studies in British Maritime Ascendancy*. Cambridge: Cambridge University Press, 1965.
Graham, G. S. *The Walker Expedition to Quebec, 1711*. London: Navy Records Society, 1953.
Grainger, J. D. 'The Navy in the River Plate, 1806–1808'. *The Mariner's Mirror* 81, no. 3 (1995): 287–99.
Grainger, J. D., ed. *The Royal Navy in the River Plate, 1806–1807*. London: Navy Records Society, 1996.
Gray, C. and R. W. Barnett, eds. *Seapower and Strategy*. Annapolis: Naval Institute Press, 1989.
Gray, C. S. 'History for Strategists: British Seapower as a Relevant Past'. *Journal of Strategic Studies* 17 (1994): 7–32.

Gray, C. S. 'Sea Power for Containment: The U.S. Navy in the Cold War'. In *Navies and Global Defense: Theories and Strategy*, edited by K. Neilson and E. J. Errington, 181–208. Westport, CT: Praeger, 1995.
Green, A. *Writing the Great War: Sir James Edmunds and the Official Histories, 1915–1948*. London: Frank Cass, 2003.
Greene, J. and A. Massignani. *The Naval War in the Mediterranean, 1940–1943*. Barnsley: Frontline, 2011.
Greenhill, B. and A. Giffard. *Steam, Politics and Patronage: The Transformation of the Royal Navy, 1815–54*. London: Conway Maritime Press, 1994.
Gregory, D. *Minorca, the Illusory Prize: A History of the British Occupation of Minorca between 1708 and 1802*. London: Associated University Presses, 1990.
Gretton, P. *Maritime Strategy: A Study of British Defence Problems*. London: Cassell, 1965.
Grimble, I. *The Sea Wolf: The Life of Admiral Cochrane*. London: Blond and Briggs, 1978.
Grint, K. *Leadership: A Very Short Introduction*. Oxford: Oxford University Press, 2010.
Grove, E. 'The Battleship Is Dead; Long Live the Battleship. HMS Dreadnought and the Limits of Technological Innovation'. *The Mariner's Mirror* 93, no. 4 (2007): 415–27.
Grove, E., ed. *The Defeat of the Enemy Attack on Shipping, 1939–1945*. London: Navy Records Society, 1997.
Grove, E. *The Future of Seapower*. London: Routledge, 1990.
Grove, E. 'The Royal Navy in the Twenty-First Century: Does It Have a Role beyond the Defence of Britain's Seas?' *Mariner's Mirror* 97 (2010): 298–313.
Grove, E. 'The Superpowers and Secondary Navies in Northern Waters during the Cold War'. In *Navies in Northern Waters, 1721–2000*, edited by R. Hobson and T. Kristiansen, 211–21. London: Cass, 2004.
Grove, E. *Vanguard to Trident: British Naval Policy since World War II*. London: Bodley Head, 1987.
Grove, E. and P. Hore, eds. *Dimensions of Sea Power: Strategic Choice in the Modern World*. Hull: University of Hull Press, 1998.
Guarnieri. G, *I Cavalieri Di Santo Stefano Nella Storia Della Marina Italiana (1562–1859)*. Pisa: Nistri-Lischi, 1960.
Guilmartin, J. F. *Gunpowder and Galleys: Changing Technology and Mediterranean Warfare at Sea in the Sixteenth Century*. Cambridge: Cambridge University Press, 1974.
Guilmartin, J. F. 'The Military Revolution in Warfare at Sea during the Early Modern Era: Technological Origins, Operational Outcomes and Strategic Consequences'. *Journal for Maritime Research* 13, no. 2 (2011): 129–37.
Guilmartin, J. F. 'The Military Revolution: Origins and First Tests Abroad'. In *The Military Revolution Debate: Readings in the Military Transformation of Early Modern Europe*, edited by C. Rogers, 299–333. Boulder: Westview Press, 1995.
Guimerá, A. 'Gravina and the Naval Leadership of His Day'. *Journal for Maritime Research* 7, no. 1 (2005): 44–69.
Haas, J. M. *A Management Odyssey: The Royal Dockyards, 1714–1914*. New York: University Press of America, 1994.

Haas, J. M. 'The Royal Dockyards: The Earliest Visitations and Reform, 1749–1778'. *Historical Journal* 13 (1970): 191–215.

Hackman, W. K. 'British Military Expeditions to the Coasts of France, 1757–61'. PhD diss., University of Michigan, 1969.

Hackman, W. K. 'The British Raid on Rochefort, 1757'. *The Mariner's Mirror* 64, no. 3 (1978): 263–75.

Hagan, K. J. *This People's Navy: The Making of American Sea Power*. New York: Free Press, 1991.

Haggie, P. *Britannia at Bay: The Defence of the British Empire against Japan, 1931–1941*. Oxford: Oxford University Press, 1981.

Haley, K. H. D. *The Dutch in the Seventeenth Century*. Library of European Civilization, edited by G. Barraclough. London: Thames and Hudson, 1972.

Hall, C. D. *Wellington's Navy: Sea Power and the Peninsula War, 1807–1814*. London: Chatham Publishing, 2004.

Halpern, P. 'French and Italian Naval Policy in the Mediterranean, 1898–1945'. In *Naval Policy and Strategy in the Mediterranean: Past, Present and Future*, edited by J. B. Hattendorf, 78–107. London: Cass, 2000.

Halpern, P. 'The French Navy, 1880–1914'. In *Technology and Naval Combat in the Twentieth Century and Beyond*, edited by Phillips Payson O'Brien, 36–52. Abingdon: Routledge, 2001.

Halpern, P. *A Naval History of World War I*. London: UCL Press, 1994.

Halpern, P. *The Naval War in the Mediterranean, 1914–1918*. London: Allen and Unwin, 1987.

Hamilton, C. I. *Anglo-French Naval Rivalry, 1840–1870*. Oxford: Clarendon Press, 1993.

Hamilton, C. I. *Making of the Modern Admiralty: British Naval Policy-Making, 1805–1927*. Cambridge: Cambridge University Press, 2011.

Hamilton, C. I. 'Naval Hagiography and the Victorian Hero'. *The Historical Journal* 23, no. 2 (1980): 381–98.

Hamilton, W. M. *The Nation and the Navy: Methods and Organisation of British Navalist Propaganda, 1889–1914*. New York: Garland, 1986.

Harbron, J. D. 'Spain's Forgotten Naval Renaissance'. *History Today* 90, no. August (1990): 29–34.

Harbron, J. D. *Trafalgar and the Spanish Navy*. London: Conway Maritime Press, 1988.

Harding, R. 'Amphibious Warfare, 1930–1939'. In *The Royal Navy 1930–2000: Innovation and Defence*, edited by R. Harding, 42–68. London: Cass, 2005.

Harding, R. 'British Maritime Strategy and Hanover, 1714–1763'. In *The Hanoverian Dimension in British History, 1714–1837*, edited by B. Sims and T. Riotte, 252–74. Cambridge: Cambridge University Press, 2007.

Harding, R. 'Contractors, Warships of the Royal Navy and Sea Power, 1739–1748'. In *The Contractor State and Its Implications, 1659–1815*, edited by R. Harding and S. S. Ferri, 159–74. Las Palmas: Universidad de Las Palmas de Gran Canaria, 2012.

Harding, R. *The Emergence of Britain's Global Naval Supremacy: The War of 1739–1748*. Woodbridge: Boydell and Brewer, 2010.

Harding, R. *The Evolution of the Sailing Navy, 1509–1815*. British History in Perspective, edited by J. Black. Basingstoke: Macmillan, 1995.

Harding, R. 'The Expeditions to Quebec, 1690 and 1711: The Evolution of British Trans-Atlantic Amphibious Power'. In *Guerres Maritimes (1688–1713)*, 197–212. Vincennes: Service Historique de la Marine, 1992.

Harding, R. *Seapower and Naval Warfare, 1650–1830*. London: University College London Press, 1999.

Harding. R. 'The Society for Nautical Research: Where are we now and where are we going?' *Mariner's Mirror* 97 (2011): 10–21.

Harland, K. 'The Establishment and Administration of the First Hospitals of the RN', Vol. 1. PhD, Exeter, 2003.

Harland, K. 'The Royal Naval Hospital at Minorca, 1711: An Example of an Admiral's Involvement in the Expansion of Naval Medical Care'. *Mariner's Mirror* 94, no. 1 (2008): 36–47.

Harris, B. 'Patriotic Commerce and National Revival: The Free British Fishery Society and British Politics, 1749–1758'. *English Historical Review* 114, no. 456 (1999): 285–313.

Harris, D. G. 'Admiral Frederic Af Chapman's Auxiliary Vessels for the Swedish Inshore Fleet'. *The Mariner's Mirror* 75, no. 3 (1989): 211–29.

Harris, D. G. *F. H. Chapman: The First Naval Architect and His Work*. London: Conway Maritime Press, 1989.

Hart, M. t'. 'Mobilising Resources for War: The Dutch and British Financial Revolutions Compared'. In *War, State and Development. Fiscal-Military States in the Eighteenth Century*, edited by R. Torres Sánchez, 179–200. Barañáin: EUNSA, 2007.

Hartelie, O. 'Notes from Naval Novels'. *The Mariner's Mirror* 6, no. 11 (1920): 339–43.

Harvey, R. *Cochrane: The Life and Exploits of a Fighting Captain*. London: Constable, 2000.

Hattendorf, J., ed., *The Oxford Encyclopaedia of Maritime History*, 4 vols. New York: Oxford University Press, 2007.

Hattendorf, J. B. 'Admiral Sir George Byng and the Cape Passaro Incident, 1718: A Case Study in the Use of the Royal Navy as a Deterrent'. In *Guerres Et Paix*, 19–39. Vincennes: Service Historique de la Marine, 1987.

Hattendorf, J. B. 'The Bombardment of Acre, 1840: A Case Study in the Use of Naval Force for Deterrence'. In *Les Empires En Guerre Et Paix, 1793–1860: IIes Journées Franco-Anglaises D'histoire De La Marine*, edited by E. Freeman, 205–26. Vincennes: Service Historique de la Marine, 1990.

Hattendorf, J. B., ed. *Doing Naval History: Essays towards Improvement*. Newport: Naval War College Press, 1995.

Hattendorf, J. B. 'Educating the Royal Navy: Eighteenth- and Nineteenth-Century Education for Officers'. *Journal of Military History* 73, no. 3 (2009): 945–6.

Hattendorf, J. B. *England in the War of the Spanish Succession: A Study of the English View and Conduct of Grand Strategy, 1702–1712*. New York: Garland Publishing, 1987.

Hattendorf, J. B. *The Evolution of the U.S. Navy's Maritime Strategy, 1977–1986*. Newport: Naval War College, 2004.

Hattendorf, J. B. *Faces of the Naval War College: An Illustrated Catalogue of the US Naval War College's Collection of Portrait Paintings and Busts*. Newport: US Naval War College, 2009.

Hattendorf, J. B. '"In a Far More Thorough Manner": The Professionalization of the U.S. Navy at the Dawn of the Twentieth Century'. *Naval History* 19, no. 2 (2004): 38–43.

Hattendorf, J. B., ed. *The Influence of History on Mahan*. Newport: Naval War College Press, 1991.

Hattendorf, J. B., ed. *Maritime History Volume 2: The Eighteenth Century and the Age of Sail*. Malabar: Krieger Publishing Company, 1997.

Hattendorf, J. B. 'Rear Admiral Henry E. Eccles and the "Lessons of Suez", 1956–1968'. In *Talking about Naval History: A Collection of Essays*, edited by J. B. Hattendorf, 291–303. Newport: Naval War College Press, 2011.

Hattendorf, J. B. *Talking about Naval History: A Collection of Essays*. Newport: Naval War College Press, 2011.

Hattendorf, J. B., ed. *Ubi Sumus? The State of Naval and Maritime History*. Newport: Naval War College Press, 1994.

Hattendorf, J. B. 'The United States Navy in the Twenty-First Century: Thoughts on Naval Theory, Strategic Constraints and Opportunities'. *Mariner's Mirror* 97 (2011): 285–97.

Hattendorf, J. B. 'The Uses of Maritime History in and for Navy'. *International Journal of Naval History* 2, no. 1 (2003), http://www.ijnhonline.org/wp-content/uploads/2012/01/article_hattendorf_pdf_apr03.pdf (accessed 19th May 2015).

Hattendorf, J. B. 'Whither with Nelson and Trafalgar? A Review Article on the Bicentenary Scholarship of the Nelson Era'. *Journal for Maritime Research* 9, no. 1 (2007): 37–66.

Hattendorf, J. B. and J. Goldrick, eds. *Mahan Is Not Enough: The Proceedings of a Conference on the Works of Sir Julian Corbett and Admiral Sir Herbert Richmond*. Vol. 10, Historical Monographs Series. Newport: Naval War College Press, 1993.

Hattendorf, J. B. and R. S. Jordan, eds. *Maritime Strategy and the Balance of Power: Britain and America in the Twentieth Century*. London: Macmillan, 1989.

Hattendorf, J. B. and M. Murfett, eds. *The Limitations of Military Power: Essays Presented to Professor Norman Gibb on His 80th Birthday*. London: Macmillan, 1990.

Haudrere, P. 'Francais Et Anglais Aux Mascareignes Apres Le Traite De Paris, 1814–1823'. In *Les Empires En Guerre Et Paix, 1793–1860: IIes Journées Franco-Anglaises D'histoire de la Marine*, edited by E. Freeman, 59–69. Vincennes: Service Historique de la Marine, 1990.

Haxhaj, E. 'More Bang for a Bob: The Decision to "Go Nuclear" and Its Impact on Chatham Dockyard'. *The Mariner's Mirror* 91, no. 4 (2005): 554–71.

Haycock, D. B. and S. Archer, eds. *Health and Medicine at Sea, 1700–1900*. Woodbridge: Boydell Press, 2009.

Hearn, C. H. *Gray Raiders of the Sea: How Eight Confederate Warships Destroyed the Union's High Seas Commerce*. Camden, ME: International Maritime Publishing, 1992.

Hebb, D. D. 'The English Government and the Problem of Piracy, 1616–1642'. PhD, London, 1985.

Hebb, D. D. *Piracy and the English Government, 1616–1642*. Aldershot: Scholar Press, 1994.

Heinrichs, Jr., W. H. 'The Role of the United States Navy'. In *Pearl Harbor as History: Japanese-American Relations, 1931–1941*, edited by D. Borg and S. Okamoto, 203–9. New York: Columbia University Press, 1973.

Henige, D. 'The Alchemy of Turning Fiction into Truth'. *Journal of Scholarly Publishing* 39, no. 4 (2008): 354–72.

Henry, D. 'British Submarine Policy, 1918–1939'. In *Technological Change and British Naval Policy, 1860–1939*, edited by B. Ranft, 80–107. London: Hodder and Stoughton, 2003.

Henwood, B. *Bagnards À Brest*. Rennes: Ouest France, 1986.

Herrick, R. W. *Soviet Naval Strategy: Fifty Years of Theory and Practice*. Annapolis: Naval Institute Press, 1968.

Herrick, R. W. *Soviet Naval Theory and Policy: Gorshkov's Inheritance*. Newport: US Naval War College, 1988.

Herwig, H. 'Admirals Versus Generals: The War Aims of the Imperial German Navy, 1914–1918'. *Central European History* 5, no. September (1972): 208–33.

Herwig, H. *The German Naval Officer Corps: A Social and Political History, 1890–1918*. Oxford: Oxford University Press, 1973.

Herwig, H. 'The German Reaction to the Dreadnought Revolution'. *The International History Review* 13, no. 2 (1991): 273–83.

Herwig, H. *'Luxury Fleet': The Imperial German Navy, 1888–1918*. New York: Humanity Books, 1987.

Herwig, H. and D. F. Trask. 'The Failure of Imperial Germany's Undersea Offensive against World Shipping, February 1917- October 1918'. *Historian* 33, no. 4 (1971): 611–31.

Hezlett, A. *Aircraft and Sea Power*. London: Davies, 1970.

Hill, R. *Maritime Strategy for Medium Powers*. London: Croom Helm, 1986.

Hiranandani, G. M. *Transition to Eminence: The Indian Navy 1976–1990*. New Delhi: Lancer, 2005.

Hiranandani, G. M. *Transition to Guardianship: The Indian Navy, 1991–2000*. New Delhi: Lancer, 2009.

Hiranandani, G. M. *Transition to Triumph: The Indian Navy 1965–1975*. New Delhi: Lancer, 2000.

Hobbs, D. *The British Pacific Fleet: The Royal Navy's Most Powerful Strike Force*. Barnsley: Seaforth, 2011.

Hocker, F. *Vasa: A Swedish Ship*. Stockholm: Medstroms Bokforlag, 2011.

Holland Rose, J. 'The Indecisiveness of Modern Naval War'. In *The Indecisiveness of Modern War and Other Essays*, edited by J. Holland Rose, 1–28. London: Bell, 1927.

Holland-Rose, J. *Naval History and National History*. Cambridge: Cambridge University Press, 1919.

Holmes, G. *Augustan England: Professions, State and Society, 1680–1730*. London: Allen and Unwin, 1982.

Hooper, E. B., D. C. Allard and O. P. Fitzgerald. *The United States Navy and the Vietnam Conflict: Setting the Stage to 1959*. Washington, DC: Naval Historical Centre, 1976.

Hore, P., ed. *Seapower Ashore: 200 Years of Royal Navy Operations on Land*. London: Chatham Publishing, 2001.

Hore, P. *Sydney, Cipher and Search: Solving the Last Great Naval Mystery of the Second World War*. Rendlesham: Seafarer Books, 2009.

Horten, D. 'Errfahrungen Im Deutschen Einigungsprozess. Die Auflösung Der Volksmarine 1990/91'. In *Deutsche Marinen Im Wandal: Von Symbol Nationaler Einheit Zum Instrument Internationaler Sicherheit*, edited by W. Rahn, 657–72. München: R. Oldenbourg, 2005.
Hough, R. *Admirals in Collision*. London: White Lion, 1959.
Howard, M. *The Continental Commitment*. London: Temple Smith, 1972.
Howat, G. M. D. *Stuart and Cromwellian Foreign Policy*. London: Black, 1974.
Howcroft, I. 'The Role of the Royal Navy in Amphibious Assault in the Second World War'. PhD, Exeter, 2003.
Howell, R. *The Royal Navy and the Slave Trade*. London: Croom Helm, 1987.
Hughes, G. 'The Act for the Increase and Encouragement of Seamen, 1696–1710: Could It Have Solved the Royal Navy's Manning Problem?' In *Guerres Maritimes (1688–1713)*, 25–34. Vincennes: Service Historique de la Marine, 1996.
Hunt, B. D. *Sailor-Scholar: Admiral Sir Herbert Richmond, 1871–1946*. Ontario: Wilfred Laurier University Press, 1982.
Hunter, M. C. *Policing the Seas: Anglo-American Relations and the Equatorial Atlantic, 1819–1865*. Research in Maritime History, edited by L. Fischer, R. Vol. 36. St John's: International Maritime Economic History Association, 2008.
Hunter, M. C. 'The U.S. Naval Academy and Its Summer Cruises: Professionalization in the Antebellum U.S. Navy, 1845–1861'. *Journal of Military History* 70 (2006): 963–94.
Hulme, P. 'The Malaspina Expedition'. *Studies in Travel Writing* 10, no. 1 (2006): 71–81.
Hyde, F. E. 'Economic Theory and Business History: A Comment on the Theory of Profit Maximisation'. *Business History* 5 (1962): 1–10.
Igancio Rivas, I. 'Mobilising Resources for War: British and Spanish Intelligence Systems Druing the War of Jenkins's Ear (1739–1748)'. PhD, University College, London, 2008.
Ingram, E. 'Illusions of Victory: The Nile, Copenhagen and Trafalgar Revisited'. *Military Affairs* 48, no. 3 (1984): 140–3.
Ingram, E. *In Defence of British India: Great Britain and the Middle East, 1775–1842*. London: Frank Cass, 1984.
Inikori, J. E. 'Slavery and the Development of Industrial Capitalism'. In *British Capitalism and Caribbean Slavery: The Legacy of Eric Williams*, edited by B. L. Solow and S. L. Engerman, 79–102. Cambridge: Cambridge University Press, 1987.
International Commission of Military History. 'The First International Colloquium in Naval History, 24th-28th August 1987'. Athens, 24–28 August 1987.
Irwin, D. A. 'Strategic Trade Policy and Mercantilist Trade Rivalries'. In *Trade in the Pre-Modern Era, 1400–1700*, edited by Douglas A. Irwin, 407–12. Cheltenham: Elgar Reference Collections, 1996.
Isby, D. C., ed. *The Luftwaffe and the War at Sea, 1939-45: As Seen by Officers of the Kriegsmarine and Luftwaffe*. London: Chatham Publishing, 2005.
Ishimaru, T. *Japan and Britain Must Fight*. Translated by G. V. Rayment. London: Hurst and Blackett, 1936.
Isley, J. A. and P. A. Crowl. *The US Marines and Amphibious War: Its Theory and Its Practice in the Pacific*. Princeton: Princeton University Press, 1951.

Israel, J. I. *Dutch Primacy in World Trade, 1585–1740*. Oxford: Clarendon Press, 1989.
James, A. *Navy and Government in Early Modern France, 1572–1661*. Studies in History. Woodbridge: Boydell and Brewer, 2004.
James, G. F. and J. J. Sutherland Shaw. 'Admiralty Administration and Personnel, 1619–1714'. *Bulletin of the Institute of Historical Research* 14 (1936–7): 166–83.
James, W. *The Naval History of Great Britain during the French Revolutionary and Napoleonic Wars; Volume 6*. 6 vols. Vol. 6. London: Conway Maritime Press, 1990. 1824: Richard Bentley, London.
Jamieson, A. G. 'American Privateers in the Leeward Islands, 1776–1778'. *American Neptune* 53 (1983): 20–30.
Jamieson, A. G. 'The War in the Leeward Islands, 1775–1783'. D.Phil, Oxford, 1981.
Jason Kendall, M. 'Maritime Rivalry, Political Intervention and the Race to Antarctica: US-Chilean Relations, 1939–1949'. *Journal of Latin American Studies* 33, no. 4 (2001): 713–38.
Jellicoe, J. *The Grand Fleet 1914–16: Its Creation, Development and Work*. London: Cassell, 1919.
Jenks, T. 'Contesting the Hero: The Funeral of Admiral Lord Nelson'. *Journal of British Studies* 39, no. 4 (2000): 422–53.
Jenks, T. *Naval Engagements: Patriotism, Cultural Politics and the Royal Navy, 1793–1815*. Oxford: Oxford University Press, 2006.
Jenkins, E. H. *A History of the French Navy*. London: Macdonald, 1973.
John, A. H. 'War and the English Economy, 1700–1763'. *Economic History Review* 7, no. 3 (1955): 329–44.
Johnman, L. and H. Murphy. *British Shipbuilding and the State since 1918: A Political Economy of Decline*. Exeter: University of Exeter Press, 2002.
Johnman, L. and H. Murphy. 'The Rationalisation of Warship Building in the United Kingdom, 1945–2000'. *Journal of Strategic Studies* 24, no. 3 (2001): 107–27.
Johnman, L. and H. Murphy. 'Welding and the British Shipbuilding Industry'. In *The Royal Navy 1930–2000: Innovation and Defence*, edited by R. Harding, 89–116. London: Frank Cass, 2005.
Johnston, J. A. 'Parliament and the Navy, 1688–1714'. PhD diss., Sheffield, 1968.
Johnston, J. A. 'Parliament and the Protection of Trade 1689–1694'. *The Mariner's Mirror* 57, no. 4 (1971): 399–413.
Jones, D. W. *War and Economy in the Age of William Iii and Marlborough*. Oxford: Blackwell, 1988.
Jones, E. 'Royal Naval Psychiatry: Organisation, Methods and Outcomes, 1900–1945'. *Mariner's Mirror* 92, no. 2 (2006): 190–203.
Jones, J. R. *The Anglo-Dutch Wars of the Seventeenth Century*. London: Longman, 1996.
Jones, V. C. *The Civil War at Sea*. 3 vols. New York: Holt, Rinehart, Winston, 1960–62.
Jordan, R. S. *Alliance Strategy and Navies: The Evolution and Scope of Nato's Maritime Dimension*. London: Pinter, 1990.
Jordan, J. *Warships after Washington: The Development of the Five Major Fleets, 1922–1930*. Barnsley: Seaforth, 2011.

Jordan, G. and N. Roger. 'Admirals as Heroes : Patriotism and Liberty in Hanoverian England'. *Journal of British Studies* 28 (1989): 201–24.

Kagan, D. 'Athenian Strategy in the Peloponnesian War'. In *The Making of Strategy: Rulers, States and War*, edited by Williamson Murray, Knox MacGregor and Alvin Bernstein, 24–55. Cambridge: Cambridge University Press, 1994.

Kahn, D. *Seizing the Enigma: The Race to Break the German U-Boat Codes, 1939–1943*. London: Faber, 1998.

Kane, T. *Chinese Grand Strategy and Maritime Power*. London: Frank Cass, 2002.

Karau, M. D. *Wielding the Dagger: The Marinekorps Flandern and the German War Effort, 1914–1918*. Westport: Praeger, 2003.

Karpoff, J. M. 'Public Versus Private Initiatives in Arctic Exploration: The Effects of Incentives and Organizational Structure'. *Journal of Political Economy* 100, no. 11 (2001): 38–78.

Karsten, P. *The Naval Aristocracy: The Golden Age of Annapolis and the Emergence of Modern American Navalism*. New York: Free Press, 1972.

Karsten, P. 'The "Naval Aristocracy" and the "Young Turks" of the "Fin De Siècle": A Dotting of the "I"S and Crossing of the "T"S'. *The Journal of Military History* 66, no. 4 (10 January 2002): 1177–80.

Keegan, J. *The Battle for History: Re-Fighting World War II*. London: Pimlico, 1997.

Kemble, J. H. 'Maritime History in the Age of Albion'. In *The Atlantic World of Robert G. Albion*, edited by B. W. Labaree, 3–17. Middleton: Wesleyan University Press, 1975.

Kennedy, P. *The Realities Behind Diplomacy: Background Influences on British External Policy, 1865–1980*. London: Fontana, 1981.

Kennedy, P. *The Rise and Fall of British Naval Mastery*. London: Allen Lane, 1976.

Kennedy, P. *Strategy and Diplomacy, 1870–1945*. London: Fontana, 1984.

Kenyon, J. *The History Men*. London: Weidenfeld and Nicholson, 1983.

Keyes, R. *The Naval Memoirs of Admiral of the Fleet Sir Roger Keyes: The Narrow Seas to the Dardanelles, 1910–1915*. 2 vols. London: Thornton Butterworth, 1934–5.

Kipp, J. W. 'The Imperial Russian Navy, 1696–1900: The Ambiguous Legacy of Peter's "Second Arm"'. Chapter 9 in *The Military History of Tsarist Russia*, edited by F. W. Kagan and R. Higham, 151–82. Basingstoke: Palgrave, 2002.

Klado, N. *The Russian Navy in the Russo-Japanese War*. London: George Bell and Sons, 1905.

Knight, J. 'Nelson and the Eastern Mediterranean, 1803–1805'. *Mariner's Mirror* 91 (2005): 195–215.

Knight, R. J .B. 'The Building and Maintenance of the British Fleet during the Anglo-French Wars, 1688–1815.' In *Les Marines de Guerre Européennes XVII-XvIIIe Siècles*, edited by M. Acerra, J. Merino, and J. Meyer, 35–43. Paris: Presses de l'Université de Paris-Sorbonne, 1985.

Knight, R. J .B. 'The Introduction of Copper Sheathing into the Royal Navy, 1779–1786'. *The Mariner's Mirror* 59, no. 3 (1973): 299–309.

Knight, R. J. B. 'The Performance of the Royal Naval Dockyards in England During the Ameican War of Independence'. In *The American Revolution and the Sea: Proceedings of the 14th Conference of the International Commission for*

Maritime History (7th-13th July 1974), 139–44. London: National Maritime Museum, 1974.

Knight, R. J .B. 'Pilfering and Theft from the Dockyards at the Time of the American War of Independence'. *The Mariner's Mirror* 61, no. 3 (1975): 215–25.

Knight, R. J. B. 'The Royal Dockyards in England at the Time of the American War of Independence'. PhD, London, 1972.

Knight, R. J .B. 'The Royal Navy's Recovery after the Early Phase of the American Revolutionary War'. In *The Aftermath of Defeat: Societies, Armed Forces and the Challenge of Recovery*, edited by G. J. Andreopoulos and H. E. Selsky, 10–25. New Haven: Yale University Press, 1994.

Knight, R. J .B. 'Sandwich, Middleton and Dockyard Appointments'. *The Mariner's Mirror* 57, no. 2 (1971): 175–92.

Knight, R. *Britain against Napoleon: The Organization of Victory, 1793–1815*. London: Allen Lane, 2013.

Knight, R. 'Changing the Agenda: The "New" Naval History of the British Sailing Navy'. *The Mariner's Mirror* 97, no. 1 (2011): 225–42.

Knight, R. 'Devil Bolts and Deception? Wartime Naval Shipbuilding in Private Shipyards, 1793–1815'. *Journal for Maritime Research* 5, no. 1 (2003): 34–51.

Knight, R. *The Pursuit of Victory: The Life and Achievement of Horatio Nelson*. London: Allen Lane, 2005.

Knight, R. and M. Willcox. *Sustaining the Fleet, 1793–1815: War, the British Navy and the Contractor State*. Woodbridge: Boydell Press, 2010.

Knight, R. and M. Willcox. 'Changing the Agenda: The "New" Naval History of the British Sailing Navy'. *The Mariner's Mirror* 97, no. 1 (2011): 225–42.

Knight, R. and M. Willcox. 'War, Government and the Market: The Direction of the Debate on the British Contractor State, c.1740–1815'. In *The Contractor State and Its Implications, 1659–1815*, edited by R. Harding and S. S. Ferri, 175–98. Las Palmas: Universidad de las Palmas de Gran Canaria, 2012.

Kowner, R. 'The Impact of the War on Naval Warfare'. In *In the Impact of the Russo-Japanese War*, edited by R. Kowner, 269–89. London: Routledge, 2007.

Krajeski, P. C. *In the Shadow of Nelson: The Naval Leadership of Sir Charles Cotton, 1753–1812*. Westport, CT: Greenwood Press, 2000.

Kyo-Ryul, R. 'The Establishment of Naval Port Jinhae and the Imperial Japanese Navy'. Conference paper: *Naval Expertise and the Making of the Modern World*. Wolfson College, Oxford, 2013.

Labaree, B. W. *A Supplement (1971–1986) to Robert G. Albion's Naval and Maritime History: An Annotated Bibliography*. Mystic, CT: Mystic Seaport Museum, 1988.

Lacour-Gayet, G. *La Marine Militaire De La France Sous Le Règne De Louis XV*. Paris: H. Champion, 1902.

Ladd, J. D. *Assault from the Sea 1939-45: The Craft, the Landings, the Men*. Newton Abbot: David and Charles, 1976.

Lagadec, Y. and D. Hopkin. *La Bataille De Saint-Cast (Bretagne, 11 Septembre 1758) Entre Histoire Et Memoire*. Rennes: Presses Universitaires de Rennes, 2009.

Lambert, A. *Admirals: The Naval Commanders Who Made Britain Great*. London: Faber and Faber, 2008.

Lambert, A. 'Australia, the Trent Crisis of 1861 and the Strategy of Imperial Defence'. In *Southern Trident: Strategy, History and the Rise of Australian*

Naval Power, edited by D. Stevens and J. Reeve, 99–118. Crow's Nest, NSW: Allen and Unwin, 2001.

Lambert, A. *Battleships in Transition: The Creation of the Steam Battlefleet, 1815–1860*. London: Conway Maritime Press, 1984.

Lambert, A. *The Challenge: Britain against America in the Naval War of 1812*. London: Faber, 2012.

Lambert, A. 'The Construction of Naval History 1815–1914', *The Mariner's Mirror* 97, no. 1 (2011): 207–24.

Lambert, A. *The Crimean War: British Grand Strategy, 1853–1856*. 1st edn. Manchester: Manchester University Press, 1990.

Lambert, A. 'The Crimean War Blockade: 1854-56'. In *Naval Blockades and Seapower: Strategies and Counter-Strategies, 1805–2005*, edited by B. A. Elleman and S. C. M. Paine, 46–59. London: Routledge, 2006.

Lambert, A. *The Foundations of Naval History: John Knox Laughton, the Royal Navy and the Historical Profession*. London: Chatham Publishing, 1998.

Lambert, A. *Franklin: Tragic Hero of Polar Navigation*. London: Faber, 2009.

Lambert, A. '"History Is the Sole Foundation for the Construction of a Sound and Living Doctrine": The Royal Naval College, Greenwich, and Doctrine Development down to BR1806'. In *The Changing Face of Maritime Power*, edited by A. Dorman, M. L. Smith and M. R. H. Uttley, 33–56. Basingstoke: Macmillan, 1999.

Lambert, A. *The Last Sailing Battlefleet: Maintaining Naval Mastery, 1815–1850*. London: Conway Maritime Press, 1991.

Lambert, A. 'The Magic of Trafalgar: The Nineteenth Century Legacy'. In *Trafalgar in History: A Battle and Its Afterlife*, edited by D. Cannadine, 155–74. Basingstoke: Palgrave, 2006.

Lambert, A. *Nelson: Britannia's God of War*. London: Faber, 2004.

Lambert, A. 'Responding to the Nineteenth Century: The Royal Navy and the Introduction of the Screw Propeller'. *History of Technology* 21 (1997): 1–28.

Lambert, A. 'The Royal Navy, 1856–1914: Deterrence and the Strategy of World Power'. In *Navies and Global Defense: Theories and Strategy*, edited by N. Keith and E. J. Errington, 69–92. Westport, CT: Praeger, 1995.

Lambert, A. 'Politics, Technology and Policy Making 1859–1865: Palmerston, Gladstone and the Management of the Ironclad Naval Race'. *Northern Mariner* 8, no. 3 (1998): 9–38.

Lambert, A., ed. *Steam, Steel and Shellfire: The Steam Warship, 1815–1905*. London: Conway Maritime Press, 1992.

Lambert, N. *Planning for Armageddon: British Economic Warfare and the First World War*. Cambridge, MA: Harvard University Press, 2012.

Lambert, N. *Sir John Fisher's Naval Revolution*. Columbia: University of South Carolina Press, 1999.

Lambert, N. *The Submarine Service, 1900–1918*. London: Navy Records Society, 2001.

Lambi, J. N. *The Navy and German Power Politics, 1862–1914*. London: Allen and Unwin, 1984.

Lana, E. O. *Los Corsarios Españoles Durante la Decadencia de los Austrias: El Corso Español Del Atlántico Peninsular En El Siglo XVII (1621–1697)*. Madrid: Ministero de Defensa, Centro de Publicaciones, 1992.

Lane, F. C. *Profits from Power: Readings in Protection Rent and Violence-Controlling Enterprises*. Albany: State University of New York Press, 1979.

Langensiepen, B. and A. Guleryuz. *The Ottoman Steam Navy*. Annapolis: Naval Insitute Press, 1995.

Langley, H. D. *A History of Medicine in the Early U.S. Navy*. Baltimore: Johns Hopkins University Press, 1995.

Langley, H. D. *Social Reform in the United States Navy*. Chicago: Illinois University Press, 1967.

Lansing, J. S. 'Complex Adaptive Systems'. *Annual Review of Anthropology* 32, no. 1 (2003): 183–204.

Larrabee, H. A. *Decision at the Chesapeake*. London: William Kimber, 1965.

Laughton, J. K. 'Scientific Study of Naval History'. *Journal of the Royal United Services Institution* 18 (1874): 508–27.

Lavery, B. *Nelson and the Nile: The Naval War against Bonaparte 1798*. London: Chatham Publishing, 1998.

Lavery, B. *The Ship of the Line*. Vol. 1: The Development of the Battlefleet, 1650–1850. London: Conway Maritime Press, 1983.

Lavery, B. *The Ship of the Line*. Vol. 2: Design, Construction and Fittings. London: Conway Maritime Press, 1984.

Lavery, B. 'The Ship of the Line'. In *The Line of Battle: The Sailing Warship, 1650–1840*, edited by R. Gardiner, 11–26. London: Conway, 1992.

Layman, R. D. *Naval Aviation in the First World War*. London: Chatham Publishing, 1996.

Le Fevre, P. 'Gibraltar, Tangier and the English Mediterranean Fleet, 1680–1690'. *Transactions of the Naval Dockyards Society* 2, no. December (2006): 19–30.

Le Fevre, P. and R. Harding, eds. *British Admirals of the Napoleonic Wars: The Contemporaries of Nelson*. London: Chjatham Publishing, 2005.

Le Goff, T. J. A. 'Les Gens de Mer Devant Le Système des Classes (1755–1763): Resistance ou Passivite?'. In *Les Hommes et la Mer Dans L'europe du Nord-Ouest de L'antiquité á Nos Jours*, edited by A. Lottin, J-C. Hocquet and S. Lebecq, 463–79. Paris: Revue du Nord, 1986.

Le Goff, T. J. A. 'Problemes de Recrutement de La Marines Francais'. *Revue Historique* 283, no. 574 (1990): 205–33.

Le Moing, G. *La Bataille Navale Des 'Cardinaux' (20 Novembre 1759)*. Paris: Economica, 2003.

Leighton, R. M. and R. W. Coakley. *Global Logistics and Strategy, Vol. 1 (1940–1943); Vol. 2 (1943–1945)*. 2 vols. Washington, DC: Department of the Army, 1955 and 1958.

Lemnitzer, J. M. *Power, Law and the End of Privateering*. London: Palgrave Macmillan, 2014.

Letenneur, J.-F. and P. Decencière. 'Un Panorama Inédit De La Bataille Navale De Velez-Malaga (24 Août 1704)'. *Neptunia* 267, no. Septembre (2012): 6–15.

Levine, P. *The Amateur and the Professional: Antiquarians, Historians an Archaeologists in Victorian England, 1838–1886*. Cambridge: Cambridge University Press, 1986.

Lewis, M. *England's Sea Officers: The Story of the Naval Profession*. London: Allen and Unwin, 1939.

Lewis, M. *The Navy in Transition: A Social History, 1814–1864*. London: Hodder and Stoughton, 1965.

Lewis, M. *A Social History of the Navy, 1793–1815*. London: George Allen and Unwin, 1960.
Lewis, A. R. *Omaha Beach: A Flawed Victory*. Chapel Hill, NC: University of North Carolina Press, 2001.
Liddell Hart, B. *The British Way in Warfare*. London: Faber and Faber, 1932.
Liddell Hart, B. *The Strategy of the Indirect Approach*. London: Faber and Faber, 1941.
Lijo, J. M. V. *La Matricula De Mar En La Espana Del Siglo XVIII: Registro, Inspeccion Y Evolution De Las Classes De Marineria Y Maestranza*. Madrid: Ministerio de Defensa, 2006.
Lincoln, M. *Naval Wives and Mistresses*. London: National Maritime Museum, 2007.
Lincoln, M. 'The Origins of Public Maritime History'. *Journal for Maritime Research* 4, no. 1 (2002): 52–66.
Lincoln, M. *Representing the Royal Navy: British Sea Power, 1750–1815*. Aldershot: Ashgate, 2002.
Lincoln, M., ed. *Science and Exploration in the Pacific: European Voyages to the Southern Ocean in the Eighteenth Century*. Woodbridge: Boydell Press, 1998.
Linebaugh, P. and M. Rediker. 'The Many-Headed Hydra: Sailors, Slaves and the Atltantic Working-Class in the Eighteenth Century'. In *Jack Tar in History: Essays in the History of Maritime Life*, edited by Colin Howell and Richard J. Twomey, 11–36. Fredericton: Arcadiensis Press, 1991.
Linebaugh, P. and M. Rediker. *The Many-Headed Hydra: Sailors, Slaves, Commoners and the Hidden History of the Revolutionary Atlantic*. Boston: Beacon Press, 2000.
Little, C. H. *The Influence of Sea Power on the Conquest of Quebec*. Halifax: Maritime Museum of Canada, 1958.
Littlewood, K. and B. Butler. *Of Ships and Stars: Maritime Heritage and the Founding of the National Maritime Museum Greenwich*. London: Athlone Press, 1998.
Llano, Jose Alcal Zamora y Quelpo de. *Espana, Flandres y el Mar del Norte (1618–1639): La Última Ofensiva Europea De Los Austrias Madrileños*. Barcelona: Planeta, 1975.
Llewellyn-Jones, M. *The Royal Navy and Anti-Submarine Warfare, 1917–1949*. London: Cass, 2005.
Lloyd, C. *The British Seaman 1200–1860*. London: Collins, 1968.
Lloyd, C. *The Navy and the Slave Trade: The Suppression of the African Slave Trade in the Nineteenth Century*. London: Longman, 1949.
Lloyd, C. *St Vincent and Camperdown*. London: Batsford, 1963.
Lloyd, C. C., J. Keevil and J. L. S. Coulter. *Medicine and the Navy, 1200–1900*. 4 vols. Edinburgh: Livingstone, 1957–62.
Loades, D. *The Making of the Elizabethan Navy, 1540–1590: From the Solent to the Armada*. Woodbridge: Boydell Press, 2009.
Loades, D. *The Tudor Navy: An Administrative, Political and Military History*. Studies in Naval History. Aldershot: Scholar Press, 1992.
Lone, S. *Japan's First Modern War: Army and Society in the Conflict with China, 1894-95*. Basingstoke: Macmillan, 1994.
Long, D. F. 'The Navy under the Board of Navy Commissioners, 1815–1842'. In *War and Peace: Interpretations of American Naval History*, edited by Kenneth J. Hagan, 63–78. Westport, CT: Greenwood, 1984.

Lovering, T., ed. *Amphibious Assault: Manoeuvre from the Sea*. Woodbridge: Seafarer Books, 2007.
Lunn, K. and A. Day, eds. *History of Work and Labour Relations in the Royal Dockyards*. London: Mansell, 1999.
Luraghi, R. *A History of the Confederate Navy*, translated by P. E. Coletta. Annapolis: Naval Institute Press, 1996.
Luttwak, E. N., ed. *The Political Uses of Sea Power*. Baltimore: Johns Hopkins University Press, 1974.
Luttwak, E. N. *Strategy: The Logic of War and Peace*. Cambridge, MA: Harvard University Press, 1987.
Luvaas, J. *The Military Legacy of the Civil War: The European Inheritance*. 2nd edn. Lawrence, Kansas: University Press Kansas, 1988.
Lyon, D. *The First Destroyers*. London: Chatham Publishing, 1996.
Lyon, D. 'Underwater Warfare and the Torpedo Boat'. In *Steam, Steel and Shellfire: The Steam Warship, 1815–1905*, edited by R. Gardiner, 134–45. London: Conway Maritime Press, 1992.
MacDonald, J. *Feeding Nelson's Navy: The True Story of Food at Sea in the Georgian Era*. London: Chatham Publishing, 2006.
Macdonald, J. W. *The British Navy's Victualling Board, 1793–1815: Management Competence and Incompetence*. Woodbridge: Boydell Press, 2010.
Mackay, R. F. *Admiral Hawke*. Oxford: Oxford University Press, 1965.
Mackay, R. F. and M. Duffy. *Hawke, Nelson and British Naval Leadership, 1747–1805*. Woodbridge: Boydell Press, 2009.
MacKenzie, D. *Inventing Accuracy: A Historical Sociology of Nuclear Missile Guidance*. Cambridge, MA: MIT Press, 2000.
MacKenzie, D. 'Missile Accuracy: A Case Study in the Social Processes of Technological Change'. In *The Social Construction of Technological Systems: New Directions in the Sociology and History of Technology*, edited by W. E. Bijker, T. P. Hughes and T. J. Pinch, 195–222. Cambridge, MA: MIT Press, 1987.
Mackesy, P. *British Victory in Egypt 1801: The End of Napoleon's Conquest*. London: Routledge, 1995.
Mackesy, P. *Statesmen at War: The Strategy of Overthrow, 1798–1799*. London: Longman, 1974.
Mackesy, P. *The War for America, 1775–1783*. London: Longman, 1964.
Mackesy, P. *The War in the Mediterranean, 1803–1810*. London: Longman Green, 1957.
Mackesy, P. *War without Victory; The Downfall of Pitt, 1799–1802*. Oxford: Clarendon Press, 1984.
Mackinder, H. J. *Britain and the British Seas*. London: William Heinemann, 1902.
Macleod, R., ed. *Government and Expertise: Specialists, Administrators and Professionals, 1860–1910*. Cambridge: Cambridge University Press, 1988.
Madsen, C. *The Royal Navy and German Naval Disarmament, 1942–1947*. London: Frank Cass, 1998.
Maffeo, S. E. *Most Secret and Confidential: Intelligence in the Age of Nelson*. London: Chatham Publishing, 2000.
Mahan, A. T. *The Influence of Sea Power upon History, 1660–1763*. Boston: Little Brown, 1890.
Mahan, A. T. *The Influence of Sea Power upon the French Revolution and Empire, 1793–1812*. 2 vols. Boston: Little Brown, 1892.

Mahan, A. T. *Sea Power in Its Relations to the War of 1812*. 2 vols. London: Sampson Low, Marston, 1905.
Mainwaring, G. E., ed. *The Life and Works of Sir Henry Mainwaring*. 2 vols. Vol. 1. London: Navy Records Society, 1920.
Mainwaring, G. E., ed. *The Life and Works of Sir Henry Mainwaring*. 2 vols. Vol. 2. London: Navy Records Society, 1921.
Maiolo, J. A. *The Royal Navy and Nazi Germany, 1933–1939: A Study in Appeasement and the Origins of the Second World War*. London: Palgrave, 1998.
Malcomson, R. *Warships of the Great Lakes, 1754–1834*. London: Chatham Publishing, 2001.
Mallett, R. *The Italian Navy and Fascist Expansionism, 1935–1940*. London: Cass, 1998.
Mallmann Showell, J. P. *U-Boat Command and the Battle of the Atlantic*. London: Conway Maritime Press, 1989.
Malony, S. M. *Securing Command of the Sea: Nato Naval Planning, 1948–1954*. Annapolis: Naval Institute Press, 1995.
Maltby, W. 'Politics, Professionalism and the Evolution of Sailing Ship Tactics, 1650–1714'. In *The Tools of War: Instruments, Ideas and Institutions of Warfare, 1445–1871*, edited by J. A. Lynn, 56–73. Urbana: University of Illinois Press, 1990.
Manuele, P. *Il Piemonte Sul Mare: La Marina Sabauda dal Mediovvo All'unita D'italia*. Cueno: L'Arciere, 1997.
Manwaring, G. E. *Bibliography of British Naval History: A Biographical and Historical Guide to Printed and Manuscript Sources*. London: Routledge, 1930.
Marchena Giménéz, J. M. *La Marina De Guerra de los Austurias; Una Approxima Bibliografica*. Madrid: Ministerio de defensa, 2010.
Marcus, G. *Quiberon Bay: The Campaign in Home Waters, 1759*. London: Hollis and Carter, 1960.
Marder, A. J. *The Anatomy of British Sea Power: A History of British Naval Policy in the Pre-Dreadnought Era, 1880–1905*. New York: Alfred A. Knopf, 1940.
Marder, A. J. *From Dreadnought to Scapa Flow: The Royal Navy in the Fisher Era, 1904–1919*. 5 vols. Oxford: Oxford University Press, 1961–70.
Marder, A. J. *Old Friends, New Enemies: The Royal Navy and the Imperial Japanese Navy: Strategic Illusions, 1936–1941*. Oxford: Oxford University Press, 1981.
Marder, A. J. *Portrait of an Admiral: The Life and Papers of Herbert Richmond*. Cambridge, MA: University of Harvard Press, 1952.
Marina, Ufficio Storico dell Regina. *La Marina Italiana Nella Grande Guerra*. 8 vols. Florence: Vallecchi, 1935–42.
Marley, D. F. 'A Fearful Gift: The Spanish Naval Build-up in the West Indies, 1759–1762'. *The Mariner's Mirror* 80, no. 4 (1994): 403–17.
Marley, D. F. 'Havana Surprised: Prelude to the British Invasion, 1762'. *The Mariner's Mirror* 78, no. 3 (1992): 293–305.
Marolda, E. J. and O. P. Fitzgerald. *The United States Navy and the Vietnam Conflict: From Military Assistance to Combat, 1959–1965*. Washington, DC: Naval Historical Centre, 1976.
Marshall, P. J. *The Making and Unmaking of Empires: Britain, India and America, 1750–1783*. Oxford: Oxford University Press, 2005.
Marteille, J. *Galley Slave*. Barnsley: Seaforth, 2010.

Martel, G. 'The Meaning of Power: Rethinking the Decline and Fall of Great Britain'. *The International History Review* 13, no. 4 (1991): 662–94.
Martin, C., and G. Parker. *The Spanish Armada*. 2nd edn. 1999 ed. London: Hamish Hamilton, 1988.
Massam, D. R. 'British Maritime Strategy and Amphibious Capability, 1900–1940'. D.Phil, Oxford, 1995.
Masson, P. *Histoire De La Marine:* Vol. 1: *L'Ere de la voile*. Paris: C. Lavauzelle, 1981.
Masson, P. 'La Pensée Navale Française De 1871 À 1940'. *Revue Historique des Armees* (1982): 42–51.
Masson, P. *Les Galeres De France: Marseilles, Port De Guerre (1481–1781)*. Paris: Librairie Hachette, 1938.
Masson, H. *Les Sous-Marins Francais Des Origines (1863) a Nos Jours*. Brest: Editions de la Cite-Brest-Paris, 1980.
Masson, P. and J. Muracciole. *Napoleon Et La Marine*. Paris: J.Peyronnet & Cie, 1968.
Mather, I. R. 'The Role of the Royal Navy in the English Atlantic Empire, 1660–1720'. D.Phil, Oxford, 1995.
Matzke, R. B. *Deterrence through Strength: British Naval Power and Foreign Policy under Pax Britannica*. Lincoln, Nebraska: University of Nebraska Press, 2011.
Maund, L. E. H. *Assault from the Sea*. London: Methuen, 1949.
Mayntz, R. and T. P. Hughes, eds. *The Development of Large Technical Systems*. Boulder: Westview, 1988.
McBride, W. M. 'Normal Medicine, Science and the British Treatment of Sea Scurvy, 1753–75'. *Journal of the History of Medicine and Allied Sciences* 46 (1991): 157–77.
McClay, K. 'Combined Operations: British Naval and Military Co-Operation in the Wars of 1688–1713'. PhD, Glasgow, 2003.
McCranie, K. D. *Admiral Lord Keith and the Naval War against Napoleon*. Gainsville: University Press of Florida, 2006.
McCranie, K. D. *Utmost Gallantry: The US and Royal Navies at Sea in the War of 1812*. Annapolis: Naval Institute Press, 2011.
McCusker, J. J. and K. Morgan, eds. *The Early Modern Atlantic Economy*. Cambridge: Cambridge University Press, 2000.
McGee, W. L. and S. McGee, eds. *Pacific Express: The Critical Role of Military Logistics in World War Two*. Tiburon, CA: BMC, 2009.
McGowan, A. P., ed. *The Jacobean Commissions of Enquiry, 1608 and 1618*. London: Navy Records Society, 1971.
McGowan, A. P. 'The Royal Navy under the First Duke of Buckingham, Lord High Admiral, 1618–28.' PhD, London, 1967.
McGuffie, T. H. *The Siege of Gibraltar, 1779–1783*. London: B. T. Batsford, 1965.
McIntyre, W. D. *The Rise and Fall of the Singapore Naval Base*. London: Macmillan, 1979.
McKee, C. *A Gentlemanly and Honorable Profession: The Creation of the US Naval Officer Corps, 1794–1815*. Annapolis: Naval Institute Press, 1991.
McKee, C. 'The Pathology of a Profession: Death in the United States Navy Officer Corps 1797–1815'. *War and Society* 3 (1985): 1–25.
McKillip, R. W. 'Undermining Technology by Strategy: Resolving the Trade Protection Dilemma of 1917'. *Naval War College Review* 44, no. 3 (1991): 18–37.

McLean, D. *Education and Empire: Naval Tradition and England's Elite Schooling*. London: British Academic Press, 1999.
McLean, D. *Public Health and Politics in the Age of Reform: Cholera, the State and the Royal Navy in Victorian Britain*. London: I. B. Tauris, 2006.
McLeod, A. B. *British Naval Captains of the Seven Years War: The View from the Quarterdeck*. Woodbridge: Boydell Press, 2012.
McNeill, J. R. *Atlantic Empires of France and Spain: Louisbourg and Havana, 1700–1763*. Chapel Hill, NC: University of North Carolina Press, 1985.
McNeill, J. R. 'The Ecological Basis of Warfare in the Caribbean, 1700–1804'. In *Adapting to Conditions*, edited by M. Ultee, 26–42. Tuscaloosa: University of Alabama Press, 1986.
McPherson, J. M. *War on the Waters: The Union and Confederate Navies, 1861–1865*. Chapel Hill, NC: The University of North Carolina Press, 2012.
Melleuish, G., K. Sheiko and S. Brown. 'Pseudo History/Weird History: Nationalism and the Internet'. *History Compass* 7, no. 6 (2009): 1484–95.
Menning, B. 'Russian Military Innovation in the Second Half of the Eighteenth Century'. *War and Society* 2 (1984): 23–41.
Menon, R. *Maritime Strategy and Continental Wars*. London: Frank Cass, 1998.
Menzies, G. *1421: The Year China Discovered the World*. London: Bantam Press, 2003.
Meril, F. J. *The Alabama, British Neutrality and the American Civil War*. Bloomington: Indiana University Press, 2004.
Meril, F. J. *Great Britain and the Confederate Navy, 1861–1865*. Bloomington: Indiana University Press, 1970.
Merino, J. P. *La Armada Espanola En El Siglo XVIII*. Madrid: Fundación Universitaria Española, 1981.
Merrill, J. M. 'British-French Amphibious Operations in the Sea of Azov, 1855'. *Military Affairs* 20, no. 1 (1956): 16–27.
Meyer, J. *Colbert*. Paris: Hachette, 1981.
Meyer, J. 'Gens De Mer En Mediterranee au xviiie Siecle: La France et L'espagne, Essai De Comparison'. In *Le Genti Del Mare Mediterraneo*, edited by R. Ragosta, 905–36. Naples: Pironti, 1981.
Meyer, J. 'La Marine Française De 1545 À 1715'. In *Histoire Militaire De La France (Des Orgines À 1715)*, edited by P. Contamine and Andre Corvisier, 486–526. Paris: Presses Universitaires de France, 1992.
Meyer, W. R. 'English Privateering in the War of 1688 to 1697'. *The Mariner's Mirror* 67, no. 3 (1981): 259–72.
Meyer, W. R. 'English Privateering in the War of Spanish Succession, 1702–1713'. *Mariner's Mirror* 69 (1983): 435–46.
Meyers, A. R. *Parliaments and Estates in Europe to 1789*. Library of European Civilization, edited by G. Barraclough. London: Thames and Hudson, 1975.
Middleton, C. R. 'The Administration of Newcastle and Pitt: The Departments of State and the Conduct of the War, 1754-60, with Particular Reference to the Campaigns in North America'. PhD, Exeter, 1968.
Middleton, C. R. *The Bells of Victory; The Pitt-Newcastle Ministry and the Conduct of the Seven Years War, 1757–1762*. Cambridge: Cambridge University Press, 1985.
Middleton, C. R. 'British Naval Strategy, 1755–1762: The Western Squadron'. *Mariner's Mirror* 75 (1989): 349–67.

Middleton, C. R. 'Naval Resources and the British Defeat at Yorktown, 1781'. *Mariner's Mirror* 100, no. 1 (2014): 29–43.
Miller, A. *Dressed to Kill: British Naval Uniforms, Masculinity and Contemporary Fashion, 1748–1857*. London: National Maritime Museum, 2007.
Miller, C. A. *Ship of State: The Nautical Metaphors of Thomas Jefferson*. Lanham: University of America Press, 2003.
Miller, G, A. 'From Jack Tar to Bluejacket: Impressment, Manning and the Development of Continuous Service in the Royal Navy, 1815–1853'. PhD, King's College, 2011.
Miller, J., ed. *Absolutism in Seventeenth Century Europe*. London: Macmillan, 1990.
Miller, E. S. *War Plan Orange: The U.S. Strategy to Defeat Japan, 1897–1945*. Annapolis: Naval Institute Press, 1991.
Millett, A. R. 'Assault from the Sea: The Development of Amphibious Warfare between the Wars'. In *Military Innovation in the Inter-War Period*, edited by W. Murray and A. R. Millett, 50–95. Cambridge: Cambridge University Press, 1996.
Milner, M. *The Battle of the Atlantic*. Stroud: Tempus, 2005.
Mitchell, D. W. *A History of Russian and Soviet Sea Power*. London: Andre Deutsch, 1974.
Modelski, G. and W. R. Thompson. *Seapower in Global Politics, 1494–1993*. Seattle: University of Washington Press, 1988.
Moinville, H. *Naval Warfare Today and Tomorrow*. Oxford: Blackwell, 1983.
Mollat, M., ed. *Course Et Piraterie*. Paris: Centre National de la Recherche Scientifique, 1975.
Monaque, R. 'Latouche-Tréville: The Admiral Who Defied Nelson'. *The Mariner's Mirror* 86, no. 3 (2000): 272–84.
Monasterev, N. and S. Terestchenko. *Histoire De La Marine Russe*. Paris: Payot, 1932.
Monkkenon, E. H., ed. *Engaging the Past: The Uses of History across the Social Sciences*. Durham, NC: Duke University Press, 1994.
Monte, P. 'Die Rolle Der Marine Der Bundesrepublik Deutschland in Der Verteidigungsplanung Für Mittel- Und Nordeuropa Von Den 50er Jahren Bis Zur Wende 1989/90'. In *Deutsche Marinen Im Wandel*, edited by W. Rahn, 565–98. Munchen: R. Oldenbourg, 2005.
Moore, R. *The Royal Navy and Nuclear Weapons*. London: Frank Cass, 2001.
Moran, J. and G. L. Rottman. *Peleliu, 1944: The Forgotten Corner of Hell*. Oxford: Osprey, 2002.
Moretz, J. *The Royal Navy and the Capital Ship in the Interwar Period*. London: Frank Cass, 2002.
Morgan, G. W. 'The Impact of War on the Administration of the Army, Navy and Ordnance in Britain, 1739–1748'. PhD, University of Leicester, 1977.
Morgan, K. *Slavery, Atlantic Trade and the British Economy, 1660–1800*. Cambridge: Cambridge University Press, 2000.
Morgan, W. J. 'American Privateering in America's War for Independence, 1775–1783'. In *Course Et Piraterie*, edited by M. Mollat, 556–71. Paris: ECNRS, 1975.
Morillo, S. and M. F. Pavkovic. *What Is Military History?* Cambridge: Polity, 2006.
Morison, S. E. *History of US Naval Operations in World War II: Sicily-Salerno-Anzio, January 1943–June 1944*. History of the United States Naval Operation in World War II. Boston: Little Brown, 1954.

Morriss, R. *The Foundations of British Maritime Ascendancy: Resources, Logistics and the State, 1755–1815*. Cambridge: Cambridge University Press, 2011.
Morriss, R. *Guide to British Naval Papers in North America*. London: Mansell, 1994.
Morriss, R. *Naval Power and British Culture, 1760–1850: Public Trust and Government Ideology*. Aldershot: Ashgate, 2004.
Morriss, R. 'Practicality and Prejudice: The Blockade Strategy and Naval Medicine During the French Revolutionary Wars, 1793–1801'. In *Science and the French and British Navies, 1700–1850*, edited by P. van der Merve, 77–87. London: National Maritime Museum, 2003.
Morriss, R. *The Royal Dockyards during the Revolutionary and Napoleonic Wars*. Leicester: University of Leicester Press, 1983.
Morriss, A. J. A. *The Scaremongers: The Advocacy of War and Rearmament, 1896–1914*. London: Routledge and Kogan Paul, 1984.
Morriss, R. *Science, Utility and Maritime Power: Samuel Bentham in Russia, 1779-91*. Corbett Centre for Maritime Policy Studies. Abingdon: Ashgate, 2015.
Morriss, R. and D. Saxby, eds. *The Channel Fleet and the Blockade of Brest, 1793–1801*. London: Navy Records Society, 2001.
Mort, M. *Building the Trident Network: A Study of the Enrolment of People, Knowledge and Machines*. Cambridge, MA: MIT Press, 2002.
Moskin, J. R. *The Story of the U.S. Marine Corps*. New York: Paddington Press, 1979.
Motte, M. *Une Éducation Géostrategique : La Pensée Navale Française de la Jeune École a 1914*. Paris: Economica, 2004.
Munch-Petersen, T. *Defying Napoleon: How Britain Bombarded Copenhagen and Seized the Danish Fleet in 1807*. Stroud: Sutton Publishing, 2007.
Murfett, M. 'Gunboat Diplomacy: Outmoded or Back in Vogue?' In *The Changing Face of Maritime Power*, edited by A. Dorman, M. L. Smith and M. R. H. Uttley, 81–93. Basingstoke: Macmillan, 1999.
Murfett, M. *In Jeopardy: The Royal Navy and British Far East Defence Policy 1945–1951*. Kuala Lumpur: Oxford University Press, 1995.
Murfett, M. *Naval Warfare, 1919–1945: An Operational History of a Volatile War at Sea*. London: Routledge, 2008.
Murfett, M. H. 'Gunboat Diplomacy: Outmoded or Back in Vogue?'. In *The Changing Face of Maritime Power*, edited by Andrew Dorman, Mike Lawrence Smith and Matthew R. H. Uttley, 81–93. Basingstoke: Macmillan, 1999.
Murphy, E. *Ireland and the War at Sea, 1641–1653*. Woodbridge: Boydell and Brewer, 2012.
Murphy, E. 'The Navy and the Cromwellian Conquest of Ireland, 1649–53'. *Journal for Maritime Research* 14, no. 1 (2012): 1–13.
Murphy, H. and D. J. Oddy. *The Mirror of the Seas: A Centenary History of the Society for Nautical Research*. London: Society for Nautical Research, 2010.
Murray, L. *The Making of a Civil Servant: Sir Oswyn Murray GCB, Secretary of the Admiralty, 1917–1936*. London: Methuen, 1940.
Murray, O. A. R. 'The Admiralty: Introductory'. *Mariner's Mirror* 23, no. 1 (1937): 13–35.
Murray, O. A. R. 'The Admiralty: Part II'. *Mariner's Mirror* 23, no. 2 (1937): 129–47.
Murray, O. A. R. 'The Admiralty: Part III'. *Mariner's Mirror* 23, no. 3 (1937): 316–31.
Murray, O. A. R. 'The Admiralty: Part IV'. *Mariner's Mirror* 24, no. 1 (1938): 101–4.

Murray, O. A. R. 'The Admiralty: Part V'. *Mariner's Mirror* 24, no. 2 (1938): 204–25.
Murray, O. A. R. 'The Admiralty: Part VI'. *Mariner's Mirror* 24, no. 3 (1938): 329–52.
Murray, O. A. R. 'The Admiralty: Part VII'. *Mariner's Mirror* 24, no. 4 (1938): 458–75.
Murray, O. A. R. 'The Admiralty: Part VIII the Modern Board of Admiralty and the Nature of Its Responsibilities'. *Mariner's Mirror* 25, no. 1 (1939): 89–111.
Murray, O. A. R. 'The Admiralty: Part IX the Admiralty Departments and Their Functions'. *Mariner's Mirror* 25, no. 2 (1939): 216–28.
Murray, O. A. R. 'The Admiralty: Part X the Naval Staff'. *Mariner's Mirror* 25, no. 3 (1939): 328–38.
Murray, W. and M. Knox. 'Thinking about Revolutions in Warfare'. In *The Dynamics of Military Revolution, 1300–2050*, edited by M. Knox and W. Murray, 1–14. Cambridge: Cambridge University Press, 2001.
Murray, W. and A. R. Millett, eds. *Calculation: Net Assessment and the Coming of World War II*. New York: The Free Press, 1992.
Musson, A. E. 'Technological Change and Manpower'. *History* 67, no. 220 (1982): 237–51.
Nailor, P. *The Nassau Connection: The Organization and Management of the British Polaris Project*. London: HMSO, 1988.
Nash, P. V. *Development of Mobile Logistics Support in Anglo-American Naval Policy, 1900–1953*. Gainsville: University of Florida Press, 2009.
Neilson, K. '"Unbroken Thread": Japan. Maritime Power and British Imperial Defence, 1920–1932'. In *British Naval Strategy East of Suez, 1900–2000: Influences and Actions*, edited by G. Kennedy, 65–9. London: Cass, 2005.
Nerzic, J.-Y. 'Le Service De Santé De La Marine Du Roi'. *Chronique d'histoire maritime* 55, no. June (2004): 44–59.
Nerzic, J.-Y. and C. Buchet. *Marins Et Flibustiers Du Roi-Soleil – Carthagene 1697*. Paris: Pyrégraph, 2002.
Nicholas, N., ed. *The Despatches and Letters of Lord Nelson*. 6 vols. London: Colburn, 1844–7.
Nicholson, A. *Men of Honour: Trafalgar and the Making of the English Hero*. London: Harper Collins, 2005.
Nish, I. *The Anglo-Japanese Alliance: The Diplomacy of Two Island Empires, 1894–1907*. London: Athlone Press, 1965.
Nish, I. *Japanese Foreign Policy 1869–1942: Kasumigaseki to Miyakezaka*. London: Routledge, 1977.
Nordman, C. 'L'essor De La Flotte De Guerre Suedo-Finlandais'ae Au XVIIIe Siécle'. In *Les Hommes De La Mer Dans L'europe Du Nord-Quest*, edited by A. Lottin, J.-C. Hocquet and S. Lebecq, 343–68. Paris: Revue de Nord, 1986.
North, D. C. 'Institutions'. *Journal of Economic Perspectives* 5, no. 1 (1991): 97–112.
North, D. C. and B. R. Weingast. 'Constitutions and Commitment: The Evolution of Institutional Governing Public Choice in Seventeenth Century England'. *Journal of Economic History* 49, no. 4 (1989): 803–32.
North, D. C. and B. R. Weingast. 'Introduction: Institutional Analysis and Economic History'. *Journal of Economic History* 60, no. 2 (2000): 414–17.
Nuxoll, E. M. 'The American Navy, the "War of Finance", and the Quest for Specie'. In *New Interpretations in Naval History*, edited by W. B. Cogar, 28–44. Shrewsbury: Tri-Service Press, 1989.

O'Brien, P. 'The Nature and Historical Evolution of an Exceptional Fiscal State and Its Possible Significance for the Precocious Commercialization and Industrialization of the British Economy from Cromwell to Nelson'. *The Economic History Review* 64, no. 2 (2011): 408–46.

O'Brien, P. K. 'Fiscal and Financial Preconditions for the Formation of Developmental States in the West and the East from the Conquest of Ceuta (1415) to the Opium War (1839)'. *Journal of World History* 23, no. 3 (2012): 513–33.

O'Brien, P. K., and S. L. Engerman. 'Exports and the Growth of the British Economy from the Glorious Revolution to the Peace of Amiens'. Chapter 8 In *Slavery and the Rise of the Atlantic System*, edited by B. L. Solow, 177–209. Cambridge: Cambridge University Press, 1991.

O'Brien, P. K. and X. Duran. 'Total Factor Productivity for the Royal Navy from Victory at the Texel (1653) to Triumph at Trafalgar (1805)'. In *Shipping and Economic Growth, 1350–1850*, edited by R. W. Unger, 279–307. Leiden: Brill, 2011.

Offer, A. 'Morality and Admiralty: "Jacky" Fisher, Economic Warfare and the Laws of War'. *Journal of Contemporary History* 23 (1988): 99–118.

O'Hara, G. '"The Sea Is Swinging into View': Modern British Maritime History in a Globalised World'. *English Historical Review* 124, no. 510 (2009): 1109–34.

Olender, P. *Sino-French Naval War, 1884–1885*. Petersfield: Mushroom Model Publications, 2012.

Olesa-Munido, F.-F. *La Organizacion Naval De Los Estados Mediterraneos Y En Especial De Espana Durante Los Siglos XVI Y XVII*. 2 vols. Madrid: Editorial Naval, 1968.

Olivier, D. H. *German Naval Strategy 1856–1888: Forerunners of Tirpitz*. London: Frank Cass, 2004.

Onwuka Dike, K. 'Gerald S. Graham: Teacher and Historian'. In *Perspectives of Empire: Essays Presented to Gerald S. Graham*, edited by J. E. Flint and G. Williams, 1–8. London: Longman, 1973.

Oppenheim, M. *A History of the Administration of the Royal Navy, 1509–1660*. London: Bodley Head, 1896.

Oppenheim, M., ed. *The Naval Tracts of Sir William Monson*. Vol. 1–4. London: Navy Records Society, 1902–13.

O'Shaughnessy, A. J. *An Empire Divided: The American Revolution and the British Caribbean*. Philadelphia: University of Pennsylvania Press, 2000.

Otero Lana, E. *Los Corsarios Espanoles Durante la Decadencia de los Austrias: El Corso Espanol Del Atlantico Peninsular En El Siglo XVII (1621–1697)*. Madrid: Editorial Naval, 1992.

Overdale, R. *British Defence Policy since 1945*. Manchester: Manchester University Press, 1994.

Owen, J. H. *War at Sea under Queen Anne, 1702–1708*. Cambridge: Cambridge University Press, 1938.

Padfield, P. *Broke and the Shannon*. London: Hodder and Stoughton, 1968.

Padfield, P. *Maritime Dominion and the Triumph of the Free World: Naval Campaigns That Shaped the Modern World, 1852–2001*. London: Murray, 2009.

Padfield, P. *Maritime Power and the Struggle for Freedom, 1788–1851*. London: John Murray, 2003.

Padfield, P. *Maritime Supremacy and the Opening of the Western Mind: Naval Campaigns That Shaped the Modern World, 1588–1782*. London: John Murray, 1999.
Padfield, P. *Tides of Empires, 1482–1654*. London: Routledge and Kegan Paul, 1979.
Padfield, P. *Tides of Empires, 1654–1763*. London: Routledge and Kegan Paul, 1982.
Palmer, M. A. *Command at Sea: Naval Command and Control since the Sixteenth Century*. Cambridge, MA: Harvard University Press, 2005.
Palmer, M. A. *Origins of the Maritime Strategy: American Naval Strategy in the First Postwar Decade*. Washington, DC: Naval Historical Center, 1988.
Palmer, M. A. *Stoddert's War: Naval Operations during the Quasi-War with France, 1798–1801*. Columbia: University of South Carolina Press, 1987.
Paoletti, C. 'Prince Eugene of Savoy, the Toulon Expedition and the English Historians: A Dissenting View'. *Journal of Military History* 70, no. 4 (2006): 939–62.
Papastratigakis, N. *Russian Imperialism and Naval Power: Military Strategy and the Build-up to the Russo-Japanese War*. London: I. B. Tauris, 2011.
Pares, R. 'American Versus Continental Warfare, 1739–1763'. *English Historical Review* 51, no. July (1936): 429–65.
Pares, R. *Colonial Blockade and Neutral Rights, 1739–1763*. Oxford: Oxford University Press, 1938.
Pares, R. 'The Manning of the Navy in the West Indies, 1702-63'. *Transactions of the Royal Historical Society (Fourth series)* 20 (1937): 31–60.
Pares, R. *War, Trade and the West Indies, 1739–1763*. Oxford: Oxford University Press, 1936.
Parkinson, R. *The Late Victorian Navy: The Pre-Dreadnought Era and the Origins of the First World War*. Woodbridge: Boydell Press, 2008.
Parker, G. 'The Dreadnought Revolution of Tudor England'. *Mariner's Mirror* 82 (1996): 269–300.
Parkinson, C. N. *War in the Eastern Seas, 1793–1815*. London: George Allen and Unwin, 1954.
Parrill, S. *Nelson's Navy in Fiction and Film: Depictions of British Sea Power in the Napoleonic Era*. Jefferson, NC: McFarland and Company, 2009.
Parris, H. *Constitutional Bureaucracy*. London: Allen and Unwin, 1969.
Parrott, D. *The Business of War: Military Entreprise and Military Revolution in Early Modern Europe*. Cambridge: Cambridge University Press, 2012.
Parry, J. H. *The Age of Reconnaissance: Discovery, Exploration and Settlement, 1450–1650*. London: Weidenfeld and Nicholson, 1963.
Parry, J. H. *The Spanish Seaborne Empire*. London: Hutchinson, 1966.
Parry, J. H. *Trade and Dominion: European Overseas Empires in the Eighteenth Century*. London: Sphere Books, 1974.
Parshall, J. and A. Tully. *Shattered Sword: The Untold Story of the Battle of Midway*. Dulles: Potomac, 2005.
Paullin, C. O. *Paullin's History of Naval Administration, 1778–1911; a Collection of Articles from the U.S. Naval Institute Proceedings*. Annapolis: Naval Institute Press, 1968.
Pebbles, R. H. 'Navy Shipbuilders "Discover" Welding'. In *Naval History: The Sixth Symposium of the U.S. Naval Academy*, edited by D. M. Masterson, 157–66. Wilmington, DE: Scholarly Resources Inc., 1987.

Peck, L. L. *Court Patronage and Corruption in Early Stuart England*. London: Routledge, 1991.
Penn, C. 'The Medical Staffing of the Royal Navy in the Russian War, 1854–6'. *The Mariner's Mirror* 89, no. 1 (1 January 2003): 51–8.
Penn, C. D. *The Navy under the Early Stuarts and Its Influence on English History*. London: Grieves, 1920.
Penrose, E. *The Theory of the Growth of the Firm*. Oxford: Blackwell, 1959.
Pérez-Llorca, J. *1898: La Estrategia Del Desastre*. Madrid: SILEX, 1998.
Perrett, W. G. 'French Naval Policy and Foreign Affairs, 1930–1939'. PhD, Stanford, 1977.
Perrin, W. G., ed. *The Autobiography of Phineas Pett*. London: Navy Records Society, 1917.
Perrin, W. G., ed. *Boetler's Dialogues*. London: Navy Records Society, 1929.
Perrow, C. *Complex Organizations: A Critical Essay*. 3rd edn. New York: McGraw Hill, 1986.
Perry, M. F. *Infernal Machines: The Story of Confederate Submarine and Mine Warfare*. Baton Rouge: Louisiana State University Press, 1965.
Peters, M. 'Early Hanoverian Consciousness: Europe or Empire'. *English Historical Review* 122 (2007):632–68.
Pfister-Langanay, C., ed. *Revue historique de Dunkerque de du littoral, no. 37; Colloque Jean Bart et son temps*. Dunkerque, Société Dunkerquoise d'Histoire et d'Archélogie, 2004.
Phillips, C. R. 'Iberian Ships and Shipbuilding in the Age of Discovery'. In *Maritime History 1: The Age of Discovery*, edited by J. B. Hattendorf, 215–38. Malabar: Krieger Publishing Company, 1996.
Phillips, C. R. '"The Life Blood of the Navy": Recruiting Sailors in Eighteenth Century Spain'. *The Mariner's Mirror* 87, no. 4 (2001): 420–45.
Phillips, C. R. *Six Galleons for the King of Spain: Imperial Defence in the Early Seventeenth Century*. Baltimore: Johns Hopkins University Press, 1986.
Phillips, E. J. *The Founding of Russia's Navy: Peter the Great and the Azov Fleet, 1688–1714 (Tables)*. Westport: Greenwood Press, 1995.
Philpott, M. *Air and Sea Power in World War I*. London: I. B. Tauris, 2012.
Pierson, P. 'The Development of Spanish Naval Strategy and Tactics in the Sixteenth Century'. In *Politics, Religion and Diplomacy in Early Modern Europe: Essays in Honor of De Lemar Jensen*, edited by M. R. Thorp and A. J. Slavin. Sixteenth Century Essays and Studies, 191–218. Kirksville: North-West Missouri State University, 1994.
Pietsch, R. *The Real Jim Hawkins: Ships' Boys in the Georgian Navy*. Barnsley: Seaforth Publishing, 2010.
Pike, R. *Penal Servitude in Early Modern Spain*. Madison: University of Wisconsin Press, 1983.
Pilgrim, D. G. 'The Uses and Limitations of French Naval Power in the Reign of Louis XIV: The Administration of the Marquis De Seignelay, 1683–1690'. PhD, Brown University, 1969.
Pincus, S. C. A. *Protestantism and Patriotism: Ideologies and the Making of English Foreign Policy, 1650–1668*. Cambridge: Cambridge University Press, 1996.
Piñera y Rivas, A. de la. 'Los Marinos Medina Y Doz En La Observation De Venus Desde California En El Ano 1769'. In *Temas De Historia Militar: 2o Congres De Historia Militar*, 87–99. Madrid, 1988.

Podsoblyaev, E. F., F. King and J. Biggart. 'The Russian Naval General Staff and the Evolution of Naval Policy, 1904–1914'. *Journal of Military History* 66, no. 1 (2002): 37–69.

Poirier, J-L. 'Questions Sanitaires Pendant La Guerre De Crimée'. In *Les Empires En Guerre Et Paix*, edited by E. Freeman, 245–66. Vincennes: Service Historique de la Marine, 1989.

Ponting, C. *The Right to Know: The inside Story of the Belgrano Affair*. London: Sphere, 1986.

Pool, B. *Navy Board Contracts, 1660–1832*. London: Longman, 1966.

Pope, D. *The Black Ship*. London: Weidenfeld and Nicholson, 1963.

Pope, D. *At Twelve Mr Byng Was Shot*. London: Secker and Warburg, 1962.

Powell, J. R. 'Blake and the Defence of Lyme Regis'. *The Mariner's Mirror* 20, no. 4 (1934): 448–74.

Powell, J. R. 'Blake's Reduction of Jersey in 1651'. *The Mariner's Mirror* 18, no. 1 (1932): 64–80.

Powell, J. R. 'Blake's Reduction of the Scilly Isles in 1651'. *The Mariner's Mirror* 17, no. 3 (1931): 205–22.

Powell, J. R. 'The Expedition of Blake and Montagu in 1655'. *The Mariner's Mirror* 52, no. 4 (1966): 341–69.

Powell, J. R. *The Navy in the English Civil War*. London: Archon Books, 1962.

Powell, J. R. 'Penn's Expedition to Bonratty in 1646'. *The Mariner's Mirror* 40, no. 1 (1954): 4–20.

Powell, J. R. *Robert Blake: General-at-Sea*. London: Collins, 1972.

Powell, J. R. 'The Siege of the Downs Castles in 1648'. *The Mariner's Mirror* 51, no. 2 (1965): 155–71.

Powell, J. R. 'Sir George Ayscue's Capture of Barbados 1651'. *The Mariner's Mirror* 59, no. 3 (1973): 281–90.

Powell, J. R. and E. K. Timings, eds. *Documents Relating to the Civil War, 1642–1648*. London: Navy Records Society, 1963.

Powley, E. B. *The Naval Side of King William's War*. London: John Baker, 1972.

Pratt, L. 'Naval Contemplation'. *Journal for Maritime Research* 2, no. 1 (2000): 84–105.

Pratt, L. R. *East of Malta, West of Suez: Britain's Mediterranean Crisis, 1936–1939*. Cambridge: Cambridge University Press, 1975.

Prazniak, R. 'Menzies and the New Chinoiserie: Is Sinocentrism the Answer to Eurocentrism in Studies of Modernity?' *The Medieval History Journal* 13, no. April (2010): 115–30.

Preston, A. *Sea Combat Off the Falklands: The Lessons That Must Be Learned*. London: Willow, 1982.

Preston, A. and J. Major. *Send a Gunboat: The Victorian Navy and Supremacy at Sea, 1854–1904*. 2nd edn. London: Conway Maritime Press, 2007.

Prestwich, M. 'Diplomacy and Trade in the Protectorate'. *Journal of Modern History* 22 (1950): 103–21.

Price, A. *Aircraft versus Submarines in Two World Wars*. Barnsley: Pen and Sword, 2004.

Pritchard, J. 'The French Navy, 1748–1762: Problems and Perspectives'. In *Changing Interpretations and New Sources in Naval History*, edited by R. W. Love, 142–55. New York: Garland, 1980.

Pritchard, J. *Louis XV's Navy, 1748–1762: A Study of Organization and Administration*. Kingston and Montreal: McGill-Queen's University Press, 1987.

Prud'homme van Reine, R. 'Michiel Adriaenzoon De Ruyter and His Biographer Gerard Brandt'. In *De Ruyter: Dutch Admiral*, edited by J. R. Bruijn, R. Prud'homme van Reine and R. van Hővell tot Westerflier, 37–55. Rotterdam: Karwansaray, 2011.

Pryor, J. H. 'The Geographical Conditions of Galley Navigation in the Mediterranean'. In *The Age of the Galley: Mediterranean Oared Vessels since Pre-Classical Times*, edited by R. Gardiner, 206–16. London: Conway, 1995.

Puddefoot, G. *No Sea Too Rough: The Royal Fleet Auxiliary in the Falklands War; the Untold Story*. London: Chatham Publishing, 2007.

Puleston, W. D. *Mahan*. London: Cape, 1939.

Pugh, P. *The Cost of Seapower: The Influence of Money on Naval Affairs from 1815 to the Present Day*. London: Conway Maritime Press, 1986.

Quinn, D. B. and A. N. Ryan. *England's Sea Empire, 1550–1642*. London: Allen and Unwin, 1983.

Quirk, R. J. *Literature as Introspection: Spain Confronts Trafalgar*. New York: Peter Lang, 1998.

Quilley, G., ed. *Art for the Nation: The Oil Paintings Collections of the National Maritime Museum*. London: National Maritime Museum, 2006.

Radogna, L. *Storia Della Marina Militare Delle Due Sicilie*. Milan: Mursia, 1978.

Rahn, W., ed. *Deutsche Marinen Im Wandel: Von Symbol Nationaler Einheit Zum Instrument Internationaler Sicherheit*. München: R. Oldenbourg, 2005.

Rahn, W. 'German Naval Strategy and Armaments, 1919–1939'. In *Technology and Naval Combat in the Twentieth Century and Beyond*, edited by P. P. O'Brien, 109–28. London: Cass, 2001.

Ranft, B. 'The Protection of British Seaborne Trade and the Development of Systematic Planning for War, 1860–1906'. In *Technical Change and British Naval Policy, 1860–1939*, edited by B. Ranft. London: Hodder and Stoughton, 1977.

Rasor, E. L. 'The Falklands/Malvinas Campaign: A Bibliography'. Westport, CT: Greenwood, 2002.

Rasor, E. L. 'The Manning Question in the Royal Navy in the Early Ironclad Era'. In *Changing Interpretations and New Sources in Naval History*, edited by R. W. Love, 208–15. New York: Garland, 1980.

Raudzens, G. *Empires, Europe and Globalization, 1492–1788*. Stroud: Sutton, 1999.

Raudzens, G. 'Military Revolution or Maritime Evolution: Military Superiorities or Transportation Advantages as Main Causes of European Colonial Conquests to 1788'. *Journal of Military History* 63 (1999): 631–41.

Raven, G. J. A. 'That Expensive Asset: A Short History of Netherlands Naval Personnel'. *Revue Internationale d'Histoire Militaire* 58 (1984): 167–85.

Raven, G. J. A. 'A Summary of the Development of Netherlands Naval Organization'. *Revue Internationale d'Histoire Militaire* 58 (1984): 155–65.

Raven, G. J. A., and Rodger, N. A. M., eds. *Navies and Armies: The Anglo-Dutch Relationship in War and Peace*. Edinburgh: Donald, 1990.

Rayner, J. '"Entrusted with the Ruling of the Waves": Images of the Post-War Royal Navy in the NMM Film Archive'. *Journal for Maritime Research* 10, no. 1 (2008): 50–66.

Rayner, J. *The Naval War Film: Genre, History and National Cinema*. Manchester: Manchester University Press, 2007.

Reader, W. J. *Professional Men: The Rise of the Professional Classes in Nineteenth Century England*. London: Weidenfeld and Nicholson, 1966.
Redford, D. *The Submarine: A Cultural History from the Great War to Nuclear Combat*. London: I. B. Tauris, 2010.
Redford, D., ed. *Maritime History and Identity: The Sea and Culture in the Modern World*. London: I. B. Tauris, 2013.
Redford, D. *A History of the Royal Navy: World War II*. London: I. B. Tauris, 2014.
Redford, D. and P. D. Grove. *The Royal Navy: A History Since 1900*. London: I. B. Tauris, 2014.
Rediker, M. *Between the Devil and the Deep Blue Sea: Merchant Seamen, Pirates and the Anglo-American Maritime World, 1700–1750*. Cambridge: Cambridge University Press, 1987.
Reitan, E. A. *Politics, War and Empire: The Rise of Britain to a World Power, 1688–1792*. Arlington Heights: Harlan Davidson, 1994.
Rentfrow, J. A. *Home Squadron: The U.S. Navy on the North Atlantic Station*. Annapolis: Naval Institute Press, 2014.
Reynolds, D. *In Command of History: Churchill Fighting and Writing the Second World War*. London: Allen Lane, 2004.
Reynolds, C. G. *Command of the Sea: The History and Strategy of Maritime Empires*. New York: Morrow, 1974.
Rice, D. and A. Garvshon. *The Sinking of the Belgrano*. London: Secker and Warburg, 1984.
Richardson, D. 'The Slave Trade and British Economic Growth, 1748–1776'. *Journal of Interdisciplinary History* 17, no. 4 (1987): 739–69.
Richardson, D. 'The Slave Trade, Sugar and British Economic Growth, 1748–1776'. In *British Capitalism and Caribbean Slavery: The Legacy of Eric Williams*, edited by B. L. Solow and S. L. Engerman, 103–33. Cambridge: Cambridge University Press, 1987.
Richmond, H. W. *The Navy in India, 1763–1783*. London: Ernest Benn, 1931.
Richmond, H. W. *The Navy in the War of 1739-48*. 3 vols. Cambridge: Cambridge University Press, 1920. Gregg Revivals, Aldershot, 1993.
Richmond, H. W. *Sea Power in the Modern World*. London: G. Bell and Sons, 1934.
Riley, J. C. *The Eighteenth Century Campaign to Avoid Disease*. London: Macmillan, 1987.
Robbins, K. 'History, the Historical Association and the "National Past"'. *History* 66, no. 218 (1981): 413–25.
Roberts, J. *Battlecruisers*. London: Chatham Publishing, 1997.
Roberts, W. H. *Civil War Ironclads: The US Navy and Industrial Mobilisation*. Baltimore: Johns Hopkins University Press, 2002.
Robinson, D. E. 'The Secret of British Power in the Age of Sail: Admiralty Records of the Coasting Fleet'. *American Neptune* 48 (1988): 5–21.
Robson, M. *A History of the Royal Navy: The Napoleonic Wars*. London: I. B. Tauris, 2014.
Rodger, N. A. M. 'The Continental Commitment in the Eighteenth Century'. In *War, Strategy and International Politics: Essays in Honour of Sir Michael Howard*, edited by L. Freedman, P. Hayes and R. O'Neill, 39–55. Oxford: Oxford University Press, 1992.

Rodger, N. A. M. 'Commissioned Officers' Careers in the Royal Navy, 1690–1815'. *Journal for Maritime Research* 3, no. 1 (2001): 85–129.

Rodger, N. A. M. 'The Development of Broadside Gunnery, 1450–1650'. *Mariner's Mirror* 82 (1996): 301–24.

Rodger, N. A. M. 'Honour and Duty at Sea, 1660–1815'. *Historical Research* 75 (2002): 427–47.

Rodger, N. A. M. 'Image and Reality in Eighteenth Century Naval Tactics'. *Mariner's Mirror* 89 (2003): 280–97.

Rodger, N. A. M. 'Officers and Men'. In *Maritime History: The Eighteenth Century and the Classic Age of Sail*, edited by J. B. Hattendorf, 137–44. Malabar, FL: Krieger, 1997.

Rodger, N. A. M. 'Officers, Gentlemen and Their Education, 1793–1860'. In *Les Empires En Guerre Et Paix, 1793–1860*, edited by E. Freeman, 139–54. Vincennes: Service Historique de la Marine, 1990.

Rodger, N. A. M., ed. *Naval Power in the Twentieth Century*. London: Macmillan, 1996.

Rodger, N. A. M. 'Patronage and Competence'. In *Les Marines de Guerres Européenes XVII-XVIIIe Siècles*, edited by M. Acerra, J. Merino and J. Meyer, 237–48. Paris: Sorbonne, 1985.

Rodger, N. A. M. 'Queen Elizabeth and the Myth of Sea Power in English History'. *Transactions of the Royal Historical Society* 14 (2004): 153–74.

Rodger, N. A. M. 'Training or Education: A Naval Dilemma over Three Centuries'. In *Hudson Papers*, edited by P. Hore, 1–34. Oxford: Oxford Unversity Hudson Trust, 2001.

Rodger, N. A. M. *The Wooden World: An Anatomy of the Georgian Navy*. London: Collins, 1986.

Rodriguez Gonzalez, A. R. *Politica Naval de la Restauracion (1875–1898)*. Madrid: Editorial San Martin, 1988.

Rodriguez Gonzalez, A. R. *El Desastre Naval de 1898*. Madrid: Arco/Libros, 1997.

Rodriguez Gonzalez, A. R. *La Reconstruccion De La Escuadra: Planes Navales Espanoles, 1898–1920*. Madrid: Galland Books, 2009.

Rodriguez Salgado, M. J. 'The Spanish Story of the 1588 Armada Reassessed'. *Historical Journal* 33, no. 2 (1990): 461–78.

Rogers, C. J., ed. *The Military Revolution Debate: Readings on the Military Transformation of Early Modern Europe*. Boulder: Westview Press, 1995.

Rogers, N. 'Impressment and the Law in Eighteenth Century Britain'. Chapter 4 in *Law, Crime and English Society, 1660–1830*, edited by N. Landau, 71–94. Cambridge: Cambridge University Press, 2002.

Rogers, N. *The Press Gang: Naval Impressment and Its Opponents in Georgian Britain*. London: Continuum, 2007.

Rohwer, J. and M. S. Monakov. *Stalin's Ocean-Going Fleet: Soviet Naval Strategy and Shipbuilding Programmes, 1935–1953*. London: Frank Cass, 2006.

Romans, E. 'The Internal Economy of the Royal Navy in the Twentieth Century'. *The Mariner's Mirror* 94, no. 1 (2008): 79–88.

Ronald, D. A. B. 'The Symbolic Power of Youth as Represented in the Naval Chronicle (1799–1818)'. PhD, Exeter, 2011.

Ronald, D. A. B. *Young Nelsons: Boy Sailors during the Napoleonic Wars*. Oxford: Osprey, 2009.

Ronciere, C. de la. *Histoire De La Marine Francaise VI: Le Crespucule Du Grand Regne. L'apogée De La Guerre De La Corse*. Paris: E. Plon, Nouritt et cie, 1932.
Ropp, T. *The Development of a Modern Navy: French Naval Policy, 1871–1904*. Annapolis: Naval Institute Press, 1987.
Rose, C. 'The Meanings of the Late Victorian Sailor Suit'. *Journal for Maritime Research* 11 (2009): 24–50.
Rose, J. H. *The Indecisiveness of Modern War and Other Essays*. London: G. Bell and Sons, 1927.
Rose, J. H. *Naval History and National History*. Cambridge: Cambridge University Press, 1919.
Rose, K. 'Nostalgia and Imagination in Nineteenth-Century Sea Shanties'. *Mariner's Mirror* 98, no. 2 (2012): 147–60.
Rose, S. *England's Medieval Navy: Ships, Men and Warfare*. Barnsley: Seaforth, 2013.
Rose, S. *Medieval Naval Warfare, 1000–1500*. Warfare and History, edited by Jeremy Black London: Routledge, 2002.
Rose, S. *Medieval Naval Warfare, 1000–1500*. London: Routledge, 2001.
Roskill, S. *Naval Policy between the Wars 1: The Period of Anglo-American Antagonism, 1919–1929*. London: Collins, 1968.
Roskill, S. *Naval Policy between the Wars 2: The Period of Reluctant Rearmament, 1930–1939*. London: Collins, 1976.
Roskill, S. W. *The Art of Leadership*. London: Collins, 1964.
Roskill, S. W. *The Strategy of Sea Power: Its Development and Application*. Lees-Knowles Lectures. Cambridge: Cambridge University Press, 1962.
Rossiter, M. *Sink the Belgrano*. London: Bantam Press, 2007.
Rossler, E. *The U-Boat: The Evolution and Technical History of German Submarines*. London: Arms and Armour Press, 1981.
Rottman, G. L. *The Marshall Islands: Operation Flintlock, the Capture of Kwajalein and Eniwetok*. Oxford: Osprey, 2004.
Rottman, G. L. *Saipan and Tinian: Piercing the Japanese Empire*. Oxford: Osprey, 2004.
Ruger, J. *The Great Naval Game: Britain and Germany in the Age of Empire*, edited by Jay Winter. Cambridge: Cambridge University Press, 2007.
Rush, N. O. *Spain's Final Triumph over Great Britain in the Gulf of Mexico: The Battle of Pensacola, March 9 to May 8, 1781*. Florida State University Studies. Tallahassee: The Florida State University, 1966.
Ryan, A. N. '"An Act of Parliament Cannot Make Men": The Quota Acts of 1795–1796'. In *Les Empires En Guerre Et Paix, 1793–1860*, edited by E. Freeman, 103–06. Vincennes: Service Historique de la Marine, 1990.
Ryan, A. N. 'The Copenhagen Expedition, 1807'. M.A. Liverpool, 1951.
Ryan, A. N. 'The Defence of British Trade with the Baltic, 1808–1813'. *The English Historical Review* 74, no. 292 (1959): 443–66.
Ryan, A. N. 'The Navy at Copenhagen in 1807'. *The Mariner's Mirror* 39, no. 3 (1953): 201–10.
Ryan, A. N. 'Trade with the Enemy in the Scandinavian and Baltic Ports during the Napoleonic War: For and Against'. *Transactions of the Royal Historical Society* 12 (1961): 123–40.
Sadao, A. 'The Japanese Navy and the United States'. In *Pearl Harbor as History: Japanese-American Relations, 1931–1941*, edited by D. Borg and S. Okamoto, 225–59. New York: Columbia University Press, 1973.

Sadkovich, J. J. 'The Indispensable Navy: Italy as a Great Power, 1911-43'. In *Naval Power in the Twentieth Century*, edited by N. A. M. Rodger, 66–76. Basingstoke: Macmillan, 1996.

Sadkovich, J. J. *The Italian Navy in World War II*. Westport, CT: Greenwood, 1994.

Salerno, R. M. 'The French Navy and the Appeasement of Italy, 1937–9'. *English Historical Review* 112 (1997): 67–104.

Sanders, G. E. 'The Spanish Defense of America, 1700–1763'. PhD, Southern California, 1973.

Sanderson, M. W. B. 'English Naval Strategy and Maritime Trade in the Caribbean 1793–1802'. PhD, London, 1968.

Sapolsky, H. M. 'The Origins of the Office of Naval Research'. In *Naval History. The Sixth Symposium of the U.S. Naval Academy*, edited by D. M. Masterson, 206–25. Wilmington: Scholarly Resources Inc., 1987.

Sas, N. van. 'Between the Devil and the Deep Blue Sea: The Logic of Neutrality'. In *Colonial Empires Compared: Britain and the Netherlands, 1750–1850*, edited by B. Moore and H. van Neirop, 33–44. Aldershot: Ashgate, 2003.

Satsuma, S. *Britain and Colonial Maritime War in the Early Eighteenth Century; Silver, Seapower and the Atlantic*. Woodbridge: Boydell Press, 2013.

Saul, N. E. 'The Impact of the Napoleonic Wars upon Russian Priorities on Naval Development'. In *New Interpretations in Naval History*, edited by W. B. Cogar, 45–60. Shrewsbury: Tri-Service Press, 1989.

Saul, N. E. *Russia and the Mediterranean, 1797–1807*. Chicago: University of Chicago Press, 1970.

Saul, N. E. 'The Russian Navy, 1682–1854: Some Suggestions for Future Study'. In *New Aspects of Naval History*, edited by C. L. Symonds, 130–9. Annapolis: Naval Institute Press, 1981.

Savours, A. *The Search for the North West Passage*. London: Chatham Publishing, 1999.

Saxby, R. 'The Blockade of Brest in the French Revolutionary War'. *The Mariner's Mirror* 78, no. 1 (1992): 25–35.

Scammell, C. '"Anglo-American Strategic Cooperation: The Role of Carrier Aviation in Western Strategy, 1945–1955"'.London: King's College, 2001.

Scammell, G. V. *The First Imperial Age: European Overseas Expansion, c1400–1715*. London: Routledge, 1989.

Scammell, G. V. 'The Sinews of War: Manning and Provisioning English Fighting Ships c.1550–1650'. *The Mariner's Mirror* 73, no. 4 (1987): 351–67.

Scheina, R. L. *Latin America: A Naval History, 1810–1987*. Annapolis: Naval Institute Press, 1987.

Schencking, C. J. *Making Waves: Politics, Propaganda and the Emergence of the Imperial Japanese Navy, 1868–1922*. Stanford: Standford University Press, 2005.

Scheybeler, C. 'A Study of Spanish Naval Policy During the Reign of Ferdinand VI'. London: King's College, 2014.

Schoenfeld, M. P. 'The Restoration Seaman and His Wages'. *American Neptune* 25 (1965): 278–87.

Schofield, B. B. *Operation Neptune: The inside Story of Naval Operations for the Normandy Landings 1944*. Barnsley: Pen and Sword, 2008.

Schokkenbroek, J. C. A. 'Portraits: Celebrities'. In *The Oxford Encyclopedia of Maritime History*, edited by J. B. Hattendorf, 311–19. New York: Oxford University Press, 2007.

Schroeder, J. H. *Shaping a Maritime Empire: The Commercial and Diplomatic Role of the American Navy, 1829–1861*. Westport, CT: Greenwood, 1985.

Schurman, D. M. *The Education of a Navy: The Development of British Naval Strategic Thought, 1867–1914*. London: Cassell, 1965.

Schurman, D. M. 'An Historian and the Sublime Aspects of the Naval Profession'. In *Dreadnought to Polaris: Maritime Strategy since Mahan*, edited by A. M. J. Hyatt, 1–11. Annapolis: Naval Institute Press, 1973.

Schurman, D. M. 'Historians and Britain's Imperial Strategic Stance in 1914'. In *Perspectives of Empire: Essays Presented to Gerald S. Graham*, edited by J. E. Flint and G. Williams, 172–88. London: Longman, 1973.

Schurman, D. M. *Imperial Defence, 1868–1887*. London: Frank Cass, 2000

Schurman, D. M. *Julian S. Corbett, 1854–1922*. London: Royal Historical Society, 1981.

Schurz, W. L. *The Manila Galleon*. New York: Dutton, 1939.

Schurz, W. L. 'Mexico, Peru, and the Manila Galleon'. *Hispanic American Historical Review* 1, no. 4 (1918): 389–402.

Scott, H. M. 'The Importance of Bourbon Naval Reconstruction to the Strategy of Choiseul after the Seven Years War'. *International History Review* 1 (1979): 17–35.

Scott, J. *When the Waves Ruled Britannia: Geography and Political Identities, 1500–1800*. Cambridge: Cambridge University Press, 2011.

Scott, P. *The Battle of the Narrow Seas: A History of the Light Coastal Forces in the Channel and North Sea, 1939–1945*. London: Country Life, 1945.

Seeley, J. *The Expansion of England*. London: Macmillan, 1907.

Self, R. *British Foreign and Defence Policy since 1945: Challenges and Dilemmas in a Changing World*. Basingstoke: Palgrave Macmillan, 2010.

Seligmann, M. S. 'Germany and the Origins of the First World War in the Eyes of the American Diplomatic Establishment'. *German History* 15, no. 3 (1997): 307–32.

Seligmann, M. S. 'New Weapons for New Targets: Sir John Fisher, the Threat from Germany, and the Building of HMS Dreadnought and HMS Invincible, 1902–1907'. *The International History Review* 30, no. 2 (2008): 303–31.

Seligmann, M. S., F. Nagler and M. Epkenhans, eds. *The Naval Route to the Abyss: The Anglo-German Naval Race 1895–1914*. London: Navy Records Society, 2014.

Seligmann, M. S. 'A Prelude to the Reforms of Admiral Sir John Fisher: The Creation of the Home Fleet, 1902-3'. *Historical Research* 83, no. 221 (2010): 506–19.

Semmel, B. *Liberalism and Naval Strategy: Ideology, Interest, and Sea Power during the Pax Britannica*. London: Allen and Unwin, 1986.

Serrano-Mangas, F. *Los Galeones De La Carrera De Indias, 1650–1700*. Seville: Escuela de Estudios Hispano-Americanos de Sevilla, 1985.

Shaffer, B. *Energy Politics*. Philadelphia: University of Pennsylvania Press, 2009.

Shankland, P. *Beware of Heroes: Admiral Sir Sidney Smith's War against Napoleon*. London: William Kimber, 1975.

Sharrer, G. T. 'The Search for a Naval Policy 1783–1812'. In *In Peace and War: Interpretations of American Naval History, 1775–1978*, edited by Kenneth J. Hagan, 27–45. Westport, CT: Greenwood Press, 1984.
Shaw, J. J. S. 'The Commission of Sick and Wounded and Prisoners, 1664–1667'. *The Mariner's Mirror* 25, no. 3 (1939): 306–27.
Sherwig, J. M. *Guineas and Gunpowder: British Foreign Aid in the Wars with France, 1793–1815*. Cambridge, MA: Harvard University Press, 1969.
Shoemaker, R. L. 'Diplomacy from the Quarterdeck: The US Navy in the Caribbean, 1815–1830'. In *Changing Interpretations and New Sources in Naval History*, edited by R. W. Love, 169–79. New York: Garland, 1980.
Showell, J. P. M., ed. *Fuehrer Conferences on Naval Affairs, 1939–1945*. London: Chatham Publishing, 1990.
Sicking, L. *Neptune and the Netherlands: State, Economy and War at Sea in the Renaissance*. Leiden: Brill, 2004.
Sims, W. *Victory at Sea*. Garden City: Doubleday, 1920.
Singh, R. J. *French Diplomacy in the Caribbean and the American Revolution*. New York: Exposition Press, 1977.
Sklair, L. 'Competing Conceptions of Globalization'. *Journal of World Systems Research* 5, no. 2 (1999): 143–63.
Sluiter, E. 'Dutch-Spanish Rivalry in the Caribbean Area, 1594–1609'. *Hispanic American Historical Review* 27 (1948): 165–96.
Smelser, M. *The Campaign for the Sugar Islands, 1759*. Chapel Hill, NC: University of North Carolina Press, 1955.
Smelser, M. *The Congress Founds a Navy, 1787–1798*. Notre Dame, IN: University of Notre Dame Press, 1959.
Smith, A. 'Mountbatten Goes to the Movies: Promoting the Heroic Myth through Cinema'. *Historical Journal of Film, Radio and Television* 26, no. 3 (2006): 395–416.
Smith, A. W. 'The Sinister Submarine as a Motif in Contemporary Legend and Popular Imagination'. *Contemporary Legend* 3 (2000): 64–82.
Smith, G. A. 'A Means to an End: Gunboats and Thomas Jefferson's Theory of Defense'. *American Neptune* 55 (1994): 111–21.
Smith, G. S. 'Uncertain Passage: The Bureaus Run the Navy 1842–1861'. In *In Peace and War: Interpretations of American Naval History, 1775–1984*, edited by K. J. Hagan, 79–106. Westport: Greenwood Press, 1984.
Smith, M. R. and L. Marx. *Does Technology Drive History?: The Dilemma of Technological Determinism*. Cambridge, MA: MIT Press, 1994.
Smith, P. *Task Force 57*. London: William Kimber, 1969.
Solow, B. L. 'Capitalism and Slavery'. In *British Capitalism and Caribbean Slavery: The Legacy of Eric Williams*, edited by B. L. Solow and S. L. Engerman, 51–78. Cambridge: Cambridge University Press, 1987.
Solow, B. L., ed. *Slavery and the Rise of the Atlantic System*. Cambridge: Cambridge University Press, 1991.
Solow, B. L. and S. L. Engerman, eds. *British Capitalism and Caribbean Slavery: The Legacy of Eric Williams*. Cambridge: Cambridge University Press, 1987.
Sondhaus, L. *The Habsburg Empire and the Sea: Austrian Naval Policy, 1797–1866*. West Lafayette, IN: Purdue University Press, 1989.

Sondhaus, L. 'Napoleon's Shipbuilding Programme at Venice and the Struggle for Mastery in the Adriatic, 1806–1814'. *Journal of Military History* 53 (1989): 349–62.
Sondhaus, L. *The Naval Policy of Austria-Hungary, 1867–1918: Navalism, Industrial Development and the Politics of Dualism*. West Lafayette, IN: Purdue University Press, 1994.
Sondhaus, L. *Naval Warfare, 1815–1914*. London: Routledge, 2001.
Sondhaus, L. *Navies in Modern World History*. London: Reaktion Books, 2004.
Sondhaus, L. *Preparing for Weltpolitik: German Sea Power before the Tirpitz Era*. Annapolis: Naval Institute Press, 1997.
Sontag, S. and C. Drew. *Blind Man's Buff: The Untold Story of Cold War Submarine Espionage*. London: Routledge, 1999.
Spavens, W. *The Narrative of William Spavens: A Chatham Pensioner by Himself*. London: Chatham Publishing, 1998.
Spector, R. *Professors of War: The Naval War College and the Development of the Naval Profession*. Newport: US Naval War College Press, 1977.
Spector, R. *At Sea at War: Sailors and Naval Warfare in the Twentieth Century*. London: Allen Lane, 2001.
Speller, I. *The Role of Amphibious Warfare in British Defence Policy, 1945–56*. London: Palgrave, 2001.
Speller, I. 'The Royal Navy, Expeditionary Operations and the End of Empire, 1956–75'. In *British Naval Strategy East of Suez, 1900–2000: Influences and Actions*, edited by G. Kennedy, 178–98. Abingdon: Cass, 2005.
Speller, I. and C. Tuck. *Amphibious Warfare: The Theory and Practice of Amphibious Operations in the 20th Century*. Staplehurst: Spellmount, 2001.
Spinardi, G. *From Polaris to Trident: The Development of the US Fleet Ballistic Missile Technology*. Cambridge: Cambridge University Press, 1994.
Spinney, D. *Rodney*. London: Allen and Unwin, 1969.
Sprout, H. and M. Sprout. *Towards a New Order of Sea Power: American Naval Policy and the World Scene, 1918–1922*. Westport, CT: Greenwood, 1976. Princeton University Press, 1943.
Stacy, C. P. *Quebec 1759: The Siege and the Battle*. Toronto: Macmillan, 1959.
Stanford Shaw, J. 'Selim III and the Ottoman Navy'. *Turcica* 1 (1969): 212–41.
Starkey, D. 'War and the Market for Seafarers in Britain, 1736–1792'. In *Shipping and Trade, 1750–1950: Essays in International Maritime Economic History*, edited by Lewis Fischer and Helge W. Nordvik. Pontefract: Lofthouse Publications, 1990.
Starkey, D. J. *British Privateering Enterprise in the Eighteenth Century*. Exeter: University of Exeter Press, 1990.
Stauffer, D. A. *The Art of Biography in Eighteenth Century England*. Princeton: Princeton University Press, 1941.
Steele, B. J. 'Ontological Security and the Power of Self-Identity: British Neutrality and the American Civil War'. *Review of International Studies* 31, no. 3 (2005): 519–40.
Steele, I. K. *The English Atlantic, 1675–1740*. Oxford: Oxford University Press, 1986.
Stein, R. 'Measuring the French Slave Trade, 1713–1792/3'. *Journal of African History* 19, no. 4 (1978): 515–21.

Stein, R. 'The State of French Colonial Commerce on the Eve of the French Revolution'. *Journal of European Economic History* 12 (1983): 105–17.
Still, W. N. Jr. *American Sea Power in the Old World: The United States Navy in European and near Eastern Waters, 1865–1917*. Contributions to Military History. Edited by T. E. Griess. Westport, CT: Greenwood Press, 1980.
Still, W. N. Jr. *The Confederate Navy: The Ships, Men and Organization, 1861–65*. London: Conway Maritime Press, 1997.
Stoker, D. *The Grand Design: Strategy and the US Civil War*. New York: Oxford University Press, 2010.
Stokesbury, J. L. *British Concepts and Practice of Amphibious Warfare, 1867–1916*. Durham, NC: Duke University, 1968.
Stoler, M. A. 'The American Perception of British Mediterranean Strategy, 1941–1945'. In *New Aspects of Naval History*, edited by C. L. Symonds, 325–39. Annapolis: Naval Institute Press, 1981.
Storrs, C. *The Resilience of the Spanish Monarchy, 1665–1700*. Oxford: Oxford University Press, 2006.
Storrs, C., ed. *The Fiscal-Military State in Eighteenth Century Europe: Essays in Honour of P.G.M. Dickson*. Aldershot: Ashgate, 2009.
Stout, N. R. 'Goals and Enforcement of British Colonial Policy, 1763–1775'. *American Neptune* 27 (1967): 211–20.
Stout, N. R. 'Manning the Royal Navy in North America, 1763–1775'. *American Neptune* 23 (1963): 174–85.
Stout, N. R. *The Royal Navy in America, 1760–1775: A Study of Enforcement of British Colonial Policy in the Era of the American Revolution*. Annapolis: Naval Institute Press, 1973.
Stradling, R. A. *The Armada of Flanders: Spanish Maritime Policy and European War, 1568–1668*. Cambridge: Cambridge University Press, 1992.
Suid, L. *Sailing on the Silver Screen: Hollywood and the US Navy*. Annapolis: Naval Institute Press, 1996.
Sumida, J. T. 'British Naval Procurement and Technological Change'. In *Technology and Naval Combat in the Twentieth Century and Beyond*, edited by P. P. O'Brien, 128–47. London: Cass, 2001.
Sumida, J. T. *In Defence of Naval Supremacy: Finance, Technology and British Naval Policy, 1889–1914*. Boston: Unwin Hyman, 1989.
Sumida, J. T. *Inventing Grand Strategy and Teaching Command: The Classic Works of Alfred Thayer Mahan Reconsidered*. Baltimore: Johns Hopkins University Press, 1997.
Sumida, J. T. 'Reimagining the History of Twentieth Century Navies'. In *Maritime History as World History*, edited by D. Finamore, 167–82. Tallahassee: University of Florida Press, 2004.
Sumrall, R. F. 'The Battleship and Battlecruiser'. In *The Eclipse of the Big Gun: The Warship, 1906-45*, edited by R. Gardiner, 14–24. London: Conway, 1992.
Sullivan, B. 'Italian Warship Construction and Maritime Strategy'. In *Technology and Naval Combat in the Twentieth Century and Beyond*, edited by Phillips Payson O'Brien, 3–21. Abingdon: Routledge, 2001.
Sullivan, F. B. 'The Origins and Development of Education in the Royal Navy from 1702 to 1902'. PhD, Reading, 1975.
Surry, D. W and J. D. Farquhar. 'Diffusion Theory and Instructional Technology'. *Journal of Instructional Science and Technology* 2, no. 1 (1997): 24–36.

Sutherland, G., ed. *Studies in the Growth of Nineteenth Century Government*. London: Routledge, 1972.
Swanson, C. E. 'The Competition for American Seamen During the War of 1739–1748.' *Man and Nature/L'homme et la nature* 1 (1982): 119–29.
Swanson, C. E. *Predators and Prizes: American Privateering and Imperial Warfare, 1739–1748*. Columbia: University of South Carolina Press, 1991.
Sweetman, J., ed. *The Great Admirals: Command at Sea, 1587–1945*. Annapolis: Naval Institute Press, 1997.
Symcox, G. *The Crisis of French Seapower, 1688–1697: From Guerre D'escadre to the Guerre De Course*. Hague: Nijhoff, 1974.
Symcox, G. 'The Navy of Louis XIV'. In *The Reign of Louis XIV: Essays in Celebration of Andrew Lossky*, edited by P. Sonnino, 127–42. Atlantic Highlands, NJ: Humanities Press, 1990.
Symonds, C. L. *The Civil War at Sea*. New York: Oxford University Press, 2012.
Symonds, C. L. *Lincoln and His Admirals: Abraham Lincoln, the U.S. Navy, and the Civil War*. Oxford: Oxford University Press, 2008.
Symonds, C. L . *Navalists and Antinavalists: The Naval Policy Debate in the United States, 1785–1827*. Newark: University of Delaware Press, 1980.
Syrett, D. *Shipping and Military Power in the Seven Years War: Sails of Victory*. Exeter: University of Exeter Press, 2008.
Syrett, D., ed. *The Siege and Capture of Havana*. London: Navy Records Society, 1970.
Syrett, D. 'The Victualing Board Charters Shipping 1775–1783'. *Historical Research* 68 (1995): 212–24.
Syrett, D. 'The West Indian Merchants and the Conveyance of the King's Troops to the Caribbean, 1779–82'. *Journal of the Society for Army Historical Research* 65 (1967): 169–76.
Taaffe, S. *Commanding Lincoln's Navy: Union Naval Leadership during the Civil War*. Annapolis: Naval Institute Press, 2009.
Taillemite, E. 'Colbert Et La Marine'. In *Un Nouveau Colbert*, edited by R. Mousnier, 216–28. Paris: SEDIE, 1985.
Taillemite, E. 'Les Problèmes de la Marine de Guerre au XVIIIe Siecle'. *XVIIIe Siecle* 86, no. 7 (1970): 21–37.
Taillemite, E. 'Une Bataille De L'atlantique Au XVIIIe Siècle: La Guerre De Succession d' autriche, 1744–1748'. In *Guerres Et Paix*, 131–48. Vincennes: Service Historique de la Marine, 1987.
Taillemite, E. 'Une Marine Pour Quoi Faire? La Stratégie Navale de Louis XIV'. In *Guerres Maritime*, edited by P. Le Fevre, 93–102. Vincennes: Service Historique de la Marine, 1996.
Tamnes, R. 'Major Coastal State – Small Naval Power: Norway's Cold War Policy and Strategy'. In *Navies in Northern Waters, 1721–2000*, edited by R. Hobson and T. Kristiansen, 222–48. London: Cass, 2004.
Tanner, J. R., ed. *Two Discourse on the Navy, 1638 and 1659*. London: Navy Records Society, 1896.
Tarrant, V. E. *The U-Boat Offensive, 1914–1945*. London: Cassell, 1989.
Taylor, S. *Storm and Conquest: The Battle for the Indian Ocean, 1809*. London: Faber and Faber, 2007.
Taylor, S. A. G. *The Western Design: An Account of Cromwell's Expedition to the Caribbean*. Kingston: Solstice, 1969.

Teitler, G. *The Genesis of the Professional Officers Corps*. London: Sage, 1977.
Temple Patterson, A. *The Other Armada: The Franco-Spanish Attempt to Invade Britain in 1779*. Manchester: Manchester University Press, 1960.
Terraine, J. *Business in Great Waters: The U Boat Wars, 1916–1945*. London: Leo Cooper, 1985.
Terraine, J. 'History and the Indirect Approach'. *Journal of the United Services Institution* 116 (1971): 44–9.
Terrill, C. 'Captain Columbine, Alexander Dalrymple and the Troubled Birth of the British Admiralty Hydrographic Service'. In *Guerres et Paix*, 245–57. Vincennes: Service Historique de la Marine, 1987.
Thomas, D. *Cochrane: Britannia's Sea Wolf*. London: Cassell, 2001.
Thomas, C. S. *The German Navy in the Nazi Era*. London: Routledge, 1990.
Thomas, G. *Records of the Royal Marines*. London: PRO Publications, 1994.
Thomas, R. D. 'Empire Naval Pageantry and Public Spectacles – the Launch of Hms Iron Duke'. *Mariner's Mirror* 88 (2002): 202–12.
Thompson, J. *No Picnic: 3 Commando Brigade in the South Atlantic*. London: Leo Cooper, 1985.
Thrush, A. 'In Pursuit of the Frigate, 1603-40'. *Historical Journal* 64 (1991): 29–45.
Thrush, A. 'Naval Finance and the Origins and Development of Ship Money'. In *War and Government in Britain, 1598–1650*, edited by M. C. Fissel, 133–62. Manchester: Manchester University Press, 1991.
Thrush, A. 'The Navy under Charles I, 1635–1640'. PhD, London, 1991.
Till, G. *Air Power and the Royal Navy, 1914–1945: A Historical Survey*. London: Jane's, 1979.
Till, G. *The Future of British Sea Power*. Annapolis: Naval Institute Press, 1984.
Till, G., ed. *The Development of British Naval Thinking: Essays in Memory of Bryan Ranft*. Abingdon: Routledge, 2006.
Till, G. 'The Return to Globalism: The Royal Navy East of Suez, 1975–2003'. In *British Naval Strategy East of Suez, 1900 – 2000*, edited by G. Kennedy, 244–68. Abingdon: Cass, 2005.
Till, G. 'Richmond and the Faith Reaffirmed: British Naval Thinking between the Wars'. In *The Development of British Naval Thinking: Essays in Memory of Bryan Ranft*, edited by G. Till, 103–33. London: Cass, 2006.
Till, G. *Seapower: A Guide for the Twenty-First Century*. 3rd ed. London: Routledge, 2013.
Till, G. 'Sir Julian Corbett and the Twenty-First Century: Ten Maritime Commandments'. In *The Changing Face of Maritime Power*, edited by A. Dorman, M. L. Smith and M. R. H. Uttley, 19–32. London: Macmillan, 1999.
Till, G. *Understanding Victory: Naval Operations from Trafalgar to the Falklands*. New York: Praeger, 2013.
Tilley, J. A. *The British Navy and the American Revolution*. Columbia: University of South Carolina Press, 1987.
Tillman, B. *Clash of Carriers: The True Story of the Marianas Turkey Shoot of World War II*. New York: NAL Caliber, 2005.
Tilly, C. *Coercion, Capital and European States*. Oxford: Oxford University Press, 1990.
Tilly, C., ed. *The Formation of National States in Western Europe*. Princeton: Princeton University Press, 1975.

Towle, P. 'The Evaluation of the Experience of the Russo-Japanese War'. In *In Technical Change and British Naval Policy, 1860–1939*, edited by B. Ranft, 65–79. London: Hodder and Stoughton, 1977.
Tracy, N. *Attack on Maritime Trade*. London: Macmillan, 1991.
Tracy, N. *The Battle of Quiberon Bay 1759: Hawke and the Defeat of the French Invasion*. Barnsley: Pen and Sword, 2010.
Tracy, N. 'British Assessments of French and Spanish Naval Construction, 1763–1768'. *Mariner's Mirror* 61 (1974): 73–85.
Tracy, N. 'The Capture of Manila in 1762'. *The Mariner's Mirror* 55, no. 3 (1969): 311–23.
Tracy, N. *Manila Ransomed: The British Assault on Manila in the Seven Years War*. Exeter: University of Exeter Press, 1995.
Tracy, N. *Navies, Deterrence and American Independence: Britain and Seapower in the 1760s and 1770s*. Vancouver: University of British Columbia Press, 1988.
Tracy, N. *Nelson's Battles: The Art of Victory in the Age of Sail*. London: Chatham Publishing, 1996.
Tracy, N., ed. *Sea Power and the Control of Trade: Belligerent Rights from the Russian War to the Beira Patrol, 1854–1970*. Vol. 149. London: Navy Records Society, 2005.
Tramond, J. *Manuel D'histoire De La Marine De La France Des Origines a 1815*. Paris: Clio, 1947.
Tredrea, J. and E. Sozaev. *Russian Warships of the Age of Sail, 1696–1860: Design, Construction, Careers and Fates*. Barnsley: Seaforth Publishing, 2010.
Trim, D. J. B. and M. C. Fissel, eds. *Amphibious Warfare, 1000–1700: Commerce, State Formation and European Expansion*. Leiden: Brill, 2006.
Truvas, T. M. *Defying Empire: Trading with the Enemy in Colonial New York*. New Haven: Yale University Press, 2008.
Tucker, S. C. *The Jeffersonian Gunboat Navy*. Columbia: University of South Carolina Press, 1993.
Tucker, S. C. 'The Jeffersonian Gunboats in Service 1804–1825'. *American Neptune* 55 (1995): 97–110.
Tucker, S. C. and F. T. Reuter. *Injured Honor: The Chesapeake-Leopard Affair June 22, 1807*. Annapolis: Naval Institute Press, 1996.
Tully, A. P. *Battle of Surigao Strait*. Bloomington: University of Indiana Press, 2009.
Tunstall, B. *Admiral Byng and the Loss of Minorca*. London: Philip Allan, 1928.
Tunstall, B. *Naval Warfare in the Age of Sail: The Evolution of Fighting Tactics, 1650–1815*. Conway Maritime Press: London, 1990.
Turnbull, A. 'The Administration of the Royal Navy from 1660 to 1673'. PhD, Hull, 1975.
Tweedie, H. *The Story of a Naval Life*. London: Rich and Cowan, 1939.
Ubbelohde, C. *The American Colonies and the British Empire, 1607–1763*. London: Routledge, 1968.
UNCTAD. *Review of Maritime Transport 2013*, http://unctad.org/en/PublicationsLibrary/rmt2013_en.pdf (accessed 17 May 2015).
Vagts, A. *Landing Operations: Strategy, Psychology, Tactics, Politics, from Antiquity to 1945*. Harrisburg, PA: Military Services Publishing Company, 1946.
Vale, B. *The Audacious Admiral Cochrane: The True Life of a Naval Legend*. London: Brassey, 2004.

Vale, B. 'The Conquest of Scurvy in the Royal Navy 1793–1800: A Challenge to Current Orthodoxy'. *The Mariner's Mirror* 94, no. 2 (2008): 160–75.

Vale, B. *A War Betwixt Englishmen: Brazil against Argentina on the River Plate, 1825–1830.* London: I. B. Tauris, 2000.

Valle, J. E. 'The Navy's Battle Doctrine in the War of 1812'. *American Neptune* 44 (1984): 171–78.

Van der Merwe, P., ed. *Science and the French and British Navies, 1700–1850.* London: National Maritime Museum, 2003.

Van Zijverden, J. 'The Risky Alternative: Dutch Privateering During the Fourth Anglo-Dutch War, 1780–1783'. In *Pirates and Privateers: New Perspectives on the War on Trade in the Eighteenth and Nineteenth Centuries*, edited by D. Starkey, E. S. van Eyck Heslinga and J. A. de Moor, 186–205. Exeter: University of Exeter Press, 1997.

Vego, M. N. *Austro-Hungarian Naval Policy, 1904–1914.* London: Frank Cass, 1996.

Vergé-Franceschi, M. 'Les Officiers Generaux de la Marine Royale (1669–1774)'. *Revue Historique* 278, no. 564 (1987): 335–61.

Vergé-Franceschi, M. *Les Officiers Généraux de la Marine Royale, 1715–1774.* 7 vols. Paris: Libraire de l'Inde, 1990.

Vergé-Franceschi, M. *Marine et Education Sous L'Ancien Regime.* Paris: CNRS, 1991.

Vergé-Franceschi, M. *La Marine Francaise au XVIIIe Siecle.* Paris: SEDES, 1996.

Villar, R. *Merchant Ships at War: The Falklands Experience.* London: Conway, 1984.

Villiers, P. 'Deux Opérations Amphibies Contre L'île de Minorque: Les Débarquements De 1756 Et De 1781/82'. *Neptunia* 266, no. June (2012).

Villiers, P. 'La Course En Martinique Et En Guadeloupe Pendant La Guerre De Succession D'autriche'. In *Commerce et Plantation Dans La Caraibe, XVIIIe Et XIXe Siècles*, edited by P. Butel, 45–64. Bordeaux: Maison des Pays Iberiques, 1992.

Villiers, P. 'La Guerre De Course en France de Louis XIV á Napoleon 1er'. In *Marine Et Technique Au XIXe Siecle*, 91–140. Vincennes: Service Historique de la Marine, 1995.

Villiers, P. 'La Lutte Contra La Course Anglaise En Atlantique Pendant La Guerre D'indépendance Des Etats Unis D'Amerique, 1778–1783'. In *Course et Piraterie*, edited by M. Mollat, 572–83. Paris: Editions du Centre National de la Recherche Scientifique, 1975.

Villiers, P. 'Marine de Colbert ou Marine de Seignelay. Victoire de Barfleur et Progres Technique'. In *Guerres Maritimes (1688–1713)*, 173–92. Vincennes: Service Historique de la Marine, 1996.

Villiers, P. *Marine Royale, Corsaires et Trafic dans l'atlantique de louis Xiv a Louis XVI.* 2 vols. Dunkerque: Société Dunkerquoise d'Histoire et l'Archeologie, 1991.

Villiers, P. 'The Slave and Colonial Trade in France Just before the Revolution'. In *Slavery and the Rise of the Atlantic System*, edited by B. L. Solow, 210–36. Cambridge: Cambridge University Press, 1991.

Viner, J. 'Power Versus Plenty as Objectives of Foreign Policy in the Seventeenth and Eighteenth Centuries'. In *Trade in the Pre-Modern Era II*, edited by D. Irwin, 303–31. Cheltenham: Edward Elgar, 1996.

Vincent, C. P. *The Politics of Hunger: The Allied Blockade of Germany, 1915–1919*. Athens, OH: Ohio University Press, 1985.
Voelcker, T. *Admiral Saumarez Versus Napoleon: The Baltic, 1807–1812*. Woodbridge: Boydell Press, 2009.
Von T. A. *My Memoirs*. 2 Vols. London Hurst and Blackett, 1919.
Walser, R. *France's Search for a Battle Fleet: Naval Policy and Naval Power, 1898–1914*. New York: Garland, 1992.
Walton, O. '"A Great Improvement in the Sailor's Feeling Towards the Naval Service": Recruiting Seamen for the Royal Navy, 1815–1853'. *Journal for Maritime Research* 12 (2010): 27–57.
Walton, O. 'New Kinds of Discipline: The Royal Navy in the Second Half of the Nineteenth Century'. In *Naval Leadership and Management, 1650–1950*, edited by H. Doe and R. Harding, 143–56. Woodbridge: Boydell and Brewer, 2012.
Ward, M. C. *The Battle for Quebec 1759*. Stroud: Tempus, 2005.
Ward, P. *British Naval Power in the East, 1794–1805: The Command of Admiral Peter Rainier*. Woodbridge: Boydell Press, 2013.
Ware, C. *Admiral Byng: His Rise and Execution*. Barnsley: Pen and Sword, 2009.
Ware, C. *The Bomb Vessel: Shore Bombardment Ships in the Age of Sail*. London: Chatham Publishing, 1994.
Wareham, T. *Frigate Commander*. Barnsley: Pen and Sword, 2004.
Warner, O. *The Glorious First of June*. London: Batsford, 1961.
Warner, O. *Nelson's Battles*. Newton Abbot: David and Charles, 1971.
Warwick, P. *Voices from the Battle of Trafalgar*. Newton Abbot: David and Charles, 2005.
Waters, M. *Globalization: Key Ideas*. London: Routledge, 1995.
Wathen, B. *Sir Francis Drake: The Construction of a Hero*. Cambridge: D. S. Brewer, 2009.
Watson, S. '"England Expects": Nelson as a Symbol of Local and National Identity with the Museum'. *Museum and Society* 4 (2006): 129–51.
Watt, J. 'The Health of Seamen in Anti-Slavery Squadrons'. *The Mariner's Mirror* 88, no. 1 (1 January 2002): 69–78.
Watt, J. 'Surgeons of the Mary Rose: The Practice of Surgery in Tudor England'. *The Mariner's Mirror* 69, no. 1 (1983): 3–19.
Watt, J. 'Surgery at Trafalgar'. *The Mariner's Mirror* 91, no. 2 (2005): 266–83.
Watts, A. J. *The Imperial Russian Navy*. London: Arms and Armour Press, 1990.
Webb, P. 'Construction, Repair and Maintenance of the Royal Navy, 1793–1815'. In *The British Navy and the Uses of Naval Power*, edited by J. Black and P. Woodfine, 207–19. Leicester: University of Leicester Press, 1989.
Webb, P. 'The Naval Aspects of the Nootka Sound Crisis'. *The Mariner's Mirror* 61, no. 2 (1975): 133–54.
Webb, P. L. C. 'The Rebuilding and Repair of the Fleet 1783–1793'. *Bulletin of the Institute of Historical Research* 50 (1977): 194–209.
Webb, S. S. *1676: The End of American Independence*. New York: Alfred A. Knopf, 1984.
Weick, K. E. and K. H. Roberts. 'Collective Mind in Organizations: Heedful Interrelating on Flight Decks'. *Administrative Science Quarterly* 38 (1993): 357–81.
Weir, G. *Building American Submarines, 1914–1940*. Washington, DC: Naval Historical Center, 1991.

Weir, G. *Building the Kaiser's Navy: The Imperial Navy Office and German Industry in the Von Tirpitz Era*. Annapolis: Naval Institute Press, 1992.
Weir, G. *Forged in War: The Naval-Industrial Complex and American Submarine Construction, 1940–1961*. Washington, DC: Naval Historical Center, 1993.
West, N. *The Secret War for the Falklands: The SAS, MI6 and the War Whitehall Nearly Lost*. Boston: Little Brown, 1997.
Westcott, A. *Mahan on Naval Warfare: Selections from the Writings of Rear Admiral Alfred T. Mahan*. London: Sampson Low Marston, 1919.
Wester-Wemyss, L. *The Navy in the Dardanelles Campaign*. London: Hodder and Stoughton, 1919.
Wheeler, J. Scott. *The Making of a World Power: War and the Military Revolution in Seventeenth Century England*. Stroud: Sutton Publishing, 1999.
White, C. 'The Navy and Naval War Considered'. In *Home Fires and Foreign Fields*, edited by P. Liddle, 115–34. London: Brassey, 1985.
White, J. *Endgame: The U Boat Inshore Campaign, 1944–1945*. London: The History Press, 1998.
White, C. *Nelson: The Admiral*. Stroud: Sutton, 2005.
White, C., ed. *Nelson: The New Letters*. Woodbridge: Boydell Press, 2005.
Whitfield, P. *The Charting of the Oceans: Ten Centuries of Maritime Maps*. London: British Library, 1996.
Wiest, A. 'Haig's Abortive Amphibious Assault on Belgium, 1917'. *The Historian* 54, no. 4 (1992): 669–82.
Wiest, A. A. *Passchendaele and the Royal Navy*. Westport: Greenwood Press, 1995.
Wilkinson, C. *The British Navy and the State in the Eighteenth Century*. Woodbridge: Boydell Press, 2004.
Williams, E. *Capitalism and Slavery*. Chapel Hill, NC: University of North Carolina Press, 1945.
Williams, G. '"To Make Discoveries of Countries Hitherto Unknown": The Admiralty and Pacific Exploration in the Eighteenth Century'. *The Mariner's Mirror* 82, no. 1 (1996): 14–27.
Williamson, J. A. *A Short History of British Expansion*. London: Macmillan, 1922.
Williamson, J. A. *The Ocean in English History*. Oxford: Clarendon Press, 1941.
Willis, S. 'The Capability of Sailing Warships Part 1 Windward Performance'. *Northern Mariner* 13, no. 4 (2003): 29–39.
Willis, S. 'The Capability of Sailing Warships: Manoeuvrability'. *Northern Mariner* 14, no. 3 (2004): 57–68.
Willis, S. *Fighting at Sea in the Eighteenth Century: The Art of Sailing Warfare*. Woodbridge: Boydell Press, 2008.
Willis, S. 'The High Life: Topmen in the Eighteenth Century Navy'. *The Mariner's Mirror* 90, no. 2 (2004): 152–66.
Willis, S. B. A. 'Fleet Performance and Capability in the Eighteenth-Century Royal Navy'. *War in History* 11, no. 4 (2004): 373–92.
Willis, S. B. A. *The Glorious First of June: The First Battle in the Reign of Terror*. London: Quercus, 2012.
Willmott, H. *The Battle of Leyte Gulf: The Last Fleet Action*. Bloomington: University of Indiana Press, 2005.
Willmott, H. *Grave of a Dozen Schemes: British Naval Planning and the War against Japan, 1943–1945*. Annapolis: Naval Institute Press, 1996.

Wilson, C. *Anglo-Dutch Commerce and Finance in the Eighteenth Century*. Cambridge: Cambridge University Press, 1941.
Wilson, M. 'Early Submarines'. In *Steam, Steel and Shellfire: The Steam Warship, 1815–1905*, edited by Robert Gardiner, 147–57. London: Conway Maritime Press, 1992.
Wilson, K. 'Empire, Trade and Popular Politics in Mid-Hanoverian Britain: The Case of Admiral Vernon'. *Past & Present* 121 (1988): 74–109.
Wilson, K., ed. *A New Imperial History: Culture, Identity and Modernity in Britain and the Empire, 1660–1840*. Cambridge: Cambridge University Press, 2004.
Wilson, C. *Profit and Power: A Study of England and the Dutch Wars*. London: Longman Green and Co., 1957.
Wilson, A. R. 'The Maritime Transformation of Ming China'. In *China Goes to Sea: Maritime Transformation in Comparative Historical Perspective*, edited by A. S. Erickson, L. J. Goldstein and C. Lord, 238–85. Annapolis: Naval Institute Press, 2009.
Wise, S. R. *Lifeline of the Confederacy: Blockade Running During the Civil War*. Columbia: University of South Carolina Press, 1989.
Wolters, T. S. *Information at Sea: Shipboard Command and Control in the U.S. Navy from Mobile Bay to Okinawa*. Baltimore: Johns Hopkins University Press, 2013.
Wood, W. *The Logs of the Conquest of Canada*. Toronto: Champlain Society, 1909.
Woodman, R. *A Brief History of Mutiny*. London: Robinson, 2005.
Woodward, E. L. *Great Britain and the German Navy*. Oxford: Clarendon Press, 1935.
Woodward, S. and P. Robinson. *One Hundred Days*. London: Harper Collins, 1992.
Wooley, P. J. *Japan's Navy: Politics and Paradox, 1971–2000*. Boulder: Lynne Rienner, 2000.
Wormell, D. *Sir John Seeley and the Uses of History*. Cambridge: Cambridge University Press, 2008.
Wright, D. *The Battle for Iwo Jima, 1945*. Stroud: Sutton, 1999.
Wright, R. N. J. *The Chinese Steam Navy 1862–1945*. London: Chatham Publishing, 2000.
Yarrington, A. 'The Commemoration of the Hero 1800–1864: Monuments to the British Victors of the Napoleonic Wars'. PhD diss., Cambridge, 1980.
Yarrington, A. 'Nelson the Citizen Hero: State and Public Patronage of Monumental Sculpture, 1805–1818'. *Art History* 6, no. 3 (1983): 315–29.
Yener, E. *From Sail to Steam: Naval Modernization in the Ottoman, Russian, Chinese and Japanese Empires, 1830–1905*. Saarbrucken: Lambert Academic Publishing, 2010.
Yerxa, D. A. *Admirals and Empire: The United States Navy and the Caribbean, 1898–1945*. Columbia: University of South Carolina Press, 1991.
Young, M. B. *Servility and Service: The Life and Work of Sir John Coke*. Woodbridge: Royal Historical Society, 1986.
Zapatero, J. M. *Historia de las Fortificaciones de Cartagena de Indias*. Madrid: Centro Iberoamericano de Cooperacion, 1979.

Zapatero, J. M. 'La Fortificación y la Defensa del Islmo Centralamericano En La Contienda Angloespañola del Siglo XVIII'. *Revista ASINTO* 7, no. 25 (1960): 5–30.

Zimm, A. D. *Attack on Pearl Harbor: Strategy, Combat, Myths, Deception.* Philadelphia: Casemate, 2011.

Zorlu, T. *Innovation and Empire in Turkey: Sultan Selim III and the Modernisation of the Ottoman Navy.* London: I. B. Tauris, 2011.

INDEX

administration, naval 74, 88–92, 97, 102, 116–17, 120, 123
Afghanistan 59
Africa 14, 67
  North Africa 28, 82
  West Africa 59, 100
America 3, 13, 22, 24, 66–8, 78, 80, 85–7, 89, 90, 93, 96–7, 99, 100, 122, 125
America, Central 68
America, South 27, 82
American Civil War (1861–5) 31–3, 39
American Independence, War of (1775–83) 15, 92, 101–5, 108
Amiens, Treaty of (27 March 1802) 19
Anglo-American War of 1812 17, 24–5
Anglo-Dutch Wars (1652–4, 1664–8 and 1670–2) 78–81, 83
Anglo-Spanish War (1739–48) 93–4
Atlantic, Battle of the (1940–5) 6, 51–5
Atlantic history 94
Atlantic Ocean 3, 13, 18, 25, 32, 37, 46, 59–60, 70, 74, 81, 84, 93–4, 99–100, 103–5, 112, 121–2
Austerlitz, Battle of (2 December 1805) 20
Austria (inc. Habsburg Empire and Austria-Hungary) 23, 30–1, 36, 40, 67, 70–1, 76, 81, 89, 90, 98
Austrian Succession, War of (1740–8) 92, 94, 97–8

Baltic Sea 19, 21, 30, 37, 52, 67, 70, 72–3, 83, 85–6, 91, 100–1, 104, 106, 122
Bantry Bay, Battle of (1 May 1689) 85
Barfleur and La Hogue, Battles of (19, 23–24 May 1692) 85, 89
Batavian Republic, *see* Netherlands
Beachy Head, Battle of (30 June 1690) 85
Belgian Revolution (1830–2) 27
Belgium 90, *see also* Belgian Revolution (1830–2)
Black Sea 29–30, 34–5, 91, 106
blockade 6, 17–18, 20–4, 30, 32–7, 39, 44–5, 61, 70, 74, 78, 100, 102, 104, 109, 129
Brazilian-Paraguayan War (1864–70) 34

Camperdown, Battle of (11 October 1797) 18
Campo Formio, Treaty of (1797) 18
Caribbean Sea 24–5, 68–9, 78, 95, 102, 104
Cartagena de las Indias 87
Chesapeake, Battle of (5 September 1781) 101
Chesme, Battle of (6 July 1770) 38, 104–6, 108
Chile 34
China 7, 28, 60–1, 68
China Sea 6, 45, 66, 111
Cold War (1945–91) 6–7, 9, 27, 30, 52, 59–61, 97, 129
Colomb, John (1838–1909) and Philip (1831–99) 5
Cook, James (1728–79) 105, 114
Copenhagen, Battle of (2 April 1801) 19

INDEX

Copenhagen, bombardment of (September 1807) 22
Corbett, Sir Julian 5, 9, 43, 45, 59, 96, 99
culture and navies xi, 2–3, 7, 10, 55, 86, 116, 124–8, 132

Darwin, Charles 114
Denmark 67, 80, 85–6
discipline and punishment at sea 35, 92, 104, 124–5
Dreadnought 42–3, 106, 113, 128

East Indies 20, 23, 33, 80, 90, 101
economics xi, 62, 74, 93, 115, 132–3
Egypt 19, 23, 128

Falkland Islands 43, 58, 60, 100, 105
fiction, and navies xi, 2, 128
film, and navies 6, 53, 128–9
First of June, Battle of (1 June 1794) 18
First World War (1914–18) 3, 5–6, 26, 33, 40, 42–6, 49–50, 56, 109
Fisher, Admiral Sir John (1841–1920) 42–4, 46
France 7, 14–18, 22, 24, 30, 37–41, 46–8, 57, 64, 67, 76, 78–9, 81, 84–7, 89–90, 92–4, 97–102, 105, 107, 112, 119, 122
Franco-Austrian War (1859) 30
Franco-Prussian War (1870–1) 35, 39
French Revolution, War of (1792–1802) 15–19
Friedland, Battle of (14 June 1807) 20

galleys 70–2, 82–3, 86, 106, 113
Gallipoli 35, 44, 46, 49
Germany 5–7, 14, 16, 20, 22, 35, 37, 40–1, 44–5, 48–9, 52, 57, 64, 84, 96–7, 109, 119
Gibraltar 50, 80, 87, 93, 101–3
globalization xi, 2–4, 7–9, 14, 64, 66, 68, 70, 108–11, 125, 128–9, 133
Good Hope, Cape of 20

Great Britain 4–5, 14–20, 23–30, 34, 37–42, 47–9, 51–2, 56–8, 60, 63, 65, 68–9, 78, 84, 86–7, 89–90, 92–4, 96–7, 99–102, 104–6, 111–12, 114, 117, 121–2, 125, 127, 129
Great Lakes 24
Great Northern War (1700–21) 85–6
Greece 27–8
guerre de course 22, 39, 100
Gulf Wars (1990–1 and 2003–13) 59–60

Hakluyt Society 69
Halifax (Nova Scotia) 87
Hango Head, Battle of (7–9 August 1714) 86
Havana 37, 87, 98, 100
health at sea 111, 122–4
Hornblower, Horatio 2
Howe, Admiral Earl William (1726–99) 18

India 14, 57, 98, 101, 103
Indian Ocean 21, 61, 66, 102–3, 112
Industrial Revolution 38, 111–12, 115, 118
Ireland 73, 78
Italy 20, 22–3, 28, 40–1, 47–9, 64, 67, 90, 94
Iwo Jima, Battle for (February 1945) 55

Jamaica 78, 87, 102–3
James, William (historian) 17
Japan 6, 13, 30, 35–8, 40–3, 47–50, 53–5, 57, 64, 111
Jervis, Admiral John, Earl St Vincent (1735–1823) 18–19, 26
jeune école 22, 39–40
Jutland, Battle of (31 May–1 June 1916) 41, 43–6

Korea 36–7, 60, 111
Korean War (1950–3) 58–60

Lagos Bay, Battle of (18 August 1759) 98, 108

INDEX

Laughton, John Knox 5
Lepanto, Battle of (7 October 1571) 71
Leyte Gulf, Battle of (October 1944) 50, 53
Lissa, Battle of (20 July 1866) 30, 36
logistics 55, 69, 86, 88, 91–2, 103, 117

Mahan, Alfred Thayer 5, 9, 15–16, 20, 22, 36, 40–1, 59, 89, 91, 102, 108–9
Malaga, Battle of (13 August 1704) 85
Malaspina, Alexandro (1754–1810) 105
Malta 19, 70
Manila 37, 68, 98, 100
Marines, Great Britain 55
Marines, United States 49, 55
Martinique, Battle of (15, 19 May 1780) 108
medicine at sea 122
Mediterranean 4, 19–20, 28, 40, 44, 50, 56, 67, 69–72, 78, 82–7, 93–4, 100, 104–6, 122, 124
mercantilism 110
Mexico 32
Midway, Battle of (4–7 June 1942) 53
military revolution 7, 81–3
Minorca 5, 87, 101–2
Moonlight Battle (16–17 January 1780) 101
mutiny 18, 78, 124

Napoleonic War (1803–15) 7, 14–16, 22–3, 92–3, 108, 128
NATO 58–61
Naval Chronicle 17
navy: Canada 52
navy: China 2, 7, 9, 35–8, 60–1
navy: Denmark 19, 22, 28, 35, 85
navy: France 9, 15, 18–19, 22–3, 267, 28–30, 34–5, 38–9, 48–9, 62, 69–70, 79–80, 84–5, 89, 93–4, 98, 100–5, 107–8, 118, 120, 122, 125
navy: Germany 22, 26, 28, 30, 37, 40–5, 48–9, 52, 62, 66, 96, 119

navy: Great Britain (and England pre-1707) xii, 4, 14–15, 84, 127
1500–1650 69, 73–4
1650–1713 78, 80, 83, 112
1713–1793 82–9, 92, 94, 97, 100–4, 108, 115–24
1793–1815 15, 18–21, 23–4
1815–1914 25–6, 28, 35, 38, 42, 125–6
1914–1918 41, 43–4
1919–1939 47–8
1939–1945 49–50, 52, 56
1945–2010 62, 129
navy: Italy 30–1, 39, 45, 49, 57, 62
navy: Japan 9, 35–8, 40–2, 45, 47–9, 53–5, 57, 111
Navy League 5
Navy Records Society 5, 69, 73–4
navy: Russia 1, 9, 29–30, 34–8, 40, 42, 49, 57, 83, 85–6, 91, 93, 104–6, 108, 111, 125
navy: Sweden 67, 71–2, 80, 83–6, 88, 93, 105–6
Nelson, Horatio 19, 21, 25–6, 38, 92, 99, 119, 128
Netherlands (inc. United Provinces) 14, 18, 67, 77, 79, 85–6, 89–90, 93, 95, 97, 101, 107, 122
Nine Years, War (1688–97) 84, 89

officer corps 15, 35, 42, 69, 73, 103, 106, 118–20, 124
Okinawa, Battle for (April–June 1945) 53
Ottoman Empire 53

Pacific Ocean 6, 13, 37, 45, 50–1, 53–7, 61, 68, 103, 105, 114, 118
Papal States 28
Pares, Richard (1902–58) 93, 95–6, 122
Paris, Peace of (1763) 99
Paris, Treaty of (1856) 32, 34
Parkinson, Cecil Northcote (1909–93) 2, 20
Peloponnesian War (431–404 BCE) 4
Philippine Sea, Battle of (19–21 June 1944) 53
Portugal 18, 23, 78, 80, 85

INDEX

privateering 21–2, 24, 32, 84–5, 89, 97, 121
Prussia 18, 20, 232, 28, 35, 39, 76–7, 93, 97–8
Prussian-Danish War (Schleswig Holstein War, 1864) 28
Punic War (219–167 BCE) 4

'Quasi-War' (United States and France, 1798–1801) 24
Quebec 85, 98–100
Quiberon Bay, Battle of (20 November 1759) 98–9, 108

religion 59, 67, 70–1, 73, 123–4
Richmond, Admiral Herbert (1871–1946) 9, 47, 95–6
Russia (inc. Soviet Union) 6, 9, 13, 16, 20, 22–3, 28–30, 34–5, 37–8, 40, 42, 57, 64, 83, 85–6, 91, 93, 104–6, 108, 111, 125
Russo-Japanese War (1904–5) 37, 42
Russo-Swedish War (1741–3) 93
Russo-Swedish War (1788–90) 106

Saintes, Battle of (12 April 1782) 101, 103, 108
St Vincent, Battle of (14 February 1797) 19, 26, 98
seamen 7, 26, 37, 69, 73, 84, 92, 118, 120–7
Second World War (1939–45) 6, 46, 48–58, 87, 97, 129
Seeley, Sir John (1834–95) 14
Seven Years, War (1756–63) 15, 92, 94, 96–7, 99–100, 102, 104, 114
Sicily 51, 55
Sino-French War (1884–5) 34
Sino-Japanese War (1894–5) 35
Sinope, Battle of (30 November 1853) 29–30
slave trade 18, 27, 34, 112, 124
Social Darwinism 4, 13, 92
social sciences x, 1, 6
Society for Nautical Research xi, 5
Soviet Union, *see* Russia

Spain 13–15, 18, 20, 23, 36–7, 42, 64, 68–9, 75–81, 85–7, 89–90, 92–4, 97–8, 100–2, 105, 108, 122
Spanish-American War (1898) 37, 42
Spanish-Peruvian/Chilean War (1864–6) 34
Spanish Succession, War of (1701–13) 84–6, 89
submarine 29–30, 33, 38, 46–8, 50, 52–4, 58–60, 62, 111, 113, 128

television, navies and 129
thalassocracy 7–8, 10, 64, 76, 92
Thirty Years, War (1618–48) 73, 75
torpedo 33–6, 38–9, 50, 54, 114
Trafalgar, Battle of (21 October 1805) 20, 26, 38, 43, 93, 127–128
Tsushima, Battle of (27–28 May 1805) 20–1, 26, 28, 43, 92, 127–8

U-Boat 30, 44, 46, 52, 54, 96
ULTRA 52
United Provinces, *see* Netherlands
United States 9, 13–15, 17, 24–5, 32–4, 36–7, 40–2, 45–50, 52–3, 55, 57–9, 62–4, 87, 91, 97, 102, 105, 113–15, 119–20
Utrecht, Treaty of (1713) 89–90

Venetian-Turkish War (1714–18) 86, 93
Venice 23, 40
Vera Cruz 28
Vietnam War (1955–75) 58–60

Walcheren 22–3, 55
Warsaw Pact (1955–91) 58, 61
Washington Naval Treaty (February 1922) 47–8
West Indies 18, 20–1, 24, 42, 84–5, 93–5, 100–2, 104, 122

Yalu River, Battle of (17 September 1894) 36–7

Zeebrugge, raid on (1 April 1918) 46